AN ANIMATED LIFE

RAY HARRYHAUSEN
AN ANIMATED LIFE
ADVENTURES IN FANTASY

**RAY HARRYHAUSEN
&
TONY DALTON**

AURUM PRESS

First published in Great Britain
2003 by Aurum Press Ltd
25 Bedford Avenue, London WC1B 3AT

A catalogue record for this book is available from the British Library.

ISBN 1 85410 940 5

3 5 7 9 10 8 6 4 2
2005 2007 2006 2004

Printed in Singapore by CS Graphics

Design by Two:Design, London

CONTENTS

FOREWORD BY RAY BRADBURY 6

PREFACE BY TONY DALTON AND RAY HARRYHAUSEN 7

INTRODUCTION 9

1 **DISCOVERY OF A GIANT APE** 11

2 **ANOTHER APE AND A BEAST** 31

3 **FROM BENEATH THE SEA TO OUTER SPACE** 65

4 **SINBAD HAS BEEN GOOD TO ME** 101

5 **ANOTHER LOST LAND** 131

6 **ALMOST HUMAN** 149

7 **ABSOLUTELY IMPERIAL** 175

8 **DINOSAURS, DINOSAURS, EVERYWHERE DINOSAURS** 193

9 **RETURN TO LEGENDS** 215

10 **GOODBYE OLD FRIEND** 235

11 **IN THE LAP OF THE GODS** 259

12 **LOST PROJECTS, LOST WORLDS** 283

  FILMOGRAPHY 299

  GLOSSARY 302

Ray Harryhausen Revisited

By Ray Bradbury

What is there to be said that is new about Ray Harryhausen?

Simply the fact that he was always new and has never grown old.

Looking back at our life together, which began when we were eighteen and just out of high school, I have sometimes felt that there were never two Rays, but one with a single dream. Dinosaurs were it.

It's not easy to follow the trail of great monsters through time, tracking them through history, but nevertheless Ray and I did just that. My happiest memories are of Ray calling me during the years just out of high school and telling me that *King Kong* was playing somewhere, in some obscure theater in L.A., so we had to rush over and buy 15-cent seats to watch that glorious animal perform again with all those beautiful monsters.

Some of my favorite recollections are of those early days, going to visit Ray's house, his garage and seeing the miniature monsters there, ready to perform on stop-motion film, where his father enacted roles and his mother made the costumes.

My love of dinosaurs led me to write a story called 'The Fog Horn', which I gave to John Huston back in 1953. His reaction to my dinosaur caused him to give me the job of writing *Moby Dick* for the screen. So you see, I thank God for those great beasts and for Ray Bradbury's involvement with Ray Harryhausen. The morning I met John Huston I had just come back from a visit to a local bookstore, looking for books on dinosaurs.

We had for many long years been neglected by Hollywood. I especially remember Ray and I visiting a small studio where an arrogant producer told Ray to hand over his experimental film of dinosaurs in a dark projection room without introducing himself or getting up to say hello. Ray and I sat in the dark watching his beautiful beasts perform, and when it was over the producer simply said, 'Get your film and get out of here.' Ray got his can of film and we walked across the studio lot in the hot sun on that day in the early 1950s, grumbling and cursing. I later wrote a short story called 'Tyrannosaurus Rex' to revenge Ray Harryhausen on this unthinking producer.

But the real reward was at a preview at the Picwood Theater several years later when by accident my wife and I attended a movie preview. The film was about dinosaurs and was dreadful. On the way out I saw a crowd of yes-men collected around that same arrogant producer who had cold-shouldered Harryhausen and myself. I went over and plowed through the yes-men, stuck out my hand and said,

'Mr Lippert?'

He looked up and said, 'Yes?'

I replied, 'Ray Bradbury. Your picture...'

He said, 'Yes?'

'It won't make a dime.' And turned and walked away. Comeuppance time.

So you see, Ray and I have waited for a lot of years to share our love with a lot of people.

Finally, I remember the night several years back when the Academy decided to give Ray a special Oscar for his long career in animation. Tom Hanks was the Master of Ceremonies that night and professed his love for Ray and myself. I made the speech introducing Harryhausen, telling people of the history of our long and loving friendship, which prevailed against many years of neglect. When I finally gave Ray his Oscar, we were both weeping because it was a great moment, not only for him, but for me. A shared moment of love after so much time.

There is nothing else to say.
My love remains.

Ray Bradbury
1 May 2003

Preface

The Authors

This book has taken us very nearly five years to complete, methodically working through the enormous collection of memorabilia so that we can add flesh to the bones of a story that has been told many times through numerous interviews and articles over many years. Now, with new information and illustrations, for the first time here is the true and complete story of how it was all accomplished. How one man, who has remained very secretive about his work, dedicated his life to creating dreams and nightmares and how those wonderful inventions of Ray's mind came to be put on the screen.

Since I was old enough to see over the top of the cinema seat in front of me, I had sought out Ray's films, always knowing that they would transport me to a realm that few other films-makers could even imagine. I was never disappointed. The motion picture industry calls Ray's work 'Special Effects'. I call it magic.

I have been fortunate to know Ray and Diana for over thirty years, since I interviewed him for a magazine. At the time I was working for the British Film Institute, where I was one of the few people to have heard of Ray Harryhausen and his movies. After much cajoling, my BFI bosses conceded in letting me hold a lecture with Ray at various Regional Film Theatres. They were an enormous success and we have stayed close friends ever since. He is one of the most unassuming and genial persons I know, and since that first meeting with Ray I have always enjoyed his company. His study, or laboratory of creations, always fills me with wonder, even after all this time, and I marvel at his ability to ignore them whilst I sit there in awe and recollect the scenes in which they starred.

Even when I thought I knew everything about Ray's work, each new chapter produced some fresh revelation. As Ray would say, I now know more about him than he does himself. Thanks for your confidence, Ray.

Tony Dalton, London, 2003

The art of motion has always intrigued me. How a body – when it throws its weight from side to side and sits down – actually sits down. What muscles interact to bring that simple movement to its conclusion. Movement is a fascinating process and each creature I have made and animated has had its own character according to its physiognomy. The animator takes a foam and metal object, makes minute adjustments in its position and creates a performance. He puts himself in the model, giving it a mind and soul. He brings statues to life. This unique blend of sculpture and theatre raises stop-motion to the level of a true art form – an art form that was born with the motion picture and which, like film itself, has yet to reach its full potential.

Stop-motion was my first love, but it wasn't just the challenge to animate some bizarre creature into life, my ambitions were much more than that. Animation provided a focus, a centre point, but just as important were the landscapes and the people who populated those forgotten lands. Special effects on their own are not enough.

The years of preparation and the months spent in animation would seem to some a daunting career, but for me the last sixty years have been an adventure: creating worlds of untold fantasy for others to marvel at. To bring a creation to life is a rare gift, indeed a miracle that the very gods of Olympus would have been envious of. I was blessed with wanting to do just that and, even more incredibly, being able to. There have been times when I wanted to produce much more lavish and spectacular subjects, but time and tight budgets forced me to work on a level I have not always been pleased with. There have been times when frustration and compromise have nearly defeated my aims, but looking back over the majority of the films I have worked on, they came out to my general satisfaction and are in the most part what we wanted them to be.

The gratifying thing is that most of the films have now gained a unique recognition within the industry. After so many years of submitting each film to the Academy of Motion Picture Arts & Science (AMPAS®) for a nomination and each time being rejected, I think that I can modestly say that they have achieved their own recognition as landmarks in the history of cinema. Too late for the box office, but gratifying for the people who did so much to make them work. This recognition became a reality for me on Friday, 13 December 1991 when I made my way to the stage after Ray Bradbury had announced that I was to be the recipient for that year of the Gordon Sawyer Award, and received a 'Special' Oscar® for a lifetime of technical excellence. This, along with all the awards and tributes that have been presented to me, I treasure and hold as a tribute to all who worked on the films: the actors, screenwriters, directors, art directors, cameramen, in fact all the technicians and, of course, Charles Schneer, the producer of most of them.

I am often asked if I would have liked to have been involved with *Jurassic Park*. The plain answer is no. Although excellent, it is not with all its dollars what I would have wished to do with my career. I was always a loner and worked best that way. Since the very beginning I fought and struggled under constant pressure to keep the design and final result within my hands. As time moved on this became more difficult, until I was forced to bow to the fact that my method of working, in the financial sense, was no longer practical. Model animation has been relegated to a reflection, or a starting point for creature computer effects that has reached a high few could have anticipated. However, for all the wonderful achievements of the computer, the process creates creatures that are too realistic and for me that makes them unreal because they have lost one vital element – a dream quality. Fantasy, for me, is realizing strange beings that are so removed from the 21st century. These beings would include not only dinosaurs, because no matter what the scientists say, we still don't know how dinosaurs looked or moved, but also creatures from the mind. Fantastical creatures where the unreal quality becomes even more vital. Stop-motion supplies the perfect breath of life for them, offering a look of pure fantasy because their movements are beyond anything we know. Willis O'Brien once told me that you should never attempt to create what you can photograph in real life – a piece of advice I have always applied to my creatures. Nothing is real, and none of them could have been a man in a suit.

Aside from providing the reader with a chronological story of how our pictures were made (giving away a few secrets in the process), there are two vital points that I have endeavoured to make very clear in this book. The first is to show that my effects were not constructed in retrospect, but were conceived and designed before or alongside the screenplay. This is an attempt to illustrate clearly that many effects technicians, especially in this field, are there from the start and are not simply brought in to visualize what is in the script after all the live action has been completed. The second point is that each film has been constructed using a combination of talents and should not be seen as one man's picture. No picture truly is. On most of our projects there were always three, sometime four, personality inputs into the film's construction: Charles, myself, the writer and on occasions the director, depending on when he was brought into the production. I will be at great pains to make clear that these were not in the usual sense the directors' pictures or for that matter producers' pictures or the special effects technicians' pictures but a combination of ideas and thoughts from a collective group of people. The writer would produce thirty of forty pages of script and we would all sit down for our famous 'sweatbox sessions' and pull it apart and then try to improve it.

The unsung hero is Charles. He is a man I respect immensely, adding so much more to the films than he is usually given credit for. He would supply the practical element, backed up with copious amounts of memos, and always knew what would work and what wouldn't. Without his help and foresight, much of what we planned together would not have seen the light of day. Charles' true talent lay in his meticulous planning, which enabled us to complete, even with a year of animation, on budget. No easy task. His success in maintaining what he promised enabled us to make more movies and his enthusiasm for them was unbounded. Producers always bear the brunt of much animosity from both the team and the front office during production, and Charles was no exception. No matter what, he would just get on with the job and, rather surprisingly for a producer, he never minded getting his hands dirty. It would amaze me to see him on location stopping the traffic and directing the trucks. My long association with my friend has been very fruitful. Thank you, Charles.

I have never considered myself 'a special effects' person, only an animator and film-maker, which is a special field encompassing its own special brand of expertise. It is a profession in its own right. My career in this strange field has seen many ups and downs – battling the critics, the unbelievers and above all the budgetary problems – but it has all been so worthwhile when I see so many people inspired by the films we made. There were times when it didn't seem worthwhile, but now I view it all as a huge odyssey of how we struggled against the enormous odds, much as Jason, Sinbad and Perseus had done. The best way that I can sum it all up is to quote Burgess Meredith in *Clash of the Titans* through the pen of Beverley Cross: 'This would make a fine heroic poem.'

Ray Harryhausen, London, 2003

Introduction

My work, and therefore to a large extent my life, have been tied to a specific film and the man responsible for it. The film is *King Kong* (1933), and although Merican C. Cooper produced and in part conceived the basic idea, it was Willis O'Brien who created Kong and breathed life into him. Both the film and the easy-going Obie, as he was known to his friends, were the catalysts for my career: the very inspiration for all my ideas and techniques. But perhaps more than that, the film set a standard by which I was to gauge my own ideas. And so, before beginning my own story, it is important to at least touch on the early pioneers and present the reader with a brief background of how Obie became the undoubted father of stop-motion animation and the commercial instigator of the process.

Stop-motion dimensional animation is as old as the motion picture itself, and is an art more easily seen than achieved. Like the simple animated cartoon, the illusion of movement is created by shooting each frame of motion picture film separately. But unlike the hand-drawn cartoon, a dimensional jointed model is used, carefully changing its position through a few millimetres of space and then exposing a single frame of film to the new position. Light levels, background positioning and foreground area are identical in each exposure. Viewed at 24 frames per second (the speed at which sound film is projected), the motion becomes fluid, giving the viewer the 'illusion' of movement.

Although there are gaps and uncertainties that make it impossible to determine the exact origins of model animation, it may have begun in France. In the 1890s the innovative Georges Méliès was developing stop framing. By accident he had discovered that when film stopped in the camera, after which it might be seconds before he began cranking again, the events passing before the lens magically 'skipped', so creating the illusion that the people moving in front of the camera when it stopped simply disappeared or skipped to the other side of the screen. The magician in him saw this as a wonderful tool, a masterstroke of illusion, and although he may not have been the first to discover the trick, he used it to its fullest extent and in so doing set the stage for fantasy films.

At more or less the same time in America, Thomas Edison's technicians were discovering that the same 'stop-motion' effect that moved people across the frame would also move inanimate objects as though they were alive. Using simple dimensional objects like wooden toys and nuts and bolts, they moved them fractionally while the shutter of the camera was closed, which when projected at normal speed appeared to move on their own. Speed of movement would depend on the distance between each move. A little later another American cinema pioneer, E.S. Porter, also dabbled in the technique by animating six tiny teddy bears for his 90-foot film *The Teddy Bears* (1907). Others were to experiment over the next few years, but even with such inventiveness by the early pioneers, the technique of three-dimensional stop-motion animation would remain a novelty and curiosity for some time to come, whereas the technique of cartoon animation was establishing itself as not only an art, but also as a financial success.

It wasn't until 1914/15 that the next and most vital step in model animation was made, one that would turn the process from a novelty into the embryo of an art form. The young Willis O'Brien, employed at the time in a San Francisco marble shop, one day idly sculptured several clay figures. Seeing what he was doing, a colleague challenged him to a desk-top mock fight with the figurines; from that Obie began to see how he might 'move' them with film, by stopping the film each frame or so and producing the 'illusion' of movement. In Obie's words: 'out of this came the idea of movies with animated models'. By accident he had started on a path to which he would devote the rest of his life.

It required a great technician with a good vivid imagination, both of which Obie had in plenty, to combine the concept of animating models with creatures that had become extinct 65 million years ago – the dinosaur. Experimenting with a borrowed camera, Obie filmed his first stop-motion film in 1914 on top of the Bank of Italy building in San Francisco. The film included a dinosaur and a caveman, both of which were made of clay over a flexible wooden frame. The next stage was easy: all he had to do was find the money, and the impossible would become possible. Although crude, the film impressed Herman Wobber, owner of a Nickelodeon, who gave O'Brien $5000 and asked him to re-shoot it with better miniatures and models. *The Dinosaur and the Missing Link* (1914), a prehistoric comedy about a caveman, a dinosaur and an ape-like creature, took a total of two months to make.

The 5-minute film was sold to Edison, who offered him a job. Over the next three years Obie produced a number of 500-foot short subjects, among which were *Birth of a Fliver* (1915), in which a caveman comes up with the idea of a dinosaur-driven transport; *Prehistoric Poultry* (1916), with Neanderthals and an ostrich-like dinosaur; *R.F.D 10,000 B.C.* (1917), about a prehistoric post office; and *Morpheus Mike* (1917), about a contemporary daydreamer who fancies himself eating in a Stone Age café.

In early 1918 Obie was contacted by New York film producer Herbert M. Dawley, who gave him a three-month contract and $3000 to make a film based on Dawley's own story, *The Ghost of Slumber Mountain*. The simple adventure tells of a mountain climber falling asleep and dreaming of a ghost who reveals, through the aid of a mysterious telescope, life on the mountain as it was a million years before. The film included several prehistoric creatures, including a dymtryx (a giant bird-like creature), a brontosaurus and a fight between a tyrannosaurus and a triceratops. The film was an enormous box-office hit in 1919 and grossed a staggering $100,000. It was Obie's first commercial success, and it is said, although never verified, that Obie appeared in the film as the ghost of Mad Dick, the old hermit, but as the character is so made up, it could be anyone.

In 1920 O'Brien joined Watterson R. Rothacker's company, obstensibly to produce a number of stop-motion shorts, but instead he suggested a more exciting application for the process – a full-length feature based on the Arthur Conan Doyle adventure novel *The Lost World*. This was a very ambitious move for model stop-motion animation. After all, it wasn't until 1937 that Disney made the same step for cartoon animation with *Snow White and the Seven Dwarfs*. Rothacker was caught by Obie's imaginative idea and successfully negotiated with First National Pictures to finance the project.

Principal photography for the film began in 1923 and continued for fourteen months, with the picture eventually being released in 1925. The two-hour film proved to be the hit of the year, but the animation was the real star of the picture. According to Obie, the screenplay writer Marian Fairfax approached Obie during animation and said that in case the dinosaurs turned out not to be very good, she had written the screenplay in such a way that they could be left out! How do you make *The Lost World* without dinosaurs?

Unfortunately, despite the film's success, Obie's career was to enter a low lasting almost six years. But in 1930 Obie was reunited at RKO with Harry Hoyt when they planned a project called *Creation*. The story premise involved a yachting party and the crew of a Chilean submarine who are swept up by a gigantic storm into a massive extinct volcano containing a land full of dinosaurs. Obie and his team

worked for over a year on concepts and tests, but in 1931 the production was cancelled. Nevertheless, it led to what would be the pinnacle of his career. Some of the ideas and concepts from the doomed film were used in Obie's next project, *King Kong*, and so *Creation* was the basis on which the techniques to make Kong were established.

Obie never gave up hope on any of his projects, even when their future seemed bleak. *Creation* was no exception. Discovering that Merion C. Cooper (or Coop to Obie) had a pet project about a gorilla and Kimodo dragons, which the RKO front office were reluctant to produce, Obie and Bryon Crabbe prepared an oil painting of a scantily-clad native woman and an explorer being attacked by a huge ape. He showed the work to Coop and told him that the ape could be made as large as he wanted with his special effects. However, Coop still needed to sell the complete idea to the front office, and so a test reel was made of two sequences: Kong shaking men off a huge log that breached a chasm, and a fight with an allosaurus. Both these scenes turned out to be so exciting that Cooper had little selling to do for the picture and the RKO money men approved continuation of the production. Willis O'Brien was named chief technician and most of his crew from *Creation* were maintained. The rest is history. *King Kong*, one of the most enduring creations of the cinema, became reality.

So much has been written about the film that I can add very little to the record. Obie was a private man, not given to talking about his career, and I was always too shy to ask about his own personal recollections of the film. However, towards the end of his life he did say of it, '*King Kong* represents the goal of more than twenty years', and later, his wife Darlyne commented: '*King Kong* was Obie. It was his personality. I could just see Obie in Kong's every movement, every gesture.' Obie was in love with the medium he was working with, and I think that love shows in this film more than any other he was involved with. It was his crowning glory, the fruits of all those tortured years of development, disappointment and frustration, and although he would work on many other projects, none would be as successful nor as personal as this.

Close on the tail of Kong, perhaps a little too close, came *Son of Kong*, the disastrous sequel. Following on, in 1935 O'Brien was the supervisor of effects for Cooper and RKO on *She* and *The Last Days of Pompeii*. In 1938 he again worked with Merian C. Cooper on *War Eagles*, based on an original idea by Cooper about the discovery of a lost world in a huge extinct volcano in Antarctica. It was at this time that I first met Obie, arriving at his office clutching my models, to be confronted by so many wonders of film-making – my hero surrounded by the tools of the trade. Sadly, fate intervened with the advent of war in Europe, and the project was cancelled by MGM. In 1941 John Speaks' Colonial Picture Company secured a co-production deal with RKO to make one of O'Brien's own original storylines about cowboys discovering dinosaurs in a lost valley. The project was to be called *Gwangi*, but once again the project never struggled past the development phase, as the studio went through an executive shake-up.

Shortly after the war, Cooper and Schoedsack were reunited, and along with John Ford began plans to make *Mr Joe Young of Africa* (later *Mighty Joe Young*), hiring Obie as creator of special effects. It had been

thirteen years since the success of *King Kong*. As the project required careful planning and the development of complex special effects, Obie found that he had little time for the actual animation itself, and so decided, along with Cooper, to hire an assistant to complete the major animation. As I had remained in touch with him since my visit during *War Eagles* and had worked alongside him on a George Pal *Puppetoons* film, he contacted me asking if I would be interested. Of course I said yes, and so began my professional career under his watchful gaze, working my way up from mounting storyboards during pre-production to the animation of much of the film. Obie's ability as a designer and continuity artist was equalled only by his talents for being able to put on the motion picture screen, in dimensional form, the most amazing photographic illusions, all fired by his immense imagination. He taught me that there should be no limits to my own imagination.

At the age of sixty-four O'Brien's unique talents were recognized for the first time by his peers. On 23 March 1950 the Academy of Motion Picture Arts and Sciences awarded *Mighty Joe Young* an Oscar® for Best Special Effects. I was fortunate to have accompanied him on that special night, the only one from the team. We both rented our tuxedos and went to the ceremony together. The effects award was contested between *Mighty Joe Young* and a film called *Tulsa* that had effects by John Fulton, whose father had worked on our production. As the nominations were read out I felt Obie tense up, and when the film was announced everyone stood up and clapped as Obie nervously collected the statuette from the stage. I clapped perhaps harder than most, proud that his work had at long last been appreciated, as it should have been for *King Kong*. Even then the statue did not bear his name, only the title of the picture, so the statue was really the producers. However, a few days later Cooper presented it to Obie, and that statue was always proudly displayed in his home.

At the age of seventy-six Willis O'Brien suffered a fatal heart attack on 8 November 1962. He was watching television when Darlyne heard a gasp and turned to see Obie fall on his side. I was filming in Spain at the time, and because I didn't bother to read the papers, I didn't hear of his death until months later. It is one of the greatest regrets of my life that I didn't have the opportunity to attend his funeral and pay my final respects.

Willis O'Brien was never fully appreciated by his contemporaries. He was a man with a vision and with the imagination to go with it. So many ideas and so many wonderfully visual creatures to put up there on the screen, yet so many of them unrealized. In Darlyne's words: 'He was still just a boy and a dreamer. He never seemed to grow up.' He could see the end result but could never really handle Hollywood people, and his enthusiasm was misinterpreted. I have always been amazed that, in spite of all that happened to him, he was always such a happy man. He was inspired, so nothing else seemed to matter. He could execute marvellous drawings, paintings and even cartoons under the direst circumstances – circumstances that a lesser person would find unbelievably depressing. Only now is his work fully recognized by both movie historians and audiences, and he is accepted today as the founder of the art of stop-motion model animation in America. His legacy lives on.

CHAPTER 1 DISCOVERY OF A GIANT APE

King Kong

The Lost World

Cave Bear

Evolution of The World

Puppetoons

Mother Goose Stories

Out of an uncharted, forgotten corner of the world, a monster… surviving 7 million years of evolution… crashes into the haunts of civilization… onto the talking screen… to stagger the imagination of man!

From the souvenir programme for *King Kong* (1933)

Fantasy is the very basis of my career, and movies allowed me to make reality of my dreams, breathing life into all the ideas that existed in my mind. Likewise, if the genre of fantasy had never existed, I would never have worked in film. Through three-dimensional, stop-motion model animation I was privileged, like Willis O'Brien before me, to realize my dreams and capture them for others to wonder at. My obsession with fantasy has been lifelong, growing during my formative years and being taken to new heights by novels, paintings and films, and was always encouraged by my parents. They nurtured this unusual passion in me by taking me to films and theatre, and later enthused about my experiments with models and animation, eventually even helping with the productions. They never tried to discourage me in any way with my obsession, and could have just as easily said: 'Get out there and be a doctor or a lawyer or follow some other profession that is going to bring in money.' Fortunately, they didn't.

My grandfather, Frederick L. Harryhausen, arrived in San Francisco from Germany in 1850 and settled in Nevada City, where my father was born. My grand-father's immigration papers listed him as a goldminer, an unusual classification bestowed on some immigrants in an attempt to encourage European refugees. With him came his brother Chris, and like my grandfather he was classified as a goldminer, although fate allowed him, at some later date, to acquire an interest in a goldmine near Jerome, Arizona. Sadly, the seam ran out, otherwise I might have become a playboy sunning myself on the Riviera.

I was an only child, born 29 June 1920 in Los Angeles when my mother, Martha (née Reske), was thirty-two years old. Born in San Francisco, one of my earliest recollections of my mother was her nervousness about earthquakes – as a young girl she lived through the big one of 1906 and lost her home. Both my parents indulged me with frequent Sunday trips to favourite haunts: museums, movie houses and one of my greatest loves, the ocean. As I have said, both were a huge influence on my chosen career, but it was my mother who directly encouraged me by channelling my interests in whatever way I wished. When I was very young, it was she who would take me to a park on the other side of town where special events and activities were held for kids. There I would learn, with gentle encouragement from her, to make moulds of animals and buildings and to use the artistic talents that I seemed to possess. She would strive to give her son every opportunity to achieve in life and to get ahead.

My father, Fred Harryhausen, was a freelance machinist by trade, and worked wherever the work took him in and around Los Angeles. Coincidentally, at one time he was briefly employed in the machine shop at the RKO studios. He was a hugely talented man, much in demand, and in his spare time he developed and patented various inventions, including a folding trunk rack for autos and a centre finder for cutting out wood. I would watch him work, and as I grew older he passed some of his mechanical talents on to me, teaching me to use my hands along with my imagination to solve difficult concepts of design. When I began working on my amateur and later professional films, he would help me, primarily in the construction of the ball and socket joints for the models, a task he continued to do right up to his death. He also built me my first camera crane out of an old car fly wheel for *The Story of King Midas*. This included a complex facility made of cogs and gears that allowed me to raise and lower the camera whilst shooting a sequence in stop-motion.

My schooling, through grammar school on 54th Street to high school at the Audobon Junior High School in Lemert Park and finally to the Manual Arts High School (where Frank Capra had been a student), was relatively straightforward, with only the occasional hint at what I was to do with my life. I suppose my initiation into the world of miniatures occurred whilst I was at grammar school. The teacher presented the class with a project that entailed constructing models of Californian Missions such as San Juan Capistrano and Carpentaria. I recollect enjoying it immensely, working with clay and mud to construct buildings and imagining the characters that would inhabit these tiny worlds. From that point in time I developed a yen for building three-dimensional objects, which eventu-ally led me to create my own prehistoric dioramas

Left hand page. *King Kong.* A paste-up image or publicity still of Kong, clutching a scantily clad Fay Wray, towering over the New York skyline from an original *Hollywood Reporter* presentation/souvenir issue that had the distinction of being covered in copper.

occupied with clay saurians with toothpick teeth. Unaware of it at the time, these miniature worlds would give me the necessary background to realize most of my dreams as I grew older.

My mother was also keen on 'encouraging' me to appreciate the world of music and dance. Again, I was grateful for this later in life. She enrolled me in tap dancing classes at the Meglan Kiddies school where I appeared in at least one stage show. Later I took violin and piano lessons. I remember the violin classes very well: there were about twelve other little horrors all screeching together to reproduce something that sounded like twelve cats being castrated – I only survived six agonizing lessons. The piano was a different matter entirely. I loved the instrument but the teacher didn't believe I had the talent. Some years later my German aunt, Tonta Hecht, gave me her old zither, on which I managed only a bad rendition of 'Nearer My God to Thee'. Of course, none of this tuition led to anything except when I was asked to clash some cymbals at a recording in 1997. Everyone seemed very impressed, and I wondered if I had missed my vocation. Probably not.

Alongside my parents, school taught me to focus on my interests from the very earliest age. I was encouraged to appreciate all aspects of the arts: film, theatre, books, painting and sometimes an entertainment out of the ordinary. I remember being taken to see the Yale Puppeteers, and later the Salzburg Marionettes, at the Orpheum Theater in downtown LA, both of which were possibly my first contact with moving puppets and models. Much later, at high school, I was initiated into the art of model making (my mother taught me how to make papier-mâché heads), movement and learning how to operate string marionettes. My English teacher wanted the class to perform a play about good and bad English, personifying it all with puppets. Apart from the devil as the bad element and a dragon in it somewhere, I remember very little about it, but it was this little production that gave me inspiration on how to bring fantasy creatures alive. Later, after I had seen *King Kong*, I adapted the film's story, constructing Kong and the dinosaurs as marionettes and performing 'highlights' of the film in front of the school.

As a small boy I was fascinated by prehistoric animals and dinosaurs. In those days I was out there on my own when it came to dinosaurs, as there wasn't the interest in them then as there is today. LA was a perfect location for helping to visualize these extraordinary

creatures, and three very important sites became a focus of my interest and imagination. The first was a most bizarre spot for a Sunday excursion, a highly active peat field in the Baldwin Hills, close to where we lived. My parents would drive me out there to watch the mist rising from them, and shrouded in the swirling steam I would imagine prehistoric landscapes occupied with strange creatures that once roamed the land. The second of my prehistoric haunts was the Los Angeles County Museum (later the Museum of Natural History), in which were displayed the bones of woolly mammoths, sabre-toothed tigers and dire wolves together with one or two dinosaur skeletons. These skeletons were my first encounter with the long dead reptiles, firing my imagination to a point where I wanted to know everything there was to know about them. I didn't realize it at the time, but this strange relationship would continue throughout my life. The Pleistocene creatures in the museum were discovered in the third of my prehistoric haunts, the La Brea tar pits, where they so long ago had been trapped in the thick oil-mud and tar bubbling up to the surface. These pits were located at Hancock Park which, when I was young, was way out at the edge of town and they were just part of the landscape, a little isolated prehistoric world all of its own. Today they are part of what is known as 'The Miracle Mile' of Wilshire Boulevard, completely obliterated by massive buildings.

Also feeding my insatiable appetite for fantasy were books. Reading was, and still is, an important pastime, but as a child it was the gateway to a world of wonder, a means by which my mind could create my own adventures. My earliest recollection was of 'The Wonder Books', which really did make me wonder! They were a beautifully illustrated series of young people's encyclopaedias that contained many different and diverse scientific developments alongside paintings and drawings of mythology, fairy tales and trips to the planets and the outer reaches of the Galaxy. From there I discovered, like so many young people of my era, H.G. Wells, who made an enormous impression on my young mind. His scientific adventures *The War of the Worlds*, *The Time Machine*, *The Island of Dr Moreau*, *First Men in the Moon* and *The Invisible Man* were all food for my imagination. One of Wells' contemporaries, Sir Arthur Conan Doyle was also a firm favourite. It was not just his scientific sleuthing in the guise of Sherlock Holmes, but also the adventures of the formidable Professor Challenger, begun in a book

that was to be very important to me, *The Lost World*.

Again, with my mother's gentle encouragement I also discovered the joys of art. Many artists have directly and indirectly affected and influenced my work, but none more so than Gustave Doré, Charles Knight and John Martin, all primarily painters of fantasy subjects. Throughout my films there are tributes to these three men, but perhaps Doré has been the most influential. Although I became aware of Doré's style (the dark foreground, medium plane and light plane in the background, creating a wonderful sense of depth), it wasn't until I met Willis O'Brien that I fully appreciated his imagination and style. Obie taught me how he had based so much of *King Kong* on Doré's work. For example, the fallen log was lifted right out of *Atala*. Doré instilled a theatricality into his illustrations that lent themselves so well to cinema compositions and in turn explains why many motion picture art directors were influenced by his engravings. Perhaps it can be said that Doré was the first real art director of the movies.

If Doré and Martin were the style, Charles R. Knight's wonderful interpretations of prehistoric creatures were the basis of my models. Long before Obie, myself and Steven Spielberg, he put flesh on creatures that no human had ever seen. His dinosaur and prehistoric animal paintings and sculptures had more than just a realistic surface quality; they also possessed scientific reality and natural beauty. He was the first to reconstruct prehistoric life in a romantic form and the first to work in close collaboration with palaeontologists to attempt to achieve scientifically accurate anatomy. His long experience in drawing and painting live animals in zoos, together with his romantic and vivid imagination, helped to instil his prehistoric reconstructions with a 'charisma' only found in living creatures. At the LA County Museum I vividly remember a beautiful Knight mural on one of the walls depicting the way the tar pits would have looked in ancient times. This, plus a picture-book about Knight's work my mother gave me, were my first encounters with a man who was to prove an enormous help when the time came for me to make three-dimensional models of these extinct beings.

The final ingredient for what would become my life and career was again due to my parents. They were avid filmgoers, taking me from the tender age of three to see both the latest popular films and more unusual subjects. So it was in 1925 that I saw *The Lost World*. This was heady stuff for such a young mind.

Right. Still of parents. My parents, Fred and Martha Harryhausen, with our dog Kong.

Far right. *The Lost World*. Although I was only five at the time, *The Lost World* made a huge impression on me, especially the scene where a huge brontosaurus falls off the plateau and into a lake of mud where it lies struggling.

Right hand page. Another illustration from an original *Hollywood Reporter* presentation/souvenir issue covered in copper. A pre-production drawing by artists Willis O'Brien and Byron Crabbe that illustrates how the Kong/tyrannosaurus sequence would look.

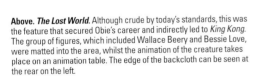

Above. *The Lost World.* Although crude by today's standards, this was the feature that secured Obie's career and indirectly led to *King Kong*. The group of figures, which included Wallace Beery and Bessie Love, were matted into the area, whilst the animation of the creature takes place on an animation table. The edge of the backcloth can be seen at the rear on the left.

Right. Still from *The Lost World*. The fight between the allosuarus and triceratops seemed so exciting when I saw this as a child.

Right hand page. Another pre-production drawing from the *Hollywood Reporter* presentation/souvenir issue, this time drawn by artists Byron Crabbe and Willis O'Brien. This would become one of the most famous scenes in the film where Kong, having secured Fay Wray for himself, tries to 'shake off' his pursuers.

Suddenly everything seemed to come together and the long-dead creatures from the La Brea tar pits came alive. The image of that brontosaurus kept reappearing in my mind's eye, and from that moment I knew I wasn't alone in my fascination with dinosaurs.

Of course there were many other films, some good and some bad, that have 'struck a cord' and allowed me to dream of adventures and fantasy. Fritz Lang's *Metropolis* (1926), with its fabulous concept of a futuristic city and the robot Maria being 'converted' into a living being. Great stuff for an impressionable boy. Another Fritz Lang fantasy film, *Siegfried* (1924), created a mythological world where the titanic hero bathes in the blood of the slain dragon. That dragon would be another image that would stay in my mind for future reference. I was sixteen when I saw the Russian film *The New Gulliver* (1935), a tour de force of stop-motion model animation which is virtually unknown today but, at the time, was one of the earliest and most complex examples of live action and puppet animation. Directed by Alexander Ptushko, it told of a small boy who dreams of the land of Lilliput where workers revolt against the monarchy. For me, the movement of the tiny characters was totally absorbing while the underlying politics went right over my head.

Other films that made an impression were Frank Capra's dream of a Utopian world *Lost Horizon* (1937), Alexander Korda's *Things to Come* (1936), *The Man Who Could Work Miracles* (1936), *The Thief of Bagdad* (1940) and *Jungle Book* (1942). It was inevitable that I would happen across a Merian C. Cooper production eventually. All of his pictures, for example *The Most Dangerous Game* (1932), *She* (1935) and *The Last Day of Pompeii* (1935), possessed high production values and never shied away from giving full rein to imagination. Cooper along with director Ernest Schoedsack filmed adventures that seemed to be much more believable to me than other similar pictures of the time, perhaps due to the fact that they had been real adventurers and explorers. It was a Cooper/ Schoedsack adventure that was to be the inspiration for my life – the one and only *King Kong* (1933). This film would set me off on the next phase of my career: the experimentation with stop-motion animation. Once I had seen the picture, my life was never the same again, and when I look back I find it all rather difficult to believe that in one afternoon a film about a giant gorilla had the influence to alter the direction of my entire life.

This turning point happened when my aunt, a nurse, was caring for the mother of Sid Grauman, the owner of Grauman's Chinese Theater (now known as Mann's Chinese) on Hollywood Boulevard and Highland Avenue. At that time it was one of Hollywood's most famous and prestigious movie theatres, renowned for its showmanship, presentation and premieres. Sid was grateful to my aunt, and to show his appreciation he gave her three complimentary tickets to the film currently showing. So at the impressionable age of thirteen I set off with my mother and aunt to see a movie about a gorilla – and I really liked gorilla movies.

I can remember every detail of that day very clearly. The forecourt was decorated with a Skull Island jungle setting: ferns, tropical plants, live pink flamingos and a full-size moving bust of Kong himself. This exotic presentation (not unusual in those great days of cinema exploitation) seemed to a young boy who had been weaned on fantasy to herald something entirely new, a fact confirmed by the front of house stills showing a huge creature towering over a city. I realized that this was going to be something very special. Sitting between my mother and my aunt in three of the best seats in the house, the lights eventually went down and a live seventeen-act show began, featuring native dancers and acrobats, all conceived and staged by Sid Grauman. It was included in the admission price and was part of the 'build-up' to the feature. I just sat there mesmerized by the sheer grandeur of it all, becoming more and more excited.

Following the one-hour show, the feature began and from the very first frame I was hooked. The adventure on Skull Island, the capture of the proud beast, the rampage through Manhattan and the death at the hands of the planes, carried me along as though this fantastic story was the most natural thing in the world. I was captivated. I had seen movies with men in gorilla suits, but when Kong appeared from behind those trees I knew he was something special, a real 'Eighth Wonder of the World'. Deep down I knew the images couldn't be real but in the back of my mind I hoped they were. I became obsessed with its magic, which some people might find a touch eccentric in one so young. Perhaps this is true, but I have found over the years that 'extravagant enthusiasm' can make all the difference in turning desire into actuality. In my case, wonderment into a career. The film stands on its own as a landmark in movie making, a pioneering technical achievement. But it's more than that: it's a triumph of storytelling, an audacious adventure into a fantastic world of make-believe that succeeds in balancing reality and fantasy. This was an ingredient that intrigued me.

After I saw *Kong*, another 'unusual' location was added to our Sunday outings. I would make my father drive me out to Culver City to the old Pathé lot to see the Skull Island wall and gate. It could be seen from the road, looming high over the other derelict movie set constructions. Friends and I would sometimes stand at the wire gate and stare at this physical symbol of Kong, reciting 'Tabe, Bala kum nono hi, Bala! Bala!' – the very words spoken by Captain Englehorn to the island's chief. For years 'Kong's wall', as it was known by everyone in Hollywood, survived, although sadly I never got to go into the studio for a closer look. It

was eventually burned for the Atlanta fire sequence in *Gone With The Wind*.

Years later my wife and I visited the Nais Islands (also mentioned in the dialogue of *Kong*). I tried using the film's speech on some of the natives, and although I didn't get my face slapped, the blank look on some of their faces suggested I was still living a dream. Ruth Rose, who co-wrote the *King Kong* screenplay, loved to 'invent' languages for films based on actual dialects from all parts of the world. Ruth once told me that she had tried to base it on an actual obscure language, but sadly I don't remember which one. Presumably not one from the Nais Islands.

I collected everything I could on *King Kong* and became aware that Kong and the other creatures inhabiting the island must have been filmed by means of 'special' techniques. Once I had realized this, it became the most important thing in my life to discover the true secrets of *King Kong*. This self-education was a painfully slow process, filtering out the mass of uninformed guesswork and misleading material and building up a true picture of the processes and the people behind it. There was one curious article in *Popular Science* that included an artist's impression of how Kong was moved. It showed a big gorilla walking through a jungle in the studio with wires coming out of its heels and a man off frame playing an organ that was supposed to have animated the creature. My first reaction was: 'That can't be true.'

Eventually I was lucky enough to meet several people (one of whom was a friend of my father) who had worked on the picture in minor capacities, and they told me about stop-motion: how the process was done, how long it took, in fact everything they knew

of the team that had animated the creatures and created the miniatures. I was also lucky that the Los Angeles Museum had at that time an exhibition devoted to various phases of motion picture production, including a section on special effects. Apart from a montage of clips showing the Dunning and Williams processes of matte shots and travelling mattes, amongst the items on display were model dinosaurs from *The Lost World*, the miniature plane and a wooden 'stand-in' figure of Kong, all of which were gifts from Willis O'Brien. I spent hours at that exhibition learning everything I could from the models and miniature props.

Once these basics had been revealed to me, the rest of the puzzle began to fit together as I read more accurate magazine articles that described in detail stop-motion, ball and socket joints and glass paintings. One crucial article was in *Look* magazine. It described scaled-down props, painted scenery on layers of glass all optically matched with real human actors and which demonstrated how miniature animals with ball and socket skeletons and rubber hides were moved in front of the camera as one frame of film was clicked off to establish motion. It was this article that mentioned the man who had pioneered the process of animation and miniatures: Willis O'Brien. As I continued to study and learn how the effects for *Kong* were achieved, I realized this was something I wanted to try for myself and perhaps be part of, so I began to construct my own miniature dioramas and models, which eventually led me to take the step in making larger moveable figures and creatures.

My first real attempt at constructing a model for animation purposes was a cave bear. Constructed of a wooden frame with the ball and socket joints made out of beads, it also featured a moving tongue, claws

Left and above. My first attempt at a stop-motion model, the cave bear. In addition to crude joints it also had the ability to move its jaws and eyes. I am glad to say that it is still with me today, although rather sadly it has along the way lost its head to another model creature.

Above. My earliest attempts at model making. These are (I still have them) my string puppets that I made to re-entact the creatures I had seen in *King Kong*. From left to right: the stegosaurus, Kong and the brontosaurus. I made them with the help of my mother, who also helped me with the backcloth and the miniature trees.

Right hand page. The stegosaurus (which I had shown to Obie) in its diorama that won 'only' second prize in the Los Angeles Museum competition.

and eyes. To cover the bear I needed some fur, so I looked around and found an old black fur coat hanging in my mother's closet. I thought, 'that's perfect', and proceeded to cut it up for my creation. Contrary to some articles about this incident, it was *not* used for a woolly mammoth, my mother *did* know all about it and I *did* have her blessing before I proceeded.

Other creations followed: a stegosaurus, brontosaurus and a woolly mammoth. The earliest was a 6-foot long brontosaurus, with a wooden frame and a hard papier-mâché torso that didn't bend. The neck and tail were made from flexible table lamps, allowing them to be moved into different positions and still hold their shape. They were the only things I could find at the time, as I hadn't learnt how to build complex metal joints. To cover the wooden frame I used bath sponges over which I slipped my mother's old silk stockings before covering the whole thing with liquid latex. Some of my other creations, although not as impressive, were a three-toed sloth and a pterodactyl. Helped by my father, these were progressively more professional in construction, attaining more flexibility for animation. It was around this time that I entered a model-making competition held by the Los Angeles Museum for junior members. I submitted my stegosaurus within a miniature prehistoric set. The model was 20 inches long with a latex cover over a wooden armature complemented with eight automobile rearview mirror hinges (the only ball and sockets I could find but a step up from angle-poise lamps) to allow it more flexibility. I thought this couldn't fail to catch the eye of the judges and was devastated when it only won second Blue Ribbon prize.

At the same time I was constructing these creatures I was also working on techniques of how to animate them on film. For this I needed a camera. My first was a 16mm Victor, borrowed from Jack Roberts, a friend of mine. It didn't possess a one-frame shaft to shoot proper stop-frame animation, so I just tapped the release button quickly and prayed that it had shot the one frame required. Sometimes this rather hit and miss method achieved two or even three frames, which when viewed at the projected speed accounted for a jerky movement in the characters. Of course, I didn't possess any lights, so my first experiments were carried out in the garden where I constructed miniature sets for the models. My very first test was with the cave bear, shot on cheap black and white stock. When I received the processed film back, only half of the picture came out. Something had happened in the developing. I was so disappointed and discouraged. Aside from lab mistakes, I also quickly learned that filming animation in the open had one major disadvantage. Once again I spent hours animating the bear, and when the film came back this time, I realized that the shadows cast by the set and the model bear were moving on the screen like time-lapse photography as the sun moved across the sky. After seeing these early films, my father consented to let me use part of the garage as a studio, and over the year or so that followed I gradually accumulated lights and other paraphernalia suitable for indoor filming. As the garage space was limited, the last experiment I filmed in the open was with my 6-foot brontosaurus. Because of its size, the only place it could be accommodated was in the open with real foliage and trees. My parents' enthusiasm never waned. My mother continued to encourage me and my father built me a little bench where I could make my models and sets.

It was about that time I purchased my own camera, a 16mm Kodak Cine II Special possessing the much needed one-frame shaft. I still have that camera today. Now owning a studio and camera, I could begin proper experiments with miniature sets, models and other adventurous techniques that I could never have done in the open. Gradually I became familiar with the intricacies of animation, and my experiments slowly began to acquire a smoothness and fluidity in movement. I also began to experiment with optical techniques, learning the basics from magazine articles. The first of these was a static matte in an experiment which reused the cave bear model and featured myself and Kong, my German shepherd, as the live action. The scenario involved the bear lumbering out of his cave and taking a swipe at me, but as he does so, I duck down, and then the bear returns to his lair. Unfortunately, Kong didn't understand why he was just standing there and ran through the matte line, totally disappearing in mid-scene.

While the sequence was crude, it was a thrill for me, as I had now introduced live characters for my models to react to. It was a major turning point and would be the basis of what would lead to my feature techniques.

Although I loved what I was doing, at the back of my mind I did wonder if this 'hobby' would stand up as a career or simply lead to a dead-end. Looking back, I always knew in my heart what I was aiming for, but alongside that was the fear I wouldn't succeed. I did consider other careers – commercial art, palaeontology, archaeology – and although I was interested in them all, none really excited and intrigued me like stop-motion. Sometimes I wondered if I was cut out for such an exacting vocation. Patience in my profession

Left and above. Mammoth. The mammoth is another model from that early period which I still possess today. Its long tusks are made of carved wood and painted to resemble ivory, and the fur, obtained from a local taxidermist, was actually Siberian goat hair.

Below left. My first brush with fame. An article in *Popular Mechanics* magazine showing a very young Harryhausen designing and animating some of those prehistoric creations.

Below right. Jupiterian. My first alien was a ridiculous creature from the planet Jupiter that possessed six arms, a grotesque face, and was completely out of proportion.

Right hand page. The brontosaurus model for *Evolution*. In this still of the brontosaurus being animated in a miniature set in my hobby house, the depth of the image is created not only by the miniature set, but also by the glass painting in the front.

Belonging to the Los Angeles Science Fiction League encouraged me to try something different from my usual dinosaur films. I created my first alien, and although it was meant to be part of a wider story, I made only one drawing of the creature, showing it attacking a rocket ship, but I did build an armatured model and photographed the sequence, making up the action as I went along. There was no storyline. Oh halcyon days!

is an absolute necessity, and this was a commodity I was sometimes short of, although over the years I learned to temper my restlessness. I remember once, in my garage studio whilst I was animating a dinosaur, that things were not going right. Gradually they got worse and worse, as they do in situations where you don't keep your temper, and in a fit of accumulated rage I threw a hammer at the floor. Unfortunately, it bounced and went straight through a huge plate glass painting I had been preparing to use in a miniature set and which I had spent weeks carefully painting. I almost cried with frustration, and there and then decided that if I wanted to make this my career, I would have to control my temper. I am not saying that I didn't lose my temper after that incident – I did – but I always tried to remember that plate glass painting. It was a timely and necessary lesson.

It was about this time that I met two people who would become lifelong friends. *King Kong* led to my friendship with Forrest (Forry) J. Ackerman, a young fantasy buff who would go on to become the editor of *Famous Monsters of Filmland* magazine. During the 1938 re-release of *Kong*, at the Hawthorn picture house, I noticed some stills on display and asked whose they were. They turned out to be Forry's, and he kindly gave me the photographs, which for years after were a basic source of inspiration. Since that time we have remained good friends. Realizing my passion for fantasy, Forry suggested that I should try out the Los Angeles Science Fiction League. At that time the League included A.E. Van Vogt and Robert Heinlein, both of whom would go on to become world-famous science fiction writers. It was at that first meeting that I met the second of my lifelong friends, Ray Bradbury.

Ray and I soon discovered we had a lot in common, but it was our mutual tenacity in the pursuit of our chosen careers – he with his writing and I with my experiments in animation and photography – that would bind us together. We would talk for hours on the phone, almost every conversation dominated by the subject of dinosaurs and making elaborate plans to produce and film outrageously complicated science fiction projects. Unfortunately, none of these ideas actually matured, and we never did work on a film together, at least not directly, although both our names were to be linked with *The Beast From 20,000 Fathoms*.

As interesting as alien creatures were, I found dinosaurs to be the ideal subject for stop-motion animation, something Willis O'Brien had discovered long before. The fact that nobody knew how those huge reptiles had moved or, for that matter, exactly how they looked meant that I could bring them alive without any fear of criticism. So it was in about 1938 that I began to think about making a full-length film entitled *Evolution of the World*. I planned it to encompass the very beginnings of life on Earth, from the swirling gases in space, through the age of dinosaurs, to the appearance of mammals. It was to have included sequences showing various creatures, including a brontosaurus and a tyrannosaurus rex, with the whole thing culminating with creatures and early Neolithic men being sucked into tar pits like La Brea. For a young teenager to attempt this enormous epic in his father's garage was far too ambitious an undertaking. But 'ignorance is bliss', and I cheerfully embarked on the project with complete neophyte enthusiasm, not thinking about the consequences.

Although the project was a challenge, it enabled me to improve the flow of movement in my models. One

Above. Tyrannosaurus. The tyrannosaurus from my ambitious *Evolution of the World* project.

Right. My sculpture called Cowboy and falling horse. This is my copy of the Remington-like sculpture of a cowboy falling from his horse.

Right hand page. War Eagles. A Duncan Gleason key drawing for the unrealized project *War Eagles*, one of many I must have seen when I visited Obie at MGM during the pre-production.

sequence shows a brontosaurus clomping through the mist (painted on glass) as tiny birds (cut from tin) fly by on invisible support wires. Another sequence shows an allosaurus, snapping and snarling, leaping into the foreground. Years later I was to recreate this sequence in *The Animal World*.

I was also experimenting with mattes, for which I had made my own crude matte box. The effect was seen in a key sequence showing a brontosaurus by a river and later climbing out of a large body of water. The river sequence was a double exposure matte in the camera, for which I matted out the area where I proposed that the water should be whilst I animated the model. I then rewound the film and Dad drove me out to Lake Sherwood to photograph the water whilst the matte box covered up the already exposed animation. Of course it wasn't very accurate, but for a teenager this was magic. There was also a down shot of the creature emerging from a black area. This area should have been water, but unfortunately I didn't get time to photograph it (which I had intended to do at the beach) before the film was developed, so all you see is what look like splashes (animated cotton wool).

Perhaps the most important experiments were in techniques that would eventually become known as Dynamation, a cheaper and more efficient method of combining the action in the foreground with depth. One surviving example of these tests used a model of an allosaurus animated against a natural background. This was later developed for *The Beast From 20,000 Fathoms*. *The Beast* was simply the sum total of years of testing an idea. In fact, soon after completing the first of my post-war Fairy Tales, I was to continue to carry out the rear projection Dynamation tests on a resurrection of the *Evolution* idea entitled the *La Brea Tar Pits* project. However, whilst making *Evolution*, I was mainly using Obie's methods of deep miniature sets and glass paintings. The true importance of the Dynamation process was still hidden from me.

All my work on *Evolution* came to an abrupt end when I went to see Disney's new animated feature *Fantasia* (1940). To my horror the wonderful 'Rites of Spring' sequence showed the dinosaurs and their demise, which was what I was trying to do with my project. I abandoned the entire project and at the same time realized that the concept of *Evolution* had been completely unrealistic for one person to try, especially when I had made no attempt to construct a script or storyboard the concept. It had taken Disney years to realize with a staff of over 300 people, and there I was attempting to visualize the dawn of our world all on my own. However, it would seem that the fickle finger of fate was at work because, as with most things, it turned out not to be a waste of time. The footage I had shot provided me with a rather unique demonstration reel as an example of what I could do on my own, and would be seen later by George Pal, Merian C. Cooper and, of course, Willis O'Brien, so enabling me to gain my first foothold into feature films.

I was still in high school when I first encountered Obie. It began after meeting a girl in social studies class who was reading a bound script of *King Kong* with illustrations. During recess I introduced myself and told her of my fanatical interest in *Kong* and how I was trying to emulate the creatures with my own experiments. It transpired that her father had worked with Obie on *The Last Days of Pompeii*, and she suggested that I simply call him at the MGM studios. I had to ask myself, 'Could contact with such a hero figure be that simple?' With some gentle encouragement from her I looked up the number. To my surprise he answered the phone. After some mumbled syllables from me, he suggested I call on him at the studio where he was in the process of preparing the adventure fantasy *War Eagles*. The time couldn't go quickly enough, but finally I found myself clutching a suitcase full of models and standing at the gate to MGM from where I was shown to the *War Eagles* production office. Knocking on Obie's door, I walked in and my jaw dropped. The walls were completely covered with paintings and drawings for the project. At that time he had three artists on the film, all producing beautiful artwork (some of which survives today).

It was all a boyhood dream. There I was sitting with the man who I admired more than any film star. I was a young kid still wet behind the ears, but he was so kind and thoughtful, putting me at my ease right away by talking about the *War Eagles* project and then asking me about my interest in stop-motion animation and encouraging me to open up and talk about my models, films and ambitions. He was aware that there were not many people interested in animation. Remembering my precious suitcase and struggling to control my nerves, I managed to produce my models. As he held the model of a stegosaurus (the one for which I had won a modelling prize) in his hands, I held my breath. Obie looked at it for a few minutes and then said: 'The legs look like wrinkled sausages. You've got to put more character into it and study anatomy to learn where the muscles connect to the bones.' This may sound brusque and unfeeling, but his criticism was gentle and constructive. I certainly didn't take offence when I looked and realized he was right. Looking at them through his eyes I could see that I seriously needed to study muscle structure, anatomy and sculpture. That day was another 'event' in my life and one that confirmed my future career, no matter what the sacrifice.

Six months later I went with my parents to visit Obie and his wife Darlyne at their home to show him some of my film experiments. Again, Obie gave me constructive criticism, helping me to realize where I had gone wrong, what I needed to improve and always enthusing over my little triumphs. Darlyne was also very supportive, and

years later she told me that after I had left clutching my cans of film, Obie looked at her sort of funny and said, 'You realize of course that you're encouraging my competition.'

In 1939 whilst still in high school I took Obie's advice and enrolled in art and anatomy night classes at the Los Angeles City College (LACC), gradually acquiring the skills to design my models with realism. It was about this time that fate led me to 'rediscover' some original O'Brien and Byron Crabbe sketches for the failed, pre-*King Kong* project *Creation*. In downtown Los Angeles in a shop next to the old Belasco Theater were three large pictures I instantly recognized as O'Brien and Crabbe's. One was an arsinotherium knocking men off a log; another was of a pterodactyl picking up a girl; and the last was of Mayan ruins with a girl pointing at a giant sloth. I almost jumped out of my shoes. A man called Goode owned the shop, and it turned out that he had attended an auction of Byron Crabbe's effects at which he had purchased the pictures. I asked the price but as I didn't have any money at that time I offered to sculpt some pieces based on the American artist Frederick Remington. He gave me some clay from which I made three separate sculptures of a cowboy on the back of a galloping horse. He made these into plaster casts that were then bronze-coated and sold in his shop.

Later still, in return for painting my portrait, I made an ape with a metal armature covered in latex and fur. Before I presented the model to him, I used it for a colour test of the creature sitting in a tree. I often wonder what happened to that ape and those pieces of plaster. Someone may still have one on their mantelpiece and not know it is a very early but original Ray Harryhausen.

I soon realized that I needed to gain more knowledge of the techniques of motion picture making, so I attended night classes at the University of Southern California (USC), where I studied art direction, photography and editing. The course was one of the earliest film schools,

operating from an old army Quonset hut, and I attended lectures given by studio technicians, directors, art designers and cinematographers like Lou Physioc, who among other techniques demonstrated the use of matte paintings and glass shots. In another fit of indecision about my chosen career I considered becoming an actor, but I was never sure if I could survive the strain. It was towards the end of high school that I first tried my hand at acting by joining the cast of the senior class performing an old-fashioned melodrama entitled *Shadow of the Rockies*. I was billed sixth, playing the character role of Judge Thompson for which I donned a bald cap wig with a rim of hair around the lower half – the shape of things to come!

Although the experience confirmed that I suffered from stage fright, I decided to take night courses in acting, the first of which was radio acting with a Miss Bird. Every Saturday we presented a short play on the local radio station, which I always found enjoyable and also stressful. My other acting class was held by Charlotte Knight, an actress, playwright and director who would become a dear friend, helping me later with scripts for several of my projects. She was a far more conservative teacher than Miss Bird, instructing me how to be less introvert, giving me confidence and persuading me to perform more naturally. In a 1959 article in *Argosy* magazine, a rather amusing quote by Charlotte reads, 'I was puzzled by this intensely introvert young man, who always chose to practice the basic animalistic passions of fear, anger and rage. It wasn't until years later when I attended a showing of *Mighty Joe Young* that I was able to put the pieces together. I could see in one of the gorilla grimaces that Ray had worked that out in our class.'

Although after the war I took up acting classes once again, at a day course at LACC, I realized that I was not really cut out for the stage. I couldn't face the terror of maybe forgetting lines and wondering if my fly was open. However, I did discover that acting was important to

understanding emotions and reactions, which I went on to instil in my models. I have always wanted audiences to feel sorry for my creatures when they are being destroyed – I suppose another legacy of *King Kong* – but the execution of that emotion is due to those acting ventures and people like Charlotte. Later, when working on *Mighty Joe Young*, I would strive for compassion in the creature, and would sit like a gorilla on the floor, acting out key scenes and timing each movement with a stopwatch. How long it would take to move my arms from one point to another, trying to synchronize it so that it looked natural and convey emotion when it came to converting the action into the animated model. The ability to instil character into creatures, no matter how alien the creature, is a key element in the animator's art. A movement of a hand, a turn of the head, the furrowing of a brow at the correct moment, these were all acted out before animation began, and all were due in some part to those teachers who attempted to teach me the finer points of acting.

By now I had begun to apply for jobs within the film industry, always searching for a career in animation, any kind of animation. I applied for a job at the Disney Studios but didn't get it. In retrospect this was the best thing that could have happened to me. It would never have suited me to end up as a cog in a machine. I don't say this to demean the Disney animators – the studio has created some memorable and remarkable films – but my path was a different one, and a job with a major studio would have been soul-destroying. Of course, I wasn't aware of this at the time, and all I wanted was a job where I could work in stop-motion model animation. My first professional employment came about in late 1938, when I applied for the position of animator on the newly formed George Pal *Puppetoons* being made for Paramount Pictures.

George Pal was Hungarian by birth but moved to the States to escape the Nazi regime. He was setting up a studio on McCadden Place and Santa Monica

Above. Ape armature. The metal armature of the ape I created for Goode in return for painting my portrait.

Right. Still from *Puppetoons*. Here I am working on the *Puppetoon Sky Princess*. The series was monotonous to work on but it did teach me patience and discipline.

Right hand page. Stills from *How to Bridge a Gorge*. By animating toy tanks, armoured cars and guns (bought at the local five and dime store) on a miniature tabletop set, my short film *How to Bridge a Gorge* showed what was possible with available engineering techniques.

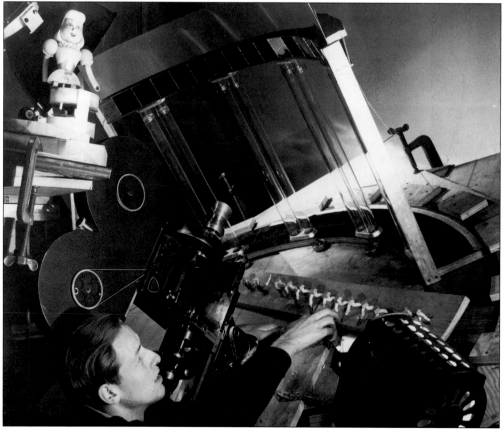

Blvd in Hollywood, and I had read that he was looking for a model animator. I rushed down there and showed him some of my models and 16mm footage of *Evolution*, and he immediately hired me as the first animator for a series of twelve 10-minute shorts. The first of these subjects were released under the generic title of *Madcap Models* but later became known as *Puppetoons*. Begun around 1938/39, they starred a very stylized, wide-eyed, innocent character called Jim Dandy, who always encountered trouble in one form or another. He featured in the first subject, *Western Daze* (in which George and I shared the animation). Several more followed before the character was abandoned because he never really caught on with the public. I felt the reason was his highly cubist appearance, which had a tendency to annihilate the warmth of the character. After that there followed *Hoola Boola* (a Dorothy Lamour send-up) with George and I sharing the animation again (after this, other animators were hired and George assumed his producer hat full time). Other titles I worked on were *Dipsy Gypsy*, *Sleeping Beauty*, *The Sky Princess*, *Mr Strauss Takes a Walk*, *Gaye Knighties*, *The Little Broadcast* and *Tulips Shall Grow* (which began life as *Nuts and Bolts*) and reflected the invasion of Holland by the Nazis.

Another *Puppetoon* character, Jasper, was a little African-American boy who eclipsed Jim Dandy. I animated three of the shorts he featured in: *Jasper and the Haunted House*, *Jasper and the Watermelons* and *Jasper and the Choo-Choo*. It was this last title on which I worked with Willis O'Brien for the first time. I had stayed in touch with him since our first meetings, but I couldn't believe my luck to be working alongside the great man. Sadly, dear old Obie didn't like the project at all and left after animating only a few scenes to work on another unrealized feature project.

I must confess that I knew how Obie felt. Although there were single puppets to be animated on occasion, Pal's main system for making the puppet films was to pre-animate most of the models on paper and from these designs the models were cut from wood. As I said, the overall design of the characters was almost cubist, with lathe-turned heads and square-cut bodies and legs. Twenty-five separate figures had to be made to assemble one complete step in the animation procedure, each model was progressively advanced from the previous one; very similar to the hand-drawn cartoon. A register pin is placed in the bottom of each puppet's foot enabling it to stand erect as well as always keeping the foot of each separate figure in the same exact place. This is accomplished by placing an accurate, pre-drilled hole in the (miniature) set that will receive the pin on the puppet. For the composition of the words and the vowels for each character there were a total of perhaps fifty heads, each one for a change of expression within each spoken word. When the film was projected at the correct speed, the words would be formed by the succession of heads to synchronize with the dialogue.

All very clever, but this method of animation was time-consuming, tedious and allowed for no originality on the part of the animator. Because the series required special departments for puppet construction, painting and set building, the costs were high, and over a year all we managed to complete were six 10-minute subjects. Although they were elegant in their own way, they were never successful, mainly because they again were too heavily stylised for public taste and were no competition to the antics of the *Tom and Jerry* cartoons.

I was being paid $16 a week when I started, which increased as Pal got to know me and recognized what I was capable of. It was hard work, sometimes animating until midnight or 2am trying to get a scene right and then to the Technicolor laboratory so that it was ready the next morning. The concentration of animation is so all-consuming and exhausting that one night whilst working alone in the wee small hours, I suddenly became giddy and fell over a camera. It was another lesson I would never forget and taught me to stop when I was tired.

I was with Pal for about two years and slowly realized that the *Puppetoons* conveyor-like process of animation was not for me. I needed to instil my own personality into the models, not laboriously animate what someone else had already planned out on paper. Obie with his experience had seen this within a few hours of his arrival at the studio. However, it had been an invaluable experience and training for me, but my stay with Pal was about to end, not because I moved to another studio, but because of the events at Pearl Harbor.

When war was declared, I realized as a twenty-two-year-old that I would be drafted, so I determined to prepare for something that I knew about: making films. Anticipating a war, Hollywood had begun classes for the training of combat cameramen, so whilst still working for Pal, I attended six months of evening classes on combat photography sponsored by Eastman Kodak at Columbia Studios. I was unaware at the time that combat photographers were as expendable as clay pigeons, but the courses did teach me a great deal about using different 35mm cameras, rapid loading and many other techniques vital in the field. What little spare time I had I used to make a 16mm 5-minute colour demonstration training film called *How to Bridge a Gorge*. I made it to illustrate how model animation could be used for troop training, and it was exactly what the title said it was, based on military photographs and articles from *Life* and *National Geographic* magazines.

Just before I began work on *How to Bridge a Gorge*

I decided that I had to find larger and more practical facilities to make my ever more complicated film projects. When I talked to my father about this problem, he was very understanding (I think he wanted the garage back for the car) and suggested that we build a small room behind the garage. So on weekends and nights my father and I (he designed and built most of it) constructed what we called the 'hobby house', purpose-built as a studio and into which I moved all my paraphernalia. When I visited LA on a trip in 1996 the hobby house was still there, although now it is used as a gym.

It was during this time that I had access to various major studios, including RKO. On a trip there to visit the still photography department I met with another hero of mine, Ernest Bachrach, one of Hollywood's great studio portrait photographers. He sat me down to have a chat, during which I inevitably talked about my obsession with *King Kong.* Reaching around the back of the couch in his office he produced the original paste-up of the log sequence.

I did consider asking Bachrach if I might buy the picture, but being bashful I thought it would be pushing my already unbelievable luck too far. If I had, I am sure he would have given it to me, but it just didn't seem right to ask him for it when he had been so kind to me. On another excursion to RKO I visited

the miniature department. As soon as I walked in I saw, high up on a shelf, all the original *King Kong* and *Son of Kong* models. I almost went out of my mind. There are many regrets in my life, but one of them has to be why I didn't ask 'Can I buy one?' Much later Forry obtained some of the models by accident when Desilu took over the RKO studios. He was told by some kid that he had taken a model of a dinosaur from the studios, so Forry instantly rang up RKO and retrieved, from a rotting pile in a damp basement, a few of the models. Nobody had any respect for what they were.

In 1942 I enlisted in the US Army and found myself assigned to the Army Signal Corps. I was sent to Fort MacArthur for training, which wasn't arduous but sometimes difficult for someone like me who was not violent by nature. However, I seem to have done pretty well, ending up with, amongst other things, a sharpshooter merit badge, due perhaps to the steady animator's hand. During training I made some enquiries about using my animation skills, and heard that the S.C.P.C. on Long Island were producing cartoon animated shorts and were experimenting in stop-motion model animation. I wrote to a Colonel M.E. Gillette on the East Coast stating my credentials and offering references from George Pal and Willis O'Brien but received no reply. Fortunately, I had

shown *How to Bridge a Gorge* to one of my teachers who in turn contacted Colonel Frank Capra and Major Sam Birkin, then starting up the Special Service Division that would be making orientation films for the US Government, with the director Anatole Litvak. Consequently the film was shown to Capra, Birkin and Litvak, resulting in my transfer from the Army Signal Corps to Special Service Division, the headquarters of which were located at the old Fox Studios at Western Avenue and Sunset Blvd. Because of my evening classes in combat photography, I was commissioned a Technical Sergeant T/3.

On the *Army–Navy Screen Magazine* series I worked as loader, clapper boy, gofer and later an assistant cameraman to such famous cinematographers as Joseph Biroc, Joseph Valentine and Joseph Vogal. I always hoped some of their expertise and professionalism would rub off onto me. We also travelled all over the States to film radio shows, concerts and theatre productions, with audiences made up from the armed forces.

After the *Army–Navy Screen Magazine*, I moved to *Why We Fight*, now a classic series, which had Capra supervising the editing with Merle White and William Hornbeck. Hornbeck was another hero figure of mine. He had worked with Alexander Korda on *The Man Who Could Work Miracles, Things To Come, The Thief Of Bagdad* and *Jungle Book.* My job was assistant

cameraman but I was also involved with travelling mattes for the connecting shots Capra required for linking archive footage together. Some of the sections were technical effects and sometimes dramatic visuals with actors. For example, one of the links had to show a Nazi soldier butting the handle of his rifle towards the centre of the screen, pretending to shatter the image like broken glass. As this first image broke into pieces, a new scene appeared behind. It was basically a wipe transition from one image to another, achieved by shooting the soldier against black velvet and making a high contrast matte from his moving image. The shattering effect was done on a light box by photographing pre-cut out black paper and animating the pieces away to resemble the breaking glass. The final composite picture was achieved in an optical printer.

To a lesser degree I also worked on another Capra war classic, *Negro Soldier*, made primarily to encourage black Americans into the forces. Basically all I did was some of the links, but at the end of the production the producer, Carlton Moss, and Capra asked me to make a sculpture of Dimitri Tiomkin, who had scored the picture. Tiomkin was a civilian attached to the Special Service Division and was the master composer on the *Why We Fight* series, going on to compose many classic feature scores. Unknown to 'Dimi', I secured photographs from his wife and from that I fashioned a 16-inch high plaster statue that portrayed him conducting from a podium with a very young black boy looking up at him.

It was presented to him at a Signal Corps special appreciation, and he was apparently so delighted with it that he kept it at home in pride of place. After the war I did keep in touch with him and often suggested him as composer for several of our films. Sadly, we could never afford him.

When I wasn't working on *Why We Fight* and another war time film *Guadalcanal*, I was always looking to diversify and learn. I found myself spending some time in the cartoon department (the Army Pictorial Service) where the famous *Snafu* series was being developed under theguidance of Major Ted Geisel, also known affectionately as Dr Seuss. Private Snafu, his name derived from 'Situation Normal, All Fouled Up'

Whilst I was working in the Special Service Division I was able to live with my parents, and went home after a day at the studios to work in my hobby house on another project called *Guadalcanal* (1943). It was a 10-minute colour short about the battle for Guadalcanal in the Pacific using model ships and planes. I hoped to demonstrate the usefulness of model animation in illustrating events and techniques for wartime use, much as I had tried to do with my earlier *How to Bridge a Gorge*. However, unlike the previous effort, this was a much more sophisticated project that used wipes, sound effects and music 'borrowed' from Max Steiner and Miklos Rozsa. For the sea I used a huge sheet of frosted ripple glass lit from below with a blue light, and for the waves on the glass I animated 'waves' of sand. The final touch was to show a Japanese ship sinking, and to simulate the distressed water I used salt, animated like the sand into ripples of white 'sea'.

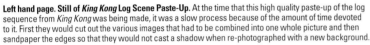

Left hand page. Still of *King Kong* Log Scene Paste-Up. At the time that this high quality paste-up of the log sequence from *King Kong* was being made, it was a slow process because of the amount of time devoted to it. First they would cut out the various images that had to be combined into one whole picture and then sandpaper the edges so that they would not cast a shadow when re-photographed with a new background.

Above left and below. Various Snafu models and set pieces I made for covers and illustrations in *Yank Army Weekly* magazine. The image on the far right below was used to warn troops about malaria.

Above right. The crew working on *Army–Navy Screen* magazine.

Right. *Army–Navy Screen* Magazine. With one of my heros Joe Biroc (cameraman) and Bill Birch (camera operator).

(in the Army there is a much stronger interpretation), was an Army cartoon character who did everything wrong. One day I was asked by Major Geisel to sculpt a model of Snafu (which I still have) to be used as a guide for the artists at the animation studio as well as for desk-top displays for Capra and Tiomkin.

As the end of war approached, we were advised that our post was soon to close and that the married men would leave first, to be followed six months later by the single men. I came into this second category, so I was shipped to Fort Monmouth in New York to await release into civilian life. Consequently, I was forced to consider what I wanted to do after leaving the services. I knew I could never go back to George Pal (although George had always said there was a job waiting if I wanted it) where I would feel trapped in the routine of animating other people's creations. Fortunately, my army career had shown me that there was a whole new world out there and that perhaps it was time to start out on my own. Television at that time was still a novelty, but according to all the industry papers (which I read regularly), it was on the threshold of becoming big. New York was the Mecca, so it occurred to me to try and adapt model animation for television commercials that I might be able to sell when I arrived in New York. In the months preceeding my departure for the East Coast and in my spare time I made a simple two-minute colour advertisement using Lucky Strike cigarettes. The whole thing was very simple, consisting of cigarettes coming to life, jumping out of the pack, dancing around the table (to the strains of 'Surrey with the Fringe on Top') and returning to the pack. When I arrived in New York I had the film tucked firmly under my arm, with high hopes that it would be snatched up by the first advertisement agency I visited.

I knew only one person in New York, my old teacher Charlotte Knight, and I asked her if she would act as my agent and tout the film around. She was delighted to help, and over the weeks that followed it was shown to countless agencies and individuals who apparently appeared to see no possibilities in it for television. At the end of my six months in New York I was feeling crestfallen that nobody had seen its potential. Only later did I discover that someone had commissioned another animator to make a film which looked remarkably like mine and which became one of the most popular of the television season. At the time I was extremely angry and considered taking legal action, although in retrospect not doing so was another lucky escape. Looking back, I can see that if my film had been accepted, I might possibly have spent the rest of my life making commercials instead of feature films.

Before leaving the Army in mid-1945, I was stationed in the same place as Charles Schneer (later the producer of many of my ideas). Although we may have met casually, at that time neither of us was aware of the other, and it wasn't until years later that we discovered, in conversation, that we had both served at the same station together.

Apart from the invaluable film-making experience I gained during my three and a half years of war service, I also acquired many friends. Being inclined to be a 'lone wolf' and a rather introverted person, I had the opportunity to understand how to work in harmony with other people, something I was going to find invaluable through the rest of my working days.

With the disappointment of the commercial and still unable to focus on a career, I made up my mind not to go straight home to Los Angeles but to see more of the world outside the States with my final army pay packet.

Via a circuitous route I arrived at the Mayan sites in Mexico. They afforded me a first-hand experience of a dead civilization, something I had only seen in countless adventure movies. My excitement at being able to climb the temples at Chichen Itza and Uxmal was overwhelming. Here were many of my fantasies and dreams of adventure, a Hollywood background come to life like something out of *The Lost World* or *She*. Gigantic stone heads were half buried in centuries of soil and monuments rose from the encroaching forests. The many images I saw on that trip would serve me later when I began making features.

After some days in the Yucatan I made my way up to Mexico City and from there reluctantly returned to California. As expected, George Pal offered me my old position on the *Puppetoons* staff, and although grateful, I demurred. I had decided on my trip to search for a fresh start, or at least look for a different direction. I still had my garage studio, my Cine II camera with its single frame and backwinding facilities and all my lighting equipment. However, I still didn't know what I was going to do with it all. The answer lay in a cupboard. With all the excitement of exotic travel I had completely forgotten that in my room I had about a thousand feet of outdated Kodachrome 16mm colour film stock retrieved from the Navy before leaving to go to New York. Having this stock forced me to think of ways to use it before it all became too old. I searched for good short subjects of about three or four minutes that would hopefully be of commercial interest to television or schools. The answer was very simple. Fairy tales were perfect storylines for short subjects and would be ideal for stop-motion model animation. Once I had decided on my subject, I searched for my first story and found it in Little Miss Muffet, which I then followed with Humpty Dumpty, Old Mother Hubbard and The Queen of Hearts.

Using models approximately 8 inches in height, I developed a special technique for filming the stories which I ambitiously called Trimentional Multiplane Animation. I had wanted to avoid the George Pal method of constructing fifty heads for every expression and vowel, so I simply did away with dialogue and lip-synchronization and opted for title cards instead. Yet I still needed expressions on the models so I made one head showing a neutral expression and then a short series of heads with extreme expressions all carved from the original neutral expression. Using quick eight-frame, in-camera dissolves from one head to the other, which nobody had done until now, I succeeded in attaining a flexibility that enabled me to instil some essence of character into the models. In all, it took me about four or five months to complete all four stories, taking eight weeks to produce 400 feet of colour 16mm film, with a soundtrack that used synchronized music cues.

Whilst I executed the designs, animation, photography and editing, my father helped construct the sets and models, whilst my mother created all the costumes and draperies for the sets. Before beginning

Left hand page. *Yank* **magazine cover.** On the basis of the models I sculpted for Ted Geisel, I was asked to model several figures of Snafu in situations for the cover of *Yank* magazine (24 December 1943 issue), distributed to the armed forces.

Above and left. Replacement heads for some of *The Mother Goose Stories*. Top left are the heads for the King of Hearts and the Knave. Top right: Old Mother Hubbard and Mother Goose. Left: heads for Little Miss Muffet and Humpty Dumpty.

Right above and below. A scene from my first Fairy Tale story. Little Miss Muffet being suitably shocked by the spider and the same scene being animated by myself.

the project I considered officially changing my name, as I thought it too long. I played around with various credit titles, including Wray Productions (you can guess why), but eventually came to realize that 'Harryhausen' provided a longer and unforgettable screen credit. I also wanted to give my parents a credit, but because I was reluctant to cover the whole film with the Harryhausen name, I credited my father as Fred Blasauf (his mother's maiden name), whilst my mother was listed as Martha Reske (her maiden name). It was a real family affair, and I believe they really enjoyed the time given to the projects, getting as much from the filming as from seeing the end result.

After the films' completion, I decided to link them all together and shoot a separate prologue and epilogue using the character of Mother Goose and her pet bird to introduce the stories with a movie projector. The four stories then became known as *The Mother Goose Stories* (1946), and were the first of a series that were to become more and more sophisticated.

The Mother Goose Stories were great fun to work on but didn't immediately earn me a living. To keep body and soul together, I took on commissions filming inserts and commercials for companies and organizations. The first of these unadventurous projects was Kenny Key, a bowler-hatted key with a bow tie, cane and cigar. This character announced a new building development called Lakewood

Amongst my other projects at that time was a sequence for a religious group, featuring a miniature set of three Biblical crosses against a dramatic sky background. After all these years I don't remember anything else about it. Yet another was an insert for a financial organization for which I animated a large silver spinning dollar (a 12-inch plaster model) that fell onto one side and was divided up into financial segments. I enjoyed none of these minor projects but they did pay for the *Fairy Tales*.

Housing, to be sold to war veterans who had no homes. I shot three 2-3 minute 16mm colour films for television advertising.

During this post-war period I knew that feature films were the only way to make a good living, and so I began to search for a method to make stop-motion animation and live action more cost-effective and therefore more appealing to producers. I had realized that Obie's methods, although groundbreaking, were becoming more and more costly, leading to projects being cancelled. For *Evolution* I had come up with an idea to insert models into real situations by using rear and front projection. One of the sequences I had planned was to show creatures and Homo Sapiens existing around the La Brea tar pits, and it was this simple idea I now considered for a short film. I planned to use existing models like the mammoth and to build several new ones, including a ground sloth, wolves, a buffalo and a camel. In the end all I shot was a colour test using a caveman model against a 16mm rear projected image of a waterfall.

Although primitive, it was the second important step towards independence and the development of what would be Dynamation. At the time I could not have realized its significance, but looking back today, I am aware of how important those tests were. The experiments revealed to me how I could combine the models with live action, allowing me to bring to life all those ideas I had crowding my imagination. The *La Brea* project never proceeded beyond that one test because around the corner awaited my first feature film: an encounter with another giant ape that would change, like *Kong* had Obie's, my entire life.

Top. The set of the Mother Goose stories.

Middle. Three crosses. To try and make some money out of my animation, I filmed a sequence for a religous group. All I can remember is that it featured a miniature set of three Biblical crosses against a dramatic sky background.

Above. RH drawing of Caveman. A drawing I originally executed for the ill-fated *Evolution* project; I later resurrected the same scene for a post-war project. It was the only scene I actually filmed and consisted of the model of the caveman walking in front of a waterfall. I had photographed the waterfall and used it as a rear-projected image in front of which I animated the model. It was the very earliest use of what would become Dynamation.

CHAPTER 2 ANOTHER APE AND A BEAST

Mighty Joe Young

War of the Worlds

The Mother Goose Stories

The Story of Little Red Riding Hood

The Story of Hansel and Gretel

The Story of Rapunzel

The Beast From 20,000 Fathoms

The Elementals

I have already tried to make clear one of animation's golden rules: bound inexplicably to the art of model animation is art itself, which in all its forms has fortunately for me always been a passion. To produce the end result on film, the first stage of fantasy film-making is to visualize on paper what is in the mind so that you yourself can see if the idea will work and, perhaps more importantly, to sell the product to the producer. Because of the bizarre subjects in my head, art was a necessary method in realizing the subjects. It allowed others to see into my imagination. Without the two-dimensional rendition, the three-dimensional version would never happen.

I had stayed in touch with Obie throughout the war and had talked to him many times whilst making *The Mother Goose Stories*, discussing amongst other things, what productions were being made and what he was working on. One day, quite casually, he mentioned he was working on a new gorilla picture. This set my heart beating twice as fast. Over the weeks and months that followed, he talked about the project until I realized that he wanted me to take an active part in the production – if it received a green light. Eventually he said to me, 'I think we ought to see if we can put you on a retainer fee', and approached producer Merian C. Cooper, who readily agreed. I think I received about enough to pay for gas, but I wasn't complaining.

Obie had realized early on that he would need someone to help with the sketches and drawings, and could foresee he wouldn't be able to carry out all the animation himself. I think he always knew I would be one of the animators on the production, and looking back, I now realize he had perhaps seen in me the passion and ability to execute the work. It was the opportunity I had waited for – not only to break into features, but also to work with my hero and mentor on a film project that had the added bonus of starring another giant ape. It was a dream come true, a dream that would last over the long pre-production and design stages through to the completion of the animation photography, a total of three years.

Mighty Joe Young, or *Mr Joseph Young of Africa* (its original title), had a turbulent production history. During the years of pre-production the picture was on, then off, then on again. We never knew whether it was going to be made until the principal photography began – and even then we all had our doubts. This roller coaster ride made me aware of the pitfalls of production and supplied me with the experience to face all these difficulties when I went solo.

Cooper had been developing the idea for some time, and though the story was Cooper's brainchild, it was ostensibly inspired by the real-life story of naturalist Augusta Maria Hoyt and her book *Toto and I*. Hoyt related how she raised an orphaned gorilla from infancy on her plantation in French Equatorial Africa and how it matured with astonishingly human traits. Even with this 'real' story as a basis, *Mighty Joe Young* was most definitely an attempt to recapture the magic of *King Kong*, and if it hadn't been for its tongue-in-cheek approach (as used in *Son of Kong*), it probably would have succeeded. It was Cooper's idea to underscore the action with a 'lighter touch', but in so doing, the script became a shadow of the strong character and pathos of Kong. The story was developed by Cooper, Schoedsack and Obie, and was again written by Ruth Rose.

Max O'Hara (Robert Armstrong) and his sidekick Greg (Ben Johnson) are searching the remotest parts of Africa for animals to appear at O'Hara's nightclub. They come across Joe Young, a ten-foot gorilla, and attempt to capture him but learn that only Jill (Terry Moore), who has raised the gorilla from infancy, can control the beast. Visualizing the possibilities for his nightclub, Armstrong ships them both to Hollywood where 'Mr Joseph Young of Africa' becomes the star attraction. There Joe performs for the audience, holding a platform above his head on which Jill plays a piano, and a tug-of-war with strongmen Primo Carnera and Man Mountain Dean. But Joe is unhappy. One night, when he is sitting in his cage, two drunken club patrons get him intoxicated and he breaks out, totally destroying the club. Joe, however, redeems himself when he later rescues a child from a burning orphanage and is returned to Africa.

To get to this final story the script went through many stages in its development. For example, in a

Left hand page. *Mighty Joe Young.* One of Obie's wonderful pre-production drawings for *Mighty Joe Young.* It shows Joe fighting with a group of lions. This was originally executed in watercolour and the fluidity of the movement in the picture is still exciting.

very early script baby Joe was found by Jill after his mother was killed by a lion. There was also to have been a sequence that showed an aircraft (carrying not only the humans but also Joe and other animals from Africa to America) crashing onto an island. Although the survivors escape unhurt, they are attacked by lions, but Joe saves the day by fighting the lions and helping the others to escape. The scene was cut because it was felt that the pace would have suffered. In retrospect, I suppose this is true.

There was one other sequence discarded by Cooper: the ending. As a young man, Obie had taken a keen interest in boxing (in fact, we had both had a fascination for boxing and often went to fights together), so he designed the finale as a fight between Joe and another gorilla on top of a cable car travelling down from the San Francisco hills. It was to have been a titanic struggle, much like the fight between the tyrannosaurus and Kong over the girl in *King Kong*. Sadly, what could have been a wonderful ending was replaced with the more sentimental burning of the orphanage. I remember how disappointed Obie was.

My actual involvement with the project began in late 1945. At the very beginning we both worked from our homes and I would meet with Obie on a regular basis to discuss suggestions for key sequences. It was a very casual time. We would often complete the tasks of the day by late morning and then retire to the Culver City nine-hole golf course and play a round. For a year my job was to cut frames for drawings, copy typing, cut mattes for production drawings, sharpen pencils – anything that needed to be done. I wasn't

complaining. One of my more important duties was to mount the story-boards Obie was producing for daily presentation to Cooper and Schoedsack at their script meetings. Sometimes he would make perhaps twenty of these drawings a day, which I would then mount and add story captions to. Obie's continuity sketches were always a delight to behold, and it never ceased to amaze me how quickly he could produce a completely acceptable drawing.

These drawings were based on a combination of ideas originating from Cooper, Schoedsack, Ruth Rose and Obie. Obie's input into the screenplay should never be underestimated: he would come up with some fabulous ideas and was a vital ingredient in the team. However, there were times when he would go into those production meetings (which I didn't attend until we were into production) and come out very dejected because his ideas had been dismissed. Yet later some of his ideas would miraculously appear in the script, though Obie never received the credit.

With Obie's encouragement I produced one or two sketches for the picture and later sculpted two clay busts of Joe that were used for reference. Gradually during the production, as Obie began to know my work, I was able to broaden my input.

By late 1946 Cooper received the go-ahead for production from the heads at RKO. A budget of $1.5 million was allocated, and in May 1947 RKO and Argosy (a company formed in 1937 between Cooper and John Ford) formed ARKO for the sole purpose of making this one picture. The old *King Kong* team was back in business: Obie as head of effects, Ernest B.

Schoedsack (who by this time was partially blind) directing, while his wife Ruth Rose wrote the screenplay. Actor Robert Armstrong (also a member of the *Kong* team) would again play an arrogant entrepreneur called O'Hara. Newcomer Terry Moore was signed to play Jill, with John Ford regular Ben Johnson playing Gregg, the hero.

Stage One (an old silent stage relegated to a warehouse) at RKO's Pathé lot in Culver City was allocated for the forty-seven-strong effects team. Besides model makers Marcel and Victor Delgado, there were a number of people who had worked on other Cooper/O'Brien productions.

Before proper production began, Cooper decided that we should experiment with the practicalities of shooting the entire picture in Technicolor. Obie and I set up the rear projectors and made several tests with one or two models. The problem was that Obie's technique using glass paintings in the foreground with the projection screen behind meant that we had to match the painting at the front with the rear plate. With the naked eye it may look perfect, but when the test came back from the labs, the projected image would have a different colour, so you always had to make very careful tests to ensure the colours matched. If the film is to be shot in black and white, you can make your own hand tests. If it doesn't match, you try to correct it by eye, shooting another test to see that the foreground matches the background. Some issues on the colour problems had been solved by Obie when he did the *War Eagles* tests before the war, so the *Joe* tests were eventually successful. However, it was

Above. Me with my model of Joe Young, which I affectionately called Jennifer. Its scale was designed to be smaller than the Kong models. The smaller the models, the smaller the rear projection images, and this in turn reduces the grain of the projected image.

Right hand page. Close up of one of the Joe Young models. This is a test still and the detail in the model illustrates how it could be used even for close-ups. Unborn calf hide was acquired to cover the Joe Young models. This was chosen because the hair was extremely fine

and therefore in proportion to the size of the model.

decided that the budget wouldn't take the additional time and expense, which was, at that time, quite considerable. When the first prints of the completed film were released, the burning orphanage sequence had a red tint produced in the laboratory, although most copies today don't seem to have kept it.

Under Obie's supervision I designed the first armature from which Harry Cunningham (who had made all the Kong armatures) machined the intricate jointed mechanism. When production began, a total of six models of Joe were made. Four were approximately 15 inches high, one was about 8 inches and one was four inches. This tiny model, used for long shots, was made so well that everything worked like the larger ones. Harry gave it every joint possessed by a real gorilla (machined from milled dural at the cost of $1200), right down to the little finger. In addition, Harry also constructed armatures for the baby girl (a two- or three-inch high model) Joe rescues, various adults, lions and horses. All possessed the same detail of movement. There was also a 15-inch high model that only detailed Joe from the waist up. This bust, attached to a board and fixed to a swivel mount, was intended for close shots. It was never used because it was found that the smaller models were of such fine and intricate quality that they could be used for all the close-ups.

Once the armatures were completed, the body muscles were built up over them by Marcel Delgado, an expert at the technique, using foam rubber, dental dam and cotton. However, before the skin was cut and glued to the model, it was treated by George Lofgren, a taxidermist who had devised a new process of rubberizing animal fur. This enabled the animator to move the model without the fur moving too much, as had happened in *King Kong*. The finishing touches to the models were the enamel-covered metal teeth and glass doll's eyes.

I had one favourite model I nicknamed Jennifer. It was the one I felt most at home with because there was something special about it that seemed to reflect the essence of the creature. It's a curious thing how one becomes attached to a mass of metal and rubber, even considering the amount of time one spends with them. The name Jennifer came about by accident when I saw some rushes being screened in the projection room we shared with another production. The scene was from *Duel in the Sun* in which Jennifer Jones' small hands appear from behind a rock. Those beautiful hands reminded me of Joe's small delicate model hands and so Joe became Jennifer. I hope Jennifer Jones doesn't mind.

To help with assessing the movements of gorillas, the production sent a cameraman to the Chicago Zoo to film Gargantua, one of the only really large gorillas in captivity at that time. Unfortunately, all he did for the camera was walk around, sit down and pick his nose. Back at the studio we studied the footage, and what few mannerisms there were helped us to instil some quirks into the beast. But it wasn't a matter of simply duplicating reality, because the script called for Joe to be a sympathetic character with human traits. A gorilla was not going to express the kind of emotion we wanted to achieve. It is these subtleties you have to add yourself from your own imagination.

My enthusiasm for the job led me to go as far as eating large amounts of celery and carrots to try and 'get into' Joe's character. It was an impulse of youth, a technique – I thought it would allow me to animate better if I felt like a gorilla.

The process of animation was begun around October 1947 and continued for about fourteen months. The first scenes I shot were of Joe in the club basement miniature. They were required as rear projection plates that would be combined with live actors. Of these scenes, the very first I animated was of a despondent Joe knocking a bowl of fruit off the table when Jill tells him to eat his food.

The scene I most looked forward to animating from this set of sequences was Joe becoming intoxicated. Unfortunately, all my plans for the drunk scene were thwarted when Cooper decided that the animation schedule needed speeding up and brought in Buzz Gibson (who had animated much of *Son of Kong*) and his brother. For some strange reason known only to Cooper, they were assigned to the basement scenes and I was transferred to animate Joe's first appearance with the lion cage. As it was, after six weeks Buzz and his brother left the production and none of the footage they had photographed appeared in the final film. Following completion of the lion cage sequence, I was reinstated to the basement scenes and completed most of what I had planned. It would not be fair to pass judgement as to why Buzz's footage was omitted, but I remember on several occasions that he mentioned to various members of the staff that the animation models were too small and he had found

them very difficult to use. On *King Kong* and *Son of Kong* the models were almost twice the size of those on *Mighty Joe Young*.

Although my removal from the basement scenes had been a blow to my confidence, to be offered the opportunity to animate the first scene in which Joe appears was a privilege and in retrospect confirmed the trust Obie had in my work. It had first been attempted by Marcel and Victor Delgado, followed by Scott Whittacker. Once again, none of their footage was used. I began tackling the complicated sequence in July 1948, which called for not only a spectacular entrance by Joe, but a technically complex set of visual effects. Joe is standing on the bank of a river in the foreground, and a real lion is seen pacing within a cage next to him. To discover what is in the cage, Joe rocks it back and forth and we see the lion moving with the cage.

Obie shot the background plate of the lion and cage with the lion (encouraged by the trainer) standing on a platform hinged on wires so that the real lion could be pulled up and down, to resemble the rocking of the miniature cage. When I received this live footage I counted the number of frames it took for the image of the lion to rock back and forth and matched them to the number of frames I needed to shoot for Joe to rock the miniature cage. Then the real lion was projected on a little screen within the miniature cage so that the two actions matched.

Later, when Joe smashes the cage, the lion becomes an animated model as it is seen escaping but changes back to a real lion on the rear projection plate behind the miniature cage. In his anger at losing the lion, Joe smashes the cage into sections, each of which had to be animated separately on wires. One small, almost insignificant touch was to animate the miniature cage so that it rocks as Joe climbs over it in pursuit of the escaping lion. Although this action took many hours to film, it provided the scene with a realistic quality.

Joe's character is never more important than in this introductory scene. It sets the mood for the rest of the picture. For example, Joe is seen pounding on the roof of the lion cage and looks up as if he doesn't know where the sound is coming from. I had noticed years before that chimpanzees do the same thing, and felt it was an action appropriate for this situation. I saw Joe as young, mischievous and unaware of his own strength, so when he hears the noise he makes, he doesn't know what it is. Another action was to have Joe pounding the ground with his fists. This was done to imply the same trait, as well as the impression of strength. Not all actions were animal traits; the way Joe looks into the cage, the way he reacts when the lion bites him, and perhaps more obvious, when he does a double take after seeing O'Hara talking to Jill in a later scene were all human qualities, some more exaggerated than others. If there is one thing that working on *Joe* taught me, it is that you have to inject something of yourself into a creature. Some of those 'personal touches' were from my own character, others were from movies I had seen, some from observation and some from acting classes.

The lion cage sequence is both my favourite and the one I am most proud of. Others liked it too. One day, after viewing some of the daily footage, John Ford came across to the animation stage and shook my hand, saying with considerable enthusiasm that he had just seen the scene and thought my work on the sequence was superb. This boosted my confidence and vindicated the years of self-training.

Following the lion cage sequence, Joe is pursued by the cowboys who attempt to lasso him western style. The sequence was an idea lifted out of Obie's failed *Gwangi* project where the cowboys lasso a dinosaur. Much of the animation for this scene was done by myself, but as the picture was on a tight schedule, both Pete Peterson and Obie, who loved horses, also took an active role.

So that the cowboys had something to rope, a fixed pole was erected to allow them to lasso the top, held at approximately the height of Joe. In the animation studio I placed the model of Joe where the pole was on the rear projection and matched the real ropes to miniature ones attached to the model. This was a trick that I would use much later in *The Valley of Gwangi*, although the pole in that was anything but static. Another trick was to have Joe in the centre of the screen with horsemen seemingly riding around him. This was achieved by having him stand in the centre of the set-up against a rear projection of horsemen riding one way, and then in the foreground I animated models of horse and rider to make it seem as though they were riding all around him. It was a simple but effective trick that gave the whole thing depth.

As the months passed, Cooper was still eager to speed up animation, so Obie assigned Pete Peterson

Left hand page. One of the basement scenes. The scene in the basement when Joe is intoxicated offered the opportunity to develop a lot of little character reactions for the inebriated ape. I had imagined a whole set of movements for Joe, like hiccuping, staggering back and forth and holding onto the bars.

Left. Scene of Joe rocking miniature cage with lion in it. Although the river was matted in, the lion was inserted in the cage by means of front projection on a second camera pass into the miniature cage – a taxing procedure. The problem was to ensure that the lion was always at the correct angle as Joe rocks the miniature cage.

Top. A still of my test for the cage sequence. The entire interior of the miniature cage is seen matted out for the insertion of the real lion in the cage.

Bottom. A test I carried out for the scene in which actors would appear in front of the rear projected image of Joe in his cage. The figure in the foreground is a plaster model, which was used to help me gauge the height of the actors and so animate the model of Joe to react to the actors when they would perform in front of the rear projection screen.

to some of the scenes. Pete had originally been hired as a grip but had slowly become fascinated with animation techniques, and when time allowed, watched the work in progress. Usually I find myself very distracted if people watch me animate, but Pete's eagerness was so catching that I found I didn't mind. Eventually he asked if he could try his hand, and Obie let him shoot a test using one of the larger models. On the basis of the results of the test he was given permission to assist, and when Cooper was pushing to speed everything up, Obie delegated scenes he thought Pete could ably animate on his own. Pete was very talented but was afflicted with multiple sclerosis, which necessitated him wearing leg braces that limited his work. Fortunately, his passion for animation carried him through the pain and he achieved some excellent footage.

One of Pete's trademarks for Joe was the rather broad humour, although much of it was cut from the final film. This talent is never more evident than during the chase sequence near the end of the picture where we see Joe sitting in the rear of the vehicle spitting at the police and drumming his knees with impatience. Pete made a good job of the scenes, but I must confess that I have never been in favour of the 'tongue-in-cheek' approach to fantasy. For me, comedy is more suited to the cartoon or the short rather than the feature-length dimensional subject. *Son of Kong* proved that to me. However, I don't believe animation should be totally devoid of subtle humour. Human traits can been seen as comic if applied to creatures, but it has to be where the scene lends itself to such humour. In *Mighty Joe Young* there

are two 'humorous' touches from my hand. The first is when O'Hara is trying to persuade Jill to go to Hollywood and Joe is at the gate of the house. When Joe sees O'Hara, he does a surprised stare with his eyes. I added this as I though it would be fun if Joe was caught out rather than the other way around. The other incident was right at the end when Joe peels the banana. Although not funny in itself, at the beginning of the film Joe is thrown bananas which he eats whole, but now after being 'civilized' by Hollywood, he peels them. Cooper liked this touch and so it stayed in the final cut.

One of the key sequences in the film was the tug-of-war between Joe and Primo Carnera, Man Mountain Dean and eight other brawny strongmen. The whole sequence was done for laughs, although never at Joe's expense. To allow Joe to 'connect', the real rope was attached to a ratchet mechanism, which not only gave something for the men to pull, but slowly pulled the rope over to Joe's side. In the animation studio I placed the model of Joe in front of where the ratchet stood in the rear projection and then matched the real rope (also on the rear projection plate) to the front of Joe's hands, as well as adding a miniature rope appearing from the other side of Joe's hands. In other words, the model's hands covered the exchange from real to miniature.

One sequence I was really not looking forward to was when we see Joe perform on stage as an outsized organ grinder monkey with Jill turning the handle of the organ. The audience is encouraged to throw large cardboard coins which bounce off Joe as he tries to

ward off the objects. In the end a drunk throws a bottle instead of a coin and Joe takes off his hat and growls at the audience. When I read it in the script, it seemed at face value an overly sentimental scene, although as the animation progressed, it took on a charm all of its own and became poignant. The first animation I did for the sequence was of Joe lifting his arms to block the coins from hitting his face, which, apart from the obvious movements, required a variety of emotions on his face – hurt, humiliation, shock and then anger. To complete the sequence Scott Whittacker, a former cartoonist, drew in the flying coins. He timed his coins to hit Joe so that they would correspond with the arm movements. To do this he had to analyze the sequence, frame by frame on moviola, and then rotoscope (by making single line drawings of each frame of film) my animation so that when the arm went up, the coins would bounce off in perfect timing to the arm movements. The whole process took him months to complete.

One scene I am particularly pleased with during the drunken nightclub sequence sees Joe crashing down on the bar canopy just in front of the lions. Aside from Joe, the debris that follows him all had to be animated (apart from what was on the rear projection plate), and as Joe struggles to free himself, the camera tracks in. Most people wouldn't notice the complexities of the sequence, but the effort to animate the model and to track at the same time was incredibly time-consuming. Because of the time, and therefore cost, it was a technique I was only able to apply in the Fairy Tales but never on a feature of my own.

Left and above. The tug-of-war sequence. The strongmen grappling with the rope and slowly being pulled into the water below were photographed as a rear projection plate. Joe and the stage rock on which he stands were miniature and the actions of Joe were matched with those of the men and the rope. The real rope disappears behind Joe's hand and Joe is holding the slack rope, which is a miniature.

Another favourite scene within this sequence shows Joe wrestling with lions, a mixture of models and rear projection. Three or four lions leap onto his back, whereupon he pulls them off and throws them.

After his nightclub orgy, Joe escapes from the police with the aid of Jill, Gregg and O'Hara, who has by now realized that keeping the gorilla locked up was a mistake. There follows the chase for which Pete animated the lighter scenes whilst I was responsible for much of the rest, including the tramp sequence and his arrival at the burning orphanage.

The orphanage building was a beautifully detailed 5-foot high plaster miniature shot at high speed (96 frames per second) to allow the flames to seem as though they were in proportion to the real people who were added by mattes into the lower part of the scene. Additional smoke and flame were superimposed or optically matted into the finished shots by Linwood Dunn and his photographic effects team. Again, I handled most of the animation, except some shots executed by Obie of Joe on the tree and those handled by Marcel Delgado using the 'little Joe' model as it climbs the tree in long shot.

Although Obie and I had worked on the project for much longer, the picture took nearly two years of pre-production and another year producing the animation and composite work, including three months of principal photography. *Mighty Joe Young* was released on 30 July 1949, and generally received favourable reviews worldwide, although it was never to gain the public's admiration as *King Kong* had. *The Motion Picture Herald* summed up the feeling towards

the film: 'at times the gorilla overshadows the humans in "acting," *Mighty Joe Young* is a type of unreal screen entertainment which the critics probably will attack and the patrons, especially the young in age or heart, will enjoy'.

As a twenty-nine-year-old, it was a wonderful experience and a unique training ground. In this I had been very lucky. Not only was it my first feature, but I had had the opportunity to study and work with the great Willis O'Brien. I had also been able to animate over 90 per cent of the picture due to Obie's trust in my abilities.

As a farewell gesture by Ernest Schoedsack, he wrote a poem (probably with Ruth Rose) called 'Grow Young with Joe Young'. In it he makes reference to O'Brien and myself: '…And now to make a point, Joe kindly wrecks O'Hara's joint / Of course the audience is thrilled. / Of course there is nobody killed / But this is not through lack of tryin'/ By Harryhausen and O'Brien'. Schoedsack finishes with, 'And even though Joe has no equal / We wonder who'll finance the sequel.'

The period following *Mighty Joe Young* was a time of disappointment for both Obie and myself. Obie was

used to disappointment but I wasn't. Even after he received the Academy Award for Best Special Effects for *Mighty Joe Young*, there were few, if any, producers knocking on his door. Now that I had broken into feature films I hoped others would materialize, and although I continued to work with Obie on other possible projects, none were realized, even though pre-production work was done. The first of these was called *The Great Adventure*, based on a 1949 Ruth Rose story and written by Cyril Hume. I never saw a script and in truth I remember little about it, apart from the fact that it was based on the rejected sequence from *Mighty Joe Young* in which the adventurers were stranded on an island where Joe saves them from lions. This was seen to be such a visual idea that Cyril attempted to 'flesh it out' so that it became a story of a bring-'em-back-alive showman marooned on a Pacific island inhabited by prehistoric monsters. I suspect it was dropped because the story had been too near the *Mighty Joe Young* storyline to be considered as viable.

Following that, or around the same time, came the doomed *Valley of the Mist* project in late 1949 and early 1950. Obie was tireless in producing stories from

For a while there was talk of a follow-up to *Mighty Joe Young*. Cooper had talks with producer Sol Lesser, who had begun filming a Tarzan picture at RKO/Pathé while we were doing *Joe Young*. The front office had thought it would make an unbeatable combination if the two characters were combined in one film using the very original title *Mighty Joe Young Meets Tarzan*. In 1949 Cooper and Sol Lesser announced that they were planning the film, which would star Lex Barker, and Leland Laurence was commissioned to develop a script for the idea. However, to the best of my knowledge this was as far as it ever got, presumably because box office for *Joe* proved to be less than expected.

Above. Animating Joe. A very young 28-year-old Harryhausen animating Joe. This is an excellent photograph of how I animated the model of Joe within the miniature of the corral.

Right. Sequence of rampage through nightclub. One of the key scenes was Joe's rampage through the nightclub after he becomes inebriated. It contains some of the most complex effects in the film, all carefully masterminded by Obie. Miniature and full-size settings, paintings, intricate inetrcutting of the animated gorilla with live actors, as well as live and animated lions.

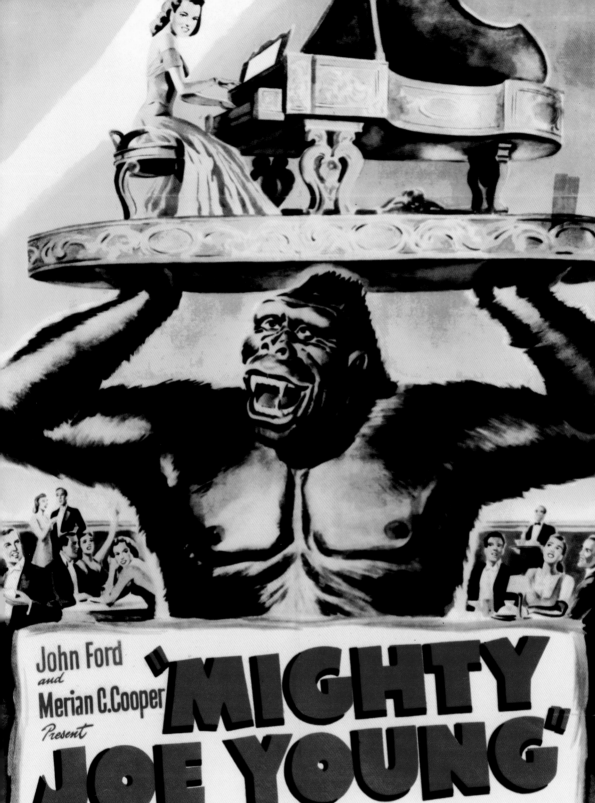

Previous two pages. Posters for *Mighty Joe Young*. Of course there was never a sequence in which Joe had a young girl in his hand while simultaneously fighting lions. This was a product of the advertising people's imagination. In fact, Joe was kind and gentle – but then that doesn't sell seats.

Above, right and right hand page. Drawings for *Valley of the Mist*. Three key drawings I made for the unrealized *Valley of the Mist* that were never used for the outline or the presentation. Over the years, my artwork had improved and each drawing contains action and depth and the influences of both Kong and Doré are evident.

his extensive imagination, and with his wife Darlyne resumed work on an outline first begun in 1944 and then abandoned. Its initial title was *Emilio and Guloso*, but was later changed to the equally uncommercial title *El Toro Estrella* (*The Star Bull*). To accompany the outline, Obie produced a handsome presentation book of sketches, all bound in cowhide. The story was yet another variation of the 'lost world' scenario:

Emilio, a Mexican boy, rears a bull calf which he calls Guloso (the boy's nickname for the bull, which means greedy). One day his father sells the bull for the bullring, which breaks the boy's heart. To get his pet back he tells the bull dealer that he will get something better for the ring and with some Indian friends sets off to find the legendary giant lizard that is supposed to inhabit a hidden valley. He finds the valley that is inhabited by various dinosaurs, one of which is a huge allosaurus that he manages to capture with the help of the Indians. When he returns triumphantly to town with his prize, the creature escapes and fights Guloso in the bullring where the bull kills the allosaurus.

Obie presented the project to Merian Cooper, who after little or no consideration told him he wasn't interested. Obie then went to see Jesse L. Lasky who became very excited with the idea, so much so that he optioned the story rights for six months and signed Obie and myself to a twelve-week retainer contract until he was able to secure proper financing of the project by a studio.

Jesse Lasky Jnr, who had worked for many years as a screenwriter for Cecil B. DeMille, worked out a screenplay based on Obie's outline, changing the title to the far more commercial *Valley of the Mist*. They produced a film synopsis (or first treatment) on 27 September 1949. The plot had changed little from Obie's original outline apart from the fact that the boy's name was now Luiz and the bull's name Bobito, and the script descriptions of the lost valley relate a lost civilization with ruined temples and huge buildings.

Lasky's idea was to shoot the entire film, including the animation, in Technicolor and in Mexico where all the miniature sets and machinery were to be made and where a good portion of the cast, including Emilio, would be recruited from the native talent. Only the script, pre-production artwork, the building of the models and the optical work were to be done in Hollywood. Obie suggested that I go to Tijuana, Mexico to get some ideas for the finale where the bull fights the allosaurus in the bullring. Having witnessed one massacre of a bull, I decided the 'sport' was not for me.

Lasky had high hopes for a deal with Paramount Pictures, the studio he helped to found, but unfortunately they turned it down, as did all the companies Lasky approached. The reasons for this lack of interest concerning the project are unclear, as on paper it seemed a good commercial prospect. My theory is that it was the high cost of *Mighty Joe Young* that frightened the studios away from becoming involved with any fantasy subject, especially one with dimensional model animation.

Mighty Joe Young had been budgeted at $1.5 million back in 1947 at the start of production, but

Above. My watercolour design for *Little Red Riding Hood*. All models and miniature items were designed in detail, with most of the animated models having a separate design for the armature.

Right. *Little Red Riding Hood* discovers that granny has been replaced by the nasty wolf. All the miniature sets were carefully constructed to allow for easy animation of the model or models.

Below. The miniature wood path set. I animated the model of Red Riding Hood as she walked through the dense forest. This still shows how much detail I put into these Fairy Tales. The trees and shrubs were painstakingly designed and constructed.

Right hand page. My design for the internal armature of the wolf. My father constructed the armatures for me so I always produced a sketch that was to scale, showing exactly how the armature would be placed within the latex model.

because the picture had been shooting for over a year and a half, all the heads of departments' salaries were literally dumped on the shoulders of the big ape. So the costs rose and rose and this then gave the appearance that the picture itself had cost over $2 million, which in 1949 was considered very costly. Whatever the reasons for the lack of interest in *Valley of the Mist*, the six months of my contract went very rapidly and then the project was abandoned altogether. The first big disappointment for me but only another in a long line of disappointments for Obie.

After completing the *Mother Goose Stories*, the offer of working on *Mighty Joe Young* halted any further thoughts for others in the Fairy Tales series, but after the failure to get *Valley of the Mist* off the ground and with no other prospect of work, I returned to what would be the second in the series, *The Story of Little Red Riding Hood*. Charlotte Knight, with whom I had stayed in touch, kindly offered to help write the narrative. I would send her an outline which she would revise and suggest alterations to until, over a period of six months, the screenplay was finally completed. I had been surprised that whilst researching the original stories of Red Riding Hood, some of the versions were very lascivious, gory, horrific and most unsuitable for educational subjects. In the end my version follows a traditional scenario, with the exception that the grandmother escapes rather than being eaten by the wolf.

Once I was satisfied with the screenplay, I began work on the general production – designing, miniature construction and model building. Once again, I received enormous help from my parents. Their names appeared again under the pseudonyms seen in the first film, whilst the camerawork was credited to one Jerome Wray (me), a combination name made up from the location of the goldmine owned by my uncle and the surname of my heroine, Fay Wray. With some of the money I had made on *Mighty Joe Young* I was able to afford bigger and better sets and spend a little time in developing new techniques, including an in-camera matte for the river and several dolly shots (one of Little Red Riding Hood as she walks through the forest and the other of the wolf as he runs to the grandmother's house), which each took upwards of a week to set up and complete. I also decided that unlike for *The Mother Goose Stories*, I needed to background the project with narration and a synchronized music track, which I felt would give the film a more professional look and therefore make it more commercial.

Being involved with *Mighty Joe Young* confirmed that I wanted to make features, but because of the rarity of such projects (Obie had taught me to rely on nothing and nobody) and their vulnerability, I decided to research the possibility of feature subjects of my own. So it was in 1950 that I searched through my story 'morgue' to see what might interest production companies and producers.

Whilst still in the Army, I had conceived the idea of filming H.G. Wells' chilling novel *The War of the Worlds* (1898), and to this end had written a basic outline in late 1942, which I updated in August and September of 1944 into a step outline. The novel was, and still is, a story I greatly admire.

Although I loved the Victorian England in which Wells had set the novel, I decided to base my version in America, a decision hugely influenced by Orson Welles' 1938 radio broadcast of the story. My hero (Randy Jordan) was a newspaper reporter and is accompanied through the onslaught of the Martian invasion by a Professor Pierson (according to my notes I had seen Claude Rains in the part). In my step outline there are scenes in an observatory, a circus (outside which the first Martian ship lands) and a farm house in New Jersey where a Martian corners the survivors in a cellar. The remainder of the action, aside from references to other parts of the States and the rest of the world, takes place in and around New York. During the conflict, the Brooklyn Bridge, the Holland Tunnel and the Statue of Liberty are shown being destroyed by the war machines (I had wanted to destroy cities even at that time), the obliteration of the latter landmark symbolically heralding the end of man's freedom.

I spent weeks experimenting with a variety of ideas for the Martians and their war machines, some outlandish ideas influenced by the covers of *Amazing Stories*.

Ultimately, my designs for both were more or less as Wells had described them because his concept had, in the end, seemed the most dramatic: articulated tripods with their canopies containing the octopus-like aliens. Looking at my concept for the creatures, I

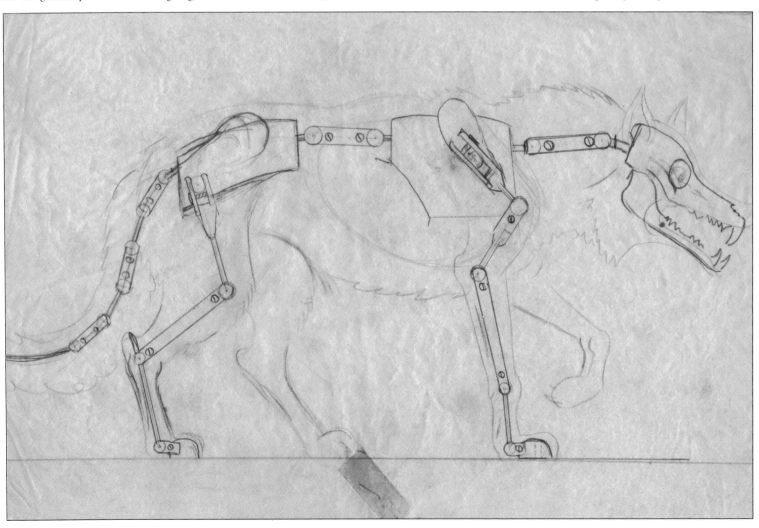

Above. Storyboard for *The War of the Worlds*. In this sequence of drawings one of the Martians is seen attacking survivors in a ruined farmhouse.

Right. Still of test. This is a black and white still taken from my original colour test footage of the Martian emerging from the capsule. The sequence shows the unscrewing of the capsule hatch and the Martian emerging and falling off the edge of the capsule.

Right hand page, left. Early rough sketch for the witch's Gingerbread House in *The Story of Hansel and Gretel*.

Right hand page, right. Colour still of Gingerbread House as it appears in the final film. For the construction of the gingerbread house I used real candy and cookies, and although I didn't have any problems with the house melting under the lights, years later, when looking through my garage, I discovered that the outer construction had been eaten away by mice.

now feel that they are a little too cartoon-like, prompting me to concede that my faithful visualization of Wells' monsters would have received laughs rather than horror from an audience. The movement of the tripod machine caused me some problems. The three metal legs would seem awkward when I animated them, so I designed the hood of the saucer to spin. The top half was to have spun one way and the lower half in the opposite direction. This would have given the whole construction a gyroscopic effect and seemed more plausible, preventing the whole thing from toppling over. As I never shot any footage of the machine, I never confirmed what legs would move when. Whether one leg would move forward and then the other two, or vice versa, I suppose I shall never know.

I drew a dozen charcoal sketches of key scenes and one storyboard of the fight in the farmhouse in which the hero and a few other survivors are trapped by a falling Martian ship. I also drew several story sequences. The next step was to demonstrate the feasibility of the project, so I decided to make a 16mm colour test based on my drawing of the Martian's first appearance as it painfully pulls itself from the cylinder. Based on my designs, my father made the metal armature over which I moulded the latex and he helped me build a plaster model of the cylinder. The test shows the hatch slowly turning and opening to reveal tentacles followed by the torso of the creature, which seems to falter in Earth's atmosphere and falls over the side of the cylinder.

I did plan to make a travelling matte of people in the foreground looking on when the creature appears, but because of lack of finance I was forced to drop the idea. However, I did manage to add a little extra drama by using a part of Shostakovich's 1st Symphony for the soundtrack, which seemed ideal for the appearance of a strange creature from another world.

With my outline, drawings and 16mm test reel I set off to see Jesse Lasky Sr. Encouragingly, he seemed impressed and indicated that he could see possibilities in the project. He took all of my materials and over the next six months or so attempted to generate interest in the project. But none of the executives or the studios, including Paramount Pictures, which owned the film rights to the Wells stories, seemed in any way interested. I even wrote to Orson Welles, whose name I hoped would stimulate an interest in producing the project, but I never received an answer. In October 1950 I visited Frank Capra at his office. He had always told me to keep in touch and to visit whenever I could. We talked about many aspects of the industry, including George Pal's film *Destination Moon* (1950), which had just been released. The mention of Pal gave me an idea. I realized that he would be the best man to approach about selling my *War of the Worlds* to Paramount. In mid-October I visited him at Paramount Studios. With me I took the outline, drawings and the test reel, plus a copy of the *Mother Goose Stories* and *The Story of Little Red Riding Hood*. We discussed the idea of Wells' story for several hours, during which he asked me how long I thought it would take to animate. Eventually he said that even though he had heard that Fox and RKO were working on the idea, I should leave everything with him and that he would be delighted to present it to the front office. A few days later I received a letter from Charlotte and a note from Obie saying that when I had taken my work to Pal he was already negotiating to make the film with Paramount. It was apparently a fight between him and another producer, Robert Fellows, who had been planning the film for two years. I was not happy that my material had been used by Pal, but because I was naïve, I decided that if it got the project made, I would be happy. Several weeks later I again visited Pal and he said that he was working on the Wells idea but that he had loved the *Mother Goose* film but was not so impressed with *Little Red Riding Hood*. However, he asked my permission to keep the films to show the bigwigs at Paramount so he could sell an idea he had about making a feature based on the fairy tale Tom Thumb. I was of course flattered that my films would be used for such a reason and gladly agreed. He also asked whether I would be interested in handling the animation for the film, to which I was even more delighted to say yes. Following months of waiting to hear from Pal, he eventually rang to say that he had not been able to enlist anyone's support for either project.

one has originally imagined or hoped it would.

After so many rejections, I was now suffering an all time low in both my own confidence and belief in the feasibility of stop-motion in feature production. I had witnessed what had happened to Obie and others in the chosen profession and my prospects seemed grim. This feeling of frustration was privately voiced in an entry made in November 1950 in my short-lived diary. I passionately reason that, 'The three-dimensional animation profession has been one of the most neglected professions of the motion picture industry. One of the prime reasons seems to be the cost of a picture using the process and by *Joe Young* which aided this erroneous myth. Now it has to be disproved in some manner, as the cost of animation need not be great if handled intelligently. All it needs is for each scene to be designed and planned to the smallest detail.' This was the first inkling that I had realized that what was required was a new idea, a new technique to move the process onwards. I had discovered that if it didn't receive one, it would die and I would have to look for another job. I knew that no producer would make a fantasy picture using Obie's techniques because they would cost millions. I had an idea how I might tackle the problem, but I needed to make more than a short film or tests to prove my point. I needed a feature project. I started to look around for such a challenge and was recommended to the producer George Moskov who was planning a dinosaur picture on a very low budget. I felt that if I could convince him of doing it my way and still keep within a reasonable budget, it would be both a commercial success and proof that it could be done. Sadly, the picture never materialized, but the opportunity to prove there was a future for stop-motion animation wasn't far away.

Until the right opportunity presented itself, I decided to return to my Fairy Tales. By 1950 the welcome

It was about the time of Paramount's lack of interest in *War of the Worlds* that I heard that Howard Hawks was making *The Thing* (1951) and that Dimitri Tiomkin, whom I had met during the war, was composing the score. I thought that Hawks might want to animate the creature, so I showed my test reel of *War of the Worlds* to Dimitri who in turn showed it to Hawks. However, it turned out that the director wasn't interested and had already decided to use an actor (James Arness) in a rubber suit.

In 1953 Pal did make *The War of the Worlds* into a film for Paramount, transposing it to a contemporary setting and using flying machines with, I might say, spectacular results. *Tom Thumb* followed in 1958 as a production for MGM using optical processing to reduce Russ Tamblyn to the size of a thumb. There seems to be a time and a place for every idea to be realized, although perhaps not quite in the same way success of *The Mother Goose Stories* and *The Story of Little Red Riding Hood* had encouraged me to be more ambitious, and so I began planning fifteen or even twenty 10-minute subjects of a similar nature aimed at television sales. Among them I considered a selection of Aesop's Fables, Rapunzel, The Three Bears (based on Goldilocks), The Sleeping Beauty and Hansel and Gretel. I chose *The Story of Hansel*

and *Gretel* as my next subject, although I once again found the details in the original story quite unsuitable for children. Not only was there a wicked stepmother (this would not have been politically correct today), but the story climaxed with the witch being thrown into the oven. I overcame both these problems by simply toning down the sequence in which the witch is pushed by Gretel into the oven and losing the stepmother completely. Charlotte Knight once again helped with the development of the screenplay, and after four rewrites we were both satisfied that we had an acceptable film for schools.

I prepared to shoot the story as I had done with *Little Red Riding Hood*, on 16mm colour stock with a simple narrative and a good full-music background. Some of the props, such as the spinning wheel (which I used again in *Rapunzel*), were built by me and my father, but the plates and other house utensils were bought at the local five and dime. For the construction of the gingerbread house I used real candy and cookies, and although I didn't have any problems with the house melting under the lights, years later I

discovered that the outer construction had been eaten away by mice. Sadly, I had to throw it out.

Once again, fate allowed me to develop and experiment with new techniques. For example, the story required that the gingerbread house magically appear and disappear. For this effect I photographed falling pieces of glitter against a black background at three times normal camera speed. This footage was then developed and rear projected upside down on a small screen so that it seemed as if the glitter was going up. A black matte was placed in front of the screen, the same size and shape as the gingerbread house. This combination was then re-photographed, in stop-frame, with suitable dissolves made in the camera to combine the house as it appears in front of the forest background. Although I am sure I was not the first to use this trick, a similar idea turned up years later in *Star Trek* as the transporter effect.

Another effect occurs when the witch opens the oven door and we see real flames from rear projection, and an anticipation of what would be Dynamation. In addition to the flames, I had to reflect the flicker of

the fire on the witch, achieved by a light and a rotating disc with slots cut into it. When animated with the model and the rear-projected flames, this gave the impression of a real fire. I was to use this trick, although with a touch more sophistication, in the Medusa sequence in *Clash of the Titans*.

Throughout all my early projects there is a special Harryhausen 'trademark', which is particularly noticeable in the Fairy Tales. A bird, or birds, can usually be seen flying across the screen in one scene or another. Until recently I hadn't realized how often I had inserted them (animated on wires), and they must have been a subconscious influence of similar effects in *The Hounds of Zaroff* and *King Kong*.

My fourth Fairy Tale, made immediately after the completion of *The Story of Hansel and Gretel*, was *The Story of Rapunzel*. When read in print it had enormous charm, but when acted out in three dimensions bordered on the absurd. Yet again I was forced to 'tone down' the violence. Whatever the reasons, the film lacks pace and charm, and is my least favourite in the series.

Above right. RH animating on *Hansel and Gretel* set. The miniature set for the woodman's house in *Hansel and Gretel* showing most of the characters and with myself placing the duck to take publicity pictures for the film.

Above and right. Rapunzel's Hair. Fortunately for *The Story of Rapunzel*, I had learned to plait many years before, so the process of her letting down her hair was simple, although everything was done in reverse.

Right hand page. An early concept for what would become *The Beast From 20,000 Fathoms*. I sketched a number of different ideas for the Beast, amongst them an octopus, but in the end I based it on various carnivorous dinosaurs, with the addition of a considerable amount of imagination.

Following page. Still of Bronze model of the Beast and lighthouse. I executed this complex bronze many years after the making of the film. All the models had been canibalized and all that was left were stills and the original model lighthouse from which to make the bronze. Making bronze copies of my models is a way of preserving them, as the latex from which they are made is prone to deteriorate over the years.

In any event, there were two specific aspects of the story that appealed to me: the pictorial attraction of the tower and Rapunzel's long golden hair being used as a rope for the witch and then the prince to ascend the tower. To use the hair as a rope it had to be plaited, and I had a visual image of the strands plaiting themselves as though by magic. Before I began filming I plaited the hair and then for filming unplaited it frame by frame. This was then reversed by the lab, thus the hair appears to plait itself.

For the time being the completion of *The Story of Rapunzel* brought to an end any intentions of filming a longer series of Fairy Tales. Just as I finished and was wondering what to do next, I received an offer to shoot the effects for a feature film about a prehistoric creature rampaging through Manhattan. I didn't know it at the time, but it was to change my life and career for a second time.

My involvement in *The Beast From 20,000 Fathoms* began when a friend (for whom I had made the Kenny Key advert) told me that producer Jack Dietz, head of a company called Mutual Films, was scripting a project called *The Monster From Under the Sea*. Apparently, he was unsure of how to visualize the main element of the picture, the creature, and didn't know whether it should it be a man in a suit or an alligator dressed up. I rang Dietz straightaway, and the next day he came over to my house to look at my models and drawings, and view sections of *Evolution* and *Mighty Joe Young*. After he had seen what I had to offer, I then enthused about the advantages of stop-motion model animation, telling him that anything and everything he wanted could be done in the process. I held my breath, not really knowing if I could actually achieve what I was promising, but I had impressed him and I was cheap, so he invited me over to the General Service Studios (a low budget independent) to chat about the project and meet the rest of the team. I was on my way. At that crucial meeting, I was introduced to Hal E. Chester, the line producer, Bernard Burton, the editor, and the director Eugene Lourie. Lourie, a Frenchman, had worked as Jean Renoir's principal designer in the 1930s and 40s, coming to Hollywood during the war. Dietz had originally employed him as art director, but because money was very tight, he was asked to direct the live-action footage. He was a good director: bright, capable and never questioned or interfered with my work. We got along very well, and in retrospect I found him more rational than most of the directors I worked with, probably because he was a designer and therefore understood what I was trying to do. He and Bernie Burton were always so co-operative, helping me to overcome my nervousness about this being my first solo feature excursion.

Without really knowing it, I think I received approval from everyone at that meeting, and it was agreed that I should read the two outlines and offer suggestions about making the story filmable and affordable using stop-motion animation. Money was the crucial issue, and Dietz wanted what everyone wanted: to make the picture for little or nothing (the budget had been set at $150,000). I took the outlines home and read them twice, trying to establish what I could do with them. The first was written by G.J. Schnitzer and called *The Monster From Under the Sea*. Reading it now, it bears no resemblance whatsoever to the final screenplay. The story was about a group of scientists who pierce the Earth's crust, unleashing an alien monster that was trapped there before time began. The creature tells humanity that it will take over the world. Secretly, one of the scientists creates a huge robot to destroy the alien, which it does, along with its creator, but in turn it has to be destroyed by an atomic bomb. It sounds like something written for a cartoon series. The second attempt was a fourteen-page outline called *The Monster From Beneath the Sea*. Although there is no writer credit, it contained enough interesting and imaginative material to make me feel able to contribute something. The outline began with a lot of boring preamble about setting off an atomic bomb at the North Pole which uncovers a creature (called a Minotaur) frozen in a huge block of ice. After the ice melts, it escapes into the sea, and after some key scenes (one of which is an attack on a light-house on Lake Michigan), it emerges at Bedloe's Island and destroys the Statue of Liberty. It is finally captured by freezing it using special jets mounted on helicopters, after which it is destroyed out at sea by another atomic bomb. It was interesting to see that the atomic bomb was the solution to all threats at that time.

After a further meeting where I detailed my ideas and how scenes could be improved, Dietz confirmed that I was the man for the job. My contract with Mutual dates 2 May 1952 and states that the work had to be completed by 19 September of the same year and all for the princely sum of $15,000, to be paid in instalments. Even though the contract included the provision of equipment, I was so inexperienced in film production finances that I undersold myself. The result was that on several occasions I had to dig deep into my own pocket as the project was realized. In a curious twist of fate, after a number of years the Fairy Tales made more money for me than *The Beast* ever did.

Many other meetings followed, at which the screenplay and key animation scenes were discussed. Dietz and Chester always asserted great emphasis on a very tight budget. I remember later that Eugene had to hire a cameraman, assistant cameraman and a grip in New York, as the money wouldn't run to an air ticket for personnel from Hollywood. In fact, it was the grip's station wagon that was used as a camera car. In Eugene, Dietz had made a good choice. Eugene was very clever with budgets. His experience in set design helped in building cheaper sets which still looked impressive on screen, and it was his idea to use a lot of still rear projections of buildings so we didn't have to take the actors to New York. Most of the film's look was due to his knowledge of simplified construction.

The first draft screenplay was written by Lou Morheim and Fred Freiberger. It was at this stage that I began to make a number of sketches of the monster. At that time no one had any idea of what the creature should look like – all they knew was that they wanted a monster, leaving me with a free hand. One early concept considered before I arrived (apart from the Minotaur) was for a Mosasaur (a marine lizard from the Mesozoic age), but it was felt that such a creature would have been too small for the storyline. They wanted it big. In the end I based the final design on several dinosaurs (mainly the tyrannosaurus), helped by a liberal dose of imagination. For some reason the creation was called a rhedosaurus, and although I can't remember where this name came from, I suspect Hal Chester or one of the writers coined it. Over the years, people have suggested that the first two letters relate to the initials of a certain animator. I have no comment.

Whilst I was designing, Morheim, Frieberger and Eugene began revising the script, which at that point still lacked substance and a good ending. I was concerned specifically about the ending, so at one of the script conferences I suggested that the Beast should be trapped within the roller coaster on Coney Island. It was a dramatic landmark, and besides, every creature should die on or near a landmark. To my surprise, everyone agreed.

After all the rewrites, the final script was delivered on 4 August 1952 and was ready for production:

A rhedosaurus is brought to life by an atomic bomb test in the Arctic. Bewildered and disorientated, the creature makes its way to its original prehistoric home, which over the millennia had become New York City. On its journey it destroys a ship, a bathysphere and a lighthouse, and once in New York it destroys all in its path until it is lured into Coney Island fairground where it is killed with a radioactive isotope amid a burning roller coaster.

Because of the budget limitations, the cast was relatively unknown apart from the delightful Cecil Kellaway who played Professor Elson, a palaeontologist who meets with an unfortunate accident in a bathysphere about halfway through the film. Kenneth Tobey (fresh from *The Thing*), who always turned out a good, reliable performance, was cast as the army officer in charge of the chase. Others in the cast were Paul Christian as the hero and Paula Raymond as the heroine. I always thought it sad that Christian never managed to 'make it' in movies, as I considered him a fine and believable actor who turned in an engaging performance. Among the other players was a very young Lee Van Cleef who made his debut in *The Beast* as the sharpshooter who has to hit the rhedosaurus with the deadly isotope.

In parallel to my designs for the creature and the key scenes, I set about devising my approach to how I would deliver the combination scenes of the creature and the environment in which it found itself, namely New York and its people. I knew what I wanted to do – to 'sandwich' the stop-motion model or models between foreground and background images of the live-action projection plate – but would it look as good as I had promised? To make sure everything would work, the first test I made was shot on 16mm in my hobby house studio. I used an early design for the Beast as a model, together with a stock footage background plate of a river. I split the screen in front of the 16mm camera by using a glass with blacked out portions where the model was standing. After photographing one portion, I would rewind the exposed film, black out the already exposed half, and then photograph the blacked out portion of the projection plate. Theoretically, the whole thing would look as if the model was part of the picture. However, there was one other problem to overcome: when the Beast was inserted it was naturally sharper than the rear projected image. Luckily, the answer was simple: I made the Beast a little out of focus and by doing so, the two images matched. The overall result was a non-armatured, completely static model of the Beast in a river, and it worked. I was both delighted and relieved with the result, and I now knew the picture was a practical possibility and my promises would be kept. If I was honest with myself, I suppose I had always known that it was a practical idea, but to realize it was confirmation.

For the actual shooting of *The Beast* I attained a more sophisticated technical approach for the 35mm camera, although it was not too much more sophisticated. The model of the creature was placed on the animation table and I aligned its feet with a specific portion of the background plate. The table was then masked off by mattes and countermattes, which I opaqued onto large panes of glass in front of the camera. When all the stop-motion animation was completed, the film was backwound, along with the projected footage. At this stage, whatever parts of the plate had been held back were now rephotographed into the unexposed areas frame by frame. Thus the creature (or model) could appear to roam behind parked cars and buildings by matting out those shapes and exposing them back in. The system capitalized on the fact that the camera's two-dimensional eye saw the rear projected image and the animation model as being in the same plane. The method also had the advantage that people's actions on the plate were not necessarily restricted to certain boundaries; if heads were cut off during the stop-motion pass, they were put back in on the second rear projection pass.

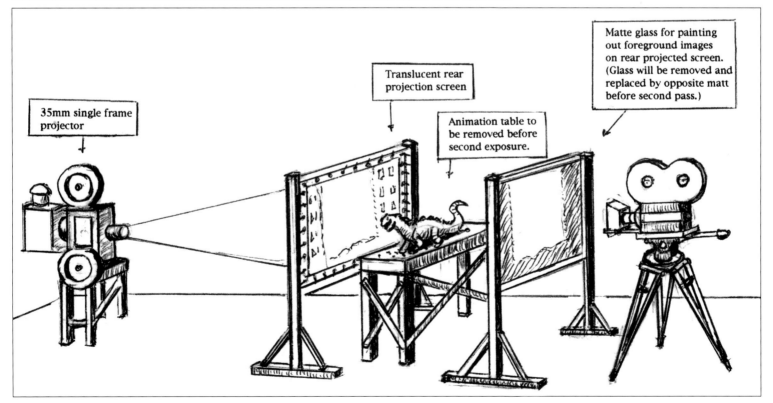

Matte glass for painting out foreground images on rear projected screen. (Glass will be removed and replaced by opposite matt before second pass.)

Translucent rear projection screen

Animation table to be removed before second exposure.

35mm single frame projector

Above. Sketch showing process of what would become Dynamation.

To comply with my contract, Dietz and Chester bought the equipment (from RKO) I had asked for. Included were two 1-horsepower stop-motion motors, a 35mm special single-frame projector (built by Cunningham for *Mighty Joe Young*), various lenses and a dolly for the projector. I looked around for a suitable but cheap studio (my hobby house was totally unsuitable) and eventually rented a newly built store on Washington Blvd, near Lincoln Blvd in Culver City, which I converted into a studio. The building was chosen for its length, as it had to be long enough to accommodate the throw of the rear projection.

Once approval had been given for the design of the creature, I then had to construct the armatured model. My father built the armature, cannibalized from old model parts and newly machined sections, and when that was ready, I built up a cotton-padded framework which I then layered with a sponge rubber muscle structure. The final layer was a scaly latex skin moulded from alligator. In addition to the one articulated model, I also constructed a 7-inch hand puppet

of the head and neck section to use for close-ups. I was never happy about using this glove puppet, as it was impossible to achieve a realistic effect with it, but fortunately it is only seen as a rear projection plate in a few live action scenes where the Beast stares through the lighthouse and tugboat windows. Because time didn't allow me to build the miniature sets, I farmed the job out to Willis Cook, a studio technician (he built a lot for my subsequent pictures and also did the floor effects and explosives for this picture). Most of the miniature props were either specially made by me or bought from toy shops (for example, the boxcars in the dockside sequence).

The film begins with the atomic explosion that releases the Beast, after which it is seen fleetingly during a snowstorm. The second time we see it a man is standing in the foreground with his back to the camera. This was in fact Hal Chester who played the part rather than pay an actor for a day's shoot. He did the shot against a black velvet backcloth and I then had a travelling matte made of it to be printed optically

into the combined picture. The third sighting in the Arctic sees the Beast on an ice cliff, which crumbles and causes an avalanche. Coincidentally, the ice cliff and avalanche were both stock shots from the 1935 *She*.

The Beast is next seen when it destroys a fishing boat near the Grand Banks. Two men see the Beast through the window of the bridge, then the Beast attacks and sinks the vessel. The scene was inserted to keep the action moving and to illustrate that the creature was alive and well and on its way. The hand puppet was used for the full-scale rear projection of the Beast's face. It was combined with a pane of rippled glass, which created the illusion of rain running down the windows of the bridge. When the Beast attacks the vessel, he appears to rock it, suggesting almost a playful attitude, like a dog with a stick. Naturally, the rocking of the vessel creates splashes. They were actually real waves, previously shot on a beach in Malibu, which were matted in separately.

Perhaps the best known scene in the film is the Beast attacking and destroying a lighthouse. The

Above and right hand page. Still of the model and set of the Beast.
These two very rare stills show the Beast in the process of being animated in front of a model building (on the right in each picture) and cut-out photos of buildings on the left and in the rear. Although this was how I animated these scenes for *The Beast From 20,000 Fathoms* this

was in fact a test for the later proposed project *The Elementals* to try and establish if 3-D might work in stop-motion animation. The two 35mm cameras seen in the picture were mounted so as to produce a 3-D image. I am glad to say that the process didn't really work and the idea was dropped.

scene was designed to be atmospheric because the Beast is curious about the light. The whole sequence begins with the sea crashing over rocks and the silhouette of the lighthouse towering behind with its light revolving and piercing the gloom. Slowly the black shape of the beast pulls itself up from the darkness beside the structure and rears up to its full height to study the light. It roars and then pushes the tower over, so extinguishing the light. The movement contained in this scene seems simple enough, but on closer inspection it was achieved through a complex set of actions. I allowed the model rhedosaurus to pull itself forward and then sit on its rear legs so its head could be level with the light. This sequence of movements would be natural for most four-legged creatures, but I had to reproduce it so that it seemed natural to the audiences watching a dinosaur doing it. The movements had to be slightly exaggerated.

The whole sequence is a perfect example of Dynamation. It consists of a combination of model (on a stand), a miniature lighthouse (also on a stand) and a projected plate of a rocky promontory with the sea crashing over rocks (a library stock shot) which was front-projected onto a large white card during a second camera pass and a static background photograph of a night sky. To blend with the projected images I used a fog filter to create a misty quality.

After a final encounter in which the Cecil Kellaway character dies in a bathysphere, the poor thing finally arrives at its breeding ground, which by an unhappy coincidence is now Manhattan. Emerging from the Hudson River in full daylight, the Beast's huge shape appears from behind a stationary group of boxcars. This projected background was photographed in New York at an actual pier. A hard line matte was used to place the creature behind the boxcars, and after the animation was completed the creature and stand were removed and the projected image of the pier was then rewound, along with the film in the camera. The matte was exchanged with an opposite delineation and the lower part of the boxcars were exposed on a second pass. There is a cutaway of a close shot that shows the men fleeing before we cut back to the creature hauling itself onto a duplicate miniature pier. In one scene we see the Beast crushing an automobile standing in the foreground. This particular model was specially made of lead, a perfect metal for animation, as it allows the animator to slowly crush it. In this case the leg of the model rhedosaurus crushes the object as it descends.

What follows are a string of scenes in which the creature stalks the canyons of New York, presumably looking for a mate. A few of the scenes stand out from the rest. A lone policeman advances towards the beast in a feeble attempt to kill it with his gun. As the gun jams, the creature reaches down and clamps the unfortunate officer between its teeth. We see his legs waving in the jaws of the beast. To do this we hoisted the actor on a wire, and this was then used as a rear projection plate in front of which I animated the model so that the mouth seemed to grip him. It was a matter of perspective, a key tool in the animator's box of tricks. With the policeman in its mouth it pulls

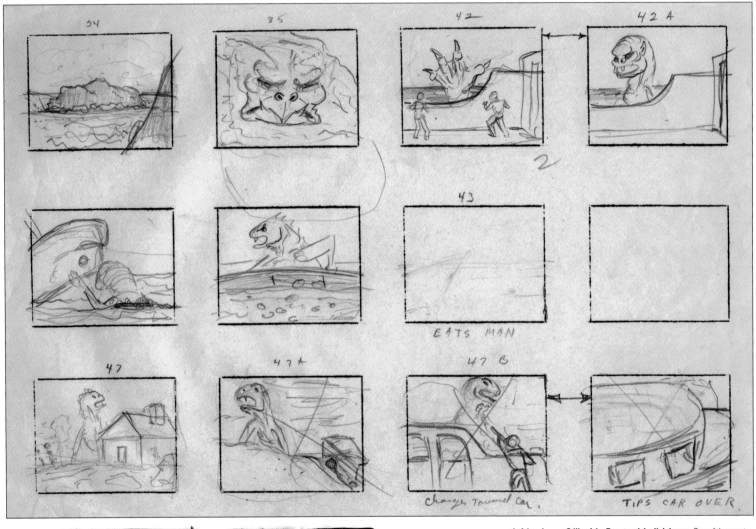

back its head and gulps the tasty morsel down. At this point the policeman was an animated model in the mouth of the model beast. This model was by necessity only about 1 1/2 inches high with a copper wire armature. The action of the Beast rearing back to swallow the food was an action seen in dogs and other carnivorous animals and one I had studied and used in my very early dinosaur tests.

Another scene sees the creature crashing through a building and emerging from the other side. Like the lighthouse before it, the building was a miniature constructed to allow sections (attached to wires) to fall away. These sections were animated down the wires at the same time as I was animating the Beast. The effect when projected is that the building seems to crumble. To add an extra touch of authenticity I double printed a dust cloud over the action.

The climax of the film sees the creature trapped in a scenic railway on Coney Island where the unfortunate Beast eventually meets its end. All the live action for the sequence was filmed at an amusement park near Long Beach, not on Coney Island. Based on my designs, Willis Cook built two beautifully detailed miniatures of the roller coaster. The first, used for the burning of the structure, was about 20 feet long by 5 feet high and was built on a studio stage. Separate sections of the structure were designed to collapse or fall away by the use of wires. The flames were achieved by applying liquid rubber cement all over the structure, which gives off a small flame (this has to be in proportion to the structure) and then the whole thing was shot at high speed so the flames would look realistic. Willis Cook also constructed another miniature roller coaster to be used for the animation sequences and therefore in proportion to the model Beast. Sections of this model were made of balsa wood, enabling the model to hold or appear to tear away from the structure with his mouth.

The task of instilling pathos into a creature that was, after all, an innocent victim of circumstances was something I had set myself from the outset, although I was restrained by the script. Eugene had the same feelings for the Beast, so in him I had an ally, and what little pathos there is for the creature is due solely to Eugene and myself. The Beast is a poor lost soul brought back to life by man and then destroyed by man. If this sounds familiar, it is. *King Kong* was a huge influence, as he would be in all the other creatures I would be father to. Without the pathos it would have been a two-dimensional character that just destroys, and although the effects may hopefully be good, there is no real content to the film. So whenever the opportunity arose that allowed me to impart the creature with something 'special', I would try to infuse some element of human dignity into him, which is (I hope) especially evident when the Beast dies amid the burning roller coaster.

The animation was completed within five months, which looking back seems very short considering the volume of animation I had to produce. The Beast actually cost me money, but it was a good 'teething ring', offering solo experience that was to stand me in good stead for the rest of my career. I really enjoyed

Left hand page. Beast out of the Hudson. This is the first clear image we have of the Beast as it emerges out of the Hudson River and onto a pier. In this still, which is in fact a test, the creature can be seen in the centre against a rear projection plate of the Brooklyn Bridge and the Hudson. The foreground is all a miniature (based on the actual pier), but in this test I have used a toy car that was purchased from a five and dime store (it would appear later in the film when it is crushed). When I shot the scene for the picture, the foreground included rail freight cars and boxes.

Above. The Beast attacks the Coney Island roller coaster. This image is made up of a rear-projection plate of the large miniature roller coaster on fire against which the model Beast is animated. The section of the roller coaster in the foreground is another, separate model and the flames in the extreme foreground were double printed in.

making the film and felt vindicated that I had managed to prove that a feature with dimensional animation could be made on a very low budget. Jack Dietz and Hal Chester were delighted with the results of my efforts, as was Eugene. His work on the film gave it a quality few other directors at that time could have come anywhere near. His economical use of sets and people was a miracle, and even by today's standards it is a thoroughly enjoyable and feasible film.

At the end of the production Jack Dietz was concerned about the changing face of the cinema screen. He was worried that our picture, which had been shot in black and white, had no big-name stars and had been filmed in the usual standard cinema ratio, would not have public appeal. Audiences were becoming used to colour and large screen formats (Cinemascope and 3-D had just appeared). Consequently, Dietz made the decision to sell the film outright to Warner Brothers for the princely sum of $400,000, which, as the film had only cost a total of $210,000, seemed like a good deal. They were so pleased that

they awarded me a 'small' hard-earned bonus. For the same reasons that Dietz had sold the picture, Warner were nervous of its commercial possibilities. Their publicity department came up with the novel idea of declaring on all the posters and adverts 'In Glorious Sepiatone', which was, in fact, an old-fashioned tinting process used for many years. The entire 500 original US release prints for the picture were dyed in sepia brown, and in some of the prints an additional tint of green was added to the underwater scenes.

The picture opened on 1 June 1953, with Warner spending $200,000 on a huge publicity campaign, matching its negative costs, and making the film the hit of the year. Most of the reviews were ecstatic. The *Hollywood Reporter* called it 'a highly saleable exploitation thriller', and with specific reference to the effects, 'Special effects and montage are ably and admirably used in a gasp-provoking scene when the animal surfaces off Fulton St'. The *Motion Picture Herald* said, 'the real stars of "The Beast From 20,000 Fathoms" are the special and technical effects men, in this case

Willis Cook and Ray Harryhausen, who have put together as weird a monster as anyone need have to disturb their nightmares'.

Dietz had had no confidence in the film and hadn't bargained that it would initiate a new trend in popular cinema and become the 'sleeper' of 1953, grossing in excess of $5 million. Even today it continues to gross huge sums, making a mint for Warner Bros.

Regretfully, I don't know what Obie thought of the picture. With *The Beast* I had changed forever the method of using model animation, whereas Obie continued to design projects that would use a thirty-man team. We would work together again, but it was never the same as it had been when I was a young apprentice and he was the master. Now I had learnt and had naturally moved onto another way of producing effects, as others would pass onto other methods. That is the law of technology. *The Beast From 20,000 Fathoms* had brought O'Brien's *The Lost World* into the atomic age and was the first 'monster-on-the-rampage' movie of the 1950s, inspiring the

Above. Still of 'The End'. Eugene Lourie summed up the end of the film perfectly in his book *My Works in Film*. 'It was emotionally strong, like the finale of a tragic opera. The Beast dies like an opera tenor.'

Right hand page. The poster for the film *The Beast From 20,000 Fathoms*. This is perhaps one of the first examples of 1950s fantasy exploitation posters. It exaggerates everything, but at the same time makes you

want to see the film, which is, of course, what such advertising is all about. Posters and campaigns of this kind are now a lost art.

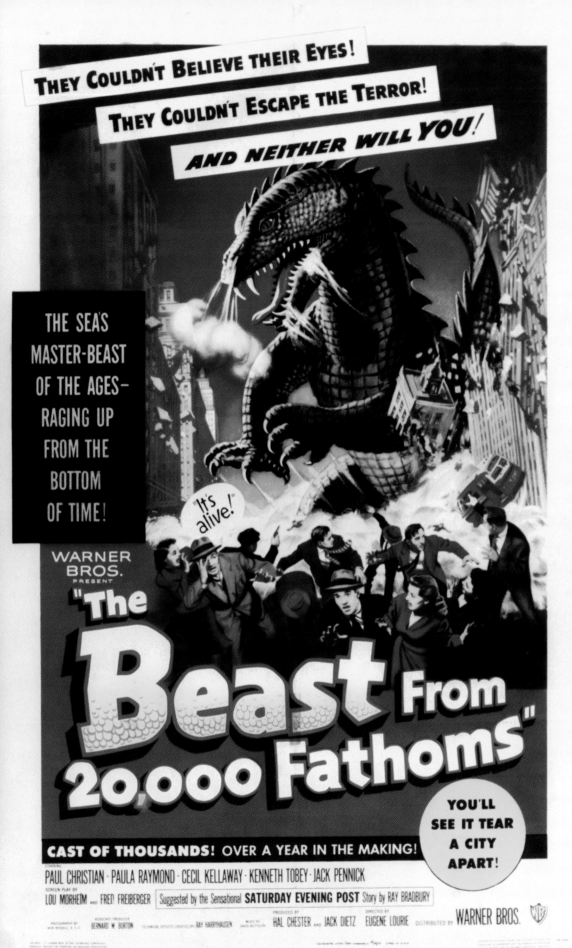

Japanese Godzilla cycle and establishing the basic formula which subsequent 'monster' films were to duplicate. It also had the effect of typecasting my work for some considerable time, although at that point I was not complaining.

Irreversibly fired by the excitement of feature film production, I determined to get one of my own ideas off the ground. Following completion of *The Beast*, Jack Dietz told me he was looking for another subject as a follow-up, so I sat down to look through my 'mortuary' of old storylines for the right plotline to appeal to both Dietz and what he saw as the reasons why audiences had flocked in such numbers to *The Beast*. Eventually I came across an old storyline tentatively titled *The Elementals* and which contained a flock of flying beasts. An added bonus of the story was that I had placed the action in France, beginning in the Pyrenees Mountains and ending in Paris. The whole thing seemed to be perfect. If Eugene was to direct, he would, I felt, wholeheartedly support the project (not only because it was based in France, although I was sure

this would help), which would hopefully guarantee its realization. I have to confess that there was another reason I thought the story perfect, and that was because I wanted a trip to France. I had always wanted to travel around Europe, so it seemed a perfect ploy to develop a story incorporating a plot involving at least one European city.

I rewrote my original ideas into a feasible five-page outline, along with several drawings, and sent it to Dietz on 20 February 1953. The story did need 'fleshing out' but the basic premise was sound:

An entomologist accompanied by his wife and faithful dog Buck are searching for specimens in the Pyrenees Mountains of France. By chance they discover the crater of a crashed spacecraft around which are lying dead giant worms and nearby, hanging from trees, are eight-foot live chrysalises. They take one of the chrysalises back to their laboratory where it hatches overnight into a bat-like creature and carries the doctor off in its talons. Fortunately the weight is too much and it crashes to the ground, stunning itself. The doctor cages

the creature and goes back to destroy the other chrysalises, but he discovers that they too have hatched and the creatures have flown off. In Paris he presents the specimen to the scientific world but learns that the other bat creatures are attacking the city from their nests in the Eiffel Tower. Eventually a huge fire of petrol is lit on the waters of the Seine. The flames attract the creatures and they fly into it, like moths to the flame.

To encourage Dietz to make the project I decided to make a test animation sequence to illustrate the project's practicality and add it to the presentation. Financing it myself and acting as cameraman (with help from my father), actor and editor, I made a 35mm Eastmancolor 5-minute test reel. The live action for the test was shot locally on the prow of a hill against the skyline, and whilst my father operated the camera, I stood on the hill and waved a large stick as though protecting myself from a creature which only I could visualize as attacking me. Back in my hobby house, having constructed an armatured model of

both the creature and myself, I animated it on wires to correspond with my arm movements, and as a climax I had the creature carry me (a model) off into the sunset.

Once I had finished, I took the test, the outline and a number of drawings designed to illustrate the overall concept to Dietz to sell him the idea. To my delight he was so enthusiastic about the concept, he paid me the staggering option fee of $200. On the recommendation of Ray Bradbury, Dietz assigned Gerald Heard to develop a treatment from my basic outline, but after some months Dietz was not getting what he had wanted from Heard, so he brought in Lou Morheim who presented a twenty-three-page treatment on 13 July 1953 called *Terror By Night*. This treatment changed my original concept from alien to prehistoric bat-like creatures, although most of my other key ideas remained.

Lou Morheim wrote a screenplay which was dated eight days later, 21 July 1953, but Dietz was still not happy with it and some months later commissioned screenwriter David Duncan, who brought a sixty-two-page treatment titled *Dark Wings* but which seemed to vary little from either mine or Morheim's versions.

Whilst all this was going on I worked happily away at storyboards agreed at script sessions, but one day Dietz came to me and suggested we should film the story in 3-D (he was afraid we would be left behind if we didn't experiment). Of course, I balked at the idea. Not only was I being asked to film the impossible, but now I was under pressure to make the three-dimensional models really look three dimensional! 3-D is not an easy medium to use with any storyline, let alone animation. It requires the use of two cameras, both mounted precisely at the same distance apart to represent the human eyes. When projected in the cinema, the audience wears either red and green tinted glasses or Polaroid, depending on which 3-D process is being used. Not only would I have had to animate, I would also have had to develop techniques for two cameras to operate simultaneously and design three-dimensional situations for the creatures so that audiences would not be disappointed.

Not wanting to jeopardize the project and swallowing my objections, I agreed to make a quick test to see what problems might present themselves by combining 3-D with rear projected backgrounds with animated models. For the test I used the model of the rhedosaurus from *The Beast*, which I placed on the animation table facing the cameras and with a flat image of a building projected onto the rear screen. The test proved that it was possible to film a model in 3-D but that it also required complex three-dimensional backgrounds. Using a flat image for the rear projection was useless if the model was seen in three dimensions. What would be required was either three-dimensional projected images or three-dimensional sets. The first would be prohibitively expensive and the second would destroy the point of Dynamation. I am glad to say Dietz finally decided it would all be too expensive and take far too long to produce any worthwhile results. The fates were not kind to most of the 1950's 'gimmicks' such as 3-D. They were difficult to watch and the audiences got tired of them, so they faded into disuse with only the occasional re-emergence. The 3-D

Left hand page. Short scene storyboard drawings for the discovery of the chrysalis, for *The Elementals*.

Left. Short scene storyboard drawings for the bat creatures' eyrie in the Eiffel Tower and Notre Dame cathedral, for *The Elementals*.

Above and left. A selection of key drawings illustrating various planned scenes for *The Elementals*. These include an attack on a cart, a sighting by a pilot and one of the creatures looking down on Paris.

Below. A rough sketch for the finale of *The Elementals*. The bat creatures would be attracted by a ring of fire on the waters of the Seine and would be consumed by the flames.

Right hand page. A 35mm test for *The Elementals*. The bat creatures attack a young man (me) and after trying to fight it off, I (or my model, it's hard to tell) am carried off into the sunset. Even this exciting test didn't manage to sell the idea. Over the years I did appear in some of my pictures, but I am usually seen only in tests. It was the Hitchcock influence.

process was one of the first to succumb to the advent of 20th Century-Fox's new Cinemascope widescreen process, which gave width and a certain amount of depth but needed no cumbersome glasses. By the time we would have finished *The Elementals*, the complicated 3-D process would have been 'old hat'.

With all my efforts to get *The Elementals* off the ground, in the end it was never made. Dietz spent almost a year searching for finance, but none was forthcoming. It seemed strange at the time, and still does now that, in spite of the huge box-office success of *The Beast From 20,000 Fathoms*, the project never

found a backer. In 1956 I was asked by Columbia Pictures if I would be available for a project called *The Flying Claw* about a huge bird that attacks New York and Paris, picking up trains and destroying buildings. The project sounded so like *The Elementals* that I wrote to Sam Katzman to decline the project and to explain that I was still hoping for finance to make my project. In the end it had little or no similarities to *The Elementals*.

Parallel to *The Elementals*, I had been developing another idea called *The Giant Cyclops* that I had also offered to Dietz, who had declined it. This story told of a Venusian creature brought back to Earth in a

spaceship where it grows to an enormous size. That project, in another form, in another country and with another title, wasn't due to see the light of day until a little later.

Above. Rough sketch of an Elemental. This is a very rough sketch of how I conceived an Elemental to look. On the right hand side is a tiny man, which would have given me an approximate comparison to a human.

CHAPTER 3 FROM BENEATH THE SEA TO OUTER SPACE

The Story of King Midas

It Came from Beneath The Sea

Animal World

Earth Vs the Flying Saucers

20 Million Miles to Earth

In early 1950s Hollywood the influence of the studios had begun to decline, although they were still a force to be reckoned with, and any technicians were usually working for a studio. I seemed to be the odd one out, even with the unexpected success of *The Beast From 20,000 Fathoms*. The film had done little to change opinion about stop-motion animation, and I was seen as a lone special effects technician, working away in my tiny studio, creating these curious effects which others more talented than myself had thought up. Only the team that had worked on *The Beast* knew the full extent of my involvement and contribution to the picture, and they weren't going to broadcast my virtues to the Hollywood moguls. Obie always suffered from a lack of proper recognition and I had seen the appalling way he had been treated by producers and the studio front office. He seemed to register in people's minds as a technician, not a creator. On reflection, some of his problems have to be laid at his own doorstep. Like most artists, he was rather shy and retiring, and in Tinseltown, where most of the ideas that reach the screen are sold by bluff or aggression, this was definitely a disadvantage.

Seeing Obie suffer taught me that I didn't want to be 'used' by Hollywood as he had been, and following the collapse of *The Elementals* and the apparent lack of enthusiasm for *The Giant Cyclops*, plus the absence of job offers, I returned to the Fairy Tale series. Here I could be my own boss, experiment and work unhindered. Instead of the usual Northern European tales, I determined to make a version of the ancient Greek legend of King Midas. My version saw Midas as a gold-hungry miser who is visited by a mysterious stranger whilst counting his money. The stranger asks Midas what he wants above all, whereupon Midas replies, 'to be the richest man in the world'. The wish is granted but the greedy king discovers that not only does he turn inanimate objects to gold, but also his beloved daughter. All ends happily when the stranger reverses the curse, so restoring the princess to life and leaving the king to contemplate his foolishness.

I had already begun a rough first draft of the story, then called *The Golden Touch*, in November 1951. When I decided to film the story in 1952, I again asked Charlotte Knight if she would help with the screenplay, which she did by the usual letters. Once again, it was a family affair, with my parents helping with the costumes, sets and armatures. The film, now called *The Story of King Midas*, opens with a 'crane-shot' high above Midas' throne. As the narrative unfolds, the camera moves slowly downward and forward, ending up as a medium shot of the King unhappily contemplating his greed. To achieve this very ambitious crane shot movement, my father made a special camera crane device consisting of a long metal arm on which was mounted my 16mm camera. The whole device could be moved both forward and down on a ratchet device so that the minute movements could be changed for each frame shot. The sequence took over four days to photograph, requiring over 800 frames to be shot in the one cut.

A scene of which I was particularly fond shows Midas hurrying to his treasury deep underground. The camera tracks down as he descends a stone spiral staircase, and he looks back over his shoulder to make sure he isn't being followed. I designed it because I thought that Midas descending was visually interesting (I would take the spiral staircase a step further in *The 7th Voyage of Sinbad*). Once in his money room, Midas is seen greedily counting his gold coins, and when one rolls off the table and hits the ground, a mysterious stranger (who had a resemblance to Conrad Veidt) materializes from it. The materialization takes place through a smoke effect, a matte in the area occupied by the model into which I dissolved real smoke, a trick I would use again in later features. *The Story of King Midas* was the most elaborate and the best of all my short subjects.

On the film's completion I had begun to realize that to shoot fifteen or twenty 10-minute subjects, as originally planned, would take three or four years, and I was not prepared to devote that much time to short subjects, no matter how enjoyable they were to work on. To have a career I needed to make features. It was the only way people would sit up and listen to my way of doing stop-motion model animation. For some years I felt that dimensional animation had still to

Left hand page above and below. King Midas. I had always been fascinated by the story of King Midas, and decided to set my version in a stylized semi-mediaeval setting with a fairy tale king, a princess and a dark stranger representing the god Dionysus.

Above. Midas sitting in his counting room. In this photo you are able to see the full miniature set, lights and even my rough storyboard on the left, showing various sequences. In the foreground are my 16mm camera and the stop-frame motor alongside.

Right. The miniature set for the throne room showing Midas hugging his daughter.

Right hand page. Original drawing for *Sinbad the Sailor*, which would become *The 7th Voyage of Sinbad*. Once I had the key scenes for *Sinbad the Sailor*, I sat down to visualize them by drawing several charcoal concepts, including a fight on a spiral staircase between Sinbad and a living skeleton.

realize its full potential, and it was about this time that I played around with it for feature films. Whilst thumbing through some of my Gustave Doré illustrated books, I came across an engraving of a knight atop a broken spiral staircase. Struck by its very dramatic pose, a rather melodramatic thought occurred to me: why not have the Knight fight with a living skeleton (a form I had long wanted to animate)? I realized that a living skeleton in a contemporary situation might seem comical, but if I placed the idea within a mythological tale, it would make an exciting visual screen image. I had always been intrigued with the Arabian Nights stories, and decided that the character of Sinbad, as the personification of fantasy adventure, would fit the bill as the skeleton's adversary. Sinbad's encounters with fantastic creatures during his voyages would also enable me to develop an outline for a feature-length story by stringing the skeleton and other creatures together into an acceptable plotline. The visual situations seemed almost infinite. I ransacked the Arabian Nights stories and wrote a rough step outline of two pages entitled *Sinbad the Sailor* which took him on a mythical adventure that would for the first time see real men battling with fantastic creatures.

Armed with my outline and drawings, I took the idea to producer Edward Small but never even got past his secretary. Next I tried George Pal, who was very interested but heavily involved in another project. Jesse Lasky Snr was intrigued but wasn't sure he could do anything with it, as it would need special sets and costumes that would take a lot of financing. I also talked with Obie about the idea, but he seemed uninterested, perhaps because he saw model animation as more suited to dinosaurs. I didn't approach Cooper because I didn't want to interfere with Obie's relationship with him, and besides, I don't really think he would have been interested. In fact, nobody seemed to be able to grasp the originality of the concept, and after months of discouragement, I reluctantly filed Sinbad under 'story possibilities', believing it would never see the light of day.

As there were no offers of feature film work, I reluctantly began work on another Fairy Tale subject. I had begun planning *The Tortoise and the Hare* almost as soon as I had finished *The Story of King Midas*, and like its predecessor, the story wasn't strictly speaking a traditional fairy tale but an Aesop's Fable. It was a story into which I felt I could instil some comic touches, both in the narration and the attitudes of the animated characters. If I couldn't work in features, I would make this film the most ambitious and best of the series.

Unlike most of my other Fairy Tales (even those I never realized), I am unable to find any reference to narrative or the story pattern in my files. All that exists is a basic step outline and a few crude sketches of camera angles and character designs for the first half of the story. The second half seems never to have been developed, so I assume I must have begun the project without the necessary preliminary story outline, which is unlike me. I always have everything planned to the last detail. I began shooting scenes, but in the end only about 200 feet of colour stock was shot (nearly 4½ minutes) because once again luck had smiled on me and I was about to meet someone who was to prove one of the most important people in my life.

Out of the blue I received a call from an old army friend, Lou Appleton, with whom I had worked on the Capra Unit. He wanted me to meet a young producer working at Columbia Studios who was interested in making a film with me. The producer had seen *The Beast* and had been very impressed with the visual effects and was keen to speak to me about a

In late 1953, at the instigation of Ray Bradbury, I began correspondence with Paul Kohner and director John Huston concerning the possible animation of the whale for their forthcoming production of *Moby Dick*. Ray was writing the screenplay and suggested that model animation might be a solution to overcome the problems of making the whale look believable. I had several meetings and conversations with both Kohner and Huston, but the correspondence illustrates I must have been struggling to convince them of the advantages of stop-motion. In one letter Kohner suggested experimenting with live sharks fitted with rubber latex coverings to give the appearance of a Sperm Whale! As politely as I could, I made the point that we had used stock footage of an octopus to the mouth of a shark for *The Beast From 20,000 Fathoms*, but it always looked as if the shark was trying to shake the octopus off. In another letter to Huston in which I describe the process of dimensional animation, I suggested that the whale be a rubber model and combined with travelling mattes of the ocean to give them the control they needed. I must have also been aware that Huston planned to use the new Cinemascope lens, because I mention that 'it may cause "unforeseen problems" and some experimental work would have to be done to see what limitations the process may cause'. I even sent a costing and several sketches for a test (the scene I envisaged was the whale destroying one of the rowing boats) to Huston's associate producer, Lehman Katz, which was for two and a half weeks at the cost of $2,520. In the end nothing materialized and eventually the effects were executed in England using a model whale, a tank and high-speed photography.

project of his own involving another rampaging beast, this time an octopus. Because I had begun *The Tortoise and the Hare*, my prime wish was to finish it. However, the temptation of a feature was too great. I finally decided to phone this Columbia producer, Charles Schneer.

Charles and I have one major thing in common: a love of motion pictures. Inspired by the success of *The Beast From 20,000 Fathoms*, it was Charles who conceived the idea of a giant octopus, released by an atomic test, flattening San Francisco. The idea was certainly challenging and I do like a challenge, so in December 1953 I agreed to meet with Charles, then working at Columbia's Sam Katzman unit, whom I found to be a forceful but pleasant person full of ideas and enthusiasm. His love of the movie business simply oozed out of him. He explained the story and his ideas, and before I knew it I was drawn into a two-way session on how we could accomplish the complex effects. Here was someone who understood. He could see the story and commercial possibilities of the effects. I left the meeting knowing I would agree to do

the project. It was much more financially rewarding to be a monster man than a Fairy Tale man. Next day I rang Charles and said 'yes'. From that first picture together, Charles and I had a good working relationship. He had a respect for me and my work, and I realized he could keep the budget under control and not let it run wild the way so many pictures had done.

The title for the project at that stage was *Monster of the Deep*, and I wrote to Charles just before Christmas 1953 telling him that I estimated the effects to take five or six months depending on the final screenplay. I also mentioned that as he wanted to film it in colour, Eastman would be my suggestion, although I would have to carry out colour tests. If he wanted the film to be made in Cinemascope (which he had mentioned in passing), we would be faced with an even longer series of tests, which would push the costs up even further. Charles persuaded Katzman to carry out tests, so in April 1954 I experimented with some colour plates and in October of the same year I also tried some simple model shots with Cinemascope using seabed and static building plates. Like my 3-D tests

for Dietz, both these techniques took considerable time to shoot and match, so Charles dropped the idea. Aside from my fee and the use of my equipment, it cost $26,000 for the miniatures, the three octopus models, three character models and separate tentacles, which by today's budgets would be the cost of coffee for the crew. Charles accepted my quote and so I began the first stage of animation by studying real cephalopod molluscs at the Hermoso Beach Aquarium to see how they moved, and then produced sketches based on key scenes from a rough step outline written by Steve Fisher.

Charles had several meetings with Sam Katzman to discuss the costs and the overall feasibility, and when he obtained the go ahead, *Monster of the Deep* became production 8260. In March 1954 Charles brought in George Worthing Yates (who had written the story for *Them*) to write the screenplay, at which point the title changed to *Monster Beneath the Sea*. George would alter the story considerably as he developed the main characters and bridged the key effects sequences, but he also dropped several scenes,

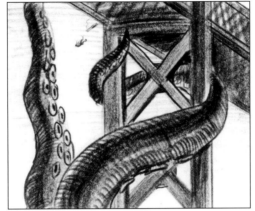

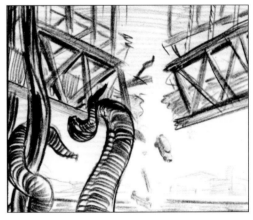

Left hand page. Drawing of an octopus based on my studies at the Hermoso Beach Aquarium. I remember that at one meeting between Charles, Katzman and myself, which was set up to present my sketches of the key scenes for *Monster of the Deep*, Katzman was disturbed that I had drawn the octopus all wrong.

He insisted that the sac of the creature should be up above the head and tentacles. It took me some time to persuade him that the image he had of an octopus was based entirely on the Popeye cartoons and bore no resemblance to a real creature.

Above. The storyboard for the Golden Gate sequence. In all, the animation took about ten days. Note how the images of the creature match similar scenes in the final film. This illustrates how I needed to plan (because of time and money restrictions) exactly how the sequence would look.

including an underwater cavern and an earthquake. After many rewrites, the final screenplay was delivered on 16 September 1954 as *Monster From Beneath the Sea*. It would finally become *It Came From Beneath the Sea* in November 1954.

A submarine is on 'shake out' trials in the Pacific when something jams its propellers. Although not damaged, it returns to port where a small section of flesh is discovered lodged in the blades. The sample is identified as an octopus, but it is realized that if the flesh is real then the creature must be hundreds of feet long. After an incident in which a tramp ship is destroyed, the creature emerges off the coast of San Francisco. After destroying the Golden Gate Bridge it makes its way to the city, causing havoc, but is eventually destroyed with a radiation torpedo.

Kenneth Tobey, who had appeared in *The Beast From 20,000 Fathoms*, was cast as the naval hero, whilst Faith Domergue provided the intelligent but attractive female interest. Donald Curtis was the scientist and Ian Keith played Admiral Burns. Robert

Gordon, who had helmed several of Katzman's features, directed, keeping the tension and managing to sustain the thrills convincingly.

The pressure on me to keep effects costs down was so intense that by necessity certain cuts to the creature had to be made. There was one obvious way: I reduced the number of tentacles on the octopus from eight to six (not five as some film historians seem to believe). Reducing appendages is a trick cartoon animators often use. For example, Mickey Mouse has only three fingers. However, to make this 'shortage' seem less obvious, I designed the animation sequences so that the octopus is mostly below the water line and at least one tentacle is kept moving at all times. This meant that most people were watching the waving tentacle, not the lack of them. No one noticed until, quite by accident, I let it slip in an interview that it was really a sixtopus! Even with this necessary 'cut', I was still pressurized to cut costs where I could, and if we had gone any further, we might have ended up with a tripod on the screen. Katzman never really appreciated my cost-cutting

attempts, a fact borne out when he once quipped that I charged $10,000 a tentacle. If only it had been true.

As you will find out later, nothing is ever thrown away, and after *It Came From Beneath the Sea* was completed, all the tentacle armatures ended up as parts of various dinosaurs in subsequent films, usually as tails! We did, however, build some detailed large-scale tentacles of various sizes, used for close-ups, and a full model of the creature's eye for the scene when the diver swims in front of it.

I rented the same store used for *The Beast From 20,000 Fathoms*, and effects production began in August 1954. As before, the first scenes I shot were for the rear projection plates, which would become part of the live action production schedule. Among these early sequences was the attack on the tramp steamer, for which I used one of the single tentacles. Against a night sky rear projection plate, the full length of the limb had to rise vertically from the sea, so all that is seen is a seemingly endless slimy tentacle of dark flesh and suckers towering over the ship. For this gradual rise I operated the limb on a threaded screw device

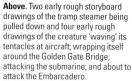

Above. Two early rough storyboard drawings of the tramp steamer being pulled down and four early rough drawings of the creature 'waving' its tentacles at aircraft; wrapping itself around the Golden Gate Bridge; attacking the submarine; and about to attack the Embarcadero.

Right. How the final scene of the attack on the tramp steamer looked. The foaming water in the foreground was created separately in a tank and matted in.

specially constructed for the film. This device allowed me to raise the model a sixteenth of an inch at a time as I shot each frame of film. To give the impression of water glistening on the flesh, I coated the latex with glycerine prior to each animation shot (under the lights, one application would last for up to half an hour before it had to be reapplied). Later the actors, who would be filmed on a section of ship deck, would react to the rear-projected tentacle rising up alongside the doomed ship on a rear projection screen.

The most dramatic sequence in the film is when the creature pulls itself up onto the Golden Gate Bridge and subsequently destroys the centre span. Photographing the live action and plates for this scene caused the most trouble for Charles. In order to obtain permission and co-operation to photograph at various San Francisco landmarks, the script had to be approved by the city fathers. We had already begun production when Charles received a firm 'no' to the use of any locations, with especial emphasis to the bridge sequences. The reason given was that a toll was charged to cross the bridge and the authorities decided that it might undermine the public's confidence in the soundness of the structure. We had to resort to smuggling cameras onto the bridge to get the shots we wanted. For the moving shots we filmed from the rear of a baker's van, which we drove backwards and forwards paying the toll each time, and for the static shots we had a solo cameraman walking across the bridge, stopping to get the required shots. Somehow the city fathers got wind of this and approached the state governor, but he could find nothing to legally prohibit the filming on the bridge, so in desperation the city refused parking privileges to the production, thus the camera crews had to be kept in constant motion. After all this, the city, although never officially forgiving Charles, made no attempt to ban the picture, and it eventually played to capacity audiences in San Francisco with no apparent harm to anyone – including the bridge.

Towards the end of the bridge sequence a tentacle pushes up through the roadway, nearly killing the scientist. This was achieved with the actor standing in front of the rear screen and reacting to the action on the screen of the tentacle pushing up the miniature road surface. For the animation I used my screw device and animated the breakaway sections of the road.

I used the largest tentacle model for the Oakland ferry gate sequence. Apart from a full-size gate on the studio lot on which I carried out my tests, we also constructed a miniature ferry gate that was a perfect replica of the real one, so the tentacle could destroy it. I again used the screw device, enabling me to gradually lift the model tentacle to allow sections of the miniature gate to break away as the tentacle forced its way through the aperture. The whole miniature was interlaced with copper wires that supported and held the pieces that would break off. These 'breakaway' pieces were on the wires, and were also animated as I turned the screw and clicked off the frames of film.

When I had completed the effects, the total cost of the movie was $150,000 which, even for 1955, was a remarkably low price considering what appears on screen. The film received excellent reviews, amongst

Above. A test strip showing how the composite was arrived at. Although not in order it shows the miniature bridge support and the model octopus. Also the rear projection plate and the split screen where the octopus would rise from to attack the bridge.

Above right. The attack of the Sixtopus. In this rare still the model octopus (here you can see it's really a sixtopus) is clinging to Charlotte Knight, who was instrumental in helping me to write many screenplays for the Fairy Tales and would again later help with the script for *20 Million Miles to Earth*.

Right. Single tentacle being animated. The single large tentacle during animation. This shows the process of animation as it is breaking through the roadway on the bridge. Below the miniature roadway was a screw device that I had devised and which allowed me to raise the tentacle gradually so that it could be shot one frame at a time.

them the *Motion Picture Herald*, which said, 'Although not unusually original, it's continuously exciting and the special effects are quite fascinating.' Like *The Beast From 20,000 Fathoms*, the film did very well at the box office, prompting Katzman to ask Charles to make another picture on similar lines.

For some time Charles had been interested in filming a science fiction film about flying saucers, a subject that seemed to feature almost daily in the newspapers. Charles was keen to use stop-motion model animation, so he asked if I would be interested in creating the saucers. Although I said yes, because it would be some time before the budget and details were sorted out, I decided to accept an offer from Irwin Allen at Warner Brothers who was working on a project that closely resembled my old *Evolution* idea.

Right. Clock Tower.
Various ideas for the attack on San Francisco harbour.

Embarcadero Sequence

Left. The complete process for the attack on the Embarcadero. Top: one of the storyboard drawings showing the Octopus attacking the tower. Next: how the final scene looked in the film. Next: the foreground (or live action) matted out and the tentacles animated as part of a split screen. Bottom: the other half of the split screen with just the foreground live action. Note that in this still some of the people have their heads cropped off because they have run through the matte line. In the event of this happening, they had to be reinstated on what is called a 'second pass' through the camera. Before this took place, however, I made enlarged photos of the heads from the 35mm frames and stuck them on a glass sheet where their heads should have been so that they were 'whole' again once the 'second pass' had taken place.

Top. The tentacles wrapping themselves around the tower. The top picture is the final composite. Below shows the model tentacles attacking the miniature tower and illustrates clearly where the matte line was drawn. In this again the head of the man on the right is cropped, so I had to reinstate him with the paste-on head during the second camera pass. The perspective of the people fleeing from the action provides a depth to the action and focuses on the tower and its attacker.

Right hand page. Poster. A typical poster of the 1950s that provides the prospective customer with an impression of explosive action. They knew how to make posters then.

Out of primordial depths to destroy the world!
COLUMBIA PICTURES presents
IT
CAME FROM BENEATH THE SEA
starring
KENNETH TOBEY · FAITH DOMERGUE with DONALD CURTIS
Screen Play by GEORGE WORTHING YATES and HAL SMITH · Technical Effects Created by RAY HARRYHAUSEN
Executive Producer SAM KATZMAN · Produced by CHARLES H. SCHNEER · Directed by ROBERT GORDON

The *Animal World* was a feature film documentary that began with the forming of the Earth, through the age of the dinosaurs, and then related the evolution of animals as we know them today. The ad line for the film was 'Two billion years in the making!' Irwin Allen was a producer, director and screenwriter who had begun in radio, advertising and then, as a talent agent, eventually turned his skills to the film industry. Before I came onto the project, Allen had commissioned Willis O'Brien as supervising animator and technical advisor to design the models and set-ups for the proposed 15-minute dinosaur sequence. I was offered the task of actual animation, which I was delighted to accept as it reunited me with Obie.

The animation sequence was to be the most expensive outlay in the budget, so Allen was eager to save money. He even considered purchasing footage I had shot for *Evolution*, which resembled what Allen was attempting to create in this picture. I had shot my footage in colour 16mm, so Allen had it blown up to 35mm, which looked great, but there was one problem. I had shot most of the material at 16 frames per second, while 35mm needed to be 24 frames per second, making the creatures move too quickly, so Allen decided it wasn't suitable for such a prestigious production.

In all, Obie and I spent about eight weeks on actual animation, the shortest amount of time I have ever spent on any project in my professional career. It was simply table-top animation, with no humans to complicate matters. This enabled us to use two cameras on each set-up, resulting in a huge amount of footage for cutting. I double-framed certain parts of the slower-moving scenes where little movement is required, but for the most part it was single-frame stop-motion. Harold Wellman was the director of photography, who lined up shots according to Obie's instructions and the requirements of the script, such as it was.

The dinosaur models were all cast from moulds using the simpler foam injection method. This is a far faster technique of covering the armatures than the Delgado 'build-up' technique that calls for the slow process of lapping each muscle over the metal armature and then covering it with properly textured skin. The 'build-up' technique gives a more realistic effect, whilst the foam injection models have little realism, evident in the photographs from *Animal World*.

For expediency's sake, mechanically operated heads, built on a much larger scale than the animation models, were crafted for all the close-ups. They always looked like what they were: mechanical things. The ceratosaurus were about 6 feet tall, and I didn't enjoy working with them, mainly because of their size. Money was also saved by casting the two ceratosaurus from the same mould, though some details were altered when the two models were painted. The allosaurus, tyrannosaurus and one of the ceratosaurus seen in the picture were in fact the same model, used in separate scenes with necessary alterations to help disguise the fact.

Because of the budget, there was little or no opportunity to instil anything into the models except basic actions. However, I did manage to insert one or two little trademarks. For example, for the introduction of the allosaurus I used a trick developed in *Evolution*. To add impact I had the allosaurus leap into the frame as a prelude to attacking the stegosaurus. This hopefully gave the audience a shock reaction to the creature.

Although there were no 'live' actors, there was one rather strange scene I had to film. Irwin Allen wanted to illustrate the enormous size of the dinosaurs, so he inserted into the script the line, 'If man *had* lived at that time…', to which I had to animate a caveman being swallowed by a brontosaurus (Allen didn't seem to realize that this creature was not a carnivore). There were several cuts made to the final release print after audiences thought the film too violent. One of the deleted animation sequences was the fight between a stegosaurus and a ceratosaurus, ending in the former's death. We animated the ceratosaurus tearing the flesh from its victim with blood oozing from the torn body and the mouth of the carnivore. Irwin Allen had told me when I was animating to make the action strong, so I did. Echoing this graphic depiction of death, there were other sequences in the live action footage in which animals are seen tearing the flesh off other creatures. This was all too much for the audiences at the previews, so all these scenes were cut, including my dinosaur dinner.

Warner first showed the completed feature in December 1955 for Academy Award consideration, hoping to repeat the success of Allen's previous winner, *The Sea Around Us*, but it failed to be nominated. It finally opened six months later in June 1956, and I am proud to say the dinosaur footage received the most praise from the critics. Obie and I were delighted to read the favourable comments about the 'grandeur' of the prehistoric sequence. Sadly, this was to be the last time I would work with Obie, although we stayed in touch.

By the time *Animal World* had been initially edited and was ready for release, I had returned in April/May 1955 to Columbia to begin work on Charles' flying saucer project. In the early 1950s there was a huge worldwide increase in UFO phenomena, especially in the States. Consequently, Hollywood was not slow to create its own little alien invasions if the box-office receipts were favourable. Charles was one of the first to 'cash in' on this craze. One of his tricks for keeping a finger on the pulse of public interest was to clip items and stories from newspapers and magazines. Charles recognized the exploitation value of a film about a flying saucer invasion and persuaded the Columbia/Katzman unit to film such a story with me shooting the effects for far less money than it would look like on screen. After the success of *It Came From Beneath the Sea*, Katzman was only too eager to have another effects film making money, so he gave the go-ahead.

Charles asked Curt Siodmak, a screenwriter with a huge reputation in the fantasy genre, to work on

Left hand page. Poor model from *The Animal World*. The dinosaur models for *The Animal World* were cast by Warner from moulds using the foam injection method, which was a poor substitute for Delgado's 'build-up' technique.

Above. Dinosaur Hatching. If there was a favourite scene in *The Animal World*, perhaps it was the hatching of the baby brontosaurus, a theme I would return to in *20 Million Miles to Earth* with the emergence of the Ymir from his jelly egg, and again in *The 7th Voyage of Sinbad* with the hatching of the Roc.

a script with the basic storyline of an invading fleet of alien saucers. Before Curt came on board, one of the ideas was to have a group of adventurers/scientists discover a crashed saucer as a prelude to an invasion of Earth. Curt changed that by concentrating on a US military space project called 'Operation Skyhook' that is threatened by the alien saucers. It was also decided that the visual climax would take place in a large city, and where better than Washington, DC, the seat of national government.

As I had to realize all the effects, I worked closely with Curt on various aspects of the script. It was me who coined the phrase 'solidified electricity' that tickled Larry Butler (Columbia's head of visual effects) so much. We were looking for a completely new and alien term, and I suddenly thought, what if you had a way of solidifying electricity? You would flash it and then solidify it through some process – it's so unthinkable that it's possible. At the same time that

Curt and I were working on a script outline, Charles bought the rights to a popular best-selling book called *Flying Saucers From Outer Space* by Donald Keyhoe, which gave us the first working title for the treatment. Research based on reported sightings was also integrated into the script, which kept the whole idea as credible as possible.

After turning down Siodmak's script, then one by George Washington Yates, Charles finally brought in Raymond T. Marcus (actually Bernard Gordon) to revise it. When this script was delivered, Charles was now satisfied that all the problems had been ironed out. It was at this point that the film became *Attack of the Flying Saucers* and Fred F. Sears was signed to direct:

Sightings of flying saucers are increasing around the globe. They are discovered to be craft of a peaceful race with technology far beyond ours who are fleeing from a dying

planet. In the US a saucer lands at a military base, only to be greeted by hostile gunfire. Declaring war on the entire planet, the aliens demonstrate their strength by using death rays, and by launching a large-scale attack on Earth with their fleet of flying saucers. Working in their under-ground rocket base, space scientist Dr Marvin (Hugh Marlowe) and his wife Carol (Joan Taylor) examine the body of a captured alien and discover that the creatures and their saucers are sensitive to high-frequency sound. They develop a machine that emits a beam that can be aimed at the saucers, and during the final battle in Washington, DC, they disable the saucers, making them crash spectacularly into various Washington landmarks, and so save the Earth.

The prime fascination of the project for me was the challenge of seeing just how visually interesting and convincing I could make a metal spaceship look on the screen. Although the possibilities were limited for

Left hand page. A drawing I made many years before the advent of *Earth Vs the Flying Saucers.*
I had conceived of an idea about adventurers discovering a saucer in a remote jungle.

Above and right. Rough sketches and designs for the saucers. Note the design for the
saucer on the right. The nodules on the underside were there for both looks and to allow me
to attach the aerial base wires for animation. The semi-circular bumps beneath the lip of the
saucers were a detail suggested by a 'real' photo of a flying saucer that had supposedly
landed in England in 1954.

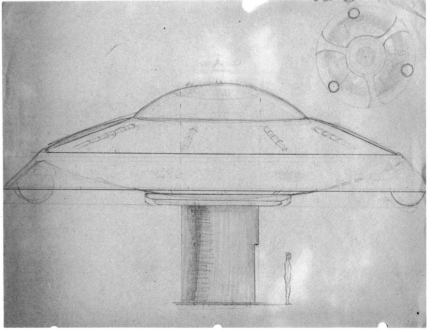

stop-motion, the idea of a fleet of saucers attacking Earth had great potential for delivering something a little different to the usual 'saucer pictures'. I had also always been fascinated with the possibilities of real flying saucers, so this made the project doubly exciting. As usual when a new project was confirmed, I did a lot of research, which in this case brought me into contact with various groups and individuals who claimed to have had actual contact with beings from outer space.

The design for the saucers was based mostly on what people expected. My research had covered all the concepts, some of which looked too earthly, for example portholes, which didn't seem right. My solution was to make the exteriors of the saucers as smooth as possible, although I did include three semi-circular bumps beneath the lip of the saucers. Aside

from their 'authenticity', being based on photos, they also broke up the smooth design of the spacecraft and served as anchors for the overhead wires that suspended the miniatures in front of the rear-projected live-action plates. Prior to magnetic tape, most recordings were made on wire, so when tape came in, I found myself with loads of this old recording wire, which I utilized for aerial shots. Whenever I look at the film I wonder if the saucer is being supported by an aria from *La Bohème* or perhaps something from Beethoven! Halfway through the film nylon wire became available, so I changed over to that. The design of the craft also had to incorporate something to show the audiences that it was moving and avoid it becoming a boring lump of metal, so in addition to the bumps I decided to give the smooth finish of the saucer something extra,

something that would 'animate' it. I designed the models so that the outer rim of the craft and the centre were independent of the inner revolving section. These rims were decorated with parallel lines that gave the saucers, when animated, a strange stroboscopic effect.

I constructed three sizes of saucer models: a 12-inch ship for close shots, three medium and three smaller models for the long shots, so that we could have a fleet of them. My father did a great job of machining the models out of aluminium on a small lathe at home, and also constructed an 18-inch model out of wood (I would have liked at least one model bigger than 18 inches to achieve more close-shot detail, but the budget didn't allow for it). To finish them off I then had the models anodized (a process of coating the metal with an oxide film by electro-

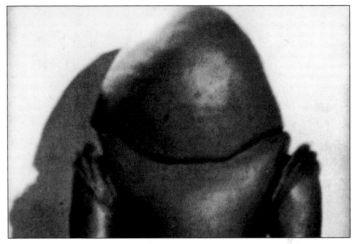

Left hand page. One of the most recognized scenes in *Earth Vs the Flying Saucers*. This scene would be copied in one form or another in many other saucer pictures because Columbia, for whom the film was made, later sold the shots for stock footage.

Left. Worm Men key drawing. This was a drawing that I completed many years before the advent of *Earth Vs the Flying Saucers*. The idea was that humans were kidnapped by worm-like aliens. The only reason I liked the idea was that the creatures were an interesting animation prospect.

Above right. The Aliens. I was never happy with these creations. They always looked phoney and stiff, like men in costumes, which is what they were.

Above. One of the actual models used in the film. Note the slits or grooves. These made it easier to animate and gave the impression when moving of some force keeping the machine airborne.

deposition), giving them a matt or buff look so they didn't reflect light. Only the large model had the capacity to lower its exit tube, whirl on its axis and extend the dish-shaped death ray. One of the smaller models had a replaceable base that held an immobile death ray projector, which was operated through stop-motion by the screw apparatus used for the tentacles in *It Came From Beneath the Sea*. I also made a separate three- to four-inch scale wooden mock-up of the death ray projector to use for close-ups.

In addition to the model and miniature set designs, I had to design the aliens. It had originally been planned to animate them, but I had trouble finding a suitable and believable alien concept. Unfortunately, the budget wouldn't stretch to animating the creatures, so I was reduced to designing a suit for actors. Following my hasty specifications,

Clay Campbell's makeup department at Columbia constructed three reinforced latex rubber suits that included a moulded alien headpiece weighing about 20lbs each. I have never been happy with these costumes – they always look collapsed and phoney, and I think that it shows how little thought or allocation of budget went into them.

Whilst the script was being finalized, I travelled to Washington, DC, in May 1955 to pick out the landmarks to be destroyed. I spent two weeks with my still camera, and when I returned to Hollywood these pictures were integrated into my storyboards. Later we sent a cameraman to Washington for ten days to shoot the 35mm background plates for the rear projection, which he faithfully photographed according to my detailed storyboards. This saved time and money.

To help build some of the miniatures, assist with the models and organize the set-ups ready for me to shoot, I decided to bring in George Lofgren whom I had met on *Mighty Joe Young*. George had started working for me as my technical assistant on *It Came From Beneath the Sea*, and because he had been a taxidermist, his work on the models and miniatures was invaluable.

The first sequences shot for *Earth Vs the Flying Saucers* were for the rear-projection plates. These plates included the saucer hovering over the desert road, to be screened behind the mock-up of the car, various flight shots for the aircraft etc., and the saucer crashing through the huge window of Union Station. I also filmed the cuts of the death ray destroying a miniature, for later use in the scene where Morris Ankrum is seen fleeing.

Above. Meeting the Alien. This is a basic storyboard for the demise of one of the scientists by an alien. The storyboards for *Earth Vs the Flying Saucers* were mostly a combination of photos with sketches added (for example the top left has a sketch of a saucer over a photo of an edge of a forest) and straightforward sketches. This process saved on time, and over the years I used this short cut several times.

Right hand page top. The saucer forcefield. This was achieved by double printing in the camera, a process I would use again when I made *The 7th Voyage of Sinbad*. A portion of the projected image was blacked out, the film in the camera rewound, the opposite matte was put in place along with a distortion glass to represent the forcefield. The glass was operated one frame at a time during the second exposure and the final image produced the effect of a force field under the cover of the saucer.

Right hand page bottom. The result of the Alien's Death Ray. The alien's death ray was not cell animation as some people believed, but an in-camera technique. I used a roman candle firework to produce the streams of light (along with a few other tricks) inserted in the second camera pass. The matte of the people effected by the ray was made and a fade out, in the camera, was made on the projected image.

The alien's death ray was an in-camera effect accomplished with roman candle fireworks. I photographed the lit candle, held horizontally (or at whatever angle was required) against a black back-ground. When this was processed, I projected it by means of rear projection and added highlights (lumps of white cotton on two wires, animated every four frames along the length of the wire in front of the rear projection screen), which gave the sparks from the roman candles more visual power. These composite shots were then used to print in wherever we required a ray effect. It was very crude but surprisingly effective.

The 'St Elmo's Fire' sequences (in the underground lab and above the house), which turn out to be the alien observation cameras, were achieved by even more unorthodox methods. The main tool was a long pole attached at one end to an electric drill and at the other end to a piece of circular plastic fitted with a

small light fixed in the centre. This then created a whirling light, which was held by George Lofgren (covered in black velvet and a black bag with two slots for his eyes over his head) who would move on my instructions towards and away from the camera in the darkened studio. When the film was processed, all the camera picked up was the whirling light, and later this footage was simply superimposed over the live action so that it corresponded with the actors' reactions to the lights. Originally, these alien observation cameras were to have been tiny saucers fashioned in the same manner as the full-size ones. These observation saucers were to fly into houses and spy on the earthlings, but the budget didn't allow the time to execute these tiny visitors.

One of the best and most successful effects in the picture was the shimmer of the saucer's defensive forcefield around the outside of the craft. It was all

done with double printing in the camera. I would photograph the scene with my miniature projection process and blot out (with a stationary matte) just outside the area where the forcefield was to be. I then rewound the film and inserted a sheet of distortion glass in front of the lens, which was then combined into the open area. The glass, which created a wavy distortion, was animated a millimetre or two, each frame, on the screw apparatus. I would turn the screw and that would raise the glass, distorting the picture within the matte. Later on I would use the saucer forcefield trick in *The 7th Voyage of Sinbad* for the barrier the Genie conjures up to hold back the Cyclops.

For the sequence in which the humans visit the saucer on the beach, I used the 12-inch model to achieve the detail. The actual beach location was at Point Dume, north of Malibu, and the high-angle

Above. Saucers in flight. The saucers were suspended by old recording wire for half the film, and being so close to the camera in order to make them appear large, these would have showed up on the screen if I hadn't painted them out on each frame of film. If the wire passed in front of a white cloud on the rear projection screen, the wires would then have to be painted the same tone. I used the more modern nylon wire for the other half, which was lighter and more translucent.

Right. People fleeing the saucers. These two pictures show how the saucers were matted into the scene of the people fleeing along the side of the Capitol building. I made a matte along the edge of building so creating the illusion of the saucers disappearing behind the building.

Right hand page top. Saucer landing in the White House grounds. This image was achieved by shooting the live action footage of the White House lawns as a background plate through the railings and then animating the model saucer against the background plate. Not much chance of doing that today!

Right hand page bottom. The Potomac scene. The scene where the saucer crashes into the Potomac river basin was achieved by using a split screen matte in the camera.

shots of the saucer sitting on the beach were shot from a plot of land I had just purchased to build a house on. We obtained permission to shoot at a military base just outside of Los Angeles, which stood in for the gate and some of the exteriors of Operation Skyhook. The underground Skyhook control centre interiors were actually the Playa del Rey Sewage Disposal Plant at Hermosa Beach. Oh, the glamour of moviemaking! All the underground pipes and complex equipment were perfect for a scientific laboratory, and all we had to do was add a few control panels to the controls for the sewage and we had a passable control room. Whilst filming in this complex, Charles and I became aware of a weird sound, or more accurately, vibration, which turned out to be the underground disintegration tanks for the disposal system. If we heard any good sounds, no matter where we were, we would have the technicians

make a recording. Later it was enhanced and used as the sound of the flying saucers.

In the finale of the film the saucers lose control because of the sonic guns and crash into various famous Washington, DC, landmarks. One saucer crashes into the huge oval window of Union Station, and for this I used a miniature based on the original window and then animated a model saucer on a wire brace so that it broke through the window. This was one of the first pieces of animation I carried out because it had to be rear projected behind actors in the foreground so they could react to the saucer. For

I am often asked how I was able to land a flying saucer in the grounds of the White House. We didn't ask permission to film but we thought that it would have been a place an alien force would land. We couldn't afford detailed miniatures, so we poked the camera through the bars of the fence at the rear of the White House. When the footage came back to me in Hollywood, I simply used it as rear projection and animated the saucer in front of the White House. All very simple, effective and inexpensive.

the scene in which the saucer crashes into the Potomac river basin in front of the Jefferson Memorial, I used a split screen matte. The whole sequence was done in two cuts. I created a matte line in the water where the saucer was to disappear and then wound the film back to expose the other half below the point where the saucer crashes, and finally double printed in the bubbles around the crashed saucer. The bubbling water was shot at high speed in a small tank with compressed air pumped up from the bottom. When the film was projected at the usual 24 frames per second, the bubbles looked as though they

could have been produced by an enormous object crashing into water. The effect of bubbling water is vital to the realism of size, but to obtain the correct size of bubble is vital so that they are in proportion to the model, achieved by varying the distance between the camera and the bubbles in the tank.

The destruction of the Supreme Court building took four days to film, mainly because I had to laboriously animate each brick or stone that fell, on separate wires. The wires were held by a specially constructed rig (usually called an aerial brace) fixed above the animation table. These wires hold the object being animated firmly in place.

The same thing had to be done with the Capitol building, which involved the use of seven wires, each running more or less vertically and attached to the building sections by wax on the back so they didn't show. I then had to animate them at an eighth or sixteenth of an inch per frame. It would have been far less time-consuming to build the miniatures about 6 or 7 feet high and then photograph the sequence in high-speed photography, but the cost of building a large enough miniature and the number of people it would have involved was prohibitive.

Earth Vs the Flying Saucers was released in July 1956 as the first half of a double bill with *The Werewolf* (another picture from the Sam Katzman unit). *Variety* said of the film: 'The technical effects created by Ray Harryhausen come off excellently... adding the required out-of-this-world visual touch'. The *Cleveland Plain Dealer* reported, 'Ray Harryhausen's photographic tricks turn the trick', and that it had 'the conviction both in direction and playing as well as in the trick camera work which makes it quite a good enough thriller to stand on its own merits without having the questionable support of *The Werewolf*'.

Left hand page. Capitol building. The destruction of the Capitol building involved wire brace work, as did a lot of the film, which I now find quite frightening every time I see it. I would never want to do that amount of work again – it was tortuous.

Above. Deconstructing Government. The main body of the Capitol Building was a large still cutout photograph with the dome missing. A miniature model of the dome completed the picture. The miniature dome was pre-broken and assembled again with wires holding it together so that when I animated the model saucer during the crash I was also able to animate the sections of dome. When the saucer hits there is an explosion. This was filmed seperately against black and added during a second exposure. In these pictures you can see that the whole set was filmed in perspective, hence the odd angles of the dome and the building. However, the stop-motion camera was in the correct perspective to make it seem as though the whole thing was as one.

I have to say that I am not enamoured with *Earth Vs the Flying Saucers*; it remains for me the least favourite of all our pictures. There is a dividing line between science fiction and fantasy, although, they can occasionally overlap. Movie science fiction generally deals with prediction (or attempts at prediction) of future events or man's relationship with gadgets and machines. Fantasy, on the other hand, has more to do with myths, the past, bizarre concepts and Gothic romance, and therefore offers more scope for a variety of visuals and ideas. Fantasy has a poetic appeal radiating romance and warmth, whereas science fiction, with all its preoccupation with machines, politics and scientific apparatus, has a tendency to reflect coldness and indifference. Most of my monster-on-the-rampage films have touched on the scientific element, but I have only been involved with two definite science fiction stories: *Earth Vs the Flying Saucers* and *First Men in the Moon*, a far superior story and production.

There were a total of seven complete and sectional miniatures, with the most spectacular being the Capitol Dome and the Washington monument. With today's spectacularly expensive special effects, it is perhaps interesting to note that the Capitol and Supreme Court building models cost $1500 each, the monument $500 and the Capitol steps $800. In the first draft scripts there was to have been an experimental space station destroyed by the saucers. Unfortunately, this was dropped because of the cost.

Above left. The End. In these three pictures you can see the complete composite above showing the saucer lying at rest inside the Capitol entrance. The miniature is shown next with the matted area for the live action, which is shown in the final still.

Right. Wire brace. The picture above shows the wire brace holding the model saucer as it descends into the Capitol. The building into which it was to crash is a model, but the Capitol dome is a photo held up with planks of wood and clamps. Below is the final composite shot.

Right hand page. Another example of how good the showmanship was in the 1950s. It's interesting to note that today many of these posters are collectable items. I suspect this will not be the case with many produced today.

FLYING SAUCERS ATTACK!

WARNING! TAKE COVER!

FLYING SAUCERS INVADE OUR PLANET! WASHINGTON, LONDON, PARIS, MOSCOW FIGHT BACK!

EARTH vs. THE FLYING SAUCERS

starring **HUGH MARLOWE · JOAN TAYLOR** with **DONALD CURTIS** · George Worthing Yates and Raymond T. Marcus

Screen Play by George Worthing Yates and Raymond T. Marcus · Screen Story by CURT SIODMAK · Technical Effects by RAY HARRYHAUSEN

Produced by CHARLES H. SCHNEER · Executive Producer: SAM KATZMAN · Directed by FRED F. SEARS · A COLUMBIA PICTURE

My next film would be one of those rare overlaps of science fiction and fantasy, and would be my first feature to materialize from one of my own ideas. *20 Million Miles to Earth* metamorphized over many years and through many different guises. Originally I had intended it to be a story about an Ymir, a giant primeval being of Scandinavian mythology, but whilst I was writing *The Elementals*, I decided to change the Ymir into a more famous mythological being and place the events into a modern setting. Hence my first outline, dated October 1954, entitled *The Cyclops*, is the story of a creature brought back to Earth in a manned rocketship but which crash lands in Lake Michigan, just off Chicago. The creature, which apparently cannot be killed, escapes and grows rapidly in Earth's atmosphere but is captured and confined in the Chicago Zoo. It again escapes and fights with an elephant, which it kills, and then, attracted by the scent of animals in the Chicago Stockyards, it is finally killed by a blockbuster bomb. Reading the treatment now, I see that the basic idea of what would become *20 Million Miles to Earth* was already in place.

As already mentioned, I had offered the treatment and a selection of key drawings to Jack Deitz but he declined the project in favour of the ill-fated *Elementals*. Because I considered the story commercially viable, I wouldn't let it die and some time later retitled it as *The Beast From Cylinder 29* and decided to see what Charlotte Knight would make of it. She liked the premise of the storyline and suggested a

number of plot and character changes. The next step outline I wrote, dated 12 November 1954, was entitled *Cyclops* and moved the location to California, in and around San Diego. Sometime soon after, I wrote a fourth outline with the story still set in America but now called *The Space Beast*. In this version the creature is described as a Satyr, which grows in the zoo, eating every living creature offered to it. Ever since the collapse of the *Elementals* project, and with it my trip to Europe, I had always planned on coming up with another project to take me across the Atlantic. I therefore decided to write a fifth outline in which I changed the location of the action to Italy. Now the creature crashes in the rocket off Sicily and is brought, by ship, to the mainland and from there to Rome. All the Italian landmarks I wanted to visit were included as backdrops to the action, including Trajan's column, the Vittorio Emanuele II monument and the Terme Di Caracalla Opera House.

The story has parallels to *King Kong*, but it was written as a tribute, not as a pale copy, and reflected my feelings about man's inhumanity to animals. This sentiment was evident in the final words of the outline: 'nature clouds well its secrets. What have we to offer other planets, our fears, our hatreds, our destruction?' Fade out. This sentiment was to survive into the final film but with a different approach.

During the filming of *Earth Vs the Flying Saucers*, I mentioned the story to Charles, who instantly saw its potential. When *Earth Vs* was completed, we began to discuss ways and means to bring the idea in on a

reasonable budget. Once we had the overall plot budgeted out, Charles brought in Bob Williams and Chris Knopt to write the final shooting script, retaining the plotline but changing the title to *20 Million Miles to Earth*. I never received any screenwriter or story credit but never pushed that fact. In those days I didn't realize modesty was a dirty word in Hollywood:

A US rocketship crashes in the sea off the coast of Sicily on its return to Earth from a mission to the planet Venus. A group of local fishermen rescue one astronaut (William Hopper) and a jelly-like specimen from the sinking hull. From the jelly a creature, or Ymir, is born, witnessed by a professor and a visiting doctor (Joan Taylor). Earth's atmosphere somehow enables the Ymir to grow to an enormous size and after terrorizing Sicily it is anaesthetized by electricity and taken to Rome zoo to be studied. Following an accident, the Ymir is brought back to consciousness, after which it battles with an elephant and wreaks havoc on the city. Finally it meets its end atop the Coliseum.

For the production of the picture Charles formed an independent company, Morningside Productions, which, to some degree, protected us from interference but continued the association with Columbia Pictures, allowing us to rely on their production funds, studio facilities and distribution. This production also allowed us a slightly larger budget, based on the commercial viability of our two previous films for Columbia.

Charles and I only disagreed on one thing about the project. From the first he had visualized it as a colour feature set in the lush locations of the Mediterranean, while I was adamantly against this idea. The reason why I was so reluctant to go to colour was that Kodak had just brought out a new 35mm black and white stock that was perfect for our specialist purposes. I could inter-cut an original negative with a second generation negative from a background plate and there would be hardly any difference between the two. A second-generation colour reproduction at that time was a very poor copy of a first generation. With this argument I managed to persuade Charles that it should be filmed in black and white, although I had the feeling that I would have to face the problems of colour sooner rather than later.

At long last I was to go to Europe – my excitement and expectations were high. My first two-week visit was spent travelling around Italy searching out suitable locations to fit the storyline. As I had anticipated, Rome, as yet relatively undiscovered by Hollywood film-makers, afforded wonderful possibilities for new and unusual background locations. The Coliseum, the Roman Forum, the Temple of Saturn and the Tiber itself, I spared nothing, even the Borghese Gallery's exterior was to be used as the background for the fight to the death between the Ymir and the elephant.

When I returned home I had to concentrate on the design for the Venusian creature. A sequence of concepts ranging from the curious to the outrageous followed. Finally I decided on a basic humanoid form because

I wanted audiences to sympathize with it, and you can't do that if it is totally alien. But to ensure that audiences knew it was alien, I added a hint of dinosaur and slowly the Ymir evolved.

There was only one fully articulated model of the Ymir constructed, this was used for all the major animation. However, I did make a second, smaller model after I began photography, which was only partially articulated, for long shots, and a third, solid, inflexible model was made for the shot in which the professor picks up the tiny Ymir from the table. Finally, a full-size latex glove of the Ymir's hand was made for the sequence when the hand comes from under the canvas cover and grabs Joan Taylor. Once again, my father made the ball-and-socket armatures with his usual professionalism, which I then covered using the sponge rubber 'build-up' method. Many months before, when I finally decided on the look of the creature, I had sculpted a plaster figure from which I made a mould of its surface texture, which supplied the thin rubber 'skin' for the model. I modelled the ele-phant after several visits to the zoo and then gave it to George Lofgren who constructed it and added latex skin.

The only other item I had to design was the rocket-ship, and I wanted it to be believable but at the same time different, practical and visually striking. Although I didn't go into as much detail as I would for the later *First Men in the Moon*, I did research many concepts and designs, and in the end the ship was based on a

Left hand page. First creature. The initial design for the Ymir in *20 Million Miles to Earth* followed my original idea of a giant Cyclops, with one eye and cloven hooves. However, when I built the first clay model, it looked totally wrong.

Top. Drawings of next concept. I eventually gave the Ymir a walrus-like moustache appendage above its mouth (used for the design of the martians in *The War of the Worlds* and later for the Kraken in *Clash of the Titans*), suggesting developed olfactory senses, a point that comes out in the script.

Above. Crew on location. The crew of *20 Million Miles to Earth* on location in Italy. Charles and myself are in the centre.

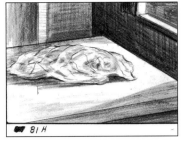

Above. Birth of Ymir. Slowly the Ymir breaks from its jelly cocoon, revealing first an arm, then its entire torso, after which it proceeds to stretch and rub its eyes. It was with this scene that we established a feeling of sympathy towards it that would continue throughout the story.

Left. Birth of the Ymir storyboard. Although planned and drawn a considerable time before shooting, this storyboard illustrates how closely the final film followed the original planning.

Left hand page. The scene of the Ymir in the Forum as it appeared in the film. Behind the Ymir is a rear projected image, and the columns in the foreground are a miniature.

combination of the World War II Nazi V2 rocket, early NASA rockets and other visualizations of what space travel might look like as seen by the scientist in the 1950s.

Once all the production preparation was completed, Charles and I returned to Italy on 21 September to begin shooting at Sperlonga, on the Italian coast (which was to stand in for the Sicilian fishing village in the script), and in Rome itself. We took only the lead actor William Hopper and two cameras, using an Italian second unit to do all the establishing and bridging shots for the background plates. Larry Butler, from Columbia's visual effects department, came along, sharing his many years of experience with second units and rear projection techniques. Other key actors were played in long shot by Italian doubles, and when we returned to Hollywood, we filmed the real actors in front of the rear projection plates we had shot for medium shots and close-ups. For the remaining scenes, we shot in California at Corriganville and Columbia Studios. Some of the interiors for the spaceship were filmed at the Edison Electrical Plant, to which we added a few balsawood girders, filled it with smoke and shot it at an angle to resemble the wrecked control room of the rocketship. Always trying to save money, Charles utilized the standing sets from the Columbia film *The Caine Mutiny* (1954) which art director Cary

Odell modified for some of the other rocketship interiors. We also saved money by once again using stock shots for the sulphur pits and the waterfall, which worked very well in rear projection. The opening of the film, with the Earth shrouded in cloud, was also a studio library stock shot.

It was only on our return to California that we secured a director, Nathan Juran. It was to be the beginning of an association that would stretch over three movies. 'Jerry' Juran was a very competent and easy director to work with because he understood what was involved in superimposing huge weird creatures into his carefully shot live action. He was the perfect choice. His understanding of our type of pictures was helped because he had been an art director (for which he won an Oscar in 1941 for *How Green Was My Valley*), because he grasped what I was doing and was a good visual director who wouldn't take any nonsense, allowing him to bring the picture in on time and within budget.

Whilst the scenes that did not include effects were being photographed, I started animation in my little studio, beginning with the opening scenes of the rocketship plunging dramatically into the sea. For this I suspended the model from wires in front of a miniature rear projection screen and slowly animated

it across the screen. The rocket's shadow on the water was added with a neutral density (a very thin sheet of smoke-coloured plastic), which I also animated along with the rocket, so that the shadow would be cast on the sea as it gets closer to crashing.

The hatching of the baby Ymir is one of the most poignant sequences I have ever filmed, apart perhaps from the homunculus in *The Golden Voyage of Sinbad*. Whereas the homunculus is an instrument of evil, here the young Ymir is so vulnerable. For the hatching I made a special little Ymir model and placed him in a mould, then poured in a mixture of white gelatine which I left to solidify. During the stop-motion animation, I cut a little section of the gelatine and shot a frame, and then cut a little more and so on, producing an effect of something emerging from the substance.

Another atmospheric scene was the barn sequence, in which the Ymir is attacked by a farmer and his dog. Some aspects of it worked well. For example, the emergence of the creature from the dark shadows towards the camera is effective and threatening. However, not all the scenes in this sequence turned out as I had originally planned. A good example of this is the fight with the dog, which takes place all in shadow. I had planned the fight to be more open and with better lighting, but because the model dog looked so

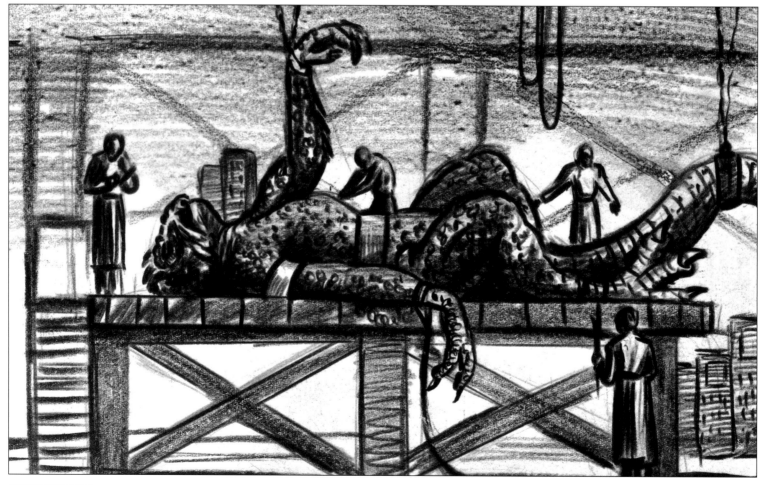

rubbery and phoney, and rather than rebuild the animal, I made the decision to animate the whole sequence in shadow. The scene begins with a real dog for the close shots, after which I brought the animated model into play in a shadow fight that can be seen on the barn wall. The result was quite dramatic, which proves that the things you least expect to work can occasionally be effective.

Later in the barn sequence the farmer plunges a pitchfork into the back of the creature as it tries to leave the barn. Because I wanted some kind of contact between the farmer and the creature, I designed it as a simple cut when the fork is about to touch the creature, and the next shot shows the impaled creature. It is so quick and dramatic that the cut is hardly noticeable. Sometimes when I deliver a lecture and criticize today's cinema of violence, I am reminded by members of the audience of this and various other scenes in our films. For the

actual fight with the farmer, when the Ymir makes physical contact with the man, I used a model based on the actor. Animating 'real' people is always difficult because the animator has to employ more realistic movements, requiring more finite moves of the model. Animating the movements for an unknown alien monster or dinosaur is far easier because the audiences have never seen one in real life. In *Mighty Joe Young* I was required to animate a model of Primo Carnera in the scene when Joe holds him over his head. The model was only 6 inches high and constructed with as many joints as a real human being. It required tiny, almost insignificant movements for the kicking arms and legs as he struggles in Joe's hands. As my first experience of such intricate armatured models, it taught me to give as much care to these small figures as time would allow.

Soon after the struggle in the barn, the creature is

captured by a metal net. The audience sees a helicopter dropping the net over the now much larger Ymir. The helicopter was real but the net wasn't. I had picked up the small net in a hardware store and painted it silver to resemble metal, which in turn gave it a rigid quality that made it possible to animate. It was suspended with six wires in front of the rear projection screen of the helicopter and above the model of the Ymir.

When the creature is brought to Rome, it is kept restrained in the elephant house in Rome Zoo. Because of an accident the creature escapes and comes face to face with an elephant, with which it has a fight. For some of the shots I used a real elephant. I had asked for a 15-foot pachyderm but could only get an 8-foot elephant, which was considerably smaller than I had anticipated. To make the real elephant look bigger we managed to find a 4½-foot actor to play the keeper. This had the effect of making the elephant look 15 or

Left hand page top left. Ymir being caught in net. I later used a similar technique in *Jason and the Argonauts* when Jason and his men drop the netting onto the flying harpies. The net was purchased from a local hardware store and painted to resemble a metal net.

Left hand page right. This example of part of the storyboard shows the cuts I had envisioned. They also establish the atmosphere of the tension, as the audience knows that the creature will force an escape.

Left hand page bottom. One of my sketches from the storyboard showing how the creature would look on the elephant table.

Left and below. Animation of creature on table. The elephant house where the Ymir is restrained was actually an almost bare sound stage in the Columbia Studios in which we constructed a huge table and observation room. These three pictures illustrate the stages that lead up to the final composite. The first shows the model Ymir on the animation table in front of the rear projection of the interior of the elephant house laboratory. The second shows the matte area that the creatures will be placed into. The third is the final composite.

Above. Fight. For some of the shots of the fight between the elephant and the Ymir I used a real elephant, but these were mainly for close-ups and long shots. Here both are models, and is a good example of animation and rear projections.

Right hand page. Elephant crushing car sketch. A very early rough tracing paper sketch for the Ymir and elephant fight. Notice that the Ymir is fatter and less human-like. This was another early concept for the creature. It is perhaps worth noting how many transitions a creature has to endure before I am totally (well, usually) satisfied with how he (or she) will look on the screen.

20 feet high – a more worthy opponent for the Ymir. Actually, I got a little carried away with the size of the elephant. If you look at the sequence, the rear-projected humans are not always in proportion to the animated model. I must have had memories of a cartoon I once saw in Merian Cooper's office during the filming of *Mighty Joe Young*. It depicted Kong in front of the cameras with the figure of Cooper jumping up and down on his hat shouting: 'Make it bigger. Make it bigger!' So, I thought, well, let's have a big elephant. It was during the elephant sequence that I made one of my rare screen appearances. On the day that we were to shoot the zoo scene with the elephant, the actor due to feed it didn't show up, so I dashed out

and started feeding it with peanuts. Because we were short of extras, I followed that up as one of the crowd fleeing from the zoo.

During the fight sequence the elephant is thrown onto a car and crushes it. I had used these specially made lead props before in *The Beast From 20,000 Fathoms* and *It Came From Beneath the Sea*, but by the time of this picture I had developed a technique of pulling the car down from the inside by a wire attached to a screw device situated under the animation table. This device gave me the desired sixteenth of an inch movement, and as I animated the creature above, I could animate the crushing of the vehicle at precisely the same time.

I was faced with a similar problem to the one I had made for myself in *Earth Vs the Flying Saucers*: to animate a crumbling structure. This time the story called for the Ymir to push up through a bridge, which not only necessitated animating the model Ymir pushing up through the structure, but also simultaneously having to move many separate pieces of model bricks and stone, each attached to wires by wax, sometimes only an eighth or sixteenth of an inch in size. When I design these scenes, they always look so interesting, but when I have finished the animation, I wonder why I make life so difficult for myself.

The Coliseum seemed a fitting place to end the short and tragic life of the Ymir. The structure's height

The fight with the elephant really reached its climax framed between the arches of Hadrian's Viaduct, when the Ymir triumphs over the unfortunate creature. The dying animal is seen on its side, breathing very deeply. This 'breathing' is an old model animation trick accomplished by inserting a hospital bladder (the type used to take blood pressure) inside the model when it is cast. The model has to be constructed with a thinner chest cavity so that the bladder is able to move it. The bladder is connected to a tube up the model's backside, which is hidden until it is required to be used, usually in a death scene. When the time comes to animate the breathing, I simply run the tube through the

animation table and hand pump it up twenty-four times and release the pump valve twelve times. When the film is run at full speed, this simulates breathing. Blood is also seen during the pachyderm's death throes. I always do this with the good old theatrical blood makeup Kensington Gore, which I mix with glycerine. The latter gives it a shine and a thick consistency with which I can animate a blood flow. Using an eye dropper I add a little to the model every time I shoot a frame of film. This, when run at the correct speed, makes it seem as though it is flowing. The technique was employed by Obie for *The Lost World* and again for *King Kong* when Kong breaks the tyrannosaurus' jaw.

and circular design lent itself to interesting compositions. Dramaturgy always demands that the 'villain' should die in the most dramatic way possible. There was only one miniature section of the Coliseum built, and that was for the final scene of him standing on top of the structure. All other shots were of the real Coliseum with the animated creature either in front of a rear projection or matted in. To film all the scenes in Rome we had to obtain permission from the Italian government. They were only too pleased to help, and even made soldiers and tanks available for the final Coliseum scene. On the day of shooting it was hot and sticky, and unfortunately the tank drivers were so enthusiastic to demonstrate their mastery of their vehicles that the tracks tore up the brand new tarmac surface around the structure. The production was responsible, so Charles had to pay for the resurfacing of parts of the roadway – he was none too pleased.

The Ymir and Kong before him are both creatures wrenched from their natural environment against their will and finally killed by man. Although these creatures must always die, they should go out with a touch of pathos. This is reflected in the last line of the picture, written at the last minute when we decided that the end needed a tagline: 'Why is it always, always so costly for men to move from the present to the future?' I think it worked rather well, although it is possibly not as good as *King Kong*'s last line. The whole film was a message about man's fear and exploitation of the unknown and that humans had assumed the Ymir was aggressive. After all, he only wanted to go home.

The film was released in June 1957, and Columbia's publicity pressbook described the effects as 'electrolitic dynamation', whatever that was. *Variety* said, 'Another "monster" to scare the kids the way they like to be scared. Good bet for the fantasy addicts.' The review added, 'realistic effects providing strong exploitation potential'. Sadly, the reviews concentrated on the monster and missed out on the compassion. In any event, it was a financial success for Morningside Productions and continues to entertain audiences, who hopefully now see in it the true intent.

Above. A chubby Ymir. Four early concepts for key scenes in the story, including the fight with the elephant. Although it is an early concept for the Ymir, I retained the drawings for the production because the scenes were incorporated into the story.

Right hand page. Poster. Once again, a good showmanship poster that tempted the audience to view sights never seen before.

This film brought to a close another chapter in my life. Not only was it to be the last black and white film I would make, but it was destined to be, with one later exception, the last 'monster-on-the-rampage' film. From now on, stop-motion animation would at last find another subject outlet to change how it was seen in the movie business. Hollywood would begin to sit up and take notice, and my dream would finally be realized.

Below. An alternative, but slightly less inspiring, poster.

SEE outerspace monster tear huge elephants apart!

SEE space-beast defy modern weapons!

SEE space-beast battle a billion volts of electricity!

SPACE CREATURE RUNS AMOK ON EARTH!

20 MILLION MILES TO EARTH

starring

WILLIAM HOPPER · JOAN TAYLOR

Screen Play by BOB WILLIAMS and CHRISTOPHER KNOPF
Story by CHARLOTT KNIGHT · Technical Effects Created by RAY HARRYHAUSEN
Produced by CHARLES H. SCHNEER · Directed by NATHAN JURAN
A MORNINGSIDE PRODUCTION · A COLUMBIA PICTURE

CHAPTER 4 SINBAD HAS BEEN GOOD TO ME

The 7th Voyage of Sinbad
The 3 Worlds of Gulliver

By now I had grown tired of destroying cities, and realized that the popularity of these 'monster-on-the-rampage' movies wouldn't last forever, so I began to think of new avenues for stop-motion model animation to wrench it away from the usual prehistoric creatures. The success of the three films Charles and I had made together had illustrated to the sceptics that model animation need not be expensive, and if I could find the right story, I might be able to persuade people that stop-motion animation was much more versatile. I decided to resurrect the Sinbad idea and present it to Charles.

Retrieving my *Sinbad the Sailor* outline and drawings, I was pleasantly surprised to find that the basic idea and images still looked good. Unfortunately, I knew it would be hard to present to the front office, especially as the 1955 RKO picture *Son of Sinbad* had bombed at the box office. Consequently, everyone said that Sinbad films and costume dramas wouldn't do well at the box office. However, Charles took one look at my material and immediately saw how original and exploitable a project populated with such bizarre creatures might be. Desperately trying not to dampen Charles' enthusiasm, I felt I had to point out that it would cost much more than our usual productions, explaining that a period fantasy couldn't be done on a shoestring. Charles, bless him, was not daunted, but knew he couldn't get it past Columbia's front office without cuts, so asked me to rewrite my rather lavish step outline into a more feasible and acceptable set of key scenes. After weeks of rewrites and redesigning scenes, we made a presentation to Columbia. The project was given an immediate go-ahead for development. So it was that *Sinbad the Sailor* became our next production.

Now that we had the green light, I was faced with designing the complex effects and opticals while Charles began looking around for someone to 'convert' the step outline into a workable screenplay. The path between an idea and a realistic screenplay is always laborious, but to produce one of our pictures the task is even more fraught. Apart from the usual script problems, the screenplay has to be tied in with effects, which entails endless 'sweat box sessions' to iron out what is and isn't possible. On a small budget there are only so many impossibles I can create. I have made a point throughout this book to detail script development, because it is at this stage of the production that the screenplay, the visuals and the budget come together. What would become *The 7th Voyage of Sinbad* is a perfect example of how a screenplay is developed in parallel with the effects. It also illustrates how ideas from all of us are used or rejected because of cost or perhaps in favour of a more simple path or because they hampered the story's flow.

Although the original *Sinbad the Sailor* step outline contained many of the basic sequences that would appear in the final screenplay, some key scenes were altered or dropped. The first of these was a sequence that had two adult Roc birds protecting their egg by dropping huge rocks on Sinbad's ship. This sequence was to survive through many stages, only to be changed in the final script in favour of the Cyclops throwing the rock. The skeleton also changed from a hooded messenger of death to a tool used by the magician in an attempt to kill Sinbad.

Other ideas that were dropped entirely from the final script included a huge toad in the underground kingdom of the sorcerer; Sinbad encountering and overcoming the Lord of Fear; and a fabulous Valley of Diamonds, which was originally the object of Sinbad's quest.

The next stage was to commission a writer, and for this Charles hired Bob Williams (who had worked on the script for *20 Million Miles to Earth*). He delivered a simple eight-page outline on 19 November 1956 entitled *Sinbad*.

Both Charles and I felt that aspects of Bob's story (especially that of Sinbad portrayed as a thief) were a little heavy for a general audience, so we asked Bob to come up with a revised outline, which he did on 27 November 1956. However, this too retained much of the same heaviness, so Charles commissioned Kenneth Kolb. Kenneth had a feel for the story and in his first outline (dated 21 January 1957) many of the story elements of the final film are contained. The only character not in the final screenplay was the Caliph's daughter, Damila, who plots with Sokurah the sorcerer to get rid of the princess, as she wants to marry Sinbad. Working closely with Kenneth we altered and inserted new scenes based on twelve key drawings, some of which I unfortunately left at the studio and never saw again. They were probably junked.

By 5 February 1957 Kenneth delivered a treatment entitled *The Adventures of Sinbad*. This contained an introduction in which it is explained that the island of Colossa is ruled over by three warring factions: the air by the Rocs, the land by the Cyclops and the underworld by the evil sorcerer. This is followed by a pre-credit sequence in which the sorcerer takes the lamp from the Cyclops' treasure cave beneath a waterfall and first meets Sinbad's men on the beach where he is being chased by the creature.

To escape the Cyclops the sorcerer travels with Sinbad to Baghdad and during an audience with the Caliph predicts a strange war that will involve Baghdad. To return to the island of Colossa, and the magic lamp, the sorcerer reduces the princess in size, telling the Caliph that the only way to restore her is with the shell of a Roc's egg. A ship is prepared and Sinbad places the princess in his pocket [I never liked this idea, as the princess would be crushed, and eventually we decided on a box or container] and sail to the island. When they land some of Sinbad's men become inebriated after drinking from a stream of champagne and are captured, roasted and eaten by the Cyclops. The remaining men are killed during a fight with the mother Roc. Sinbad acquires the lamp and summons the genie who tells him that the sorcerer has escaped to his castle in the realm of death, a cave guarded

by a dragon and many monsters. The genie helps Sinbad to slay the dragon at the cave entrance, but once inside, Sinbad encounters a skeleton with whom he has to fight to gain entrance to the sorcerer's castle. Having destroyed the skeleton, Sinbad falls into a pit of mirrors but escapes and locks the sorcerer in a dungeon. Giant rats help the sorcerer to escape and they chase after Sinbad and the restored princess. At the entrance to the cave a huge battle begins between the Rocs, the Cyclops and the rats. The sorcerer is killed and Sinbad and the princess escape in the talons of a Roc which returns them to his ship.

On the delivery of this first treatment by Kenneth he made one or two interesting points. Instead of the sorcerer predicting the future, 'there should be some

"entertainment" conjured up by the magician'. He goes on to say that 'Ray is dreaming up something for that sequence', which would eventually become the snakewoman. He also visualized the Cyclops being held by means 'similar to the Lilliputians who strapped down Gulliver', a premonition of a future project. Charles now presented the treatment and drawings to Columbia Pictures and got the go-ahead for further development, which meant a first draft screenplay that was delivered by Kenneth on 29 March 1957. This screenplay, production number 8400, still bore the title *The Adventures of Sinbad*, but there were other changes and new innovations. For example, the princess' maid, Sadi, who now has a larger role, asks Sokurah if he can make her beautiful,

which leads to the transformation into the exotic snakewoman. A crossbow that would kill the dragon is built on the voyage to Colossa. A huge tentacle rises out of the sea (can't think where this came from) as the ship nears the Island of Wailing Demons. The treasure is located behind the waterfall. The genie's story is now told – how he ran away from his mother, as a result of which she was killed and the rulers of the spirit world imprisoned him in the lamp. The dragon still guards the entrance to the cave but is now chained to a winch. The giant rats still free Sokurah but one of them dies on a rock bridge above a lava stream.

After three of four more rewrites, another screenplay emerged on 2 May 1957. Still titled *The Adventures of Sinbad*, it was this that convinced Columbia to give

the production the green light. On 28 June 1957 Kenneth delivered a final screenplay now called *The 7th Voyage of Sinbad*, a title I had suggested because the number 7 has had a magical connotation throughout history and because we all felt it was a better title for a fantasy/adventure movie. It told a bold and exciting story that linked all the key elements together.

Just prior to shooting there were scenes that were deleted:

1. The rat sequence, for which I had created a storyboard, was dropped as it was felt that it might be too frightening for kids (it should also be noted that Charles hates rats).

2. Sinbad and his men being attacked by bat-devils.

3. A fight between two Cyclops over the roasting sailors.

Left hand page. Sinbad slaying the dragon. One of twelve key drawings used to sell the Sinbad project to the studio. Sadly, my original drawing went missing after the film was completed.

Above. Wheel lock storyboards. The first two sketches are of the dragon and the wheel lock that Sinbad winds up in order to secure the dragon.

Below. Rat storyboards, a sequence that was dropped. Originally a group of giant rats were to pursue Sinbad out of Sokurah's cave. The idea was that Sokurah's association with the rats would make him seem even more diabolical, but Charles decided that rats were too frightening and, in any case, they were not necessary because Torin Thatcher played the part so well.

Right. My design for what would be the cyclops. This is a rare rough sketch I made showing the cyclops in all its glory, and again I made it to compare the height it would appear on screen with that of a man.

I was disappointed to lose this sequence above everything else, as I would have liked to execute the animation of two huge beings slugging it out over the terrified tasty morsels.

4. The Isle of Wailing Sirens was to be developed at one stage, with Sirens seen on storm-tossed rocks. I had conceived them as alluring women with fish tails, but time didn't allow for it.

5. Finally, the sequence in which Sinbad and his men are trapped in a tree by a huge serpent but saved by a Cyclops (Charles also hates snakes).

The film might have been better with these scenes included but in the final analysis it had more than its share of high adventure and didn't require any more event sequences.

Sinbad and his men land on the island of Colossa, where they rescue the sorcerer Sokurah from a huge Cyclops. The magician is ungrateful for the rescue, as he has left behind an all-powerful magic lamp which commands a genie. Following their arrival in Baghdad, Sokurah creates a snakewoman who dances for the Caliph, but later, to force Sinbad to return to Colossa for the lamp, he reduces the princess Parisa to only inches by means of magic. Returning to the island, this time with a giant crossbow, Sinbad with his men, Sokurah and the tiny princess, seek out the Giant Roc egg for an ingredient to return the princess to normal size. On the way they encounter a Cyclops who attempts to roast Sinbad's men on a spit but Sinbad manages to blind him so that he plunges over a cliff. In Sokurah's castle, which is defended by a dragon, Sinbad is forced to do battle and destroy a sword-wielding skeleton, brought to life by the sorcerer. Fleeing with the princess (who has now been restored to her full height) and the lamp, Sinbad has a final confrontation with Sokurah who tries to use the dragon to kill Sinbad. On the beach the dragon is slain by Sinbad's giant crossbow and as it falls to the ground it kills the evil magician.

When we had the final screenplay I began working on the costs for the effects. Based on a thirty-week shooting period and including equipment, drawings and storyboards, rent of the studio, George Lofgren's fee, travel, the construction of the armatures (by my father) and the building of the miniatures, the final figure totalled $75,759.30. It was reasonable then, but compared with today's costly effects it is minuscule. Charles realized that the project relied heavily on my technical knowledge, so he had me insured for an undisclosed sum of money and, like Betty Grable's legs, my hands were insured for a million dollars or thereabouts.

I knew I could deliver every event and character contained in the script but the main problem I had to overcome was that Charles insisted the film was to be in colour. Up until that point I had always managed to convince him that it was unnecessary, would take more time to shoot and therefore cost more. However, deep down I knew that a film based on the Arabian Nights wouldn't lend itself to monochrome. So I was faced with making Dynamation work in colour. Many hours and hundreds of feet of film were spent experimenting with balancing the colour between live-action and effects work. Because the human eye does not register the same colour and quality of light, colour matching with the rear projection was a big problem in those early days because of the loss of definition and colour quality when the back plates were projected and then re-photographed with the animation. With Gerald Rackett, the head of Columbia laboratories in Hollywood, I set about trying to solve the problems of how we could get less contrast and so avoid excessive colour changes. Slowly, by trial and error, we discovered that one of the solutions was Eastman Kodak's newest colour stock 5253, which had the benefits of offering a master-positive as well as a duplicate negative that would eliminate some of the problems in re-photographing projected footage on the rear projector. However, matching the animation plates with the rest of the live action was not an easy task: the plates lost a generation in the Dynamation process. We were requiring standards that simply didn't exist and were forced to use both tried and tested methods, and invent and re-invent new methods of improving the look of the film.

Frequently we would rely on flashing the more contrasty scenes so the blacks in the plate wouldn't go completely black and lose all detail. When I projected the background plates, the colours wouldn't deteriorate quite as much as they would if you projected a normal plate. Another trick we developed for *7th Voyage* was to photograph the background plates at full aperture (most live-action films are shot with part of the frame masked off). The principle is that the larger the negative, the larger the picture is going to be and the better the quality. When I shoot a Dynamation plate, I take off the academy mask, which cuts down on the grain as it produces that little bit more area. It's a small decrease, perhaps 10 per cent, but it's noticeable.

There was one other unforeseen problem. Up to that point, I would usually shoot enough footage for a cut before I would break for the day. However, on *7th Voyage* I had to work as fast as possible to get a full sequence before a cut. This was because the colour values of the film stock would fluctuate when processed due to temperature changes overnight after the set was closed down. These days, film stocks are generally not sensitive to the problem, but at the time if I couldn't get a cut, I would be forced to work on until I did, often through the night.

Shooting the picture in colour meant animation would take longer, so Charles was faced with searching for other means of producing spectacle without the money. Furthermore, by the mid-1950s most of America's good locations had been overused, and aside from the budget, we also wanted to give the film a fresh and original look, so we decided to shoot it abroad. We began with considering the Middle East (which seemed a natural place to start for an Arabian Nights story), but the area was in political turmoil. After discarding Italy, we looked at Spain, which possessed landmarks of Moorish architecture and a variety of virtually unused locations and beaches. I flew there to meet Lewis Roberts, our production manager, who showed me the facilities in Madrid and Barcelona, as well as wonderful locations at S'Agaro on the Costa Brava, the Alhambra Palace in Granada and the island of Mallorca. I had found the perfect setting for *7th Voyage*, and if the locations were perfect, the low cost of Spanish actors and labour was an added bonus. Over the years Charles and I were destined to use the Spanish coastline and landmarks for scenes in almost all our subsequent movies together. I fell in love with Spain then and have continued to love and appreciate its beauty even with the advent of mass tourism. Unfortunately, I have never mastered the language, even though my wife Diana and I have a house there. It was whilst working on *7th Voyage* that I invented my own version of Spanish, adding 'o' to nouns, for example, 'Bring me el pencil-o', which is not very efficient when you are filming. You know what you want but nobody else does, including the English-speaking members of the cast and crew. Over the years this 'habit' became even worse. Whilst shooting the cave interior for the Fountain of Destiny for *The Golden Voyage of Sinbad*, I wanted mist in the background, so I called out for 'Mucho smoko! Mucho smoko!' The words echoed around the cave, whereupon someone beside me said, 'Do you know what that means? It has something to do with picking your nose.'

Left hand page. Drawing of bat devils. Although the bat devils were eventually dropped, I used a variation years later in *Jason and the Argonauts* when we conjured up the harpies.

Left. Night filming in the Alhambra for *The 7th Voyage of Sinbad*. From left to right, myself, Charles and the director, Jerry Juran. Jerry never seemed to be down, but Charles and I look worried, probably due to the fact that filming in the Alhambra was not exactly straightforward.

Before returning to the States we stopped off in England to visit the blue screen stages at the MGM Studio at Borehamwood and the Rank Film Laboratories at Denham (at that time the world's leading travelling matte experts). It was during this visit that we found our cinematographer, Wilkie Cooper, who had been recommended by the head of the Columbia Labs in Hollywood. Wilkie turned out to be the perfect choice. On every production there are one or two nightmares the cinematographer has to face, but on this production we were not only treading new ground, requiring every effects scene to be carefully lit, but Wilkie was limited to a very tight budget. Wilkie invented new methods and always overcame the problems. For the scenes filmed in the Caves of Arta on Mallorca, we had hired the lamps in Spain from a defunct company that had them in customs, but as we left to sail to Mallorca, the net in which the lights were being loaded broke and several of them were written off when they fell into the harbour. When we got to the caves poor Wilkie had the enormous problem of lighting them with less lights than ideal. In the end he resorted to underlighting the scenes and asking the lab to overdevelop the negative. This was a very risky move, and it is a compliment to Wilkie that the scenes worked out beautifully.

Whilst Charles and I had been away, Columbia's casting department had begun on the lead parts. Several of their leading men were considered for the role of Sinbad but the part eventually went to a young contract player, Kerwin Mathews, whom Columbia had been eager to try out in a major role. The key part of Sokurah, the sorcerer, went to the distinguished British actor Torin Thatcher. Princess Parisa was played by Bing Crosby's wife Kathryn Grant, and the Genie by the very young Richard Eyer. All the other minor parts would be cast in Spain from English actors living there or, if the role was non-speaking, from Spanish extras. It was a production on which everyone got on with the job and the actors were always able to understand my complex explanation of the bizarre creatures they were unable to see,

especially Torin Thatcher, who possessed a wonderful flair for the theatrical, with his marvellous voice and appearance. He was ideal for the part, keeping the picture vital and realizing that the character required a larger than life performance.

Since Charles and I had got on well with Nathan Juran during the making of *20 Million Miles to Earth*, he was the natural choice of director. As the production was complex in visuals and storyline, we needed someone who was competent and could visualize the effects. Jerry, as always, was the perfect director.

The location photography was carried out on a very strict time schedule with no room for error that might risk our budget. Each location was allocated a set number of days and Charles had worked out the travel arrangements calculated to the day (and almost to the hour). He was always on set, which showed that he wasn't just watching the money but that he genuinely liked making films. Added to that, his understanding and confidence in how I would handle the effects was evident from our first picture, and he rarely interfered.

Live-action shooting began in Granada at the Alhambra Palace, where we filmed at night to avoid the tourists. This, however, forced us to shoot night for day, which meant a huge battery of lights (enabling us to light the day backings outside each of the windows). As the Alhambra at that time was not equipped with electricity, we were forced to generate all our own power. Later we moved to the Caves of Arta in Mallorca, and found ourselves working straight through the night and into the following day, to avoid the tourists and make the deadline for the next flight, hotel and location. The cave sequences included the idea that inspired the film, the skeleton fight, which was to be choreographed by Olympic fencing master Enzo Musumeci-Greco. Enzo had been practising the fencing with Kerwin, and we had talked about the sequence many times before we arrived on the island, but needed time to work out the choreography for the fight. Wilkie, Enzo, Charles and I tried to anticipate any problems, but because we were working so

quickly, things occasionally went wrong. I remember once, in Mallorca, when we were on location for the ascent to the Roc's nest, the props truck ended up at the wrong location for that day. They were in the middle of nowhere, with the cast, cameras and costumes but no props – specifically the swords. Tired of waiting, Jerry and I set off in a rainstorm for a local hotel, where we searched unsuccessfully for swords. However, around the back of the hotel we discovered a log pile, and with nothing else available we set about carving two swords. Fortunately, they were only required for long shots.

For Sinbad's ship, Charles had acquired the use of the replica of Columbus' Santa Maria, tied up in Barcelona harbour as a tourist attraction. The Spanish authorities had agreed to let us take the vessel out into the open sea so that we could film various onboard scenes, including a storm sequence in which Sinbad and his crew encounter the Island of the Wailing Demons, without the harbour and buildings in the background. But the vessel was not built for rough water (it had no keel, only a cement bottom), so when it hit the wake of a large ship coming into harbour, it very nearly capsized. The Spanish Commodore in charge of the vessel, and who had been most amiable up to then, frantically yelled for the ship to come about and return to its mooring. He flatly refused ever to take it out again, much to the distress of poor Charles, and so we were forced to shoot the storm scene in the harbour.

By shooting at angles we were able to avoid any buildings and overhead cables, but we still had the problem of ship movement. Jerry hit on the bright idea of getting Enzo to wave a white flag from side to side, simulating the motion of a rocking ship and so enabling the actors to all roll the same way as they would on the high sea. We then mounted the camera on a gimbal (a special rig to allow the camera to move) so that it was able to rock in the opposite direction to the white flag, thus simulating a ship at sea in a storm. To attain fierce winds we used an old aeroplane engine with its propeller fitted as a wind machine.

Right. Ship in harbour. Unfortunately, the replica of Columbus' *Santa Maria* we used as Sinbad's vessel didn't look anything like an Arabian ship. We got around this little problem by shooting the actors at angles to avoid the buildings surrounding the moored ship.

Right hand page. Drawing and notes for sequence. My design for reducing Kathryn Grant's arm. For the princess' shrinking arm on the pillow I used a long dolly track. We placed Kathryn on a support and began with a close-up, slowly pulling the camera back at an angle. All the other sequences that involved specialist techniques were similarly designed.

MORNINGSIDE PRODUCTIONS, INC.
1438 NORTH GOWER STREET
HOLLYWOOD 28, CALIFORNIA
HOLLYWOOD 2-3111

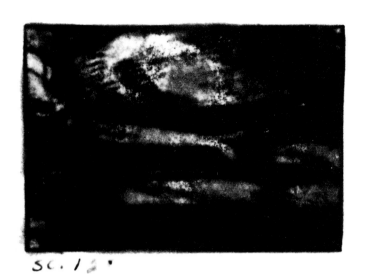

SC. 125

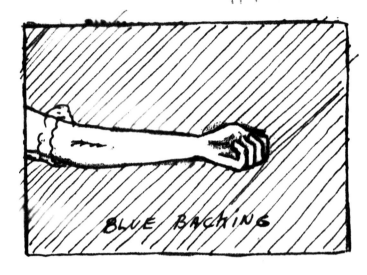

BLUE BACKING

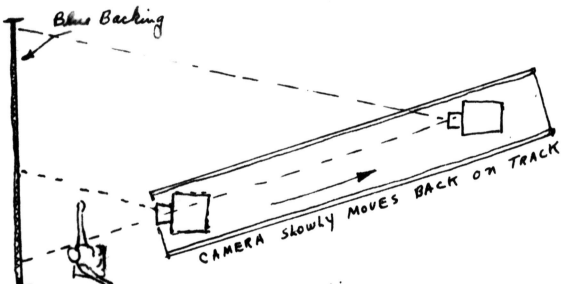

Blue Backing

(DOWN VIEW)

CAMERA slowly MOVES BACK ON TRACK

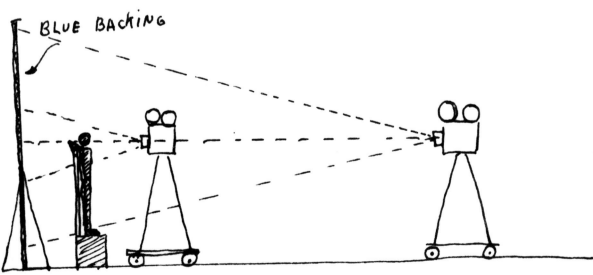

BLUE BACKING

Above. The miniature as seen in the final film. The scene was made up of a live-action foreground that included the men carrying the fifteen-foot arrow and the men standing in front of the wheel (which was also full size). I then created a split screen along the sand, around the full sized wheel and beneath the crossbow. Into this I placed the miniature crossbow; the landscape behind with the rest of the beach and the trees is the other part of the split screen. Actors were placed in front of the full size wheel to create the illusion of scale.

Right. Giant crossbow. The miniature crossbow, which is some two feet in length, was only recently returned to me from Forry Ackerman's collection. A full size, fifteen-foot arrow was also constructed so that it could be filmed on the deck of the ship and being carried to the crossbow by a group of sailors.

Right hand page. Snakewoman. The snakewoman's skin, from her hips to the end of her tail, was moulded from that of a boa constrictor. A real skin would not have been suitable because it would have been too brittle and inflexible, so I made a plastercast and a rubber-textured skin to put on the model.

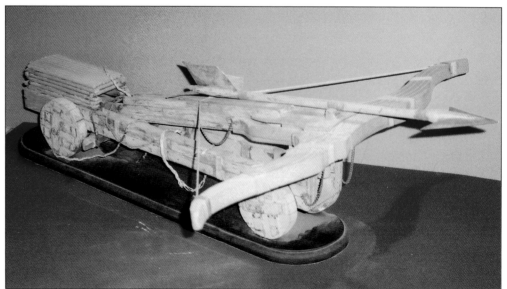

The final touch was the rain, for which we obtained the help of the Barcelona Fire Department, which aimed four or five hoses over the vessel and actors. Unfortunately, the water they were pumping was from the harbour and therefore almost raw sewage, so to try and overcome this unsavoury problem we had a chain bucket brigade to throw clean water in the actors' faces. Poor Kerwin was shouting his lines over the noise of the water and the wind machine, and every time he opened his mouth he received a considerable amount of harbour water. Days later he was running a temperature of 103°, but because he was a professional, he never let us down. We were all ill at one time or another, but we couldn't let it stop us, although on occasions it was extremely uncomfortable.

Following the location shoot, Charles, myself and key members of the cast flew to England to spend three days at the MGM Studios filming the blue screen work. Some of the backgrounds for the travelling mattes were shot in Spain and some were finished off in Hollywood, but at least one part of all the composites were shot in London. So that everyone (cast, crew and laboratories) knew what was required, I made careful notes and drawings illustrating how each travelling matte scene would work. Examples of these are the rock crevice scene with Kerwin and Torin staring up at the blue screen, into which I would later add the Cyclops. For the scene in which the princess slips down into the lamp I shot Kerwin and the lamp in Madrid, but Kathy was photographed in London. She was placed on a table against the blue screen together with a foreground blue matte.

After six weeks of location and studio work, we all returned to Hollywood to shoot the odd pick-up shot and loop over most of the dialogue. Following that, the crew and what cast that was left disbanded, and I retired to my little studio on 54th Street, near Cimarron, where I would also live during the completion of the effects work. I began by putting the finishing touches to the models and the miniatures and, assisted by George Lofgren (for the last time), prepared for the animation sequences. For *20 Million Miles to Earth* I had begun using the quicker foam injection moulding technique for the models rather than the slower build-up method used by Obie and Delgado, although the process wasn't always successful. I had to whip a mixture of liquid foam in a bowl, pour it into the mould and then pop it into an oven I had installed

at the studio so that it would harden. The secret was in the cooking time, usually about an hour, although if the oven door was opened too soon, the concoction would fall like a cake. To attain the quality I was looking for, it would often necessitate the baking of half a dozen before one came out right. I eventually overcame this problem by packing the armature in the mould with pre-shrunken foam pieces; this would avoid a fallen creature. The smell was appalling, and in later years when I carried out these 'cooking' sessions in the house, my wife Diana would reprimand me because the smell would remain in the house for days and days. Of all the models for *7th Voyage*, the skeleton was perhaps the most delicate. The bones were constructed of cotton wool soaked in latex and the head was made of resin. The only model that survives more or less unscathed is the skeleton, which reappeared as one of the seven skeletons in *Jason and the Argonauts*, although I still have part of the ball-and-socket armature that once belonged to the Cyclops, the skull of the dragon and those of both the adult and baby Roc.

The film also contained a large number of miniatures. Among them were Sokurah's cavern castle, the spiral staircase, Sinbad's ship, the cage, the Roc's egg and the cave entrance on the beach. The island of Colossa was a large miniature (about 5 feet across) mounted on a table and later combined with a matte in the foreground of sea I had shot in Spain.

The giant crossbow was a two-foot miniature (which I still have). To integrate it with live action of Sinbad's men, we constructed an 8-foot high wheel on the beach at S'Agaro, Spain, where the action was to take place. This full-size wheel was large enough to act as a background for the actors performing in front of it. Later at the studio I added the miniature crossbow into the shot, matching it with the real wheel.

Although by no means the opening scene, one of my favourites is the dancing four-armed snakewoman, created by Sokurah for the Caliph's entertainment. The sequence was to aid the audience's appreciation of the sorcerer's powers, although I designed it to be eye-catching entertainment and a substitute for the traditional, ubiquitous Hollywood dancing girls. Nobody could say this film wasn't different!

Above. Storyboard of Roc being pulled from shell. In one of the early drawings for the project, Sinbad and his men are seen pulling the baby Roc from its egg, but in the final film we had the Roc break out of the egg, which was much more dramatic. When one arrives at the final location for the sequence it is always necessary to change the original concept in some way because circumstances may dictate changes. However, the storyboard is always necessary for editing and continuity purposes.

From the very beginning the Roc sequence was always going to be a key scene. The model baby Roc was covered by George Lofgren with genuine duckling down skin obtained from a taxidermist. The delicate covering presented me with the problem of trying not to disturb it whilst I moved the model during animation. I managed this by touching and moving the model where the camera couldn't pick up the disturbance of the down. The egg itself was made of plaster, cast in sections so I could animate it cracking open and the chick appearing from inside. To animate the baby model from apparently inside the egg, it was constructed with a section at the back, away from the camera, which opened to allow me to move the model and then close it again to shoot the next frame.

The mother bird was covered in ordinary bird feathers, which I animated on an aerial brace. During the attack on the sailors, the huge bird creates a cloud of dust with the downdraft from her wings achieved with wind machines on the location shoot. These details always add a special reality to stop-motion animation unnoticed by the audiences but without which the scene wouldn't work. When they have not been possible, the scenes have suffered as a result, and are vital to bridge the credibility gap between the audience and the action.

The Cyclops was a central figure. Along with Sokurah, these creatures ruled over the island, but they also became one of the audience's favourites. Curiously, I had originally designed the Cyclops with

a more human appearance, but I changed it because we were afraid that audiences would think they were men in suits – and I always remembered what Obie had said about men in suits. To overcome this, I gave the Cyclops furry goat legs and cloven hooves, an idea lifted from my first concept of the Ymir in *20 Million Miles to Earth* (I also used the same armature for both). I designed detailed muscles, warts, veins and cracked dry skin, which all gave him a more grotesque appearance. In one of the original concepts for the story, we had wanted the island of Colossa to have a colony of Cyclops, but because of the costs of building and animating them, we decided to only hint at a population. Therefore there were only three models of varying sizes: one at the start of the film and for the

Above. The model cyclops. The model was so detailed that it allowed me to photograph it in close-up.

Following pages. Left hand page. An early key drawing for the cyclops spit roasting the unfortunate sailor. This concept for the cyclops was different from the one that appears in the film. The final version did not have the crest (it became a horn) or the vampire-like teeth, but he would possess cloven hooves, which this one appears not to have.

Following pages. Right hand page. Spit scene. The frames from sequence showing the cyclops' capture of Sinbad and his men, ending with the spit scene. This final scene was censored in Britain and was only restored many years later when the film was re-released.

spit sequence, a small one that falls off the cliff and yet another being killed by the dragon at the end.

During the location filming I used a 'monster stick', a simple stand-in device enabling actors to see how tall the creature (in this case the Cyclops) would be and assisting them to get the correct eye-line. The stick is usually just a pole on which I mark in strong colours different parts of the Cyclop's body (head, eyes, torso, arms, etc.). Later in my studio it is replaced with the model, which usually stands in front of the stick on the back projection plate. In model animation the actor's eye-line is vitally important, because if the actor is staring at something three feet below the creature's eye-line, the realism is lost, although to some extent eye-line can be corrected during the process of animation. If the scene dictated that the creature move across the screen, I would first of all talk the actors through my sketches and storyboards and mark out the ground where the creatures would eventually move, and then hold the monster stick myself and bound about all over the area, shouting what the creature was doing according to what I had designed for it – 'here comes the Cyclops… it's reaching down… This is the dragon with fire coming out of its mouth'. I must have looked crazed.

For the sequence in which Sinbad is 'picked up' by the foot and lifted out of the treasure room, we had Kerwin hoisted up on wires during the location photography. This was then used as a rear projection plate for the animation with the Cyclops. In my studio I built a miniature boot that I inserted in the model Cyclops' hand, carefully positioning it in front of the rear-

projected image of the real Sinbad boot. I then animated the model to follow the line of Kerwin's real boot. The end result is that the Cyclops appears to lift Kerwin.

A scene in which the complexity of the effects are generally missed (which means I have succeeded in my job) occurs just after Sinbad's men have been captured. The Cyclops closes the cage on the men and lifts it up to his chest and walks off with it. From the point of picking up the cage the men became models to be animated along with the Cyclops. This was achieved with the same trick used for the Roc's egg: I built a

false back to the cage, allowing me to open and close it to animate the men's frantic movements.

My favourite Cyclops moment was when we see one roasting a sailor on a spit. To give the creature character (humour was not really intended) I had him pull up a giant stool and sit down to watch his meal cooking, then added a close-up of him licking his lips with anticipation of the meal. I had designed these scenes some time before animation to instil some human qualities into the creature. It was never the intention to make it scary. Strangely, when the

film was released in the UK the censor cut this shot, along with the skeleton sequence, because 'it would be too frightening for younger audiences'. I have always thought it really silly, especially as the sailor escapes from the Cyclops and Sinbad destroys the skeleton. Years later I am glad to say that the scenes were restored for a re-release of the picture.

Along with the skeleton, the dragon was one of the earliest ideas for the project. Originally I had drawn the beast being slain outside the cave, but in the final version he goes on to take part in the finale of the

Above. Various early sketches of the dragon on the beach, the cross-bow and the dragon being slain. The concept of the dragon was a composite of many ideas about what a dragon should look like – a hint of Doré, a smidgin of St George's adversary, and a more than liberal helping of my own imagination.

Right hand page. Another design for a travelling matte sequence. This time it shows how Sinbad will walk in front of the blue backing screen, so emphasizing the dragon's great size. Kerwin was photographed against a blue screen in the studio and afterwards the dragon was animated and the two images were then optically combined.

Right hand page bottom. Dragon on the beach – the split screen process. The first shows the foreground matted out with the blank rear screen. The next shows the model dragon animated in front of the rear screen and the last is the composite.

MORNINGSIDE PRODUCTIONS, INC.
1438 NORTH GOWER STREET
HOLLYWOOD 28, CALIFORNIA
HOLLYWOOD 2-3111

SCENE 445 — 523 — 527

1. T.M. TO BE SHOT IN LONDON.

2. BACKGROUND OF DRAGON AND CAVE WILL BE SHOT IN HOLLYWOOD.

picture. The model was close to three feet in length and was a large model to animate, especially for the fight with the Cyclops, which took me two to three weeks to complete. The dragon's 'fiery breath' was never used to the full potential in the final picture. We had originally planned to have the dragon breathing fire throughout the fight with the Cyclops, but the cost would have been too high, so he only twice shows how bad his breath is. I used a flamethrower in the gardens of the Alhambra against a night sky (I couldn't find a black backcloth big enough) and shot it at a distance of 30–40 feet. Back in London I superimposed the effect onto the area in front of the dragon's mouth.

All the creatures were fantastic, strange and exciting adversaries for Sinbad, and you can't get any stranger than a skeleton sword fighting with the hero. The fight sequence was extremely complex in design, mainly because it was the first 'contact' fight I had done between an actor and a creature, so it was vital that I understood the movements of swordplay.

Because the skeleton's movements had to look as good as Kerwin's, I enrolled in a six-month fencing course. Sadly, I didn't complete the course, because the stance one is required to attain threw my hips out of joint. However, the experience, such as it was, proved invaluable, not only for *7th Voyage*, but for subsequent pictures. Prior to shooting the skeleton sequence, I had a meeting with Enzo during which we discussed my sketches and what was needed to enable me to animate the skeleton the way I wanted. Amongst other criteria, he had to ensure that Kerwin was behind the skeleton and not in front, otherwise I would have had to resort to a travelling matte, which I

Above. How the dragon looked in the final film. The dragon appears to be coming out from behind the rocks on the left. This was achieved by matting out the rocks and foreground (just below the actors' feet) and then printing it back in on the second pass.

Right hand page. The model dragon on the animation table with the 'face' entrance to the valley of the Cyclops. The minature face of the cave was later superimposed on the real cave, which had been built on the beach at S'Agaro in Spain. As you can see, the model dragon was large and took some considerable effort to animate.

didn't want to do. Enzo had the imagination to understand what I wanted from the scene and patiently worked out and broke down the fight into sections during rehearsals. When the day came to film the fight, Enzo, who stood in for the skeleton, rehearsed Kerwin on the specially constructed spiral staircase. This enabled him to be sure that every one of Kerwin's body movements was exactly right for each section. He had decided that everything must be done to the count of eight, and therefore had one of his assistants clap out eight beats. This simple idea helped Kerwin to master each movement as he would his lines, and when Enzo was satisfied that the entire sequence was perfect, we shot a black and white test that included Enzo and Kerwin. This would act as a guide when I came to animate the skeleton in the studio. When we had that in the can, Kerwin then had to go through exactly the same split-timed routine for the camera, but this time without Enzo. Since we shot the final take without sound (which was added later), Enzo clapped out the eight beats with his hands, off camera, which had the added advantage of later helping Bernard Herrmann, the film's music composer, to write the castanets concerto for the scene.

The animation for the entire skeleton sequence consisted of over twenty-five separate scenes, lasting for less than four minutes but taking nearly three months to complete. In all, the animation for the entire film took eleven months. Now it was up to the music composer to add that vital ingredient to the film that can make or break it. We had begun searching, just before I began animation, for a composer who possessed a feel for fantasy. I had wanted either Max Steiner or Miklós Rózsa, but when Charles first told me that he knew Bernie and was hoping to sign him up for *7th Voyage*, I could have not have been more pleased. However, before Bernie committed himself, he insisted on viewing what we had shot, which worried us because all we had at that stage was a black and white cut (we couldn't afford colour), and we were reluctant for someone of Bernie's standing to make a decision based on that. Viewing this rough cut, which had no creatures, just actors and the monster sticks, he emerged with a rather grim expression on his face, but to our relief he agreed to score the picture.

Bernie liked fantasy. I think he was just waiting for the opportunity to write for a fantasy picture. I believe that the music for *7th Voyage of Sinbad* was one of his finest and most inspired scores, although he always disagreed with me. It lifted the film, making it something very special and allowing the creatures an even greater dimension of size, as though they really were from a world of fantasy.

By the time we had begun the picture, Charles and I had found that the word animation was being interpreted by reviewers and cinema-goers alike to mean cartoon techniques. We felt that the time had come to distinguish between the flat drawing and the dimensional model by using a word or slogan to sell our pictures to the public. Charles came up with the perfect solution. At that time he had just bought a brand new Buick to drive the 10 miles every day to the studio. One day he was sitting in the traffic and noticed that on the dashboard there was the word DYNAFLOW, which was a logo or gimmick to describe some special feature on the automobile. Charles realized that he was looking at the answer to our prayers. He dropped the 'FLOW', left the 'DYNA' and added 'MATION', so making DYNAMATION, a magical combination of dimensional and animation. *The 7th Voyage of Sinbad* was the first film to bear the name: 'IN DYNAMATION – THE NEW MIRACLE OF THE SCREEN'. All we had done, in effect, was to christen the art of three-dimensional model animation with a fitting new name, one that everyone would now hopefully use to refer to it.

The cost of the film was a mere $650,000, which, considering what it contained, is incredible. Columbia Pictures promoted the picture in a big way, and it went on to be the 'sleeper' of the year, with people queuing to see it again and again for weeks after its opening. Part of Columbia's promotion was to release a 'pop' record sung by Ann Lenardo through their record company, which was nothing to do with Bernie's score. I am unaware as to whether it was a hit or not, but the songs were fairly awful. The B-side had a catchy little ditty called 'Sinbad Cha, Cha, Cha' and the A-side contained the timeless classic 'Sinbad Has Been Bad, But He's Been Good To Me', which, if nothing else, sums up my feeling for the character. The enormous success of the picture was also helped by the generally very favourable reviews, *Boxoffice* said on 1 December 1958, 'Columbia's nimble-minded publicists created a new word to describe this thoroughly enjoyable, action-freighted celluloid fantasy. It's Kidult, which is designed to convey the intelligence that here is a parcel of escapist entertainment that will assert a strong appeal to both kids and adults.' The *Film Daily* on 25 November 1958 said, 'Dynamation... is the star of this spectacular presentation of the Sinbad story.' It added, 'it is rich in romance, in action, in death and daring, as any in the story-books of the young folks who are, by design, the people who will make up its principal audience'. *Variety* gave us our most favourable review on 25 November 1958: '*The 7th Voyage of Sinbad*... has re-created in rich Technicolor and with the kind of gusto and bravado that certainly catches the spirit of the tale...'. And the final accolade: 'Harryhausen, who was responsible for the visual effects, emerges as the hero of the piece. He's responsible for some striking scenes that create real magic on the screen'. Praise indeed, although this honour was tempered by a review in the *Hollywood Reporter*, also on 25 November 1958, which stated, 'The models are operated both manually and electronically.' Like *King Kong* before it, the visuals were so original that few people at that time knew how they were done.

As I had hoped, the film had allowed me to take the art of model animation into a new story concept, and create not just one creature but a film full of them. I knew that what we had managed to put on the screen was so new and impressive that it would cause a stir, but I didn't expect the runaway popularity with all age groups. It was destined to be a watershed for Charles and I, allowing us to get away from second feature movies and into the mainstream, hopefully to produce subjects that we wanted to make with higher budgets.

Left hand page top. Skeleton fighting Sinbad. Kerwin Matthews was a master at shadow boxing, always maintaining the illusion that he was actually fighting with a skeleton and always managing to make the destruction of his adversaries look so simple, as any hero should.

Left hand page bottom. Some rough storyboard sketches for the skeleton fight.

Left. Enzo on *Sinbad* set. We were lucky in having Enzo Musumeci-Greco (on the left) arranging the fights. His invaluable input enabled Kerwin (right) to look like a professional and allowed me to create an imaginative and exciting fight sequence with the skeleton.

Above. Herrmann and Charles during a recording session. Bernard Herrmann and Charles during the recording session for *The 7th Voyage of Sinbad*.

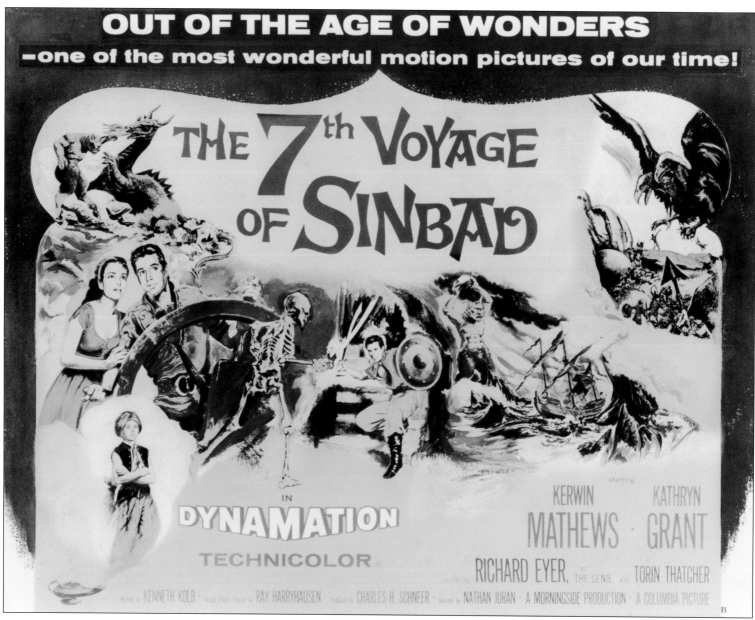

Above. Poster for *The 7th Voyage of Sinbad*.

Right. Sunny days on *The 7th Voyage of Sinbad*. Unfortunately I cannot remember everybody's name in this wonderful photograph of us all obviously having a great time. It must have been the last day of the location shoot! From left to right (third in): Maurice Gillet (electrician), Wilkie Cooper (cinematographer), Eugene Martin, myself, Charles Schneer, Kerwin Mathews, Torin Thatcher. Standing above between Kerwin and Torin is Nathan 'Jerry' Juran, the director.

My next project began with some drawings for what would become *The 3 Worlds of Gulliver*, which for us was slightly unusual because it was already written. This production of Jonathan Swift's eighteenth-century fantasy-satire had first of all been adapted as a screenplay by Arthur Ross and Jack Sher for Universal Pictures who, on reading the script, decided they weren't interested. It was subsequently acquired by Charles for Morningside Productions and Columbia Pictures. The intention was to make it as a musical with Danny Kaye, but that fell through, mainly because Kaye was contracted to Sam Goldwyn, who was asking too much for his star. So, following the huge success of *7th Voyage of Sinbad*, Charles decided to adapt the script, with Ross and Sher, to accommodate Dynamation. By June 1959 we had a shooting script:

Lemuel Gulliver (Kerwin Mathews) is an unhappy rural doctor whose fiancée, Elizabeth (June Thorburn), wants him to settle down. Hoping to make his fortune and see the world, Gulliver signs up as a ship's doctor, hoping his fiancée will forgive him when he returns a rich man. Once at sea he discovers Elizabeth is a stowaway and during a terrible storm both are swept overboard. Separated from his Elizabeth, Gulliver is washed onto a beach and awakes to find himself tied to the ground and surrounded by tiny people. Eventually the Lilliputians untie him and on visiting the Emperor he discovers that the island of Lilliput is at war with a neighbouring island over the question of which end to crack open an egg. Determined to end the petty conflict Gulliver captures the opposition's fleet, so restoring peace and harmony to the islands. Leaving on a boat prepared by the Lilliputians to search for Elizabeth, Gulliver is again cast up onto another shore belonging to the land of Brobdingnag where the people are giants. He is captured and taken by a girl to the palace where Gulliver is reunited with Elizabeth. Following a fight with an alligator, Gulliver is helped to escape by the little girl and eventually both he and Elizabeth find themselves back in England.

Columbia wanted a big name for the part of Gulliver, suggesting Jack Lemmon, who fortunately turned it down, so we again chose Kerwin who had been so easy to work with on *Sinbad*. June Thorburn was cast as Elizabeth, with a support cast that included much British acting talent: Basil Sydney, Mary Ellis, Peter Bull and Canadian actor Lee Paterson.

Charles and I made the decision to set up the production for *Gulliver* in England. *The 7th Voyage of Sinbad* had shown us that the Mediterranean countries offered unlimited and underused locations, as well as talent and cheaper labour. England at that time was still only two or three hours travelling time to Spain or Italy, with the cost being minuscule compared with flying a crew from Hollywood. And so it was that we came to Europe to do one picture and have been here ever since. There was also another reason: the Rank Film Laboratories, with Vic Margutti in charge, had developed a special matte process called 'sodium backing process', or 'yellow backing process', which was a simplified matte technology. Unlike the old blue backing process we had used in *7th Voyage*, which required from eight to ten different steps to produce a desired matte, the sodium method made an instantaneous matte in a split-beam camera. Each of these processes has its own advantages, depending on the subject and necessities of the picture, but for our next three pictures we found that the sodium process suited all of our extreme requirements. The advantages were enormous. The choice of colours available in the foreground shooting was unrestricted, whereas with the blue backing process it was necessary to avoid any costume or foreground item with the colour blue in it. Another disadvantage in the blue backing process was that delicate lines such as thin ropes or netting could be 'lost'. The sodium process minimized all these difficulties, if not eliminating them entirely, giving us a wider variety of foreground choices of composition and colour.

Pinewood Studios, just outside London, was selected as the production base where I would work on animating the complex matte scenes. We also filmed most of the interiors here, including the scene in which Gulliver captures the Brobdingnag warships.

Location shooting proceeded rapidly, helped by the pre-production planning and Charles' unshakeable schedules. We shot in several of the same locations around the Costa Brava that we had used for *7th Voyage*. Quite often there would be two separate set-ups at either end of the S'Agaro beach, perhaps one for a tiny Lilliput scene and the other for a giant Brobdingnag scene, which would necessitate Kerwin having two different costume changes and running between them. Kerwin never complained. Other locations used were the famous Palacio de Oriente at La Granja (for the water pool scene when the prospective prime ministers battle it out on a tightrope), Segovia's chateau and forests, the ancient walled city of Avilla and the mountains of Boca del Azno. Most of the miniature sets and some interiors were shot in Madrid's Sevilla Studios, with the remainder being shot at Pinewood, and Shepperton Village Square standing in for Gulliver's home town of Wapping.

Fantasy films have always been, and continue to be, a source of new ideas and more exciting ways of achieving the visual effects. The *3 Worlds of Gulliver* called for every trick in the book plus some that were not. Although the model animation scenes were few, this didn't mean that my work on the picture was a vacation and I could enjoy myself. Because of the nature of the story (small and large people), the script called for a large number of travelling mattes (more than 300), but as these are expensive to produce we cut costs by using 'forced' perspective – oversized sets and foreground miniatures, techniques that go back to the silent days.

Perspective photography is cheap but requires careful planning and use. I used a 'forced' perspective

Left. Kerwin and miniature ships. The scene where Gulliver captures the Brobdingnag warships was shot during the depths of an English winter, and although it was an interior studio tank constructed on the special effects stage, the water wasn't heated. Kerwin had a terrible time having to do retakes whilst sinking slowly into a state of hypothermia.

Above. Sand pits. I filmed the scene in which the tiny Gulliver encounters the giant Brobdingnag girl in this hole in the beach. It was to achieve the correct perspective as the camera pans up on Kerwin, but at the same time pans up on the giant girl.

Sc. 33　　　　T.M.&S.S.

F.G.-Fine sand　Studio

Use f.g. matte.

Sc. 37-41-43-55-62-72
71.　　　　T.M.

F.G. Studio

B.G. Location

set-up when the Lilliputians are standing on a tower and presenting Gulliver with a medal. For this I placed Kerwin in the foreground and the actors on the tower way off in the distance. By using a wide angled lens, I told Kerwin and the actors where to look so that we were able to shoot it at the same time without double printing. It worked and so saved a lot of expensive optical work.

Wherever possible we used 'forced' perspective, but travelling mattes were the major technical effect in the picture. One good example of this technique is a scene on the beach (in Brobdingnag) where the camera pans up from the tiny Gulliver to a giant girl looking down at him. For this I had to dig a three-foot hole in the sand so the camera would be low enough to give the height that we wanted to the girl. I then used a wide angled lens to enable us to pan up the girl, and while the tiny Gulliver was inserted later, the same pan had to be repeated for the travelling matte. On the movieola we would put the two together, giving the illusion that we were panning from Gulliver, in the foreground, up to the girl's face.

Another example of a travelling matte was the tracking shot of the Lilliputian king walking along the side of Gulliver's body, for which we photographed Kerwin on a rostrum table covered with sand on the beach and tracked along him. Back in the studio the king walked along on a treadmill whilst looking up as though at Gulliver's body. The two shots were then optically combined.

The key scene in the whole movie is where Gulliver arrives on Lilliput and is tied down to the beach. In the high shot of the scene we see Gulliver lying the full length of the beach with what looks like hundreds of tiny people around him. I managed this by shooting the people on the beach but leaving a vacant area in the centre in which I would place Gulliver. Back in England we photographed Kerwin lying on his back against a yellow backing and then the two separate shots were combined.

Another special scene took place in the magician's laboratory, where Gulliver is trapped by the magician under a glass container. So the actors had something to play to, I used a miniature of Gulliver during rehearsals, but when we were ready to shoot, I took the miniature away and shot the sequence with nothing inside the container. Back at Pinewood we shot Kerwin acting as though a real glass container was being lowered over him, and by carefully lining up the exact frame from the first piece of the sequence, as the glass goes over Gulliver we created a travelling matte with the bottom of the real glass acting as the matte line. At the point where the glass goes over the tiny Gulliver, I brought in a reflected glass effect so that it made him look as though he was inside the container. This effect was a separate pass in the printer, which we shot through distorted glass against a black velvet background.

After the many creatures seen in *7th Voyage*, this picture is a little thin on the ground in animation

Oversized sets are most effective for closer-type shots but limited for a whole film. Once again, a good example is the sequence where Gulliver plays chess with the giant king of Brobdingnag. The sequence was important to the story and so warranted the cost of building enlarged pieces. However, if one continues to employ nothing but these enlarged props, the illusion of comparative size soon falls apart unless combined with other processes such as travelling mattes or split screen which introduce live action in the form of small or large actors in the sequence. This combination of various processes, used with discretion, creates the ideal illusion.

Left hand page, top. Part of my storyboard for the capture of Gulliver by the Lilliputians.

Left hand page. Drawings of travelling matte sequence. One of the key sequences, showing Gulliver tied down on the beach, was created by use of travelling mattes and split screens. This sequence of sketches show in part, how we put together the scene. The pictures in the first row shows how the final scene should look, the second row shows the foreground images filmed in the studio, and the last row shows the background images filmed on location. Underneath these storyboards is the final composite shot as a still from the movie.

Above. Huge chessboard and pieces. We built oversized pieces in the Madrid studio for the chessboard scene.

sequences, which perhaps disappointed some fans. In fact there were only two sequences: a squirrel which sees Gulliver as a tasty acorn to be stored in his burrow and a nasty alligator that the king of Brobdingnag sets on him. Unfortunately, the squirrel sequence lacks excitement, and I have never been happy with the fact that the creature makes a sound more like a wheeze than a squeak. Having said that, I do feel that the squirrel has a certain charm, which the film needed at that point in the story.

If the squirrel is on the dull side, the alligator more than makes up for it, although it was originally meant to be a rat. In the end the whole sequence stands as one of the best in the film, perhaps one of the best in any of my early films. Armed with a sword (from the catch of a giant jewellery box) and a shield (a brooch), Gulliver parries and thrusts at the hissing reptile. Enzo Musumeci-Greco again choreographed the swordplay, which was designed to accommodate certain touches. Like all fight sequences, during rehearsals Enzo took the part of the alligator, after which Kerwin had to reproduce the movements in a shadow-boxing sequence.

To give the fight scene a sense of reality between the creature and the live action, I used a variety of tricks, including the placement of several miniature props in front of the model. This was intended to help the viewer relate to the scene. As I have mentioned before, 'contact' between the model and the actor(s) is necessary to maintain credibility. The fight between Gulliver and the alligator was designed by me and choreographed by Enzo to allow Gulliver to occasionally be seen to contact or 'touch' the creature. One such 'contact' is the struggle for Gulliver's shield as it is pulled from side to side by the alligator's mouth. To achieve the

pulling action, the shield was held by Kerwin during the live action photography and he simulated the jerking motion. On the animation table I placed a small portion of the shield (actually made of cardboard) in the creature's jaws, and then matched the live action movement on the rear projection screen with the model alligator. Another 'contact' in the fight is when Gulliver whacks the beast's snout with his sword. The 'contact' is made with a replica miniature sword, which I aligned in front of the real one held by Kerwin in the rear projection plate. When Kerwin's action reached a point that contacted with the model, I replaced his sword with the miniature one and stuck it on the nose of the alligator with a tiny piece of wax. The duration for the 'contact' lasted for about 4 or 5 frames – enough to give the illusion that the sword had hit him. I used more or less the same trick at the end of the fight when Gulliver triumphantly stabs the creature in the neck. Kerwin went through the motions of stabbing the beast, and then in the studio I replaced the real sword on the rear projection with the miniature sword at the right frame change when it made 'contact' with the model. The real sword simply disappears behind the model whilst the miniature takes over and plunges into the model.

Because of the optical work, the pressure was immense, so much so that I contracted dysentery and as a result lost a great deal of weight. Over the years I did adapt to the pressures, but even so, the same oppressive worry descended on me when I considered what could be lost if I got things wrong. Sometimes I would be so involved with a sequence that everything around me ceased to exist. During the filming of *The 3 Worlds of Gulliver* there is one incident that

illustrates how insular I could become. Whilst filming the sequence in which the Lilliputians are hauled up in a cage, the rope attached to the cage broke. Thankfully nobody was hurt. Furthermore, at one point actor Lee Patterson observed me wandering around the beach with the cage held out in front of me muttering quite loudly, 'Futility thy name is Harryhausen.' Location photography on our budgets was a little like playing Russian roulette, during which I hoped that nothing would go wrong, because if it did, I would have to redesign the action and try to smooth out the gaps and faults.

Once again Bernie Herrmann enhanced the imagery of the film by writing one of his best scores, allowing both the live action and effects to flow into one.

Since the word DYNAMATION had worked so well for *7th Voyage*, the ad men wanted something that would upstage the phrase to hopefully suggest that it was something quite new. After much discussion it was decided to name the effects SUPERDYNAMATION. Spectacular and good for the ads, but this time it really didn't mean a thing.

The 3 Worlds of Gulliver was launched at a royal premiere in England at the Odeon Marble Arch on 30 November 1960, attended by Princess Margaret and her husband at the time, Anthony Armstrong-Jones. Before the film he asked questions about my work and the effects in the film. It turned out he was a fan, but as time was short, it didn't allow for too much detailed conversation. Although the film was well received, one incident at the premiere is worth mentioning. At the end of the film Gulliver and Elizabeth come ashore and ask someone where they are. The reply is 'Wapping-by-the-Sea'. As most people

Top. Gulliver and Elizabeth face the squirrel. An image from my original storyboard. I spent some time studying squirrels in London parks and used my observations when animating the model.

Above. Squirrel model. I obtained the squirrel from a taxidermist, and after my father had made the metal armature, I fitted it inside using sponge to build up the body.

Above right. One of the creatures (I think it was a mink) Gulliver and Elizabeth encounter whilst fleeing from the King and his men.

Right hand page. Top. Part of my original storyboard for the alligator sequence. Note how little change there is between these images and what appears in the final film.

Right hand page. Centre. This shows how Gulliver's sword pierces the alligator.

Right hand page. bottom. Fight alligator sequence. Because I had little animation to do on the film, I was able to take longer and instil much more movement into the scene with the alligator than perhaps I might have done with a similar scene in another animation-packed movie. To enable me to move the alligator model, I constructed only two walls of the cage for the animation table (the front and the side facing the camera). This was then placed in front of the rear projection screen, which matched with the remaining two walls of the cage in the live action plate.

From camera POV the sword on projection plate will line up with miniature sword in throat of alligator.

Projection of live action on projection screen.

Miniature piece of sword in throat of alligator.

Animated model of Alligator.

in England know, Wapping is a real place but is on the river Thames and nowhere near the sea. I believe that even Princess Margaret was heard to snigger. You could tell the writers were American!

The picture was released in America in December 1960 with a massive publicity campaign. The *Variety* review was most praiseworthy: 'The picture is notable for its visuo-cinematic achievements and its bold, bright and sweeping score by Bernard Herrmann.' It goes on, 'Special visual effects expert Ray Harryhausen, whose Superdynamation process makes the motion-pictured *Gulliver* plausible and workable, rates a very low bow for his painstaking, productive efforts. Perspectives, optical variations and split-screen synchronization efforts are gratifying and invaluable.' Even Charles, who rarely receives the credit he deserves, comes in for praise: 'producer Charles Schneer has erected a live-action screen translation with enormous appeal for younger children and family audiences'. One review even had the headline 'Children from 6 to 60 will enjoy *Gulliver*.'

When I see the film today, I find it entertaining, but

Only recently I came across an outline by Arthur Ross entitled *The New World of Gulliver* with no date on it. It was adapted from Books III and IV of Swift's novel and relates to the further adventures of Gulliver (with his wife Elizabeth) on the Floating Island of Laputa, as a spy in the land of the Yahoos and in the mysterious land of the Houyhnhnms (talking horses). I can only assume that this was a suggested sequel to *Gulliver* that Ross asked me to look at. Reading it again, it would have been prohibitively expensive, extremely complicated to visualize and uncommercial.

Above. Close-up of the alligator. Those teeth were sharp!

Right hand page. One of the posters for *The 3 Worlds Of Gulliver*.
This poster includes the ad men's very original updated version of our stop-motion process – Superdynamation.

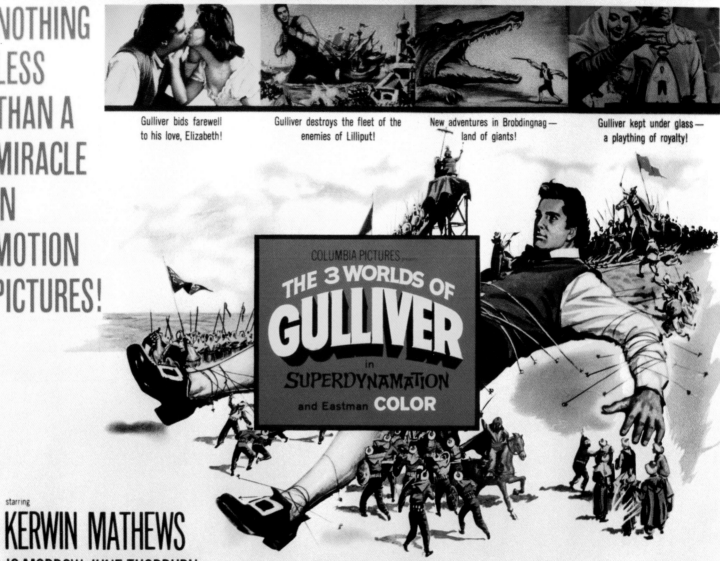

I have to say that it is not one of our best. It retains some elements of the Swift books and maintains a good eighteenth-century feel, but the pace is not right, and because of this, the film as a whole suffers. Although I am generally pleased with the overall effects, I miss the creature set pieces – another reason it lacks that all important magic quality that any fantasy film needs.

Following the completion of *Gulliver*, Charles and I went through what was becoming a usual routine of searching for a suitable subject that would suit the necessary criteria demanded by Dynamation. We talked about *Tarzan and the Ant Men* and my old favourite *Food of the Gods*, but neither of these came to anything and the search continued. It was Charles who discovered a script that had been lying around at Columbia for several years. It was an adaptation of a Jules Verne story, a sequel to *20,000 Leagues Under the Sea*, which contained possibilities for high adventure and, more importantly, for Dynamation.

Right. The Royal premiere. With the very beautiful June Thorburn at the London premiere of *The 3 Worlds of Gulliver* at the Odeon Marble Arch cinema.

CHAPTER 5 ANOTHER LOST LAND

Mysterious Island

Left hand page. Four very rough sketches for various scenes, some of which were discarded, for *Mysterious Island*. The first depicts the survivors discovering an ancient roadway in the jungle. The second shows the roadway disappearing into the sea and various ruins, suggesting an earthquake had destroyed the civilization that had built it. The third is a huge statue under the sea, which I changed for Egyptian-type statues, and the fourth is the ruined city beneath the sea, which remained, with some small changes, into the final film. All of these images were intended to evoke the idea of the lost city of Atlantis.

'Creatures, always creatures, never monsters.' I have made this statement countless times over the years. The reason for my insistence on what my creations should be called is that people often identify them as monsters, whereas for me the word 'monster' conjures up images of Frankenstein's creation, Dracula, a ghastly alien or perhaps something equally horrifying which might suggest a malevolent entity. This is not how I see most of my creations. None of them are really evil; perhaps 'odd' or grotesque, which makes them different, but not individually evil unless controlled by other forces. None of them destroy for the sake of destroying. The destruction is usually the result of the gods 'playing' a game on mankind or mankind itself meddling in things that don't concern it. An example of such a group of creatures is contained in what would be our next picture, a fantasy adventure based on a novel by the master of the genre.

Even today, Jules Verne's imaginative stories continue to be original and exciting, bridging the gap between scientific romanticism and reality. No matter how fantastic, they were always believable. Despite Walt Disney's excellent screen version of *20,000 Leagues Under the Sea* (1954) with James Mason playing Captain Nemo who apparently goes down with his submarine, the *Nautilus*, surprisingly the sequel had been somewhat neglected, perhaps because it lacked the futuristic elements of the first novel. In the mid- to late 1950s, because of Verne's popularity, Columbia decided to make a new adaptation. In 1957 Crane Wilbur wrote a screenplay that remained reasonably faithful to Verne's original, telling a straightforward story of survival on a desert island and ending in the discovery of Nemo and his nautilus. Columbia costed the script but found that it was far too expensive and shelved it. It was then offered to Charles because *7th Voyage* and *Gulliver* were seen as similar types of film and because they thought we could produce it with a more realistic budget. Frankly, I had some trepidation about filming the story, as I felt it might be compared with Disney's movie, but without us having the kind of budget they had lavished on it.

Like Verne's original, Wilbur's screenplay contained only one or two animals (one being an ape that is trained to be a servant). New and interesting creatures were something we knew about, but by injecting Dynamation creatures into the story, it meant we had to take certain liberties with Verne's original. However, we felt that we could keep the best elements of the story – the runaway balloon, the survival on a desert island and the appearance of Nemo – and still come up with a feasible and faithful storyline that would enable us to bring in Harry-hausen creatures.

In July 1958 I began drawing key Dynamation scenes, a man-eating plant, a phororhacos (a giant prehistoric bird-like creature) and a cephalopod (a prehistoric tentacled creature with a huge shell). At that early stage the idea was to integrate dinosaurs into the plot, but it was later set aside in favour of Nemo experimenting with enlarging ordinary creatures as an answer to the world's food shortage. These drawings supplied the incentive on which to begin building a new storyline, and it was at this point that Charles asked Kenneth Kolb to write a new outline and screenplay to bridge together the drawings I had made with the key elements of Verne's story.

Sometime in late 1958 and early 1959, Kenneth came up with various plot ideas but seemed to be having trouble coming to grips with Verne's original. One of his notes to Charles said, 'I still want to discuss the possibility of eliminating Nemo from the story'! If there was one thing we were certain of, it was to keep Nemo. Some of his ideas were inventive but none were really suitable or practical for the kind of budget we had. However, in one thing Kenneth was correct. In the original Verne story there was a dog called Top, which we had wanted to keep in to fight with the phororhocus. Kenneth wrote, 'I killed the dog off early (in the story) since dogs are a nuisance in a picture like this.' 'Ah,' I can hear you say, 'what a shame', but he was absolutely right. Dogs are unpredictable, and on a picture where everything has to be predicted, they are definitely not good news even if animated. Look at the problems I had with the dog in *20 Million Miles to Earth*. In the end we used very few of Kenneth's ideas, as they were far too difficult to translate onto the screen and conflicted with the overall ideas that Charles and I had in mind for the project.

Eventually Charles commissioned Daniel Ullman and then John Prebble and Raphael Hayes (who was not credited on the film) to write a new script, which was when the story really began to develop. All of Verne's main ingredients are there and, with respect, a few improvements for the modern audience. The story now became a technical version of Defoe's *Robinson Crusoe*, with Nemo creating giant food experiments on bees, oysters and even throwbacks from prehistoric times. The final story went as follows: *Richmond, Virginia, during the American Civil War. Three Yankee soldiers, Captain Harding (Michael Craig), Herbert (Michael Callan), Neb (Dan Jackson), Spilett (Gary Merrill), a war correspondent, and a captive Confederate guard called Pencroft (Percy Herbert), escape prison by hijacking an observation balloon during the great storm of 1865. The balloon carries them across the States and over the Pacific where they are marooned on a remote island. Shipwrecked on the island by the same storm are two English ladies, Lady Mary Fairchild (Joan Greenwood) and her niece, Elena (Beth Rogan). Working together they find cover and protection in a cave, which they name 'Granite House', and during the group's struggle for survival they encounter huge creatures, including a crab, bees, a nautiloid cephalopod and a prehistoric phororhacos. Eventually they discover that Captain Nemo (Herbert Lom), who is living aboard his disabled submarine, the Nautilus, has created these creatures. He tells them that the island's volcano is about to explode and that they must escape. In the finale, as the volcano wreaks its devastation, they leave the island, not on the Nautilus, but on a sunken pirate ship which they have raised with the aid of Nemo's technology. The island explodes and the castaways look on as Nemo and his secrets die in the destruction.*

Left hand page, top and above. Rough thumbnail sketches show early concepts for the storyline. Although the appearance of Nemo (top left pictures) remained, the costume was altered to apparatus that consisted of giant shells (see illustration above). The volcano and *Nautilus*, of course, remained, as did the sunken Egyptian city, but Nemo's 'mining machine' seen in three of the pictures was regrettably discarded.

During the endless 'sweatbox' sessions many ideas, both good and bad, were discarded. Everyone, including myself, Charles, the screenwriters and later Cy Endfield, the director, put up many ideas, only to have them thrown out either immediately or as the script developed. Here are a few of the discarded themes.

At first the concept was to show the island as a type of Atlantis with temples hidden in the jungle. We saw it as a mixture of the great civilizations – Egyptian, Greek, Minoan, etc. – but that the island had sunk beneath the sea in a massive catastrophe. The idea was not only to produce a visual treat, but was also intended to explain the final volcanic catastrophe that would befall the island. In a subsequent screenplay the civilization is discovered by Herbert and Pencroft when they find an urn with hieroglyphics on the beach and the tops of huge statues emerging from the sea. In the end all that survived of the civilization idea were just two sequences showing the remains of a sunken city.

In another treatment the first appearance of Nemo would be of him operating a mechanical spider-like digging machine, the purpose of which was to mine phosphorous (needed to power *Nautilus*) in the volcano's crater. We also dropped the idea of a forest of gigantic mushrooms, daffodils and buttercups. Similarly, we gave up on a man-eating plant seen devouring the Green Man, Thomas Ayrton (in another version it eats Top the dog). The idea of such a plant had been at the back of my mind for some years and the drawing was one of the earliest I executed for the project. Sadly, it was dropped when the prehistoric idea was set aside, as was a scene conceived for the climax of the film: whilst the island is being rocked by earthquakes, huge cracks appear in the ground and from them emerge prehistoric monsters. At one point there was to have been a giant semi-prehistoric mole creature which emerges from the walls of the volcano's crater to fight a huge snake creature. After a titanic battle they crash through the crust of the volcano into a lake of molten lava.

And it wasn't just the creatures that changed as the story progressed. It was left until the penultimate version of the screenplay to drop the character of Thomas Ayrton. In the original Verne story he had been marooned on the island by pirates, but in our version we decided to make him more colourful, so we had him turn green after eating the giant mushrooms – hence his name in the script, the Green Man. Because of costs, Ayrton was dropped and all that is left of him in the final film is his skeleton and diary, found by the new inhabitants of Granite House.

Finally, in Verne's original story Captain Nemo dies on his submarine of natural causes and Harding scuttles the ship. However, we decided that Nemo couldn't possibly be wasted in such a manner, so we made him a central character, letting him survive until the very end.

Sc. 195

TM.-DYN.   Sc. 199

DYN.   Sc. 200

DYN.   Sc. 201-203

DYN.   Sc. 205-210

DYN.   Sc. 206-212-215-234

Sc. 207

DYN.   Sc. 211

LARGE PROP.   Sc. 213

TM.-DYN.   Sc. 216-218-221-229

DYN.   Sc. 219-222-224-226-231

We had considered asking James Mason to reprise his role as Captain Nemo, but his fee would have been far too high for us. Herbert Lom, who had appeared in Charles' production of *I Aim at the Stars*, was cast as Nemo, playing the part with great authority. I only met him once, but it was enough to know he had a quiet presence that ideally suited the part. The rest of the cast was also excellent. Michael Craig was suitably heroic, and both he and Percy Herbert (both English actors) made a good job of the American accent. Joan Greenwood, who was a delightful person, was magnificent in the part of Lady Mary Fairchild and added an air of genteel aristocratic eccentricity to her character. Gary Merrill, who was divorcing Bette Davis at the time, was a joy to work with. He was

always playing practical jokes and thoroughly enjoying himself, and perfect for the cynical Spilett. The remainder of the cast, Beth Rogan, Michael Callan and Dan Jackson, all played their parts with conviction and gusto.

As usual, before shooting began I recced for locations. I ventured further afield to look for a desert island, visiting Tobago, Antigua, St Lucia and Martinique. As much as I enjoyed the trip, in the end the cost of shipping all the equipment, actors and crew would have been prohibitive, so it was decided that Spain, once again, would do. To give the impression of a tropical island we constructed a number of fake palm trees and rocks to help with the appearance of a rugged, deserted look. The opening of the film

was supposed to be Richmond, Virginia, but was in fact Shepperton Village Square. It was chosen not only because it was a stone's throw from the studio, but because, with some doctoring, it resembled certain areas of the Southern United States during the Civil War period.

I made several production drawings (based on a design from the period) and later storyboards of the balloon as it is swept along by the storm. As a full-sized balloon would have been too difficult to control, even in a fake storm, we resorted to other methods. The lower portion of the balloon was used in Shepperton Village, where the men are seen clambering into it during the storm. This was suspended on a large crane whilst fire hoses and wind machines

  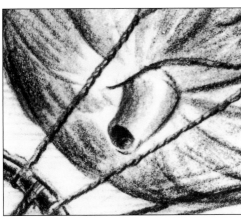

Left hand page. A section of the storyboard for the man-eating plant sequence, which was dropped from the final script. The sequence suggests that one of the men sees a venus fly trap plant. In doing so he 'wakes' a giant man-eating plant. The plant seems to emit fumes that stupefy the man and from there it prepares to eat lunch. Below right is a colour key drawing showing the plant with the Green Man in its clutches.

Above. A section of the storyboards for the take off of the balloon. Bernie Herrmann's wonderful score for the sequence helped to make the escape and flight in the balloon so exciting. It is perhaps one of the best examples of Bernie's music in our films.

Above and left. A section of the storyboard for the landing of the balloon on the island.

Below left. Live action showing the actors performing in front of the yellow backing screen.

Below centre and right. Shepperton Village stood in for Richmond during the opening sequences. We constructed the lower section of the balloon mounted on a crane, to simulate the storm and ascent. I am standing in the centre looking slightly bemused.

Right hand page top. Key drawing for log sequence. This drawing of the log sequence, used to base the matte painting on, gives a feeling of fantasy and danger to a potentially boring transition section of the plot.

Right hand page below left. Me on miniature Shepperton Square. You can get a good idea of the size of miniature sets by comparing my size to that of the model of Shepperton Square.

Right hand page below right. Key drawing for the Granite House. My original concept for the Granite House.

recreated the 'greatest storm in history'. However, we used miniatures when the script called for the balloon to be shown in full. For the opening long shots we built a duplicate of the balloon and the entire square in miniature. The characters were later added to the shot by a travelling matte, bringing the whole miniature set alive. The end result was far more effective than anything that could be staged full size. For the long shots of the balloon skimming over the waves we built another miniature of the deflated balloon and photographed it in the studio tank.

The final film used a total of seven matte paintings to help the audience visualize aspects of the island. Based on my designs, the special effects department at Shepperton Studios, headed by Wally Veveers,

executed all the paintings, the first being a high shot of the upper section of the island, which was combined in the lower part with the Spanish beach, and for an added touch, flying gulls and smoke from the volcano were matted in. I have never been happy with the painting because I considered it too fantastic, which is why I inserted the gulls and volcano smoke to give the whole thing life and movement.

Another matte painting I was never really happy about was the long shot of Granite House, which was meant to give the audience a sense that it was a good refuge. The actors below were shot against the yellow backing screen and optically inserted into the painting. For the close and medium shots of the actors in the mouth of the cave we built a 50-foot

section of the rock face, with its two 'eyes', on the S'Agaro beach.

The best of the paintings owes more than a passing tribute to *King Kong*, although even that film had lifted it from a Gustave Doré illustration. During a survey around the island, the survivors walk across a vine-covered log bridge suspended over a deep chasm with a waterfall (to add to the movement). The waterfall was real and double printed into the painting, whilst the men were shot at a distance against the yellow backing screen and then inserted onto the log via travelling matte.

In the final picture there were four encounters with creatures: the crab, the bees, the phororhacos and the cephalopod. The first of these is when the men

accidentally tread on a giant 'sleeping' crab, and for many is one of the highlights of the film. The live action for the sequence was rehearsed and photographed on the beach at S'Agaro. To enable the actors to maintain direct contact with the creature, we built two of its legs and a huge out-sized claw to pick up Dan Jackson. Such live action props are always difficult to operate convincingly, although we achieved a considerable rate of success with this by keeping the shots short and cutting into the animation whenever possible. For the long shots of Jackson in the claw, I used a three- or four-inch model of Dan, which I animated along with the crab. By editing between the full-size prop and the animation, it is possible to achieve a convincing flow of action,

but the close-ups of the claw are vital to illustrate just how huge the crab is.

The crab itself was actually real, or at least he was when we bought him, alive, in Harrods Food Hall. The reason for using a real crab was that nature had made such a good job of creating this complex creature that whatever I would come up with would never look the same. To avoid boiling the poor thing live in water, I had him professionally and humanely killed by a lady at the Natural History Museum in London. She took it apart and laid it all out on a board to show me how it fitted together. Later I 'reconstructed' it by mounting the pieces around the armature my father had built to my specifications. I attached each piece to the armature by filling the

sections with fibreglass to hold the metal armature firmly. The exterior joints were made of moulded latex, which allowed for flexibility during animation.

For the close-ups of the crab mandibles (which would have been time consuming to animate) we used four smaller live crabs photographed in the Spanish studio. We had to have more than one because they had a tendency to fall asleep under the lights. It is one of those live crabs that is seen plunging into the boiling geyser, which was a model with dry ice to simulate the steam. However, I have to confess that after we had all the shots in the can, we did sit down and have the crustaceans for supper, conscious of the fact that we were eating the stars of the scene. This is, I can assure the reader, the one and only

Above and right. Drawing for giant crab. This creature was first conceived in some notes I made dated September 1958 in which I describe him as 'a giant crab-like monster'.

Right hand page top. Roping crab. In animating the crab roping sequence, the height at which the off-screen crew member was pulling the rope had to be carefully measured so that it would exactly correspond with the model.

Right hand page below right. Testing the strength of the oversize prop claw to be sure it was safe for the actor. What I don't do for my art!

time that I have eaten the actors. Hitchcock would have approved.

To kill the beast by pushing it into the geyser, we see the man tie the rope to a full-size prop leg of the crab, following which I then had to animate the model crab with the rope tied to its leg, while on the other end we see the men tugging on the rope. During the live action we had a man off camera who was tugging on the other end of the rope on which the actors were pulling. This real rope had to be placed exactly in the correct position so that it would later match up with the animated model and the miniature rope (actually wire) that would be attached to the model crab. There is no room for error with this, as once the live action is filmed,

that's it. All direct 'contacts' such as this took time and effort, and had to be exactly planned before we began the live action. The final effect of the sequence is that the rope seems to be one between the crab and the actors. When there was no direct 'contact', the actors had to shadow box the imaginary beast, which, as always, had to be carefully 'choreographed' by me, as I was the only one who knew where the creature would be at a certain point. I spent a lot of time with the actors showing them the storyboards and running around the location to enable them to better understand the sequence and visualize the effect of the giant crab. In all such scenes, the eye-line between the actors and the creature were vital so that realism could be achieved, and so I used

my old friend the 'monster stick' for the actors to follow.

When I attended a screening of the film in 1994 in London, someone remarked after the film that he had seen a bikini-clad young lady just to the side of the frame during the crab sequence. I couldn't believe it, so we ran the picture back and, lo and behold, there she was for a fleeting second. Throughout the shoot, the animation and the edit she had gone unnoticed. It is perhaps a comment on the scene that the audience's eyes are on the action, not on the periphery. Before you rush off and check the scene on your video, I believe that the young lady would only be present in a theatrical screening when the full aperture is able to be shown.

One of the most popular sequences in the film is the giant bird, or to give the correct name, phororhacos. The poor old phororhacos has had a rough ride because most reviewers and audiences assume it to be an overgrown rooster, much like the crab and bees.

The misconception wasn't helped by the fact that he, or she, was highly coloured and possessed an awkward, hopping movement, brought about by its physiognomy (based on an ostrich). All these traits turned it into the 'comedian' of the film, which wasn't helped by the castaways eating it like a chicken. When Bernie came to write the music, he saw it as comical, although the success of the sequence owes much to his music. It is scenes such as this when Bernie's

genius comes into its own. After a serious, almost malevolent arrangement during the chase, he achieves a comic 'attitude' by using oboes from the point where the creature leaps onto the screen, thus attaining a quirky and eccentric sound. For me it's an 'awkward' theme, which was perfect for what I had visualized. When I sat with Bernie to watch the rough cut, he remarked jokingly, 'Maybe I should use "Turkey in the Straw" as the theme.' I almost gagged. In the end all the elements worked and I was delighted with the sequence.

The model itself was approximately 10 inches high, and although the prehistoric species is supposed to be brightly coloured, I didn't want it to look too gaudy, so apart from the red head feathers, the remainder

was ordinary chicken feathers. I would hasten to add that I didn't pluck these myself, but obtained them from my taxidermist. Sadly, the model doesn't exist today, as I reused the armature for something else, perhaps the ornthinimus in *Valley of Gwangi*.

To introduce the creature to the audience, Spilett is woken by a shadow crossing his face. We cannot see what he sees, but he turns and runs from the camera. The creature is eventually seen as it leaps from the left-hand side of the screen, over the camera and onto the beach. This simple action of jumping into the scene introduces the creature in a dramatic way and can add surprise or shock. I use this technique wherever appropriate, and it has been a favourite action of mine since *Evolution*. As the

Above and right. This is a good example of Dynamation. Beth Rogan, the fence and the beach area behind and just in front of the creature is the rear projection plate, which was filmed on location in Spain. A minature foreground was made so that it matched in with the background in colour and consistency, and it is on this that the animated phororhacos walks.

Left. Phororhacos. I never planned for the phororhacos to be seen as comical – in fact I had conceived it as a serious menace – but because the audience views the creature as a chicken, I can understand how the humour comes about.

Below. The Callan model on the phororhacos. The sequence was achieved by using a mix of models: both miniature and a full size section of the creature, with the actor sitting astride the mock-up and his 'substitute' model astride the model phororhacos.

creature terrorizes the two ladies, Spilett tries to fend it off, whilst Herbert leaps on its back and eventually knifes it to death. To achieve the transition of a real actor jumping onto what is in reality a model, we shot Callan in close-up leaping into nothing and then cut to an animated model of Callan on the back of the bird. The model of Callan is seen knifing the creature. Three or four inches high, because it was required for only a limited number of actions, namely stabbing movements, this basic model of Callan possessed only minimum movement possibilities. For the live action cutaways of Callan on the back of the creature, we filmed him on a full-sized mock-up of the creature's back and neck. When the creature collapses, the model of Callan is thrown off its back and the

model transforms into the real Callan. This was accomplished by digging a hole in the beach for Callan to lie in and then having him pop up out of the hole and roll across the sand. Again, I had to time this live action photography precisely so that when I photographed the animated sequence of the falling creature, the miniature Callan falls off over the far side of the bird and was then replaced by the real Callan rolling across the ground. This 'substitution' trick is another vital ingredient in convincing the audience that the animated human figure is the real thing, but it takes an enormous amount of complex preplanning.

The next Dynamation sequence is the appearance of the giant bee. First mentioned in the script dated 6 September 1960, it is described as a bumblebee. I

must have had second thoughts about a bumblebee; perhaps I considered that the creature's shape might be seen as fat and therefore comical. To have two comical sequences would not have been a good idea. In any event, it became a bee. To achieve the rapid flutter of the wings, they were shot in a two/three frame cycle, up, middle and down, and then repeated, which was possibly the easiest piece of animation in the entire picture. Just three stages of animation repeated over and over. When projected at the correct speed, the fast movement gave the wings a blurred drumming effect. Much as we had done with the phororhacos, there is an anticipation before the creature's appearance. Michael Callan and Beth Rogan are standing on a ledge outside a high cave

Above. Bee storyboard. Originally the bee was not part of the screenplay, but an idea of mine that was added much later when others were dropped.

entrance when they hear a noise, look up and flee into the cave. We then see the huge bee fly in and land on the ledge. We filmed Callan and Rogan on the edge of a real cave, near the beach, reacting to the area of the screen that would eventually disclose the object of their fear. This footage was used as the rear projection plate, in front of which I built a miniature section of the ledge for the model bee to land on. One of the secrets of achieving a proper match between the real rock and the miniature, or for that matter any miniature/live action, is achieving the correct lighting balance. If the miniature is lit darker or lighter than the rear projection, it all looks wrong. Obtaining that balance is sometimes more difficult than the animation.

Once inside the hive, we briefly see three bees. To avoid making three models, I simply used the one, and by means of mattes, split the screen, shooting three separate sets of different action in three parts of the frame. This is done by shooting the model bee on the left-hand portion of the frame and matting out the other two thirds, running the film back, matting out the action I had already photographed on the second third of the frame and animating the model again, this time with different movements, in the centre of the screen. You then run the film back for a third time and matte out the first and middle sections, and then animate the model on the third and right-hand section of the screen. This creates three bees for the price of one.

The climax to the sequence sees one of the bees 'sealing' Callan and Rogan into a honeycomb cell. For this we constructed a full-size honeycomb set, which was placed in front of the yellow backing screen. The bee is seen at the rear of the cell (by means of the yellow backing screen) seemingly regurgitating a substance and sealing them inside. This sealing process was accomplished by working backwards. I began with a 10 x 8-inch sheet of very thin paraffin wax on a wooden frame, which would represent the sealed entrance to the cell. Gradually, frame by frame, I removed tiny sections of it as I animated the bee in movements that looked as though he was taking the wax away. Afterwards the sequence was printed in reverse so it seemed the bee was sealing them in.

Top. These show the model bee descending onto the ledge of the cave and his shadow appearing on the rock. The actors and cave entrance were all on the rear projection plate but the bee lands on what seems to be the cave ledge. This ledge was in fact a miniature set up in front of the rear projection screen and it is onto this that the model lands. The false ledge had to be matched in exactly, both in shape and in colour.

Above left. Close-up of the model bee before it proceeds to seal Callan and Rogan in the honeycomb cell.

Above far right. Bee model as it looks today. Time has not been kind to him. Although several bees appear in the film, I constructed only one model, which was about 10 inches in length, 8 inches high and covered with a dyed fur.

Right. Honeycomb set. The full-size honeycomb set was made from fibreglass (giving the whole thing a translucent appearance) in the studio. The model bee, which appears to be sealing Callan and Rogan in with a waxy substance, was later matted in.

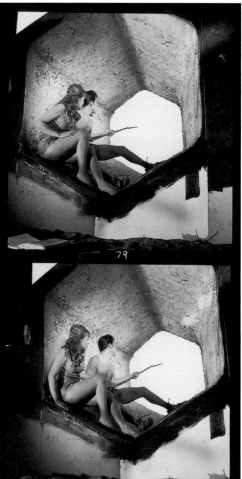

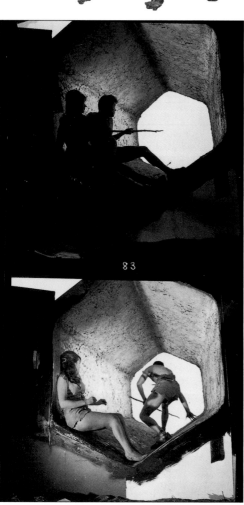

After the discovery of the *Nautilus*, Herbert and Elena make their way back to the others, only to discover pirates attacking the castaways. The live action on board the pirate ship was photographed onboard a hired vessel that was primarily a tourist attraction. However, for the sinking and then the raising of the ship we used a 7-foot model which we photographed in the sea off the S'Agaro beach. There really is no substitute for the real sea, but if you use sea and models together, you also have to wait. We waited many days! This was because the waves had to be just the right height so that they are more or less in proportion to the model. You can't have foot-high waves on a 7-foot model unless you want a storm, and we didn't. This enabled us to control the rate of

descent. All the underwater photography was shot off the coast of Benidorm, Spain, in a little bay that was famous for its clear water and underwater scenery. Egil Woxholt was in charge of the photography (he later filmed the underwater sequences for *Clash of the Titans*). The ship sections were constructed on land and then floated out into the bay on large oil drums to be sunk in the correct location. All the actors' parts for the underwater scenes were played by expert divers, one of whom was Egil. Unfortunately, I suffer from claustrophobia, so I wasn't able to dive, although I watched the action from the surface with a snorkel.

The giant underwater creature, the nautiloid cephalopod, was the other 'leftover' from when we were considering a more prehistoric theme. At

various stages of the script development the creature was to have been an octopus, then a clam or giant oyster protecting a huge pearl, but all these were thought to be a little too clichéd. In the end we settled for a sea creature I based on a pink fossilized shell, over 6 feet in diameter, in the Cologne Museum. To introduce the creature to the audience, the underwater mariners walk by a dark crevice; the camera holds on the threatening darkness, then zooms in, followed by a dissolve to the miniature as the cephalopod opens its gigantic red eye. All the live action for the sequence where the creature wrestles with the divers was filmed underwater by Egil and later combined with the animated model. Like the octopus in *It Came From Beneath the Sea*, there

Top. The nautiloid cephalopod as it appears in the film. Animated against a rear projection of the seabed off the coast of Benidorm, the creature holds one of the unfortunate explorers, which of course is a model. To create the impression that the whole scene was taking place underwater, I sometimes shot the animation at double frames rather than the usual one. This had the effect of slowing the motion of the models down and creating fluidity in the movement.

Right. Divers in gear. I designed the divers' gear to be practical (big enough to cover real diving apparatus), visual and at the same time Victorian in look. These shots were taken on the yellow backing screen stage. The actors played out the action and later the undersea effects were combined in an optical printer, in this case the fight with the nautiloid cephalopod.

should have been more tentacles, but the budget dictated that less was best. The tentacles required almost microscopic movements in order to achieve the illusion of a slow undersea effect as they curl, twist and wrap themselves around the victims. It was a painful process both for the divers and me.

I have to confess that the shells for the helmet and breathing gear was my idea. I am reluctant to own up to this, as people seem to find them amusing. In the early outline these were to have been from the nautiloid cephalopod creatures. Of course, they were completely impractical, but I hoped audiences wouldn't think about such things. The bubbles from the divers in the long shots were double printed onto the action. They were photographed with special machinery in a fish tank, against a black back cloth. To achieve moving bubbles that would be seen coming from moving divers, we constructed a tube that would produce tiny bubbles in a tank. The tube was mounted on a worm gear arrangement, which moved exactly as the divers moved in the live action. This was later matted into the travelling matte shot of the actors in the miniature background set. The underwater ray gun beam was in fact a roman candle firework. The candle was lit against a black background cloth, then the sparks double printed to fit with the direction of the gun. It was the same principle as the alien beam in *Earth Vs the Flying Saucers* but without the cotton wool.

The climax sees a volcano explode and destroy the island, Nemo and his *Nautilus*. A miniature volcano was constructed in the studio, the smoke photographed by Wilkie Cooper at 96 frames per second. Smoke, like water, has to be slowed down to seem in proportion to the model, and in this case it also gave the impression of great distance and height, both of which are vital when reproducing a volcano.

The film was released in the US in August 1961 and in the UK the following year. Most of the reviews were generally favourable, but the film didn't exactly live up to expectations. Today many fans seem to hold it in esteem, although personally I feel it could have had a smoother storyline, and, as always, there are sections which, given the opportunity, I would change. However, I am unable to do that, and as the

Top. Still of the *Nautilus* model. The disabled *Nautilus* was about 5 or 6 feet in length, and the miniature rock cave was built carefully to scale. I used dry ice in the water, which enhanced the scene and gave it a mysterious quality. During the volcanic eruptions, sections of the cave were made to fall away and high-speed photography was employed to give the whole thing a more realistic effect.

Right. The actors in diving gear on the yellow backing stage.

film stands, it is, I believe, one of our better pictures.

Special mention has to be made of two individuals who worked on the film. The first is the director Cy Endfield. He was one of three or four directors with whom I worked who I admired and got on well with. He was a good choice for the project and one of those rare directors who can handle drama, action and effects, knowing how the whole thing is going to fit together. He knew what kind of picture it was and had no pretensions about his work. He just got on with the job. His overall input into the project, including the storyline, was invaluable (it was he who came up with Nemo growing food for the world), and although we didn't always agree, he always seemed to know instinctively what I wanted for the Dynamation.

Bernard Herrmann's score was masterful in its approach to counterpointing the action in the most effective way. Although the score is not my particular favourite, it is certainly one of his best, being full of atmosphere, particularly during the balloon sequence, which contains three powerful and dominant notes. He had such variations of power. When we first see the island, Bernie used French horns, giving a sense of mystery yet beauty. The crab sequence was greatly enhanced by Bernie's score taking the sequence to heights I could not have imagined when animating it. During animation I often have a piece of music in mind for a sequence. Sometimes I will even play music, which helps me give the animation an extra sense of movement and

life. For example, in the case of the snakewoman in *7th Voyage of Sinbad*, I had a section of music (I think it was from *Salome*) that I played over and over again, trying to imagine the movements she would have made to fit the music. Along came Bernie and composed an original score perfectly fitted to the action and bearing no resemblance to what I had imagined. In the case of the crab sequence, a piece of music had been running through my head, but his score with horns and string composites to an uneven seven counts to the bar was so exciting that I couldn't have found anything like it, nor wished for anything better.

Filming *Mysterious Island* was a delight: everything seemed to come right with the cast and crew, and

Following Callan and Rogan's escape, they discover Captain Nemo's submarine, the *Nautilus*, in a giant underground sea cavern. Of course, the submarine and the cave were miniatures constructed and shot in Spain. The design of the craft was loosely based, as was Disney's, on some of the original *20,000 Leagues Under the Sea* book illustrations that gave it a sleek superstructure and large portholes. Because of copyright, I couldn't duplicate Disney's wonderful design with its jagged ramming beam, but I could revamp the novel's description. In one edition of *Mysterious Island* an illustration of the craft in the cavern shows an almost smooth hull with lights shinning up and a handrail around the top. Both Disney and I gave it a more robust and gothic look, and although it wasn't in the original illustrations, the ramming beam was seen as such a good idea (and it was felt that audiences would expect the *Nautilus* to have this feature), I designed one that was connected at the bow and which arced up into the air. The interiors of our *Nautilus* were also based very closely on Verne's description: a mixture of luxury and mechanical coldness, adding a mystique to the character of Nemo.

Far left top and middle. These pictures show a section of the full sized *Nautilus* against a yellow backing screen. The cave will later be matted behind.

Far left bottom. Myself and technicians on the miniature volcano.

Left. The model pirate ship outside the studio. This was used for the sinking scene off the S'Agaro beach. We placed concrete blocks on the seabed and pulled the model down with cables, so allowing us to control the rate of descent.

Above top. The volcano begins to erupt. This shows the miniature volcano matted in with the live action in the foreground

Above. Stills showing some of the tests for the smoke and explosions.

overall I had few difficulties with the animation. Aside from the smoothness of production, the picture holds another fond memory. Some time before the shoot I had met a young lady called Diana Bruce (who would soon become my wife), and I suggested she come out to Spain with me for a holiday whilst I was involved in the location shooting. Making movies was all new to her, and for most people it would be daunting, but being a naturally warm and friendly person she had no trouble in making friends with everyone on the production. Her presence was an inspiration to me. Diana listened to my ideas and problems, and ever since that time she has helped me during the planning of a picture and always joined me on location to give me support – something that I usually desperately needed.

Above. The original artwork for *Mysterious Island*, which I consider one of the best ads designed for any of our films. Sadly, it didn't help at the box office because the film was thrown away as a second feature.

CHAPTER 6 ALMOST HUMAN

Jason and the Argonauts

Greek and Roman mythology had never been a favourite subject of mine at school, but as I grew older I began to appreciate the legends and realize that they contained a vivid world of adventure with wonderful heroes, villains and, most importantly, lots of fantastic creatures.

In the late 1950s Charles and I discussed the possibilities of filming a Greek legend, specifically the story of Perseus. Following the lack of enthusiasm for *Mysterious Island*, we resurrected the idea and searched for a legend to form a natural storyline for Dynamation. Like *7th Voyage*, we would have to adapt and gently manipulate the story. Between us we read all of the Greek legends, and instead of the Perseus story (which we felt had some problems), we eventually decided on Jason and his search for the golden fleece, allowing us the most flexibility for high adventure and fantasy.

Having decided that it was to be 'Jason', Charles presented our idea to Columbia in December 1960. The front office was intrigued and gave us the go-ahead to prepare drawings and a treatment for the project, tentatively called *Jason and the Golden Fleece*. So it was that what would be known as *Jason and the Argonauts* was born, and of all the films that I have been connected with, it continues to please me most and is, rather gratifyingly, the film most people mention when they meet me.

was string the 'encounters' together, so providing a natural progression. I began this by visualizing some of the key sequences, and the first results included the harpies (an early version), Talos, Triton and the clashing rocks, modifying each one until I was satisfied that they would work on the screen.

Whilst I was working on the concept drawings for the key sequences, Charles commissioned a treatment and screenplay from Jan Read. At a 'sweatbox session' I showed my drawings to Jan and Charles, and between the three of us we discussed how to link them together. Jan then went off to formulate and bridge my drawings with a suitable continuity for a screenplay. During one of the preliminary discussions we considered the idea of top and tailing the story with a modern section. This, we realized later, was a mistake, but in those early days we were reluctant to plunge contemporary audiences directly into a film set in ancient times. We felt that it needed a prelude, and doggedly pursued this line of thought, which Jan then transferred into a first rough screenplay. This screenplay begins with a group of tourists visiting the Temple of Poseidon at Sounion, in Greece, and whilst looking around they come across a strange man who relates the story of Jason. As the story of the Argonauts' great adventure unfolds, the screen dissolves into the time of legend.

The earliest written notes I have relating to *Jason* were made during the filming of *Mysterious Island*, hastily written on the back of a page of the script, entitled *Sinbad in the Age of Muses*. I am not sure why I used that title (I probably thought that by keeping Sinbad in there it would lead to better box office). It was those scribbles that presumably led me to formulate some of the basic ideas that would become *Jason* and scenes for future pictures. Aside from the main premise of Sinbad and Jason setting off together on a quest for the golden fleece, there are references to 'a land of the dead with walking skeletons', 'flying on a griffen', 'Medusa the magician' and 'the harpies'.

Because myths are usually very episodic and lack strong continuity, such stories need some degree of manipulation. But the story of Jason lent itself more than most to a natural flow of instances that could, we felt, be strung together to make a cinematic story. Its central theme told of the hero Jason searching for the magical fleece, throughout the quest encountering all manner of obstacles and beasts. What we had to do

Although sections of Jan's screenplay were carried into the final picture, the bulk of the story and dialogue, especially the beginning, tried too hard to remain faithful to the legend, making it far too complex and cumbersome for the kind of picture Charles and I were looking for. Although Jan worked hard at trying to resolve the problems, we needed a writer who was familiar with the subject, so Charles

Left hand page. Two key drawings for the film. Above is my concept for the Hall of Zeus at Thessaly, and below is an early design for what would have been part of Jason's journey into the underworld. Here he is seen with Cerberus, the two-headed (it should have been three) guardian of the underworld. Although we didn't use him in *Jason and the Argonauts*, he was a creature that would pop up in *Clash of the Titans* on Medusa's Island.

decided to bring in Beverley Cross who, amongst his other talents, was an expert on Greek mythology. Although the usual 'sweatbox' script sessions continued, it was Beverley who tightened everything and wrote much of the excellent dialogue, sometimes on a day-to-day basis:

Jason (Todd Armstrong) has been deprived of his kingdom by King Pelias (Douglas Wilmer) and the only way in which he can gain his inheritance is to search for the famed golden fleece in the land of Colchis. A ship is built by Argos (Laurence Naismith), and, with the help of the goddess Hera (Honor Blackman) and the hindrance of Zeus (Niall MacGinnis), Jason sets out with the Argonauts, amongst whom are Hercules (Nigel Green) and Acastus (Gary Raymond). Stopping for water, they first encounter the giant bronze statue Talos, which nearly destroys the Argo and is only stopped when Jason releases its life blood. The second encounter is with the harpies whom the gods have sent to harass the blind seer Phineas (Patrick Troughton). In return for directions to the fleece, Jason agrees to capture these demons, which he does. Finally, Jason and the Argonauts have to find their way through the Clashing Rocks in order to reach Colchis. Just as all seems lost, the god Triton saves the Argo. Eventually they arrive in Colchis where Jason falls in love with the priestess Medea (Nancy Kovack). King Aeetes (Jack Gwillim) tries to stop Jason from taking the fleece, but after killing the hydra which protects the magical fleece, Jason and Medea escape. Aeetes pursues them and casts the teeth of the Hydra to the ground, from which spring seven warrior skeletons. Together with two of his men Jason fights the skeletons but Jason alone escapes to rejoin the Argo and Medea.

Our next task was to cast the film. For the role of Jason, Columbia suggested Todd Armstrong, a young studio contract player who had been a support actor in *Walk on the Wild Side* (1962) but had little, if any, lead experience. However, his good looks and screen presence persuaded us that he could handle the difficult role, which called for both tough physical and acting abilities. Unfortunately, when we had completed a rough edit of the film, Columbia felt that his strong American accent didn't mix with the accents of the dominant British cast (contrary to several articles that I have read over the years, he had a good speaking voice) and so they wanted to soften it. We therefore had to dub his voice using a British narrator with a slight American accent. Fortunately, the end result is a good mixture, and the general audience would not be able to tell that Todd was dubbed.

Nancy Kovack, another Columbia player, was cast as the high priestess Medea, but the rest of the cast was made up of British actors, including Gary Raymond, Niall MacGinnis, Laurence Naismith, Honor Blackman, Andrew Faulds and Nigel Green, who played a larger than life Hercules. Although Hercules doesn't feature greatly in the story, we felt that it was an important role but wanted to get away from the Italian beefcake the public had expected of him. Nigel was perfect as a slightly older and more intelligent hero, who in his ratty old lion skin was both a braggart and compassionate, especially when his friend Hylas disappears beneath the crumbling statue of Talos and he decides to stay behind to look for him.

When it came to locations, it was only natural that our first choice would be Greece, but after a recce taking me all around the country, I found it to be very bleak and grey. At that time the ancient ruins, other than the Parthenon, were mostly unrestored and in too much of a state of decay (even for the Phineas sequence, which necessitated a ruined temple) for the project. Rejecting Greece, we decided to look at what was then Yugoslavia, where once again I spent a lot of time. It seemed perfect, especially the mountain and coastal areas. We chose a number of sites located around Dubrovnik and found a standing set of an ancient city at the Yugoslav Studio, which had been built and used for an Italian feature production. However, this love affair with fresh locations didn't last long. Well into pre-production we began to have 'difficulties'. It became clear to Charles that certain production representatives were trying to 'load' our budget, whereupon Charles, quite rightly, blew his top. Although we were committed to the crew and the actors, we decided to move the production, pulling out of Yugoslavia only a month before shooting had been scheduled to begin. I can remember a feeling of panic in the air. At literally the eleventh hour we turned our sights to Italy.

By the 1960s Italy's film industry was thriving, which meant that it would be able to supply all the facilities for our production without costing countless millions. Also, having filmed *20 Million Miles to Earth* there, we knew that it had good unused locations, as well as Greek temples (mainland Italy had been

colonized by Greeks before the rise of Rome). But the question was, would they be right for *Jason* and the peculiarities of Dynamation? To save time it was agreed that Don Chaffey, the director, would recce the north whilst I travelled south. Fortunately, I found perfect Greek ruins and an abundance of good coastal locations against which we could sail the *Argo* and use as backdrops for most of the major scenes. The most striking scenery was in and around the tiny seaside village of Palinuro, south of Naples between Pisciotta and Sapri. The unusual rock formations, the wonderful white sandy beaches and the natural harbour were all within a few miles of each other, making for a convenient and economical shooting schedule. Some differences in basic composition are often a direct result of compromising with the available locations. Sometimes it can be bad but often it is good. For example, the first time I saw the temples of Paestum, which served as the background for the harpy sequence, I almost flipped. However, when the production was to be shot in Yugoslavia, we had planned to build Phineas' temple on top of a mountain, although on a much smaller scale. As it happened, the Yugoslavs had done us a favour: not only were the locations far superior, but Paestum, the icing on the cake, was far better than anything we could have built.

There are always unexpected problems with location shooting. Although there was plenty of sunshine during most of the filming, there was also a lot of rain. About six weeks of steady rain to be precise. This made it very difficult to film and get supplies to some of our remote locations, which on occasion meant that we very nearly ran out of food. At one point all we had was cornflakes and spaghetti! I also recall having to take our production trucks through an olive grove to get to one specific destination. After we had photographed the necessary scenes, an Italian farmer approached us and told us that we had squashed all the olives lying on the roadway with our trucks. These were the olives that had fallen on the ground! He probably thought that as we were a Hollywood film company, we could pay lavishly for the olives. Although unhealthy for our budget, we decided it would be wise not to incur the possible anger of the local Mafia, so Charles paid the farmer for his loss.

One of the other problems was that we were not the only crew filming in Italy at that time. On one occasion we were shooting a scene in which Jason's ship, the *Argo*, was to appear from around a rocky bluff. Everything was ready, the camera was rolling and we radioed the ship to start off. What should come around the bluff but the *Golden Hinde*! The tension was broken when Charles was heard to shout, 'Get that ship out of here! You're in the wrong century.' It transpired that another British film crew was shooting some second unit footage for the TV series *Sir Francis Drake*, and their vessel, with its more powerful engines, beat ours around the cove.

The first live-action scenes to be shot were those onboard the *Argo*, which was a focal point for a lot of the action. Because it had to accommodate cameras, crew and cast, it had to be solidly built. The outer shell of the ship was mounted over the existing framework of a fishing barge and the whole thing powered by three Mercedes-Benz engines, allowing us both to move the craft to and from locations and also to manoeuvre the vessel to catch the correct sunlight for each new set-up. The cost of building her was $250,000, a huge portion of the overall budget, but following the completion of all location filming, Charles sold it to Twentieth Century-Fox, who used it for the Actium sea battle in *Cleopatra* (1963), which offset the cost of its construction.

The Hera figurehead, located at the stern of the vessel, was designed so that the eyelids opened and the eyes moved, but I drew back from making the mouth move, as I felt most audiences would liken it to a ventriloquist's dummy, and it would then become borderline comedy. In the end we decided that Hera would communicate with Jason in his mind.

Most of the interiors were photographed in the small Palentino Studios, in Rome, but the main effects work was completed at Shepperton Studios in England. I used the yellow backing process once again, shooting all the travelling mattes against the huge screen we had rigged in our facility at Shepperton. Full-size sections of the *Argo* (the prow and the rail) were built for close-ups and matte work, along with a full-size mock-up of a section of the hydra's tail. There was also a four-foot model of the *Argo*, used for the Talos and clashing rocks sequences.

Single frame rear projection of live action of island and splashes of water. (Splashes made by skimming a stone on on the surface of the water.)

Arial device for suspending disc on wires to synchronise with splashes on screen. (Complete scene shot one frame at a time in sync with projected image.)

Matte glass to blot out rock when disc appears to go over the top and disappears. (Opposite matte inserted for second pass of film.)

Left hand page. *Argo*. The 92-foot *Argo*, built in the Anzio shipyards, was beautifully designed by Geoffrey Drake, based on ancient Greek pottery paintings.

Above. Discus throwing. This is a diagram of how I achieved the apparently simple task of throwing the discus across the water and over the rock.

THE GATEWAY TO THE GODS – MT. OLYMPUS

STANDING IN FRONT OF THE GODS AT OLYMPUS

Top. Concept drawings. The gateway to the gods on Mount Olympus, and my original drawing of Jason on Mount Olympus.

Above. Still from Mount Olympus scene. The view from the gods, Jason seen from above.

Right hand page. Still from Mount Olympus scene. Combined with the gods looking down at him, it seemed that a tiny Jason is standing in front of them.

In November 1961 I sent my father the designs for the construction of the model armatures, which he produced with his usual high quality, so much so that they still work smoothly today. In all there were fourteen complex armatures: one Talos, one Talos foot and hand, one Talos arm and hand, one hydra, two flying harpies, six fighting skeletons, one Jason and one Acastus. They arrived in February 1962, allowing me four months to make the bodies and paint them before beginning the animation.

Jason and the Argonauts has received so much attention over the intervening years, both in countless articles and on television, that I find it unnecessary to detail everything I did on the picture. As with the other films I have discussed, I have selected particular scenes because there is a story to tell, an interesting method of achieving the effect or simply because I am particularly proud of the sequence.

As an introduction to the gods, Hermes (the messenger and herald of the gods, played by Michael Gwynn) appears to Jason as an old man who then transforms himself into the god. All this takes place in a ruined temple, a set filmed on a mountain near Palinuro, overlooking the sea. The day scheduled to film the sequence saw the weather dark and stormy with intermittent rain, and because the story was set in Greece, such weather would usually be seen to be a problem. As the schedule didn't allow for any delays, we were forced to wait for the rain to stop and then shoot all the scenes, which at the time we thought would look awful. However, back at the studio we subtly added thunder to the soundtrack and this, along with the dark brooding skies, gave the scene an unexpected feeling of being in the presence of the gods.

The growth of Hermes from an ordinary man to the gigantic figure of the god was completed against a yellow backing screen as a travelling matte super-imposed into the background. We used a dolly track to move closer to Michael Gwynn, giving us the desired effect of his image growing to enormous size. Today I would have used a zoom lens, but at that time we didn't have them. When the god had apparently grown to the desired height, we drew around his outline to create a matte into which we faded in a smoke effect, previously used in *The Story of King Midas* and again in several other scenes in *Jason.*

In one of the early scripts Hermes, in the form of a man, asks Jason to climb into his chariot, whereupon Jason witnesses the transformation into a god (but without any increase in size). The journey to Olympus is also interesting. With one pull of the reins the horses are transformed into unicorns and fire spits from the wheels of the chariot, taking both Hermes and Jason into the sky. Sadly, the script was altered to save time and money, and we ended up with almost a straight transition to Olympus through a dissolve.

Once transformed into his true entity, Hermes delivers Jason to Zeus on Mount Olympus. For the establishing shot on Olympus I had designed a massive imposing archway that would lead into the palace of the gods, but once again we changed the concept to save time. Creating Mount Olympus on our budget was always going to be a problem. It had to look impressive and inspiring but not cost too much, so we used a long shot of the temple-like palace set where the gods are seen entertaining themselves, then combined that with a matte painting. Both the art director and I discussed how we could depict the actors as gods. We didn't want to cut from the mortal world to the gods with barely anything to differentiate between them, so we decided to use a variety of images and designs to give the impression that the gods were truly omnipotent and dominated the world of humans. The obvious trick was to make the gods huge versions of humans (the ancient Greeks always imagined their gods as gigantic images of themselves). We also painted the set pure white with gold embellishments, and dressed the actors in white and gold togas, which were distinctly different to the humans' more earthly colours. As a final touch we later added in the lab an edge of mist around the frame. We also wanted to have a physical means by which the gods are seen to play with the fates of mankind. We accomplished this with a chess-like board game played by Hera and Zeus and which reflected the events on Earth (in *Clash of the Titans* we used a miniature arena with tiny statues in niches as the game pieces). It was important to the story that the human characters feared the gods but also saw them as vulnerable and fickle by treating the mortals as chess pieces.

Jason arrives on Olympus in the hand of Hermes, from which he steps onto the board game that Zeus has before him. For this confrontation with Zeus we built a full-sized board set with oversized pieces on which Todd would stand and deliver his lines upwards, towards the camera, so as to appear as if he was talking to a gigantic Zeus. I used a travelling matte of Todd, against yellow backing, of him with his back to the camera as Hermes places him on the chessboard.

Once back on earth, Jason holds games to select the men who will sail with him on his voyage into the unknown. This is the first time that we are introduced to other key characters, especially Hercules and Hylas, the latter of whom challenges Hercules to see who can throw a discus the furthest. Hercules throws first and we see the discus soaring through the air and hitting a huge rock in the sea off the beach. Next Hylas throws, but artfully skims the discus across the surface of the water like a stone, so that it not only hits the rock but sends it over. Although the two actors throw real discuses in the medium shots, the long shots of the discus use a tiny animated model. Hercules' throw was fairly straightforward. We first of all photographed the sea and rock for the back projection plate and then I animated the discus (which was about an inch across) on an aerial wire, flying across the screen to apparently hit the rock. However, Hylas' throw was very different, as the discus had to skim or bounce off the water. I managed this by getting one of the crew to throw a flat stone to skim the water between the beach and the rock. This created the splashes I needed for the animation. Using the footage as a back projection plate I carefully timed the duration between the splashes and animated the tiny discus to correspond with them until it hits the rock, at which point it bounces over and disappears. To make the discus seem to disappear behind the rock, I had to insert a special matte. In actual fact the discus was animated in front of the rock but the matte allowed a line along the top of the actual rock, so blotting out the animated disc as it crossed below that line. On a second pass the image of the rock was printed in the blacked out area.

The first Dynamation sequence in the film is Talos, the massive bronze statue that comes to life on the Isle of Bronze. Talos *did* appear in the Jason legend, although he was only 7–8 feet tall and was located on the island of Crete. When he came across any strangers, he would heat his body in a fire until red hot and embrace the unfortunate intruders. We had to alter this image. We first of all did away with the hot embrace, although we did have him crush some of the Argonauts, and then I made him a huge 100-foot high adversary, which was based on the Colossus of Rhodes, one of the seven wonders of the ancient world. There are no remnants of the Colossus, but from some accounts we know that it straddled the harbour of ancient Rhodes facing the open sea – totally impractical but the stuff of cinematic dreams. Our Talos straddled a natural harbour, so preventing the exit of the *Argo*. A Colossus in reverse.

The sequence was filmed in a bay near Palinuro where, during my recce, I found a big natural rock arch on the beach. Having the action take place through a natural arch allows the audiences to believe in the effects. They suspend disbelief because they know the arch is real, therefore Talos must also be real. Of course, the mind of the viewer wouldn't ask that question, they would just accept it, which is what I always try to achieve.

When I drew the storyboards for The Isle of Bronze (just having recced the Yugoslavia locations),

Top. Frames from the Talos sequence. The statue of Talos comes alive and descends from his plinth to pursue the men on the island and then as they flee in the *Argo*.

Middle. Sections from the Talos storyboard. The action and general look of the scene is almost as it appears in the completed film. It is another example of how planning is so vital in these movies.

Left. Talos model. Talos was based on the ancient Colossus of Rhodes. It had always fired my imagination, and over the years I had tried to use the concept, which I finally achieved, to good effect in *Jason*.

Above. Test frame for the Talos sequence. This shows Talos straddling the two sections of land to block the exit of the *Argo*. In this test the miniature 'addition' to the land, which makes it look like a natural harbour, can be seen on the left hand side of the frame.

Right hand page right. The end result showing how my storyboards were filmed. The actors' reactions were crucial in making the audience believe the 'threat'.

Right hand page left. The original concept for the sequence. This is my original key drawing for Talos confronting the *Argo*. The only thing I changed was Talos' helmet, which I decided made him look more warrior-like and therefore more threatening.

I had visualized the events leading up to Talos coming to life as something slightly different. Leaving Jason and the other men to search for food, Hercules and Hylas come across the head and hand of a huge bronze torso coming out of the ground. Hercules hits the hands and it rings with a resounding metallic echo. However when the locations were changed to Italy, I had the idea of beginning the Talos sequence with Hercules and Hylas standing at the head of a valley in which we would see huge bronze statues created by Hephaestus (the god of fire and metal-working). I called it the Valley of the Titans.

The model of Talos is approximately 12 inches high. In addition to the animated model, I constructed two other fibreglass copies and sections of his body for

close-ups, including an arm and hand (which comes through the rock arch) and a foot and ankle (for the 'Achilles heel' sequence that would match the full-size one we had filmed on location). When it came to animating the model, I found myself faced with a whole new set of rules. It seems ironic that for most of my career I have been trying to perfect smooth and life-like animation action, but for Talos (which was the longest animation section in the film), it was necessary to create a deliberately stiff and mechanical movement in keeping with a bronze statue that had sprung to life.

At first I had intended all the statues in the valley, including Talos, to be freestanding, but when I began designing the sequence, I realized that it would be

more dynamic to have Talos climb off a plinth or platform. Quite often there were elements in a movement or action which owed something to an image I had subconsciously stored in my mind. It might be an animal or human reaction, a book illustration or occasionally a movement inspired by something in a movie. An example of the latter is in this scene. It begins with a low angle shot of the statue kneeling on the pedestal, then slowly this huge inanimate object turns its head to look down at Hercules and Hylas. It's an eerie action heralded by deep metallic sounds. The slow movement of the head turning was inspired by an image from a Japanese film in which a woman, sitting with her back to the camera, slowly turns her head. That one, almost supernatural,

TALOS CONFRONTS THE ARGO

movement just popped into my head during the process of animation. There was no conscious attempt to copy it, but the action was perfect for Talos. A further example of influences occurs at the conclusion of the Talos sequence, when we see the bronze giant fall forward onto the beach. This action of the object falling towards the camera gave the scene bulk and was an action inspired by a silent film I had seen in which an enormous clay statue falls on someone. However, unlike the head turning, in this case the action was designed as a dramatic end to the scene.

The highlight of the whole Talos sequence is the 'Colossus' scene, where we see the bronze giant straddle the exit to the natural harbour to prevent the *Argo* leaving. In fact the headlands to the harbour were not natural but a sleight of hand look-alike. The curve of the land, on the left-hand side, was in effect an island off the mainland, connected together with a miniature so that it looked like a natural harbour. The miniature 'bridge' was placed in front of the projection plate so that Talos appears with one foot on each piece of land. His right foot 'stands' on a platform behind a split screen of the real land and the other on the miniature.

After Talos has apparently destroyed the *Argo*, the men struggle back to the beach where Talos pursues them. His massive form appears from behind a tall jagged promontory and he turns his body to look down at the puny men on the beach. This was designed to be as impressive as possible. Like all good stories, hope is at hand when Hera tells Jason that Talos' weak point is his heel. He has to remove a cover to allow the giant's ichor (the life blood of the gods) to drain out. To enable Todd Armstrong to attack Talos' heel, we had a full-size plaster foot and ankle built in Italy, which we managed somehow to get to the beach. After much experimentation, the props department came up with a concoction for the ichor consisting of oatmeal and coloured water. For the medium shots of the animated model foot and ankle, the steaming ichor was actually cellophane. You can't animate water, so I had to find an alternative. Cellophane was the answer. First of all I constructed a round wire mesh frame onto which was mounted a circle of rolled coloured cellophane and then lit it with a red light to

Top. Frames of the Talos sequence.

Middle. Talos sequence storyboards. This section of the storyboard shows Jason locating the cover on Talos' heel and opening it, so releasing the ichor.

Above and right. Talos appears from behind the promontory. This helps the audience to quantify just how big Talos is, which in turn tells us that there is little chance of escape. The sequence is a classic mix of Dynamation using my figure of Talos cut with live action sequences. This is also another example of depth. The beach and the fleeing men take the eye to the Colossus, which is both dramatic, to say the least, and frightening.

The Talos model was shot to deliberately integrate with the landscape in the location I had scouted and chosen. The actors needed a little prompting to get the reaction I wanted, particularly so that their eyeline and head angles matched what I knew they would seem to be looking at in the final scene. the deliberate, yet mechanical movement of Talos added to this scenes dynamics. All the time the scale of the live action was upper most in my mind as I was animating the sequence.

Right hand page left centre and right. This is the original model of Talos in the position that appears in the picture of the scene on the far right. It stands against a rear projection screen onto which I projected the live action. The model was integrated into the scene by means of a split screen.

Right hand page bottom left. Talos as a bronze statue. Because the latex rubber from which the models are made deteriorates over the years (some more quickly than others) I recast Talos many years later as a real bronze statue in exactly the same dimensions as the original.

OVER SIZE PROP — STEAM 268 COMES OUT

DYN — MOULTON METAL POURS OUT STEAM RISES

DYN. — STEM RISES AT A SC.270 FOOT. TALOS LOOK

match the real slop from the full set. I animated the whole thing, moving it a fraction of an inch each frame, after which it was inserted by means of matte lines so that it seemed to be coming out of the ankle and disappearing into the sandy beach. The steam was real. It was produced during the filming of the live action by placing a smoke pot behind a board (which represented the ankle). When I came to animate the sequence, I placed the model foot in front of the board on the rear projection screen, so it seemed as if the steam was coming from the ankle.

The conclusion of the Talos sequence sees huge cracks appear all over his body as the ichor drains away, he totters and then falls forward towards the camera and onto the beach. I didn't use the main model for this but a fibreglass one that I then cut into cracked sections. The cracks were filled with clay and the whole thing painted to match the armatured model. During the animation I shot a frame and gouged out a little of the clay, then shot another frame, slowly creating the appearance of cracks opening up on the body. At the same time I animated sections falling away and finally disintegrating when the model struck the ground.

The next Dynamation scene was the torment of Phineas by the harpies. The name 'harpies' gives the impression of dislikeable creatures, and in the legend they are described as having the face of a woman, the body of a vulture, with their feet and fingers armed with sharp claws. As always, I had to take some liberties with this description, making them bat-like to give a more practical but at the same time more menacing appearance.

For the harpies sequence I designed several 'contacts' with the humans. The first is where the blind Phineas is fighting off the demons and we see his stick and belt yanked from him by the creatures. Like all good 'contacts', this was begun during the live action filming. Both objects were attached to offscreen wires and on my signal a member of the crew pulled them away from Patrick Troughton. Later in the animation studio I would animate the models on their wire braces to seem as though they were snatching the objects. In the case of the stick, I changed it (between one frame and the next) to a miniature one because

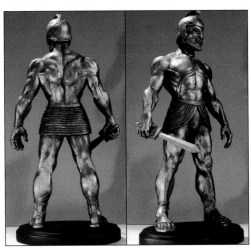

PHINEUS AND THE HARPIES

one of the harpies is seen holding it. There is also another 'contact' when the stone altar/table Phineas has been eating from is seemingly pushed over by the harpies. This again was rigged during the live action and I simply animated the model to appear to push it over.

The whole sequence was filmed in and around the largest of the three magnificent temples of Paestum (we would later use another of these temples for the exterior shots of Medusa's lair in *Clash of the Titans*). For Jason and his men to capture the harpies, the script called for nets to be stretched over the roof and sides of the temple. We had to place the actors on the top of the ancient temple columns with ladders. When the net falls onto the disorientated harpies, we see them struggling beneath it. For this I used a very fine miniature meshed net that had been specially made and strengthened with wire, which I suspended on wires and then animated in unison with the model harpies as they plummeted to the ground. Once on the ground, I combined the real and miniature nets so that the real net, which the men are seen pulling, works on the projection plate and the miniature net (in the foreground) is seen with the creatures struggling underneath. Following the encounter with the harpies, the story moves on to the clashing rocks and the god Triton.

Above. Drawing of harpies. Long before my aborted 1954 project *The Elementals* and the unrealized bat creatures in *The 7th Voyage of Sinbad*, I had wanted to do something with winged demons. The story of *Jason* provided me the opportunity of creating a duo of delightful ladies.

Left. Capture of the harpies. Although the ruins of the temples of Paestum were 2500 years old, the authorities were very co-operative, letting us climb all over the monuments. I can't imagine the Italian authorities letting any film crew do this today!

Right. Harpies sequence. For this sequence I constructed two animation models of approximately 8 inches high with a wingspan of 18 inches, and two smaller, less articulate ones to be used for the long shots.

Right hand page. The blind Phineas being attacked by the harpies.

We searched for months to find an actor to play Triton. The part required one special qualification, namely long arms, because he had to be able to reach across to the opposite miniature cliffs to prevent the destruction of the miniature *Argo*. Even on the miniature the gap was quite considerable. We eventually chose an actor who was also a swimmer and thus able to submerge himself for fairly long periods. It was not an easy role for anyone to play. The poor man had to wear an uncomfortable rubber fish tail corset and avoid all the complex mechanisms, operated by wires by a studio technician, that controlled the tail. In addition to that, his wig was heavily lacquered to prevent the water making it look like wet noodles. After the first take of

him emerging from the water he looked a little ordinary, so I told him that I wanted him to stick his lower lip out, like the Royal Hapsburgs. This would give him a majestic and sinister appearance. Although he spent hours and hours in the water tank wearing all that paraphernalia, he never complained.

The whole sequence was shot in about a week on a small stage at Shepperton Studios where we had built a special tank that included a wave device. The clashing rocks themselves were 6–7 foot high plaster sections mounted on wooden platforms that in turn were mounted on car inner tubes so they floated and allowed the whole thing to be moved backwards and forwards by studio prop men.

When we first built the set we made the sections of rocks that fall away during the clashing process of Styrofoam covered with plaster. Nobody, including myself, had considered any problems with this until we came to the first day of the shoot and found on attempting to 'clash' the rocks that they splashed into the water and just floated. Overnight the construction shop made replacement solid plaster rocks that proved to be ideal. Wilkie Cooper and I shot the sequence using high speed photography, which exaggerated the splashes, consequently giving the scene a dreamlike quality that perfectly reflects the surrealistic subject matter of a huge god holding back rocks.

Top. My conceptual drawing for the clashing rocks visualized Triton as an animated model with water matted in around him. However, I soon realized that this was too complicated for our budget and decided to use an actor filmed at high speed.

Right. Still from the film. The *Argo* along with its mariners was shot in front of a yellow backing screen in the studio. Later an optical printer was used to combine this with the action of Triton and the rocks. It was important to keep a sense of rhythm throughout the whole scene, which emphasized both the drama and the scale of what was appearing on the screen.

Right hand page. Triton stills. Although the actor playing Triton (sadly I can't remember his name) spent hours and hours in the water tank wearing all that paraphernalia, he never complained.

In these still shots one can clearly see the set and the direction being given to the actor. It was very important for us to choreograph the actor to fit in with the other elements.

Top. Key frames from the hydra sequence. I based the design of the hydra on classical vase paintings, although it went through many changes before I finally came up with the idea of making it 'serpent-like' with a distinctive tail ending.

Above left, middle and right. This illustrates the process of how I used a matte to place the hydra into the set of the golden fleece. First of all the live action was shot on the set, and then I created a matte area at the mouth of the hydra's cave. After animating the hydra model it was placed into the matte area. Todd had to make sure his eye line was right and shadow box the area according to my instructions.

Middle left. Still shot taken on set from the live action sequence with Don Chaffey and myself on the set of the hydra's lair.

Above. Original hydra model. The hydra model used a very complex armature to enable all the heads and necks to be manipulated easily during the animation process.

Right hand page. Todd Armstrong on the set of the hydra's lair. The studio lighting gantry can be seen top left. It was a beautifully made set that at first centres on the golden fleece and then becomes dominated by the hydra.

Following the clashing rocks, Jason and his Argonauts finally arrive at Colchis, where they locate the fabled Golden Fleece. In our version the guardian of the fleece is the seven-headed hydra, but in the original legend it is a dragon that never sleeps. I felt that a dragon is seen today as a medieval beast, besides which, I had already animated a dragon before, so I searched through the Greek legends and came up with the hydra, which appears in the Hercules legend when he slays it as one of his labours. Originally, it was portrayed as having more heads than I could have coped with (a hundred heads

according to Diodorus; fifty according to Simonides and nine according to Apolodorus), and as soon as Hercules cut off one head, two grew in its place. The hero finally kills it with the help of Iolaus, who applied a burning iron to the wounds, so ensuring no head would grow, but for our film this was all too complicated, so I gave him seven heads (as it's a magical number in all legends) and killed him with a sword through the heart. As with Talos, I based the basic design of the creature on classical vase paintings, although it went through many changes before I finally came up with the idea of making it 'serpent-

like' with a distinctive tail ending like a forked snake tongue. The seven heads were designed to resemble a dinosaur-like bird with curved beaks and two ear-like crests curving backwards, an image that would suggest a throwback to prehistoric times. When designing such a creature I always have to ask myself, 'Can I put this on the screen?' If I had no such limitations, my imagination would run riot, but in the end it is time and money that dictates practicality, although with the hydra I did set myself a pretty tough task.

The hydra model was over three feet long, which up to the time was one of the largest I had designed

and built, but it did allow me to photograph it in detail. It also possessed an incredibly complex armature that provided a wide range of movements, including its snake-like body, seven heads, double tail, mouths, tongues and blinking eyes. All these body elements had to be synchronized. For every frame of film, I would move the model perhaps by only a millimetre, but there were sometimes thirty-plus movements required. Each element of the body had to be moving and then I had to remember that the third head was going forward and down, the fourth was going backwards and

up, the tail was curving this way, the body another way. As if these elements were not enough, I also had to animate, at different stages of the sequence, two human figures (Acastus and Jason) who were held in the grip of one of the tails. Both scale models were based on the actors, whom we had photographed from every angle in their costumes to obtain the best likeness. For the close-ups of the characters gripped by the tail, the real actors were suspended on wires and wrapped in a full-size section of the tail.

All too soon, Jason slays the hydra by twice

plunging his sword into the creature's chest, the second thrust being fatal. The choreography for this was done on the set in Rome, although I had pre-planned it before we began filming. At a predetermined point in the action, Todd thrust his sword forward and then dropped it onto the studio floor. In the animation studio the real sword on the rear projection screen was hidden behind the animated model of the hydra and substituted with a miniature sword at the moment most appropriate to keeping the detection of the substitution minimal.

Top. Frames of the hydra sequence.

Below. The original concept drawing for this sequence.
Note how only the figure of Jason changes in the final film. The rest is more or less how it appears in the film.

Right hand page. The battle with the Hydra as it appears in the film.
Unfortunately, when a still frame of the picture is enlarged as this is it does show the grain in the rear projection. When the film is projected at 24 frames per second, then these imperfections are hardly noticeable. In the still the matte line in the ground around the base of the hydra is clearly visible, along with these miniature rocks, and the eye-line can be seen to be exactly right, as though Todd was actually looking at the creature.

Above. Three stills of the hydra emerging from its cave. The first is the model on the animation table. Notice the rocks on the floor: this was a little trick of bringing the creature into reality. The rocks seemed to be part of the cave and the surrounding rocks. The second still shows the creature against the rear projection screen with the rock background and the third is the final composite of the creature emerging from the cave, achieved by means of a matte line drawn around the mouth of the cave in the live action.

JASON BATTLES THE HYDRA

Sc.601 DOLLY SHOT OF ABET SCATTERING HYDRA'S TEETH

Sc.603 DYN. AEETES SCATTERS HYDRA'S TEETH.

Sc.604 DYN. EARTH SEPERATES AND SKELETON'S HAND + SWORD APPE

Sc.606 DYN SKELETONS GROW OUT OF EARTH.

Sc.607 DYN. REMAINDER OF SEVE SKELETONS GROW.

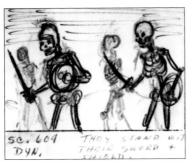

Sc.609 DYN. THEY STAND WIT THEIR SWORD + SHIELD.

Sc.611 AEETES GIVES ORDER TO CHAR

Sc.612 DYN. SKELETONS MARCH SLOWLY

The climax of the film is the battle with the children of the hydra's teeth. When Aeetes catches up with Jason he scatters the teeth whilst calling on the forces of darkness to avenge him of the crime. From out of the ground appear armed skeletons. In the legend it is rotting corpses, and despite originally designing the scene as such, we thought this would give the film a certificate that might have barred children, so we decided on seven skeletons (the same number as the hydra's heads). By today's standards the rotting corpses would not only be acceptable, but expected.

projection plate. Below each of the holes I constructed seven little platforms to which the crouching skeletons (they are crouching when they first appear up through the ground) were attached. I then fixed each of the platforms to a screw device (a mechanism I had developed for *It Came From Beneath the Sea*), allowing me to slowly animate each skeleton rising up and breaking through the cork. To allow the cork to be animated at the same time as the models, I cut each disc into sections so that when the skeletons broke through, it would seem like clods of earth had

Once Jason has killed the hydra, he flees with Medea and the fleece. When Aeetes, king of Colchis, sees the dead hydra, he calls on the power of Hecate, queen of darkness, to deliver to him the children of the hydra's teeth, the children of the night. Fireballs rain down from the sky and consume the body of the creature, reducing it to a skeleton from which Aeetes' men collect the teeth. Les Bowie (an accomplished British special effects technician) photographed the fireballs. Based on the exact angles I wanted the fireballs to appear from, Les made up a number of small balls of wadding soaked in petroleum that were lit and thrown from a platform at night. He filmed a variety of angles for me, and once we had chosen the best ones, they were added by double printing in the camera.

Each of the model skeletons was about 8–10 inches high, and six of the seven were newly made for the sequence. The remaining one was a veteran from *The 7th Voyage of Sinbad*, slightly repainted to match the new members of the family. Of course, I had to take certain liberties with the human skeleton to allow the bones to cover the metal armature. Like the skeleton in *7th Voyage*, the shape of the bones was created from cotton wool soaked in latex, which I then shaped into bones and allowed to solidify. For their appearance from the ground we built a miniature section of landscape made of plywood, covered with painted plaster and into which we cut seven random holes. These holes were covered with cork and the whole thing painted to match the area in front of King Aeetes and his men who would appear in the rear

been pushed aside. Each of the sections had copper wire passed through them, allowing me to animate them so that it seemed as if the skeleton had done it. Some of the cork pieces appear to roll away from the hole, and these were animated by using wax to hold them in place for the frame to be shot. I could, I suppose, have made the skeletons simply appear in a cloud of smoke, but the result would not have been the same. The effect of these 'children of the night' almost unwrapping themselves from the earth is far more dramatic.

When all the skeletons have manifested themselves to Jason and his men, they are commanded by Aeetes to 'Kill, kill, kill them all', and we hear an unearthly scream. What follows is a sequence of which I am very proud, although the logistics involved were immense.

Above left. One of my very earliest sketches for the fight between Jason and the skeletons on the plinth. This even precedes the key drawing that appears on the following page.

Above right. What Jason sees.

Right hand page, top. At the very earliest stage, such scenes as the skeleton fight are designed and visualized with continuity sketches. However, when these are drawn for the script, they are executed in the broadest terms, dictating only set-ups. The original storyboards show my planning of each cut with the animation of the skeletons interacting with the live action sequences.

Right hand page far top right. Lost idea. The storyboard image of the missing animation shot of the skeleton searching on the ground for his head.

Right hand page middle. Contact shot planning. In this section of the storyboard one of my pre-planned 'contact' shots is illustrated. In frame two (shot 634) we see Jason swinging his sword and in the following shot (635) the sword making contact with the skeleton's head and decapitating him (can a skeleton be decapitated?). I had planned that the shot would show Todd's lower legs and in front of this projected image I would animate a miniature sword slicing off the head.

Right hand page bottom. This was one of my key or concept drawings for this particular sequence. I based the look of the drawing on an ancient classical theme, but with touches of Doré. In the final film the temple in the background was not included. This I think was never a possibility on our budgets, but the drawing helped to sell the idea of the project.

I had three men fighting seven skeletons, and each skeleton had five appendages to move in each separate frame of film. This meant at least thirty-five animation movements, each synchronized to the actors' movements. Some days I was producing just 13 or 14 frames a day, or to put it another way, less than one second of screen time per day, and in the end the whole sequence took a record four and a half months to capture on film. There is one scene in which we see a skeleton chase Fernando Poggi, our sword-master, and jump across a ruined gateway. It looks great but took me longer to complete than any other scene in the sequence because the model had to be animated on aerial wires. I only have myself to blame, as I designed it that way.

kept things simple, there would be fewer problems.

The synchronization between the live actors and the models is, of course, vital. During the skeleton fight (or, for that matter, any fight between real actors and models), I had to count each frame of film on the rear projection plate to determine exactly where the actor's sword, which appeared on the plate, and the skeleton's sword would meet. The number of frames would determine how long it would take for the skeleton to go from point A to point B so that the swords met at exactly the right spot.

The number of frames dictates what speed is required to get the skeleton's arm up, so that when the actor's hand is in a certain place, the skeleton's sword will block it. The speed of the live-action photography

As I have made clear, little or nothing in any of our films is left to chance. Everything is pre-planned to avoid waste, which costs money. However, in the case of the skeleton fight there is one brief animation shot that was cut. It showed a skeleton on all fours, feeling around the ground for its severed skull, and was meant as light relief. When we viewed the complete sequence it was decided that it slowed the pace and was therefore cut out. It was one of the very few times that any of the filmed animation was dropped from our productions. In the UK one scene in which we see the skeletons charge the camera and hear a horrific shriek, was cut for the film's release. The censor thought it far too risky for British children, and as we wanted a children's certificate, the shot had to come out. Like the cyclops and the skeleton in *7th Voyage,* the scene was reinstated some years later.

Concentration, especially with such a complex scene as the skeleton fight, is a vital talent for any animator. The minute your mind wanders, you lose continuity and a whole scene or a day's work can be lost. If the phone rang (in the 1960s I didn't have the luxury of an answering machine), I would either let it ring or take it off the hook altogether. When I look back at the hydra sequence, it is remarkable that I ever remembered which head was going forward or backward and whether a model was accelerating or decelerating. I am often asked whether I used a flow chart (a record of movements and progression of the models) to detail the moves but the answer is no. Occasionally I would make a few basic notes when I broke for lunch, and sometimes, but rarely, used a surface gauge. Aside from that, I always found that if I

would be 24 frames per second, so I had to judge the speed of the movement for the animation accordingly. The broader the movement of the model, the faster it will appear to move when run at 24 frames. It presents a problem of timing because the models and actors must appear to have been photographed at the same time. This makes it necessary to sometimes move the model about half a millimetre per frame in order to keep in synchronization with the live actors. Sometimes I would have to 'kill' footage (killing time means that the model action is not completed) in order to get the skeleton from point A to point B to meet the actor, but occasionally I would have to do the opposite by 'fleshing out' time with subtle movements to allow synchronization with the live action and so lengthen the scene.

Sc. 633
DYN.
JASON & TWO
SKELETONS.

Sc. 634
JASON SWINGS
HIS SWORD WILD

Sc. 635
DYN.
JASON'S SWORD
CUTS OFF HEAD OF
SKELETON.

Sc. 636
DYN.
JASON BATTLES
ONE SKELETON.

Top left and above. The still above left shows the stuntmen rehearsing with Todd Armstrong, Andrew Faulds and Fernando Poggi for the skeleton fight. The stuntmen wore numbered sweatshirts so that the actors knew which skeleton they were supposed to be fighting, and this was also used as a reference for when I came to animate the 'real' skeletons. The sequence of stills above show Andrew Faulds acting out his death from one of the skeletons. The actors were relentlessly rehearsed so that when shooting the sequences, everything was as convincing as possible. Again, of course, the eyeline was crucial, as well as the smoothness of the shadow boxing.

Top right. The scene on the plinth as it appears in the final film. The plinth in the rear projection has been replaced with a model plinth exactly aligned with the real one. On and around this I placed the skeletons, matching their movements with the footage kept of the stuntmen with the actors, and so matching the actors' movements.

Right hand page top. More stills of the shadow boxing, several with a stuntman.

Right hand page. My designs for the skeleton armatures showing in detail some of the ball and socket joints. Also is a still of one of the skeletons.

Below and right hand page below. Frames from the finished film. In them can be seen the death of Andrew Faulds' character and the leap into the sea.

At the very earliest stage such scenes as the skeleton fight are designed and visualized with continuity sketches. However, when these are drawn for the script, they are executed in the broadest terms, dictating only set-ups. That's all very fine on the drawing board, but there are unpredictable factors – the actors, the weather or how the location chosen will apply itself to the set-up – none of which can be anticipated on our budgets, so everything must be kept as fluid as possible.

Planning is crucial, but one way to avoid too many variants is a reliable crew. The live-action choreography for the skeleton sequence was intensely complex but was, as usual, made less problematic by the presence of both Wilkie Cooper, our cameraman, and Fernando Poggi, our sword-master. Enzo had been our sword-master for every production since *7th Voyage*, but just before the production of *Jason*, he had decided to retire and so Poggi, who had worked alongside Enzo, took over the role. He also played one of the Argonauts in the skeleton fight sequence. I must confess that since I had visualized the skeleton sequence, I had had concerns about how we were going to photograph the live action. I needn't have worried. As soon as the location photography began, Poggi and I discussed the sequence, and when he wasn't working on a scene, he practised with the actors and the seven other stuntmen, away from the camera and crew. Poggi insisted that the seven stunt-men were dressed in numbered white sweatshirts and, like Enzo, he again used a hand clap for the beats that would determine the duration between each action. Slowly, as the fight was practised over and over, the sequence came together, with the end result that on the day of the shoot it went extremely well. As with most scenes

such as this, it was shot twice. The first was a black and white guide print of the actors and stuntmen in picture, which allowed me to keep track of exactly where the skeletons would be. The second was a duplicate of the first but without the stuntmen, showing only the actors 'shadow boxing'. It was this that would be my back projection plate so that I could align the models to the action.

I designed and animated into the skeletons certain human 'touches' to give them some character. For example, I was able to give the impression that a skeleton was mortally wounded, while another example occurs on the platform when a skeleton rolls to the edge, apparently stunned, with its bony arm hanging over the side. The arm can just be seen swinging with the force of the movement. It wasn't something I needed to do, but these 'touches' add character and occasional relief to a scene. The illusion of reality is achieved through 'contact' between the live actors and the models. It was the vital ingredient to enable the whole thing to work for the audience. Although I designed several of the 'contacts' at the planning stage, it wasn't until we arrived at the actual location that Poggi and I were actually able to define them. Apart from the obvious clashing of swords, we see one of the skeletons' heads being lopped off and there are several actions of pushing and kicking the skeletons away. However, there is one shot that puts Todd Armstrong into direct 'contact', and this is when we see him plunge his sword through a skeleton's ribcage. During the live action Todd plunges his sword down and then at a specific point in the movement lets go of it so that it drops to the ground. In the animation studio I animated the skeleton in

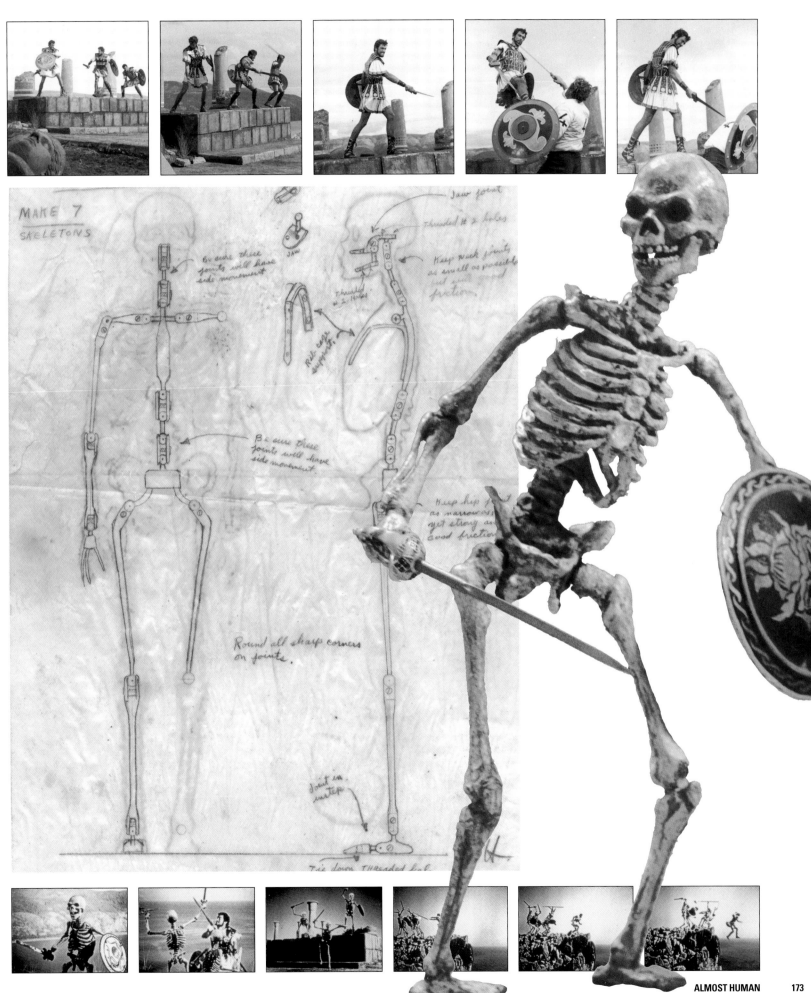

front of the sword dropping onto the ground, which appears in the back projection plate, and replaced the real sword, as it appeared to enter the skeleton, with a miniature one. Todd then pulls his arm away and the skeleton is seen clutching onto the miniature sword. Of course, you can't kill a skeleton with a sword, but the effect is exciting.

So how *do* you kill skeletons? We puzzled over this conundrum for some time and in the end we opted for simplicity by having Jason jump off the cliff into the sea, followed by the skeletons. It was the only way to kill off something that was already dead, and besides, we assumed that they couldn't swim. After filming a stuntman jump into the sea, the prop men threw seven plaster skeletons off the cliff, which had to be done correctly on the first take as we couldn't retrieve them for a second. To this day there are, somewhere in the sea near that hotel on the cliff edge, the plaster bones of seven skeletons.

The sequence is one of my favourites, although I would never want to do it again. It was painful to the extreme. Hours and hours of the same movements can wear a man down. But it was worth it. It is there on film for all to see, and no matter what technology is invented, it can never be reproduced. In stop-motion the whole scene has a supernatural quality that could only be achieved by the use of dimensional animation. My one and only regret is that we didn't photograph it at night or, even better, twilight. There is no doubt in my mind that this would have greatly heightened the overall effect.

Above. Myself and Diana on our wedding day in 1963.

Not long after I had completed Jason, in late 1963, I received a script (not from Charles) concerning the Loch Ness monster, a subject that had always fascinated me. The whole idea of a lost prehistoric creature in a Scottish loch has wonderful possibilities for model animation, but this screenplay, entitled Breakout of the Loch Ness Monster, didn't meet expectations, so I turned it down. It was just another monster-on-the-rampage movie, this time featuring a radioactive (picked up from a satellite that had crashed into the loch) plesiosaur from the Mesozoic Era, whose best scene was to emerge from the loch and attack a boat. I am not aware that it was ever made, and while the idea had some potential, it would definitely have required considerable expansion to give the creature a more credible role.

As I was nearing the completion of the animation, a rough cut of the film was sent to Bernie for him to write the music. Once again, he delivered a brilliant score possessing a vitality and originality that managed to complement the fantasy action. As was his style, he used large amounts of wind, brass and percussion (but no strings) to create an overall feeling of mystery that reflected the ancient world. The title overture is a variation of the *Argo*'s theme and is the film's most distinctive piece of music: a heroic, stirring battle march that dominates the score. The Talos sequence is composed of brass, low winds and timpani, evoking the gigantic bronze creation, and as a finale he wraps the skeleton fight in an aura of nightmarish imagination. Although we didn't know it at the time, this was to be Bernie's final score for us, but it is a tribute to his genius that I continued to animate on subsequent films with his music always in my mind.

Jason and the Argonauts took nearly two years to complete and cost an unprecedented (for us) $3 million, which made it our most expensive and lavish production to date. Although we had made the film under the title of *Jason and the Golden Fleece*, Columbia discovered that there had been an Italian sword and sandal movie starring Steve Reeves with the same title. We obviously didn't want it confused with the very image we were trying to avoid, so Columbia's publicity department came up with a list of alternatives, amongst them *The Incredible Voyage of Captain Jason*, *Journey Into the Unknown*, *The Fantastic Voyage of Jason*, *Perilous Voyage* and *Set Sail For Danger*. Eventually we decided on the simple and straightforward title *Jason and the Argonauts*. As the publicity machine began to be involved, they came up with yet another 'new' technical name for Dynamation, called Dynamation 90. It was obvious that they were running out of good ideas. Before you ask, no, I don't know what the 90 stands for, except that it was probably an attempt by the department to create a feeling that it was a widescreen process, much like Panavision 70. It was neither widescreen nor possessed any different technology from any of our other films made since *The 7th Voyage of Sinbad*.

When the film was released it generally received good reviews. In their 5 June 1963 review, *Variety* said of it, 'Here's a choice hot weather attraction for the family trade – a sure delight for the kiddies and a diverting spectacle for adults with a taste for fantasy and adventure.' They go on to add, 'an impressive display of cinematic verisimilitude for which associate producer and special visual effects expert Ray Harryhausen rates at least the motion picture equivalent of two ears and a tail. ...The money, at any rate, is on the screen.' The *Hollywood Reporter* said in their review of 5 June 1963, 'Here is a legendary adventure, expertly produced, a triumph of "cinemagic"'. On the down side, *Time* magazine reviewed the picture by commenting that 'they have dreamed up monsters Jason never saw, including a steam-powered *King Kong*, built of bronze, with a drain plug in his heel'. And that was the best part of the review! As I have gone to great lengths to emphasize, we do take 'liberties' because the film has to appeal to general audiences, and you can't do that if you stick to every exact detail, as if Greek scholars were the only ones to view the picture.

Although in Britain the film was one of the top ten big moneymakers of 1963, it was unfortunate that the film opened in the States at the same time as the public was becoming tired of the Italian muscle epics that had seldom visualized the creatures in mythology, and which we had desperately tried to avoid being associated with. Over the intervening years since the picture was made, it has become a classic (not my words) and is, as I have said at the beginning of this chapter, one of the most popular of our movies. I am often asked if we intended there to be a sequel. Fans quote the fact that Jason still had to confront Pelias, the usurper of his throne, and Zeus is heard to say, 'But for Jason there are other adventures. I have not yet finished with Jason. Let us continue the game another day.' I suppose we must have hoped that there would be a sequel, but apart from resolving the conflict with Pelias, we would have had to take even greater liberties with the second half of the legend in which Medea kills her two children by Jason, dismembers their bodies and returns to Colchis. I did, however, want to make a film of the Labours of Hercules, but like so many ideas, nothing ever came of the suggestion.

As almost a footnote, Columbia submitted the picture to the American Academy of Motion Picture Arts and Sciences for consideration as a possible special effects contender. We all fully expected it to earn at least a nomination for visual effects, but it was ignored and the picture that won was *Cleopatra*. I am told by certain Academy members that it was seen then as nothing very extraordinary, but how could that be, when at the time nothing like it had ever been done for the screen? A nomination and an award would have helped it at the box office. Disappointment on both fronts, but my private life was far more successful. After the completion of the production, on 5 October 1963 I was married to Diana. *Jason and the Argonauts* was a project that seemed to encourage marriage. Seven of us (there's that magical seven again) on the crew took the vow of wedded bliss, either during the production or shortly after.

What subject could we film next? Something different, something eye-catching and spectacular. Ever since my amateur days I had always wanted to make a film of one of H.G. Wells' novels. Although *War of the Worlds* and *The Time Machine* had been made into respectable films, another of Wells' stories, *First Men in the Moon*, had always seemed a good vehicle for Dynamation. Instead of the usual invasion from another planet, *First Men in the Moon* would enable us to explore another world and a complete alien civilization. On our budgets, this was likely to rival the tasks of Hercules!

CHAPTER 7 ABSOLUTELY IMPERIAL

First Men in the Moon

In 1901 H.G. Wells wrote the quirky space adventure *First Men in the Moon*, a novel documenting a trip taken by two adventurers to our nearest satellite by using a substance called Cavorite (a liquid that defies the force of gravity).

Apart from the Georges Méliès film *A Trip To the Moon* (1902), there had been only one other filmed version of the story: a 1919 Gaumont British film directed by J.L.V. Leigh. Since then, nobody had touched the idea. I had first read the novel in my teens and my passion for it never subsided and over the years I had often mentioned the idea to Charles.

Charles would look at me and bring up the same logical arguments, namely that there was not enough variety in it for a feature production and that space exploration had advanced to such a degree that it would be difficult to make the story seem believable to modern audiences. To try and overcome these disadvantages we at one point considered modernizing the story, much as George Pal had done with *The War of the Worlds* (1953), but it just made it worse. If we had set it in the 1960s, we would have had to bring in the bomb, which would not have fitted well with the original story.

One day, however, whilst Charles was having lunch with Nigel Kneale (writer of the BBC television science fiction series *Quatermass*, and an H.G. Wells enthusiast), he happened to mention my enthusiasm for filming the novel. Nigel was so intrigued by the idea that he promised to think about it. After some time Charles received a call from Nigel, who had come up with a viable solution for updating the story but at the same time retaining the charm of the original, and would be delighted to work on it if funding could be found. With Nigel onboard, Charles realized that the project now had promise and so approached the Wells estate to secure the rights to film the story. At that time Frank Wells, H.G.'s son, was still alive and took an avid interest in any projects based on his father's work. Frank knew our reputation and readily granted permission, after which Charles approached Columbia Pictures. This is where things came to a stop, at least for a short while. Basically they were a little reluctant to commit themselves. The main reservations were 'there is not an audience for it… there is too much space fact on television to allow any room for space fiction'. They concluded with 'real science-fiction buffs laugh at outer-space science-fiction because of lack of authenticity'. Despite these negative comments, and perhaps because of our track record and Charles' enthusiasm, the head office eventually decided to let us prepare a screenplay.

Nigel's brilliant idea to update the novel was to 'top and tail' the Wells storyline with a modern day space exploration. A United Nations spaceship makes the 'first' manned landing on the moon, and whilst exploring, the astronauts discover a British flag and a document suggesting a previous expedition during the reign of Queen Victoria. On Earth UN executives are sent to England to locate the person whose signature is on the paper, leading them to an elderly gentleman named Bedford. He relates the story of how he and his two companions, Cavor and Kate, travelled to the moon in 1899, and from that point on the essence and main body of Wells' story is left more or less intact.

Nigel also slipped in the idea that Cavor would have a cold so that when he is left behind, the bacteria wipes out the inhabitants of the moon, the Selenites, and Bedford would realize that it was Cavor's cold that terminated them when a later expedition finds the city empty and in ruins. I have always felt that not enough was made of the cold, and I feel that audiences do not get the point that it was this that wiped out the Selenites. Anyway, it was a respectful nod at Wells, who had used the bacteria idea in his *War of the Worlds*, and also neatly accounted for the fact that NASA would not find any Selenites when their astronauts landed there.

That's how it ended up on the screen, but of course the reality was that months of hard work had gone into developing the storyline and overall look of the film as per usual. Because we didn't make the usual kind of film, it was not a matter of a scriptwriter coming in and then we make the film. These films relied heavily on effects, and key sequences dictated the pace of the story. I had to determine if an idea

Left hand page top. The moonscape was based on scientific fact with a touch of cinematic licence.

Left hand page middle and bottom. Four drawings of the lunar landscape and the mooncalf. These were executed when I was in my late teens after reading the novel. They reflect that Wells' story had the travellers walking on the surface of the moon with no protective clothing. This was something we had to change for our version, as scientific fact had overtaken what Wells had written.

would work and, if so, how I could put it on the screen. I have tried throughout this book to emphasize how script development (new ideas replaced previous ones, either because they were better or because of time and budget) was so important in the story of how our films were made. All the participants usually made a contribution to the final look of any film.

If I hadn't come up with a storyline, such as in the case of *First Men in the Moon*, the first step after approval for script development would be for me to sit down and begin drawing possible key scenes. Gradually, these visuals are rejected or accepted, and Nigel would link the approved scenes with the original Wells storyline, although in the original book certain elements would have been unacceptable to modern audiences with our newfound knowledge of the moon. So Nigel's first draft treatment lifted the essence of Wells' story and strengthened it to construct an imaginative modern story for the screen.

Charles commissioned a screenplay from Nigel, which was written by him between 4 and 22 May 1962. It generally contains most of the elements in the final film, with the exception of a whirlwind created by Cavor's experiments in anti-gravity and the fact that the Grand Lunar's brain was connected to the machinery that controls the complex Lunar civilization.

In this first script the mooncalf is described as 200 feet high with 'a head as high as a man, covered with horny scales, long stalk-like appendages holding tiny witless eyes… a colossal hulk that seems to rise almost to the roof of the cavern, a mountain of translucent blubber'. It would be some time before Nigel's slug-like creature would change to the caterpillar mooncalf I eventually conceived. The Selenites are described as 'a grotesque outline that suggests a human being in a cloak, with a lowered head… it seems to consist of two enormous flat casings that are presumably its eyes, yet there are no pupils, no eyeballs, only oblong boxlike formations covered with vertical slates… the supposedly solid body was hollow! Inside out. Its rib cage folded about it like a bat's wing.' To achieve the image of a civilization reminiscent of an insect colony, Nigel describes the Lunar city thus: 'an extensive maze of angular passages and countless open topped

chambers are packed together in steeply rising tiers… a gigantic termite hill'.

The whole storyline was a far clearer and more practical visualization of the Selenites' world, although sections of it were still beyond a realistic budget. Therefore Charles decided to bring in Jan Read to help smooth out the story so that it could be made within the confines of a budget acceptable to Columbia. Between 4 and 12 December 1962 Nigel and Jan wrote the second screenplay. Following Nigel's first screenplay, the Columbia front office insisted that the story must have a woman in it, because it was felt that a female would help women identify with the story, even though neither Wells' novel nor indeed the title allowed for one. So Kate, a character who had appeared briefly in the first screenplay, was expanded to accompany the two men to the Moon. Nigel and Jan rather cleverly had her accidentally join the expedition rather than allowing her to be a professor's daughter or something equally cliché.

This new script introduced some striking new features. Firstly, Cavor is introduced to Bedford and Kate when a miniature sphere containing two floating mice bounces into their garden. The idea was that it would have been funny but also allow the audience an early realization of what Cavorite could do and prepare them for the 'leap' into space. Sadly, it was discarded during a sweatbox session as too time-consuming. We still needed to find an introduction to the powers of Cavorite, so some time later I suggested that Cavor is seen floating around his house when Bedford first visits him. This was also discarded. In the final version Cavor demonstrates his invention by painting Cavorite to the bottom of a chair on which Bedford is sitting, and when the solution dries he rises unceremoniously to the ceiling. It is in this second script that the British flag is found by UN-1. All three of the characters are captured by the Selenites, but whilst the trio are visiting the hatchery, Kate is commanded to remain in the Queens' chamber with the other females. The 'Queens' are described as 'creatures with tiny heads and swollen abdomens'. Embarrassed, Bedford and Cavor persuade the Selenites that Kate does not do that sort of thing, but when the three appear before the Grand Lunar, it

becomes apparent that the Selenites want to breed humans. Horrified, they escape and locate the sphere in a chamber containing giant cocoons (this is what happens to the mooncalves if they are not eaten). From one of the cocoons bursts a giant moth, and it is this creature that saves Bedford and Kate, whilst Cavor sacrifices himself by throwing himself into the shaft along with several Selenites. One final element of this screenplay differs from the final ending: it envisioned Bedford and Kate accidentally trapping a Selenite inside the sphere when they take off, and as the craft enters the heavier gravity of Earth, the creature's body collapses and it dies. I imagine that we considered some of this, especially the disintegration of the Selenite, far too gruesome, and would have had trouble with the certificate.

Columbia had wanted an American director, so Charles asked Nathan Juran to helm once again. Apart from being an excellent director, he also possessed a sense of humour, which allowed the film's lighter side to emerge without sacrificing the seriousness of the adventure. Many of the 'laughs' are from his mind, from actor Lionel Jeffries (Cavor) or a combination of both. In a script assessment from Jerry dated February 1963, headed 'Outline of new material', he makes several good suggestions, some of which would affect the final look of the film. They also confirm that it was Jerry who instilled some of the comic action into the film. To begin with, he has Cavor objecting to some chickens in the sphere, which begins a chaotic scene of birds and feathers filling the confined space. When Cavor and Bedford land on the Moon, the Selenites watch them. The craters of the Moon are explained as the residue of the Selenites' underground excavations. Some, although well observed on Jerry's part, were not so constructive, at least as far as my work was concerned. In the final pages Jerry wrote, 'Cavor is borne into the palace of the Grand Lunar on a magnificent golden palanquin', against which I scribbled a bold 'NO'. The time and effort to produce animated creatures holding a live man, albeit in a palanquin, was daunting to say the least. Similarly, I had written the same comment next to the line, 'As far as the eye can see, there are millions of Selenites.' I'm not surprised I objected to that one, Jerry.

Left hand page. Another of my very early amateur designs for the lunar landscape.

Left and above. A section of my storyboard for the killing of the mooncalf and what would have been Cavor's discovery of the cocoon chamber and the hatching of one of the giant moths.

Jerry was once reported to have said 'I don't believe in getting "arty"… directing films was just a way of making a living.' This might have been true, but Jerry could deliver quality when the subject matter allowed, and *First Men in the Moon* supplied him with all the necessary elements to shine. His art director's background, humour and ability to handle actors all came together to make this his best film. As I have said before, he was one of the few directors that 'understood' what I was up to. I once had a director who tried to have me removed from the picture. He had little idea what I was doing and had not, at the time, realized that the concept for the project was mine in the first place and that my role was more than effects supervisor. There are often personality problems. I never had any with Jerry.

The final screenplay was written in August and delivered in September 1963 by Nigel and Jan.

A UN expedition to the moon discovers a British flag and a letter to one Arnold Bedford, and a team is sent to the village of Dymchurch in England to find out if the paper is genuine. They find Bedford (Edward Judd) and he relates his amazing story. Bedford is attempting to write a play, but during a visit by his fiancée Kate (Martha Hyer), the house of a local eccentric, Cavor (Lionel Jeffries), explodes. Visiting the house, Bedford discovers that Cavor has invented a substance that cuts off the force of gravity and Cavor tells Bedford that he intends to travel to the Moon in a sphere coated with Cavorite, which he has already constructed. Reluctantly Bedford decides to accompany him as a partner in the enterprise and Kate joins the expedition accidentally. Once on the Moon they discover a race of insect-like creatures called Selenites, living beneath the surface. They are shown the wonders of the Selenite civilization, which ends with Cavor having an audience with the Grand Lunar, the leader of the Selenites. Bedford, however, realizes that the Selenites have no intention of letting them leave and, during a struggle with Cavor, accidentally fires a gun at the Grand Lunar. Running for their lives, Bedford and Kate manage to find the sphere and escape, but Cavor elects to stay behind. Returning to the modern day, all that is found by the UN-1 expedition is the decayed and crumbling remains of the Selenite City, presumably destroyed by Cavor's cold.

We could now commence the pre-production problems and the cast could be assembled. Martha Hyer, a beautiful and talented American actress, was chosen to play Kate opposite the equally talented and versatile British actor Edward Judd who would play Bedford. However, it was Lionel Jeffries, a delightful and sublime actor, who stole the picture as the eccentric Cavor. It was as though the role had been written specially for him. Lionel is one of those rare breed of actors who is not only accomplished in his field, but also enjoys what he is doing and has the added bonus of having an imagination. I would show him drawings of the effects scenes and he would know instantly what was required and how it would look, even offering suggestions at the same time.

Along with numerous other tasks, I was also faced with the design basics for a whole alien civilization. Because the Selenites were to be insect-like, I decided that all doors and apertures were to be hexagonal, a common structure in the insect world. Whether it was scientifically accurate was secondary to the consideration that it should look realistic, be practical and above all spectacular. These basics were relatively straightforward, but when it came to broader aspects of the story that included tunnels, lunar landscapes, lens complexes, oxygen machines and the palace of the Grand Lunar, the budget prevented any of them from being built as full sets, so I designed them as mini-atures and incorporated the actors with the aid of travelling mattes. For example, the huge bubbling vats that produced the oxygen were three- or four-foot high miniatures. However, these design headaches were nothing compared to Charles and Columbia Pictures announcing that the film, if possible, should be photographed in widescreen to give it an added attraction.

I argued against its use, knowing there were going to be major complications for the Dynamation sequences. Charles simply reminded me that I'd resisted colour for *The 7th Voyage of Sinbad* and that scope was simply another technical advance audiences expected. In the end I had to give way to the commercial arguments and began redesigning the Dynamation process. I first of all had my rear projector overhauled to accommodate widescreen, and then with the assistance of the Panavision company, who made a special anamorphic lens, I carried out a number of tests. Gradually it became apparent that the process I had employed for previous films could not be used to any great extent for the anamorphic system. The tests revealed that the lenses created a severe 'fall off' of light and definition on the sides of the rear-projected image (which is never normally seen) and there was a fluctuating focus and critical hot spot in the centre of the screen, which had to be constantly corrected. I have no doubt that with time and effort it could have been made to work, but neither of these luxuries were available to me. With the failure to find an inexpensive solution, I was forced to redesign the Dynamation sequences as travelling mattes, which would be animated within miniature sets and added in later. My troubles didn't end there. Because of the widescreen, the yellow backing or sodium vapour process was also out of the question. The widest angle of lens that could be used in a camera at that time was 75mm, which meant that I couldn't use an extreme wide-angle lens like Panavision with the sodium process because of the space for the prism. If I wanted very small people on the screen, I would have had to build an extension tunnel outside the studio door in order to get the camera far enough away to obtain the correct relationship between people and sets.

The solution was to revert to the blue backing process, where we were able to use 25mm or even 18mm lenses. The results were fine but never as good as the yellow sodium process. When the picture was completed, even Charles conceded that 'the extra time we took to do it didn't seem to merit the use of the process'.

Because of the widescreen limitations, many of the animation sequences were lost, and we were only able to retain three major animation sequences: the scientific Selenites, the mooncalf and the Grand Lunar. Among the lost sequences was a scene in which the scientific Selenites are 'put to sleep' and stored for when next they are required. The sequence would have shown them being 'filed away' by a machine that raised each Selenite up to its own hexagonal honeycomb-like chamber. In the final film it was modified into a translucent tube descending over a creature, which when raised left it covered in a cocoon-like web. This was much less spectacular.

Left hand page. The wonderfully talented actor Lionel Jeffries, who played Cavor, resplendent in the Victorian version of a spacesuit. Lionel was able to add style, humour and realism to both his character and the film as a whole.

Top. Separation of capsule. The model mothership and landing module were based on NASA designs for the proposed lunar landing. They were in total about 12 inches long, whilst the module that lands was about 18 inches high.

Right. Three stills of uncredited star Peter Finch. When British performer William Rushton was unable to turn up for the part of the writ server, we unexpectedly secured the services of one of the world's top actors. Lionel persuaded Peter Finch (they had appeared together in *The Trials of Oscar Wilde*), who happened to be shooting *The Pumpkin Eater* on the next stage, to guest in the role. To save time, Lionel wrote out Finch's lines on the back of the summons paper, and he delivered them with enormous enjoyment.

Shepperton Studios was to be used for all the live action photography, but because of the huge number of travelling mattes and miniatures to be produced, I realized I would require assistance. I approached Les Bowie, who had done some work on *Jason and the Argonauts* and previously made his name working on effects for Hammer Film Productions. Charles and I decided that it would be more convenient if I was based in Les' own studio in Slough. Rather interestingly, Les Bowie's estimated total budget for the effects work came to £26,184.25. This included pre-production, experimental work, construction of miniature sets (built by Les' technicians according to my and the art director's drawings) and studio rental. Even for 1963 that was pretty good. If you were trying to find such facilities today, it would be more in the region of $20 million. The schedule for shooting the effects was twenty weeks, during which time I completed the Dynamation in a specially built facility at the rear of the Bowie studio. It wasn't very large, but big enough for me to carry out the small amounts of animation required.

In June 1963 my father began work on the model armatures for the picture. It was to be the last film on which we were to work together, albeit with several thousand miles between us. He passed away soon after. His skill with the armatures, as with all things mechanical, was unique, and I would never again be able to match his talents. He skilfully constructed the extremely complicated mooncalf, the Grand Lunar, eight 9-inch Selenite armatures, six 4.5-inch Selenites and six 4.5-inch soldier Selenites (which were never used). My father was a very talented man and a loving parent. Without his and my mother's encouragement in my formative years, I would never have achieved what I did.

One of the things I am most proud of in the film is the scientific accuracy of the prologue. It must be remembered that it was made before the actual moon landing, and although we knew a great deal about the satellite, we didn't know everything. Much time and research went into the United Nations landing that shows a capsule detaching itself from a 'mothership', which remains in orbit around the moon, and then slowly descends to the surface. The whole sequence was based on information from NASA (with whom Charles had dealt whilst producing the film *I Aim at the Stars*, 1961), who co-operated to such an extent that they gave us blueprints for their proposed Lunar module. Of course, I enhanced their designs to meet the cinematic requirements, but generally the whole sequence reflected what would happen when the actual moon landing occurred some four years later. In fact, whilst the actual event was taking place, the sequence from our film was shown on US television to demonstrate how NASA would be accomplishing the momentous landing.

A full-sized section of authentic moonscape was constructed on a stage at Shepperton, to which we added a full-sized sphere. In addition, Les Bowie's technicians built two miniature spheres; one 8–9 inches in diameter was used for the landing, whilst the other was 24 inches in diameter, providing greater detail and used for the flight shots between the Earth and the Moon. The landing miniature was beautifully made and had little springs inserted in the bumpers which allowed it to bounce across an 8-foot square miniature moonscape. The spectacular effect of the sphere's landing was achieved by throwing the miniature onto the model moonscape whilst it was being photographed at high speed. This delightful task was mine, and I spent several enjoyable hours tossing the sphere across the moonscape from different angles, after which we selected the shots that offered the most realism. As the sphere touched the moonscape, it created plumes of dust that were actually Fullers Earth, a fine powder ideal for simulating moondust.

Both the interior and the exterior of the sphere were designed to match as closely as possible the description given by Wells, although I have to confess that we did have to take some liberties. It was fascinating just how practical the sphere concept was, providing, of course, one could devise a paint that would actually eliminate the force of gravity. In the novel he mentions an inner shell made of glass and an outer one constructed of bolted steel struts, between which the Cavorite-coated blinds operated. We discarded the glass shell as impractical because I wanted everything to look as feasible as possible for a 1960s audience, even if it had been built in Victorian times. However, I never fully believed that the railway

bumpers would keep anyone from breaking their necks when it landed on the moon, but they were a great idea and gave the sphere a wonderfully eccentric look.

The first time we witness the full force of Cavorite is when an explosion occurs in Cavor's house, causing the roof to disintegrate and rush skywards. To accomplish this spectacular introduction to Cavor's ingenious liquid, we built a detailed 6-foot balsa wood model roof, which was constructed in such a way as to break into smaller sections. We then suspended it upside down against a black backdrop. The camera was set to film at high speed so that when it was slowed down, the disintegration of the roof would seem plausible. When all was ready, we dropped a weight (off camera) into the inside of the model roof, which shattered it into sections that fell to the ground off camera. As we also had to account for the interior of the house crashing out through the roof, we dropped separate sections of miniature debris through the hole. In the film laboratory the picture was flipped over in the optical printer so that the sections of miniature roof appear to be rising, not

falling. Finally we matted out the roof on the footage of the real house, and inserted the model roof footage, which matched exactly. We used the same technique for the greenhouse sequence in which the sphere is seen crashing through the glass roof and shooting up into the night sky. The greenhouse model was about 6 feet long, again constructed of balsa wood and real glass, while the surrounding trees and foliage were constructed around it. Then the whole huge miniature was suspended upside down. Several real trees being blown about in the rush of wind were matted into the foreground later to help give the sequence some authenticity. Filming again at high speed, we dropped a specially built sphere (built in proportion to the greenhouse) into the underside of the model, creating the illusion of smashing through the roof and hurtling into space.

Once on the lunar surface, Cavor and Bedford's first realization that there is a moon civilization is the lens aperture that covers an abyss-like shaft into the interior. The lens was a miniature 2½–3 feet in diameter and constructed with sections that slide back which were supposed to allow sunlight into the prism and

shaft below. The shaft itself was a cardboard tube of approximately 24 inches diameter by about 10 feet long, and was shot horizontally against black. The beam of light with its sparkle effect (produced by glitter dropped against the light source) was shot against a black background cloth and optically printed into the shaft.

The first Selenite was designed by Nigel Kneale's brother to match the description in the screenplay of a creature with a hollow chest cavity and great multicoloured 'horsefly' eyes. The effect was very unsettling, and when I came to model the prototype it became obvious that it was too grotesque and we might be in danger of upsetting the censor and losing the younger audience.

As the reader will have realized by now, I have never been keen on using 'men in suits' as animaloid creatures, but several scenes called for masses of smaller 'worker' Selenites, which would have taken an eternity to animate. So we had to resort to using children in suits. I designed a suit made into twenty-five moulded latex costumes with reinforced sections. Although they were never really convincing, mainly because the children's arms were not spindly enough to match the animated Selenites, the low-key lighting allowed Jerry to use the suits with reasonable success.

Because no one on the production was happy with it, I designed a Selenite that was based on an ant. This was more acceptable and so much more believable.

Deep inside the Moon, just prior to the discovery of the mooncalves, the explorers come across a forest of giant mushrooms. Although it is never made clear in the script, these were supposed to be the food source for the mooncalves. In actual fact, they were a leftover (excuse the pun) from earlier scripts. I had always been disappointed that the forest of giant mushrooms had been dropped from *Mysterious Island*, but transposed here, on the moon, it seemed absolutely right to have such fungi growing deep underground.

Left hand page. The sphere being hoisted onto the full size set at Shepperton.

Above top. The descending shaft that allowed sunlight to penetrate the world of the Selenites. This was, in fact, a cardboard tube with Edward Judd matted on top.

Above. The lunar caves. The lunar caves and the angled mirror for directing the sunlight were all miniatures. The tiny figures of Bedford and Cavor were inserted by means of a travelling matte.

Right. Drawing of Selenites. My design for the Selenites, based on ants.

Aside from several scenes with Selenites, the only fully animated sequence in the film is the caterpillar-like mooncalf that attacks Cavor and Bedford. To avoid animating all the legs, I designed the scenes to show only the front portion of its body. The legs had to reflect a wave-like action that you would see in a real caterpillar, and although this gave me some sleepless nights, I achieved it by inserting tiny levers into the model so that one foot would progress forward and I would fasten it down whilst another foot was just about to lift off, and so on. In effect, each leg would be in a different position all down the line. Even though I wasn't animating the whole creature, I found the movement extremely complicated. Until then I had thought the crab in *Mysterious Island* had been bad enough, but this was horrendous. Of course, when I designed it I knew it would be difficult, but I hadn't fully realized just how frustrating it would be. It took me three or four days just to produce the charge past the camera.

Other than fans, most people forget that this film contains one of my best friends – the human skeleton, although in this story it is not an evil adversary. Whilst Martha Hyer is locked in her glass prison, the Selenites observe her through a type of X-ray machine. The screen shows a brief transition from an animated skeleton watched by a Selenite, to the real Martha Hyer as she walks into the left-hand side of the screen. The X-ray area was a matted section of the picture, into which I matched the movements of the skeleton with the actions of Martha Hyer as she stepped out of the X-ray area. Apart from an early experiment with *Baron Munchausen* in which I had animated the Baron talking to the Man in the Moon, and occasionally in the Puppetoons, this was the only time I had animated a model to match with the lines spoken by Martha: 'Let me out of here. Can you hear me?'

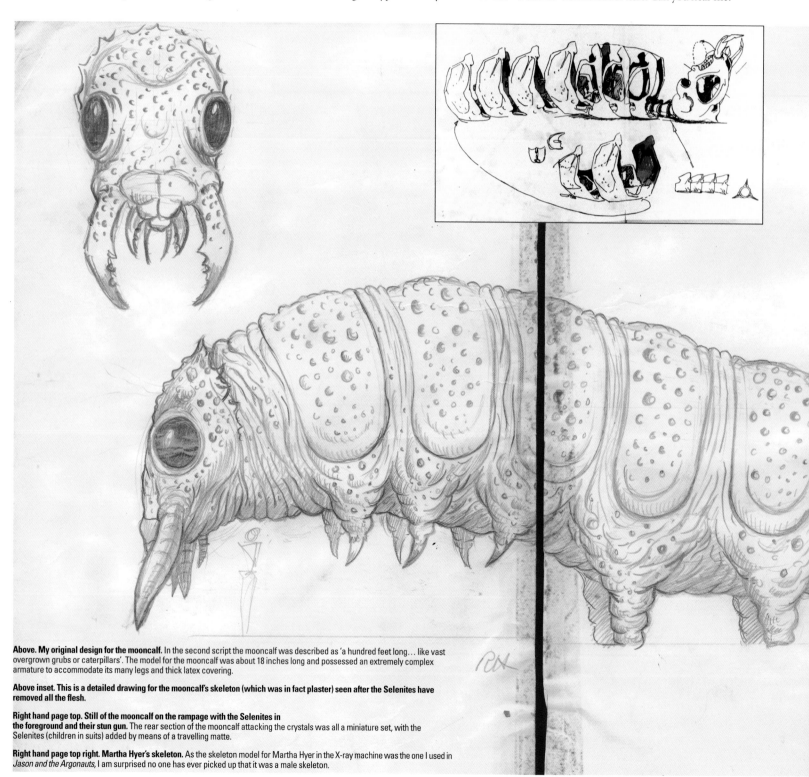

Above. My original design for the mooncalf. In the second script the mooncalf was described as 'a hundred feet long… like vast overgrown grubs or caterpillars'. The model for the mooncalf was about 18 inches long and possessed an extremely complex armature to accommodate its many legs and thick latex covering.

Above inset. This is a detailed drawing for the mooncalf's skeleton (which was in fact plaster) seen after the Selenites have removed all the flesh.

Right hand page top. Still of the mooncalf on the rampage with the Selenites in the foreground and their stun gun. The rear section of the mooncalf attacking the crystals was all a miniature set, with the Selenites (children in suits) added by means of a travelling matte.

Right hand page top right. Martha Hyer's skeleton. As the skeleton model for Martha Hyer in the X-ray machine was the one I used in *Jason and the Argonauts,* I am surprised no one has ever picked up that it was a male skeleton.

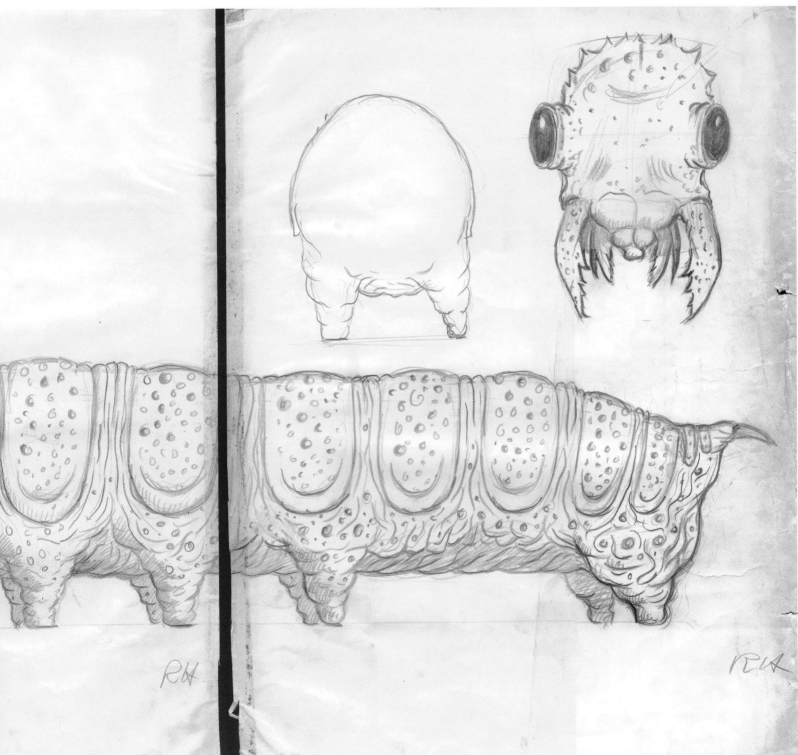

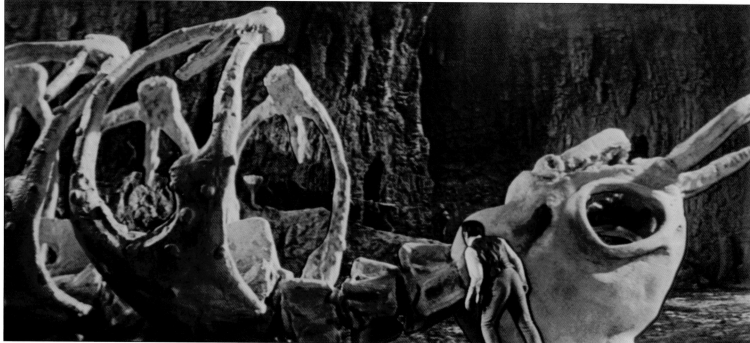

Above Top. Bedford witnesses the slaughter of the mooncalf. Edward Judd was filmed on a set that consisted of two walls separated with a blue screen. He was, in fact, looking at the blue screen. Into the area of the blue screen I placed the action of the worker Selenites killing the mooncalf and then stripping it of its flesh, which in turn was also a matte of the Selenites onto the miniature cave with its model mooncalf.

Above. The mooncalf skeleton after the Selenites had finished with him. Again, Judd was filmed against a blue screen and then added by travelling matte in front of the plaster skeleton of the mooncalf.

Right hand page. Me with my mooncalf. This was a publicity gimmick, although it was never used for any campaign that I am aware of. I remember doing almost the same thing with my allosaurus when I was making *Evolution*.

The climax of the visitors' stay on the moon is Cavor's audience with the Selenites' leader – the Grand Lunar. Cavor ascends to the Lunar palace in the distance, watched by Bedford in the foreground. It was one of the most complex shots in the picture, and was produced by passing the film through the camera no less than four times to establish the various mattes. First we shot the miniature Grand Lunar palace and underground cavern, then Cavor climbing the steps (using a wide-angled lens on a studio section of the staircase), the light beam into the palace, and finally Bedford in the foreground as a travelling matte.

When Cavor reaches the top of the first flight of steps, the palace doors open and we see another flight

Later the whole effect was combined with a miniature set of steps that led to the Grand Lunar himself.

I had always intended the meeting with the Grand Lunar to be a spectacular scene and decided that a huge, almost never-ending staircase would give the scene a grandeur that would only be rivalled by *A Matter of Life and Death* (1946) in the history of film. Actually, it was my recollections of the film *She* (1935), in which Helen Gahagan sits on a throne reached by a steep flight of steps that influenced me. The steps begin in a huge cavern where the entire Selenite Lunar city is laid out below.

of spectacular steps ascending to a shimmering image. The doors were built full-size so that Lionel could be photographed against a blue backing screen.

Arriving at the top of this last flight, Cavor is confronted by the huge shimmering prism-like area, which clears, revealing the sitting figure of the Grand

Left hand page. A section of the original concept storyboards showing Cavor climbing the steps to the Grand Lunar's Palace. With some exceptions, the storyboard is almost the same as seen in the final film.

Above. Two stills from this sequence as seen in the final film. In the top image Cavor can be seen climbing the steps inside the palace. On a set on one of the Shepperton stages, Lionel climbed a short flight of steps. This area was matted into a model of the interior of the palace. The shimmering area at the top was added separately. In the bottom image Lionel Jeffries acts out his lines in front of a blue screen. The Grand Lunar was animated on the miniature set and then matted, along with his shimmering protective field, into an area on a miniature cave set. The protective area was added over the Grand Lunar and the whole thing was matted onto the area behind Lionel that was the blue screen.

The ripple effect was achieved by moving a distortion glass, frame by frame, during the stop-motion process. The glass effect was achieved by having the animation done behind a large ball of glass, which was the residue from a glass factory. Lionel Jeffries was put into the miniature set by the travelling matt process. The scene was then put together in the optical printer at the Rank laboratory. The impressive music by Laurie Johnson helped enormously to give the final effect of the 'grand illusion' as well as the importance of the brain behind the Lunarians.

Lunar with his outsized head. We wanted something unusual and spectacular that would 'protect' the potentially vulnerable Grand Lunar, so I came up with the rippling prism-like effect, intended as a kind of forcefield. For the effect I went to a glass factory and found a large 18-inch thick slab of glass that was the residue left behind in the heating chamber after it had cooled. It was, of course, distorted, and was perfect for the prism I had envisioned. I mounted it onto the animation table in the back of the Grand Lunar model with an extra distortion glass (the same kind I had used in *Earth Vs the Flying Saucers* and *The 7th Voyage of Sinbad* for the forcefield effect) in front of the camera. I then animated the model and the distortion glass, but the block of glass remained static.

This process of animating the distortion glass against the slab of glass created variations of rippling and shimmering light effects. Following this, the whole sequence was matted into an area in the live action set. As he was the Grand Lunar and therefore royalty, we wanted him to be sitting on a throne. However, because of the shape of his body, or carapace, he would be unable to sit down as a human would, so to allow for an elongated body I cut a hole in the model throne into which he would fit. My reasoning was that as the Selenites had two legs, they would have had to sit down and so must have designed chairs to fit their anatomy. I was somewhat concerned about this, as a chair with a hole cut in it might be misinterpreted by some people as meaning something entirely different to an ordinary chair, although nobody seemed to pick this up.

Since *The 7th Voyage of Sinbad*, Bernie had scored all our subsequent pictures, but because he had raised his fees, our production simply couldn't afford his talents. Charles therefore commissioned Laurie Johnson (a friend of Bernie's). I must confess that I missed Bernie's unique interpretation of the visuals, but I believe Laurie delivered a very atmospheric score that suited the picture completely. He was extremely conscientious and visited me whilst I was working on the miniatures to talk about how it was going to look

so he could get a feel for the picture as a whole. Laurie delivered a distinctive score that captured the mood for the fantasy and spectacle as well as the period of the story. In short, it accentuated the dramatic value of the film.

Some of my fondest memories during production were the surprise visits of several personalities. The first was Frank Wells, son of H.G. Sadly, I only met him briefly, but he showed great enthusiasm for the design and animation, and we talked about his father. Another visit was by one of Hollywood's greatest directors, William Wyler. He was shooting a film on another stage, and although he wasn't there very long, I did manage to talk with him, and he seemed intrigued at what we were doing. Furthermore, when British performer William Rushton was unable to turn up for the part of the writ server, we unexpectedly secured the services of one the world's top actors. Lionel persuaded Peter Finch, who happened to be shooting *The Pumpkin Eater* on the next stage, to guest in the role. To save time, Lionel wrote out Finch's lines on the back of the summons paper, which he delivered with enormous enjoyment.

In autumn 1963 Charles sent the British Board of Film Censors the final shooting script for them to read and make comments on if it was considered that anything was unworthy of a U (General) certificate. In his reply to Charles dated 26 September 1963, John Trevelyan, the secretary to the Film Board, made several worrying points. He stated that 'the script would be all right for a "U" category up to Page 86, but that from this point on it is almost certain that your film will give us trouble for the "U" category… we may have to give you an "A" (Parental Guidance) certificate'. Page 86 barely gets the sphere off the ground, but even more worrying was the next comment. 'The trouble is of course that your moon-creatures must be rather spooky and unearthly to be effective, and must create some degree of fear in the audience. If there is more fear than young children can take we must put the film into the "A" category.'

His final comment was, 'we hope that they will not

Above left. Myself and Bowie. Les Bowie (right) and myself working on the miniature palace.

Above right. Myself, Charles and Frank Wells. Frank Wells (right), son of H.G., had taken an enthusiastic interest in the production. He visited whilst we were filming the sequence in which the Selenites were put to 'sleep'.

Right hand page. Poster for *First Men in the Moon*. We were back to Dynamation but the publicity people did manage to get in Lunacolor. To emphasize the fact that it was 'in the Moon', the poster tried to illustrate this by highlighting the 'in' and showing some of the colourful events that take place under the moon's surface. In the end, with all these specifics, the poster was rather childish and to some extent probably accounts for the poor box office.

H.G. WELLS' ASTOUNDING ADVENTURE IN
DYNAMATION!
COLUMBIA PICTURES
presents a
CHARLES H.
SCHNEER
production
H.G. WELLS'
FIRST MEN IN THE MOON
IN PANAVISION AND LUNACOLOR!
starring
EDWARD JUDD · MARTHA HYER and LIONEL JEFFRIES · Screenplay by NIGEL KNEALE and JAN READ
Associate Producer RAY HARRYHAUSEN · Directed by NATHAN JURAN · AN AMERAN

look nearly as bad as our old friend the Cyclops, which gave both you and me a lot of trouble'. Because the project had been designed as a family film, these negative comments did not bode well. Of course, Trevelyan had not seen the designs and was unaware that we had endeavoured not to make them gruesome. By today's standards they are positively insipid. In the end, when the completed film was shown to the Board there was not a problem and it received the hoped-for 'U'. The incident illustrates what problems we faced with the British censor at that time, problems hardly imagined by today's film-makers.

The film opened to generally good reviews. *Variety* said, 'Ray Harryhausen and his special effects men have had another high old time in Charles H. Schneer's Panavision, Technicolor piece of science-fiction hokum filmed in Dynamation. Family audiences should flock to the wickets. It is an astute blend of comedy, occasional thrills and special effects work. Film is a good example of the kind of fare that television cannot hope to match in the foreseeable future.' It goes on, 'Take it as you like – as an out-and-out schoolboy adventure, or as a springboard for another, more serious probe of potential Earth-Moon relationships – Schneer's production still stands up as a healthy prospect.'

On 16 October 1964 the *Hollywood Reporter* commented '"First Men in the Moon" is probably the first space fantasy comedy', which is a great compliment. It continues, 'the Charles H. Schneer film works up some fierce action in the closing passages, with the customarily excellent special effects by Ray Harryhausen'.

It was released with another of Charles' pictures, *East of Sudan*, and Columbia mounted a massive publicity campaign, part of which included Charles and I travelling all over Europe and America to promote the film. Given the reviews and campaign, *First Men in the Moon* didn't do well at the box office, either in the States or in Europe. The poster Columbia came up with really didn't help to sell it. It was too childish in its attempts to point out that it was 'in' the Moon, not 'on'. Personally, I believe it is one of the most faithful adaptations of Wells' novels, but perhaps the time was not right for such a film, or perhaps the real moon landings were too close. Hopefully, posterity will look upon it with kinder eyes.

Over the previous three or four years I had made three very different kinds of movie, but now I was about to return to a subject with which I was more than familiar: dinosaurs. Although I didn't know it at the time, the remainder of the 1960s was to be taken up with breathing life once again into prehistoric creatures.

CHAPTER 8 DINOSAURS, DINOSAURS, EVERYWHERE DINOSAURS

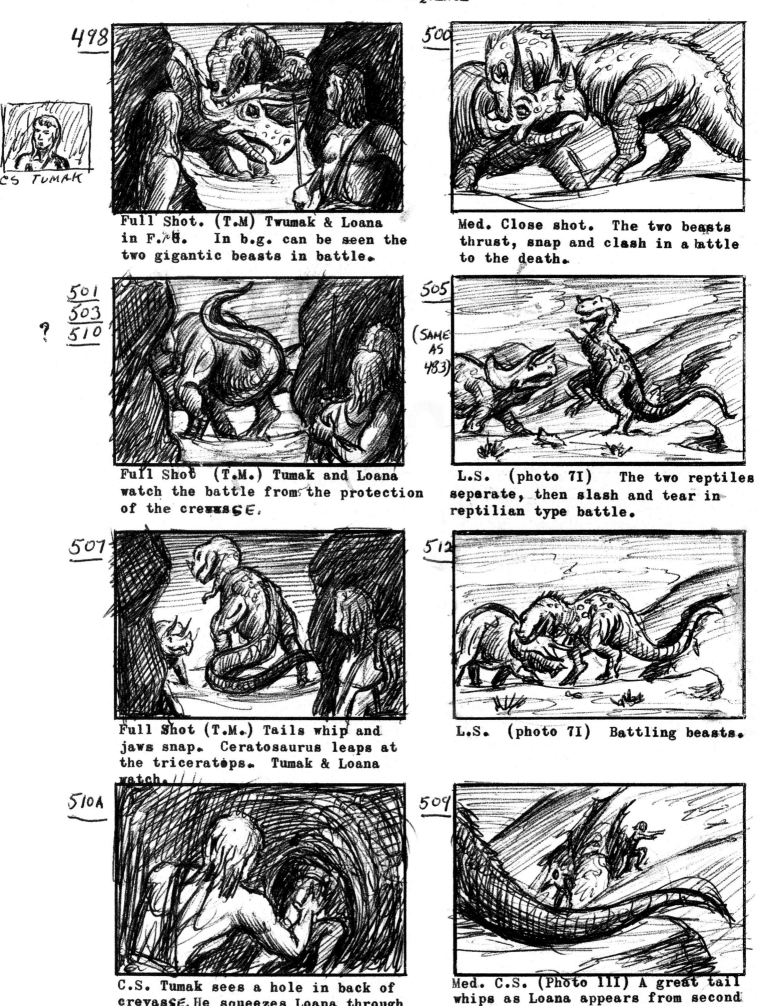

CS TUMAK

498 — Full Shot. (T.M) Twumak & Loana in F.G. In b.g. can be seen the two gigantic beasts in battle.

500 — Med. Close shot. The two beasts thrust, snap and clash in a battle to the death.

501
503
510

Full Shot (T.M.) Tumak and Loana watch the battle from the protection of the crevasse.

505 (SAME AS 483) — L.S. (photo 71) The two reptiles separate, then slash and tear in reptilian type battle.

507 — Full Shot (T.M.) Tails whip and jaws snap. Ceratosaurus leaps at the triceratops. Tumak & Loana watch.

512 — L.S. (photo 71) Battling beasts.

510A — C.S. Tumak sees a hole in back of crevasse. He squeezes Loana through it but it fills with sand before he CAN GET THROUGH.

509 — Med. C.S. (Photo 111) A great tail whips as Loana appears from second crack and runs out right. Tumak cannot ESCAPE BECAUSE OF LASHING TAIL.

One Million Years BC
The Valley of Gwangi

The most popular exhibits in any natural history museum are, without doubt, the dinosaurs. These creatures' popularity grows each year, partly because of the recent resurgence of dinosaur movies, but also because a skeleton of a full-sized tyrannosaurus rex still has the ability, even 65 million years after its death, to chill us to the bone.

For me, these enigmatic creatures have proved an enormous asset over the years. They have been the tools by which I learned my trade and which led to my career in feature films. However, although my name is synonymous with dinosaurs, it wasn't until the last half of the 1960s that I was finally able to realize my ambitions of bringing them to the screen. It was an opportunity to return to my pets and the reason why I had begun stop-motion model animation.

In the UK, Hammer Film Productions had expanded throughout the late 1950s and early 1960s with the success of its gothic horror subjects under the watchful eye of James Carreras (known as 'The Colonel'). However, his son Michael Carreras wanted to redirect the company into new areas, so he began searching for suitable projects to produce alongside their more traditional fare. He became intrigued with the idea of making a dinosaur/monster picture because he felt the time was right for a regeneration of the genre. The idea led him to a 1940 film, *One Million BC* (UK title: *Man And His Mate*), a poor attempt at fantasy adventure that saw cavemen surviving in a world of dinosaurs.

Realizing that the premise of *One Million BC* was sound and that it contained previously untapped commercial potential in the form of dinosaurs and sex, Michael secured the rights to re-make it. To give him credit, he was determined that the dinosaurs should look as real as the humans. He was aware of my work and knew that I lived in England, so he and producer Anthony Hinds viewed a number of my films, including the early monster-on-the-rampage subjects, and offered me the job of creating the set-piece dinosaurs for the project. I had not seen the 1940 film for many years and was dubious about the possibilities of making it into a respectably good film. However, I decided to see what Hammer planned to

do with it. Watching a print of it, I began to see the possibilities of updating the simple story of cavemen and dinosaurs. Although the film leaves a lot to be desired, I realized, with satisfaction, it could be improved upon, particularly in the visual impressions of the dinosaurs. One sequence, comical though it was, in particular seemed to contain potential: a flesh-eating creature (in the original script it is named as a tyrannosaurus) attacks the Shell people's camp. It was actually a man dressed in a dinosaur suit. The director must have realized that the rubber costume was obvious, so he photographed the scene with the creature behind bushes and trees in a feeble attempt to disguise it. With stop-motion animation, and the right budget, I could create dinosaurs to look as good as any caveman, hopefully better. I have always been reluctant to involve myself with anything that resembled a re-make, but when I looked at the technical possibilities this project offered, along with the opportunity to enlarge and enhance my interest in dinosaurs, I knew I couldn't say no. In any event, I decided to take the project and was duly loaned from Morningside Productions to Hammer for the duration.

Whilst I went off to devise new creatures and new situations for the key scenes, Michael began constructing a usable screenplay based on the original. Gradually the ideas came together from both sides. At the very early planning stages I made pre-production drawings of three main sequences in the film: the allosaurus raiding the village, a pteranodon sequence and a brontosaurus sequence. These, together with other sketches, helped Michael to visualize the story and gradually construct the screenplay.

Michael and Anthony Hinds realized very early on that the project would require a good director and cameraman, not only because it relied heavily on special effects, but because it had to look like a classy production rather than a cheap B-feature. I had no hesitation in suggesting Wilkie Cooper as cameraman and either Don Chaffey or Jerry Juran for director. Wilkie was contracted straight away, and as Don was based in Britain and had directed several Hollywood productions, he was chosen to direct. American actress Raquel Welch, who was then relatively

Above. A brontosaurus being attacked by villagers. This never appeared in the final film, as Michael Carreras decided that the sequence wasn't necessary. He did, however, briefly appear disappearing behind a hill when Tumak is trekking through the desert landscape.

Left. Raquel Welch as Loana. Although Michael had flown in professional photographers to take publicity stills, with an emphasis on getting the right Raquel Welch shot, in the end the one that everyone remembers was shot by our local unit photographer. I should think that this picture created more publicity for the film than any other still picture in the history of motion pictures.

unknown, was cast as the heroine Loana, and British actor John Richardson was cast as the hero Tumak. People often ask me how I got along with Miss Welch. Actually, I had very little contact with her, but when I did, I found her a very likeable person who took her acting and the film very seriously. In recent years she seems to have dismissed the film, which is sad because she was at her most beautiful in it and for my money succeeded in making the difficult role of Loana into a believable character.

In the original 1940 film the introduction is set in the 20th century and shows two lost travellers (Victor Mature and Carole Landis) stumbling into a cave during a fierce storm, where an archaeologist (Conrad Nagel) shows them primitive drawings. He tells the two about the prehistoric events that took place a million years previously. Although an interesting premise, it was decided that this was a cumbersome opening, and so we settled on the more straightforward and scientific idea of illustrating the violent forming of the Earth. The story continues:

Tumak (John Richardson), a member of the aggressive Rock people, is banished from the tribe and journeys across a harsh and uncompromising landscape, encountering a giant lizard, a spider and a brontosaurus, before reaching the sea and collapsing on a beach. Living nearby are the gentle Shell people who rescue him from being crushed by an archelon, following which the beautiful Loana (Raquel Welch) helps him to recover. One day an allosaurus invades the Shell people's camp and it is Tumak who manages to kill the beast. Although the tribe are grateful, Tumak is banished again after he forceably takes a spear. Accompanied by Loana he makes his way back to his own tribe, but on the way they witness a terrible fight between a triceratops and a ceratosaurus and become separated. Eventually they are reunited and once they reach the Rock people, Tumak and Loana try to educate them about farming. One day Loana is carried off by a pteranodon and during a fight between two of the flying creatures she is dropped into the sea. Although Tumak believes Loana has been killed, she manages to make her way back to her own people and, after a nearby volcano erupts, wiping out most of them in a terrifying upheaval, the two tribes unite.

During pre-production Michael considered shooting the entire film in Iceland, but then we heard about Lanzarote, one of the Spanish Canary Islands in the Atlantic, which at that time were relatively unknown by the film business and tourists. Michael came back from his investigation very enthusiastic, so in mid-July 1965 Michael, Don Chaffey and myself flew out to recce the islands. As soon as we saw the desolate volcanic landscapes, we knew we had found the perfect backdrop for the production. During the nine days we were there I took countless photographs of possible effects locations, and back in London I collated them into a location storyboard, sketching in some of the animation action (as I had done with *Earth Vs the Flying Saucers*) to illustrate how the sequences would look against the actual locations. To enable us to plan the action, almost everything was based on these recce photographs, allowing Michael, Don and Wilkie to relate to the scenic background in advance. The action had to fit the scenery in the broad sense, although there would always be changes once on location.

Just before the live-action shoot, Michael, Don, Wilkie, Bob Jones (the art director) and myself made another trip to the islands to finalize locations and arrangements. We nearly had a disastrous accident when walking over a lava field. Suddenly Don began to sink into the ground between Bob Jones and myself. He had stepped onto the thin crust of an underground lava tunnel that had given way under his weight. He sank up to his waist before we were able to grab his arms and save him. God knows what drop there was below – none of us wanted to look.

On 17 October 1965 the first and second units flew to Las Palmas. Accompanying me were Diana, our 18-month-old daughter Vanessa and her nanny. Lanzarote was the main action location, but the sand dunes were photographed on Grand Canary (the main island) and the remainder on Tenerife. The film has occasionally attracted adverse comments that we should have used Mesozoic type (fertile) landscape, but the only 'odd one out' would have been the brontosaurus, a known swamp dweller, and that only appears briefly. Unless one is making a scholarly documentary, these 'questionable' facts are secondary

to the making of a good adventure film. I always felt that the other dinosaurs looked quite at home in the barren, jagged landscape with its great curtains of mist and cloud running down the mountains. We were extremely lucky with those wonderful streams of clouds. Whilst travelling to a location early one morning we noticed them, whereupon Wilkie shouted, 'Quick, set up the camera, let's get this.' Also, the deep lava flows and irregular crevasses made ideal settings for the final eruption/earthquake at the end of the picture. Of course, the extinct volcano cones had to be doctored with smoke and steam, but the look was all there on tap. A movie set that had taken millions of years to create!

During the four-week shoot I spent all my time making final adjustments for the effects scenes, trying to stay just ahead of the live-action photography. I spent as much time as possible with the actors, showing them, with the use of the storyboards, what was required. Sometimes I would climb into a truck and lean out the back shouting instructions to the cast about how the creature would move and in what spot it would be at a certain moment. Raquel Welch was excellent at eyeline and continually striving to instil motivation into her character, although with just grunts it was difficult. One day, during a particularly arduous shoot and after a long conversation about her reactions and character with Don, I overheard him say to Raquel, 'That's very interesting, but I'd like you just to start at Rock A over there and go to Rock B, and look back and smile.' Whatever her feelings about the film, she was striking in the part, and it is still the film most people remember of her long and successful career.

After the completion of the shoot, the production returned to England to the ABPC Elstree Studios at Borehamwood. Here the remainder of the live-action shots were to be filmed, including the cave sequences, the Sea people's camp and all the blue-screen matte shots. During my absence, the models I had designed were being completed. For me, the anatomy of the dinosaurs had to be as near accurate in the light of what was known about them at that time. Palaeontologists always seem to be fine-tuning their vision of dinosaurs, and what seemed right in 1965 may not seem as accurate today. I did a great deal of detailed research at various museums in order to attain as much authenticity as

Left. The skeleton of a dinosaur. Again during Tumak's trek through the desert, he encounters this apparently huge skeleton of a dinosaur. Here it is seen in the foreground on a hill of sand, which was set up in front of the rear projection screen.

possible, even though some of the reptiles that are seen together in the film may not have lived in the same prehistoric period. To save some time I commissioned sculptor Arthur Hayward, who had an excellent knowledge of prehistoric animals, to carry out the task of modelling the clay and making the plaster moulds. When I returned from the location photography, I made the authentic animation models myself, carefully planning them and adding the teeth and eyes. Once they were complete, I was ready to begin the arduous task of animation in an old scene dock area way at the back of Elstree Studios near the tank, which was roped off and partitioned with a canvas screen to allow me some (limited) privacy. I spent very nearly a year working in that cramped area. In all, the animation took eight months, from 6 December 1965 to 29 July 1966. Whilst I was busy at Elstree, Les Bowie was working in his Slough studio on the pre-title sequence, for which he designed explosions and effects that were then intercut with stock footage of the sea and the sky.

In one of the early screenplays (dated July 1965) a woolly mammoth is the first creature Tumak encounters, but it was discarded because we would have had to use a real elephant dressed up in heavy furs on location, and it was felt that this rather passive creature wasn't quite spectacular enough for the very first creature the audience sees. In the end we opted for a compromise, which was to use photographically enlarged live animals, as the original 1940 film had. Apparently, Hal Roach used lizards and crocodiles with fins glued to their backs that were then photographed at high speed and rear projected behind the actors.

In our version we used two live creatures: an iguana and a large hairy spider. People always ask me about these two un-Harryhausen creatures, and I must confess the idea was mine. At the time I felt that by using real creatures we might convince the viewers that all of what they were about to see was indeed real. If we established the live action first, people wouldn't feel so critical about the dinosaurs. On reflection, it was an irrational mistake, if only because everyone picks up the fact that there I was trying to get a real lizard to do tricks. Another crucial factor was time. Using these creatures would save on animation, but in the end we shot more footage. Lizards are very lethargic and will fall asleep at the earliest opportunity, especially under the heat of the lights. Often it would only be possible to extract an occasional blink from them, let alone make them look ferocious. In the end we resorted, with the assistance of the animal trainer, to provoking them into action by prodding them.

After Tumak is exiled from his tribe, he wanders aimlessly through the forbidding landscape and encounters a huge skeleton of a dead dinosaur. This supposedly massive skeleton was actually only about 12 inches in length, made of plaster and shot against blue backing, then matted into the foreground. The skeleton was to keep the audience in anticipation of further encounters, and indeed it isn't long before we

We 'auditioned' many breeds before settling on a type of iguana that needed no additional fins or appendages. The size was also important. Many more interesting creatures had to be discarded because they were simply too small, and when they did eventually move, moved much too quickly for the camera. High-speed photography does slow them down, but there is a limit. In the end we used three identical iguanas, so if one went to sleep, we could film another. I relied on a reptile trainer to occasionally manipulate them by holding them by the tail, just outside camera range, encouraging them to move when they were reluctant to do so. There is a sequence when John Richardson is caught by the creature's tongue and the lizard is seen to be looking down at him. We tried for hours to get the wretched animal to look down but it refused to co-operate, so in the end the trainer had to grab its chin and hold its head down. I was extremely careful to not allow any cruelty to the animals, although I was told that the usual method of obtaining movement from these poor creatures is electric shock. Under no circumstances would I allow that. All things considered, I think the sequence worked well. Even the full-sized prop of the creature's massive tongue works convincingly. However, after this experience I can honestly say that using animated models is far more cost-effective and realistic than live animals. Not only is there more control of the action, but the physiognomy of the beast, if it's a dinosaur, can be more accurate and believable.

The second live creature, a tarantula, is only seen momentarily in silhouette, thank goodness, but even so, I have never been happy with the sequence. I originally wanted it cut from the film but was overruled by Michael who thought it effective. Like the iguanas, we employed three spiders because they were also prone to nod off under lights, although in their case the trainer had to tempt them with grasshoppers to get any movement. Again, it was something with which I was not completely happy. In an early screenplay there was also a sequence where Tumak encounters scorpions, for which we would have used photographically enlarged live scorpions. Like the mammoth, they were dropped at an early stage when we realized that two live species would be sufficient. In retrospect, I think the scorpions would have worked a lot better than the spider.

Top left. Still of iguana.
In all we shot 3000–4000 feet of film at high speed of the iguana, just to gain a few feet of usable screen footage. He was combined with John Richardson by means of a travelling matte.

Left and above. The archelon. The archelon model was the usual metal armature and latex, but possessed a shell made of fibreglass, and although the remains of these sea turtles show that they grew up to 12 feet long, mine was much bigger. Screen actors are always glamorized, so why shouldn't I glamorize my creatures?

Right hand page. The tribe attacking the archelon. Once again I created this shot to emphasize size, and similar scenes appear in many of my films all for the same purpose. I used a travelling matte with the actors looking up on the blue screen set and the creature baring down on them added in the optical printer.

see the first Dynamation sequence, signalled by Tumak coming across huge footprints. In the distance a brontosaurus is seen strolling through the harsh countryside. The sequence is short (originally it was to have been longer) but is a foretaste of the next encounter. When Tumak collapses on the beach, he is found by Loana. Whilst she fusses over this handsome young man who has stumbled out of the desert, from over the top of a sand dune appears an archelon, or giant prehistoric turtle. The archelon had never been used in a picture before, and it introduces the audience to the Shell people. It was never intended to be threatening, and the men of the tribe only attack it to deflect it from its course towards the unconscious Tumak. All it wanted was to reach the sea, and we were careful not to kill it, as our intention was to save the more terrifying carnivorous beast until later. Diana has always main-tained that I am cruel to my creatures because I usually devise sticky ends for them, but in the case of the huge but gentle archelon, I resisted the temptation.

In their attempt to turn the creature from its course, the men of the tribe hurl spears and rocks that bounce off its shell and hide. The spears and stones were real, until, that is, they touch the archelon. At a specific point I changed them with miniature copies (the stones were actually tiny bits of cork) suspended on wires and animated to bounce off the model. Meanwhile, the real spears and stones had fallen behind the model on the rear projection screen. Overall I am pleased with the scene, although there is one mistake (thankfully not mine) that continues to irritate me. When the creature appears, one of the actors shouts 'archelon', but of course the word wouldn't have been invented until palaeontology came along.

Following the passiveness of the archelon, there is a short respite until the 'raid' on the Shell people's village by the allosaurus. This sequence closely followed that in the original film. However, I did expand it with a combination of shots that helped build the sequence to its climax. I made him a juvenile allosaurus, which meant that he could terrorize and kill but not wipe out the village. Originally I had wanted to use a real location for the sequence, and in an early story synopsis the sequence is described as taking place in 'a swamp area'. I believe this would have enhanced the credibility of the sequence, but for some reason, before we began location shooting, it was decided to film the scene back at the studio.

To introduce the creature into the sequence, I thought about using one of my old friends, the phororhacus – the chicken-like bird in *Mysterious Island*. The idea was to have the bird escape from a corral kept by the Shell tribe, and when Tumak and Loana run after it, the unfortunate creature is pounced on by the allosaurus. While I didn't like the idea of wasting the allosaurus on simply killing the phororhacus and then disappearing until later, I did want it to have a more dynamic entrance.

As the allosaurus strides into the camp, we see it pick up a member of the tribe in its mouth. The real actor was raised on a wire and then I animated the model to correspond with the actor's movements on the rear projection plate. The process of co-ordinating a live actor with a model is more difficult than it looks because the frames, and therefore the timing, have to be carefully worked out so that the model corresponds exactly with the real movements of the man. To allow the creature to kill the man, I used a cut-away shot, after which I replaced the live actor with a model man that the creature then proceeds to place on the ground to devour. To create more movement in the

sequence I used several tracking shots showing the creature moving from left to right across the screen whilst snapping down at John Richardson who is backing away. I repeated this action later when it is seen attacking a group of cavemen. Even though I try to use different approaches to attain movement in the camera, the budget doesn't usually allow for the time involved. However, in this case the shots were not complicated because the ground wasn't shown, allowing me a little self-indulgence. Most of the action takes place on the set when John Richardson and the other men were shot backing away across the camera. On the animation table I positioned the model of the allosaurus so that it matched the eye-line, and then proceeded to animate it to seem as though it is walking but at the same time reacting to the actors' movements. This makes it sound easy, but to achieve a smoothness in the model's actions, the frames on the rear projection plate had to be counted so that the model's movements arrived at the correct point when the spear is pushed at it. To save some time in matching live-action move-ments with the models, I sometimes photograph the creature in close-up, with no men except a spear moving in and out at the edge of the frame. The spear is a miniature on a support, animated at the same time as the creature. These shots were then used as cut-aways with shots of the men threatening the dinosaur with spears. An animator has to be many things, but perhaps most importantly he should have the eye of a film editor. By using low cost shots with the full action it helps to break the sequences and keeps the action going.

During the fight, Tumak and a few other men find themselves beneath a crude shelter made of wooden supports and foliage. In an attempt to get at the men the allosaurus snaps at the roof, taking part of it away with its mouth. How was it that a model could

dismantle something real? The real shelter was built full size in the studio but rigged to collapse at a certain point during the action. In my animation studio, many months later, I constructed a miniature section of the roof that matched exactly with the section of the real roof. I then suspended the section on piano wires (painted to match in with the background) and situated it in front of the rear-projected shelter, nearest the dinosaur, so that it appeared to be part of the shelter. It is this miniature section that the creature grabs with its mouth and pulls away, and as the model makes contact with the miniature, I then took away the wires to allow the model to hold the section on its own. Meanwhile, in the rear projection plate the real shelter collapses, making it seem as though the whole thing has been caused by the allosaurus.

Also during the fight the men throw several spears that appear to pierce the creature's skin. This 'contact' was achieved by the same method I have described for the archelon. The best example of this in the allosaurus sequence is just before the creature's demise, when one man is pushing the creature back with his spear and then throws it so that it lodges in the creature's neck. The allosaurus reacts by pulling it out with its front claws.

The climax sees the allosaurus impaled by Tumak on a wooden pole. The first shot was a travelling matte in which we see Tumak on the ground in the foreground with the pole pointed at the creature as it advances towards the camera. We then cut to a medium shot of John Richardson lying on the ground holding the pole with the suspended allosaurus staked on the end. For this we had John on the studio floor with nothing in his hand, just going through the actions of holding a pole upright. In the animation studio I placed a miniature pole in front of John on the rear projection

plate so that it appeared to be in his hands. The arm seen on the visible side of the pole is a tiny arm armature that I had taken off another human model. I then suspended the allosaurus on wires on top of the miniature pole, counted the correct number of frames for its sweep over John Richardson's head and then animated it in an arc on the end of the miniature pole.

The entire fight sequence demanded the constant movement of the creature. Even when he appears to be standing still, he takes short steps forwards or backwards, or side to side, like a boxer in the ring. His tail is forever whipping the air, counterbalancing the weight of the body, and the head is always glancing from side to side, aware of its surroundings and at the same time controlling the body in a sequence of movements – ducking, snarling, pulling back, lunging and recoiling. All were integrated into a smooth, life-like flow of action, and because of this, the sequence is one of which I am very proud. Although studio based, it offers one of the most exciting scenes in the movie.

Now exiled from the Shell people's camp and having nowhere else to go, Tumak and Loana trek back to the Rock people. Along the way they witness a battle to the death between a triceratops and a ceratosaurus whilst trapped in a narrow rock cleft. We shot most of the scene on location, except the shots of Tumak and Loana looking out of the crevice at the fight, which were done back at Elstree against the blue backing screen. The triceratops/ceratosaurus fight is another of my favourite sequences in the film. Although the time taken to plan and choreograph such a fight can take weeks, the end result can be exciting and extremely satisfying. Of course, we don't really know how such huge creatures would have fought, as scientific opinion on their physical makeup is altering all the time, but that allows my imagination

free range, with some inspiration from contemporary flesh-eaters such as lizards and alligators. I also realized when I began animation that dinosaurs must always be kept moving, otherwise they can attain a stance that is cinematically dull. Like the allosaurus, there should always be constant movement in the tails, necks, heads and feet. The tail is my favourite and one of the reasons I enjoy animating the large carnivorous dinosaurs. They have such wonderfully long tails with which to counterbalance their huge bodies.

The next major sequence was the appearance of the flying pteranodon. I wanted a background that would allow the pteranodon model to stand out, and spent some time looking for the right location. Just when I thought I wasn't going to find one and we would have to shoot against a desert location, we came across a volcanic pool of deep green water in Lanzarote. It was perfect. The water would act as a place for the tribe to bathe or fish in, and the pool had a spectacular rock background against which the model pteranodon would stand out. The actors certainly didn't complain about the location: during the live action photography, it was so hot that the actors were grateful for the opportunity to swim, even though nobody knew how deep the pool was.

The sequence called for Miss Welch to be picked up by the pteranodon, but we didn't want to risk using a large crane on location, so I had to substitute, or 'convert', the real Raquel into a tiny miniature that could be held in the creature's claws. During the attack the pteranodon singles her out as a tasty morsel, and as it swoops down, she falls behind a rock, following which the claws of the creature reach down behind the rock and pick her up. Of course, the real Raquel was still in a hole obscured by the rock, while on the animation table I had replaced her with a detailed

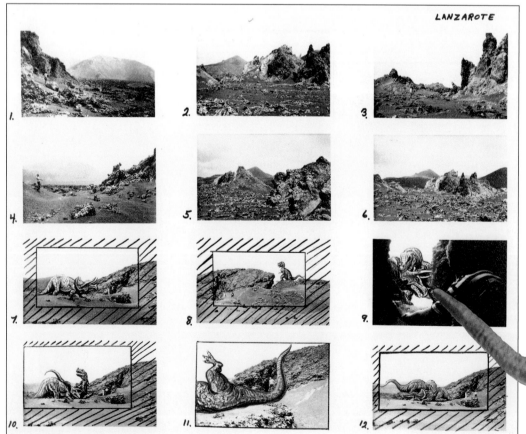

LANZAROTE

Left. Photographic storyboards showing location of fight. On a recce in Lanzarote I spotted this location where the rock formation and the cleft in the rocks were perfect for the battle of the dinosaurs. To save time and to show how the scene would work and be cut together, I made up this photographic storyboard, sketching the action that would appear in the scene over some of the shots.

Above. Ceratosaurus and triceratops fight scene. In the original 1940 film a lizard and a baby alligator, rather than a ceratosaurus and a triceratops, were used for the fight, and the humans were trapped in a crack in the ground whilst the creatures rolled over them. Here the ceratosaurus is leaping onto the triceratops back to attack its neck. The model of the ceratosaurus was suspended on an aerial wire during the process of the stop-frame animation of the leap. In the end the poor old ceratosaurus loses out to the horns of the triceratops.

miniature. Simple but effective, and it saved a great deal of money. To simulate the down draft created by the wings of such a flying reptile, we used a wind machine to disturb the water and dust at the edge of the pool. It is these little touches of detail on location that help make the sequence more acceptable. It demonstrates how an animator has to pre-plan long before the live action is begun. It would have been no use me deciding that a wind machine was required once we were on location. I simply wouldn't have got one. Another example of pre-planning was seen when the creature flies off with the poor lady in its claws. Aside from the wing movements and the wild kicking of the Raquel model, they both remained stationary in front of the back projection plate. The panning movement was actually in the projection plate, which I had carefully planned with Wilkie on location.

Carrying the poor woman to its nest on a tower of rock near the sea, she almost becomes dinner for two hungry baby pteranodons. The nest was a miniature mounted by means of a matte on top of a real rock shot on location and projected as a rear projection plate. I mounted the nest with its two chicks at a certain height and then matted the whole thing into the shot. The matte line cut off the top of the actual pointed rock. Another flying reptile, the pteradactyl (both are of the pteradactyl family), attacks the first, forcing it to drop Loana into the sea. For her fall we simply released the claws and she fell onto a mattress below, followed on screen by a long shot of her falling into the sea, which was the small model animated on wires.

In a very early outline dated 21 May 1965 the climax to the film was to have shown a brontosaurus attacking the cave of the Shell people, changed later to the Rock people, which is then followed by a cataclysmic earthquake.

The brontosaurus was to have been killed by Tumak and other members of the tribe, who force it onto a rock bridge that disintegrates under the weight, sending the poor creature plummeting into a cauldron of lava. It has to be said that brontosaurus were not carnivores (although in *King Kong* one does attack the ship's crew and eats a sailor), but it was thought that the creature would make a good visual opponent, especially as his long neck could reach deep into the cave. Some scenes of the fight with the brontosaurus (for the rear projection plates) were photographed, but at some point Michael decided that the picture had too many animation sequences and that it was going to be far too long. Something had to go, and it would be the poor old brontosaurus. To compensate for this, Michael rewrote the ending whilst we were on location, changing it to a fight

I must confess I wasn't looking forward to beginning the pteranodon sequence for a number of reasons. Animating flying creatures requires an enormous amount of preparation as well as a complex system of overhead wires. Aerial brace animation can take twice as long as a model with its feet planted on the ground, so I have never really enjoyed it. As with the conventional land-bound models, all parts of the creature's anatomy had to be animated – wings, head, body and in this case the addition of a small model of Miss Welch. The fact that everything is suspended on wires simply doubles the headaches. One rarely uses one wire, usually three or four, so the model is relatively firm, although there is always some movement after you have taken your fingers away, so you have to wait whilst it stops before you can shoot the next frame. It may only be seconds but it does take extra time. Sometimes I took advantage of the movement to avoid a strobing effect with the wings. Strobing sometimes occurs when you shoot a fast moving object. When a real person is filmed, the arms or legs, if they are moving quickly, are blurred in each frame, but when I shoot a model wing it is shot frame by frame and therefore not blurred. This lack of blurring can cause strobing. To avoid this I sometimes go to great lengths to move the model, and in the case of the flying reptiles, I used two methods of correction. I would hit the model very slightly just before I shot the frame, which had the effect of blurring it. However, this could also get out of hand. Sometimes I would hit it just too hard and end up with one big blur. The alternative was to use a little Vaseline gel on a glass set in front of the animation camera.

Top. Me animating the pteranodon in flight. I can be seen in front of the rear projection screen with the image of the sea and coast. The model pteranodon is suspended by aerial wires.

Above left. Allosaurus model. In reality the allosaurus was an enormous carnosaur that grew up to 39 feet long, but for once I decided not to think too big, because if I had, it would have destroyed everything and the men of the tribe would have been unable to offer any resistance.

Above. The allosaurus being attacked by various members of the tribe brandishing spears. For the fight the spear was an important example of 'contact'. As the spear in the rear-projected spear image 'touches' the model, it was replaced with a miniature one.

Right. The allosaurus picking up a man from the water. The real actor was suspended on wires in the studio and filmed writhing in agony. In the animation studio I matched the actor's actions with the mouth of the model allosaurus. In later scenes the real actor was replaced with a model.

between the two tribes that is interrupted by the commencement of the volcanic eruption. Now, of course, we had a brontosaurus but no scenes for him. In the end we used the brontosaurus at the beginning when Tumak watches it disappear behind a hill. Nothing is ever wasted on a Hammer film, and the live-action plates shot on location were used for publicity, with the brontosaurus added. I regret that the sequence was never completed, especially as the shape of the brontosaurus, with its long neck and tail, lends itself so perfectly to animation and provides the potential for so many exciting movements. Another creature dropped at the early planning stage was a sequence that included an arsinoitherium (a rhinoceros-like creature). To my knowledge no one had ever animated such a creature apart from tests for Obie's unrealized project *Creation*. Unfortunately, it was not seen as being prehistoric enough, but such a charging creature would have added an excellent action scene.

The chosen climax to the film required the eruption of a volcano heralding the destructive earthquake. As there were no smoking volcanoes in the Canary Islands, we had to construct our own 6–7-foot high volcano in the studio. The eruption explosions and lava flows (composed of a mixture of wallpaper paste, oatmeal, dry ice and red dye) were photographed at high speed, but in the long shots the smoke was added (as we had done for *Mysterious Island*) by simply shooting smoke at a distance against black and then double printing it into the shot. The cracks opening in the ground were achieved with miniatures and travelling mattes. The actors performed in front of a blue backing screen, combined with five or six miniature backgrounds. These blue backing shots were the last of the live-action shooting, and during the set-ups I foolishly rushed out without a coat into the cold from the heat of the studio and consequently caught pneumonia, losing me over a week during which time I was confined to my bed.

One Million Years BC was not only the 100th Hammer production (if you can believe the publicity), but also one of their most expensive, coming in at about £500,000. It was, however, to go on to be one of the most successful pictures of that year, even though it received predictably mixed, if not cautious, reviews on both sides of the Atlantic. Nobody was sure whether to go for the effects or Miss Welch. In *Variety* on 26 December 1966 the lead says, 'Adventure hokum which should do well. Gives Raquel Welch a physical, if not thespic, boost.' It goes on, 'Don Chaffey does a reliable job directorially, but leans heavily on the ingenious special effects in the shape of prehistoric animals and a striking earthquake dreamed up by Ray Harryhausen.'

Because of the film's phenomenal success Hammer did make two sequels. I wasn't involved with either, although I was approached by Michael to create the creatures for *When Dinosaurs Ruled the Earth* (1969), but by that time I was heavily involved in production for *The Valley of Gwangi*. The second sequel, *Creatures the World Forgot* (1971), also directed by Don Chaffey, told a similar story to *One Million Years BC* but dropped any references to the prehistoric creatures the title implied. The film was not a success, proving that the fascination was with the animals, not the humans.

Back once again with Charles, the success of *One Million Years BC* led us to the conclusion that we ought to search for a project to 'cash in' on the resurgence of interest in dinosaurs. That search took us back to 1941.

What became *The Valley of Gwangi* was not only a film about dinosaurs, it was also a tribute to my mentor, the late Willis O'Brien. Really it was his imaginative genius that brought it to the screen. It all began when I was searching through my 'mortuary' of old stories for a dinosaur project, and although there were a few ideas, none of them were good enough. However, my search did bring to mind an old O'Brien project he had talked about many years before: a variation on the *Lost World* story in which cowboys attempt to lasso a dinosaur. It was this fantastic image of lassoing a dinosaur that had implanted itself at the back of my mind.

Above. Raquel Welch and myself. Here I am 'choreographing' Miss Welch in how she should fall behind the rock for the pteranodon sequence so that I can later have the model pteranodon pick up a model of her from 'behind' the same rock on the rear projection.

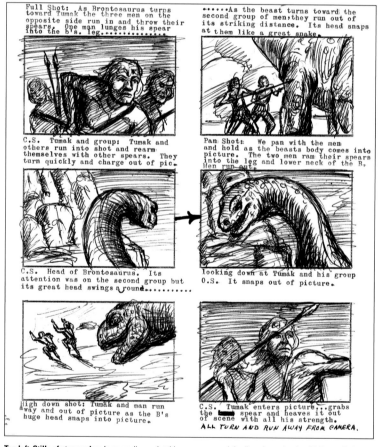

Top left. Stills of pteranodon. In an earlier script this scene was originally going to begin with Loana finding a large nest containing two hungry baby pteranodons, and believing them to have been abandoned, feeding them with a gull's egg. At that point a huge adult pteranodon would swoop down and attack her, which was all that was left in the final film.

Above. Missing brontosaurus sequence storyboards. Earlier in the sequence the creature was to have been seen with its head inside the tribe's caves. The distinctive image of a huge head and neck of the brontosaurus thrashing about in the confines of a cave seemed very exciting to me, so I regret that it was dropped.

Right hand page. Poster for *One Million Years BC*. There's that image of Miss Welch again with the creatures seemingly minute in the background. Was it the creatures or Miss Welch that sold the picture?

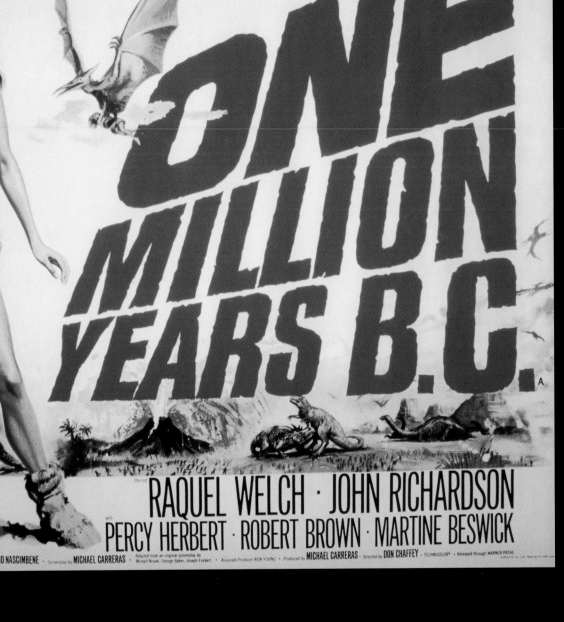

The most SPECTACULAR WESTERN of the year!

It staggers the IMAGINATION!

GWANGI

GWAN-GEE

Just prior to going into the army, Obie invited me over to RKO for a chat and to see the work that was being done on *Gwangi*, as the project was then called. The dioramas, each about two feet across, were beautiful and had been constructed to illustrate where the rear-screen projector was to be and where the live action took place. Each dimensional cardboard set-up included cut-outs of the actors and creatures so you could see just how they would work. However, when I saw his preparations for the roping sequence, I couldn't contain my excitement and heard myself saying out loud, 'My God, this is going to be great! There's been nothing like it since the wheel.' He laughed. Obie explained that the name 'Gwangi' was an American Indian word meaning lizard, and proceeded to show me other wonders, including his production sketches and hundreds of black and white continuity drawings, of which he would turn out perhaps ten or twenty a day. All were vivid testimony to his imagination and mastery of action drawing. In 1948 when I was animating the cowboy roping sequence (lifted straight out of *Gwangi*) for *Mighty Joe Young*, I talked again with Obie about the *Gwangi* project. It was then that he gave me a copy of the screenplay and told me a few of the facts about the production. The ill-fated *Gwangi* was originally to have been a Technicolor co-production between RKO Radio Pictures and Colonial Pictures, but after RKO had spent almost a year in preparation and over $50,000, they decided, for cost reasons or perhaps the war, to abandon it. Colonial then declined the option offered for a mere $30,000, after which *Gwangi* was officially terminated. Obie's disappointment was almost overwhelming, especially as it had followed on

from the cancellation of *War Eagles*. With the exception of the script and a few photographs of some of the continuity drawings, sadly most of the vast amount of pre-production and preparation work has long since been lost. However, I am told that three very large oil paintings on hardboard by O'Brien and Jack Shaw still exist. Perhaps one day these will surface and offer us a wider vision of what Obie planned for the film.

I spent several hours rummaging through the garage of my Palasades house, eventually finding the script, whereupon I sat down to read it. After twenty-five years, I was surprised that it stood up reasonably well, although it has to be said that sections of it were too slow for modern audiences:

The T.J. Breckenridge & Co Rodeo (the T.J. of the title being a woman) has just arrived in the small desert town of Zenith, which is on the edge of 'The Badlands'. Also newly arrived is an 'old friend' of T.J., Tuck Kirby. Mr Carson, the curator of Zenith's curio museum, shows Tuck and other rodeo cowboys fossils of dinosaurs, and Charlie, a Navajo Indian, tells Tuck about a herd of Lilliputian horses, which are supposed to exist in the Badlands. Tuck decides to find the herd for the rodeo and is told by Charlie, '…go due east. After three days you will sight a landmark called The Sentinel of Stones, beyond the dead forest and the river of lava'. Deep inside the Badlands, Tuck, T.J. and the rodeo cowboys find the Sentinel, a huge rock column, near the top of which they see a strange bat-like creature. In a chasm or canyon, they find the midget horses and the herd leads the explorers through a fissure entrance into a valley which Charlie had called 'The Valley

of the Ancients'. Out of the sky swoops a pterodactyl and picks up one of the cowboys but due to the weight it falls back to the ground where Tuck kills it. Gwangi, a massive allosaurus, appears and begins to eat the dead pterodactyl. The cowboys try to rope the massive creature but it breaks free and fights a triceratops which it kills. Chasing the cowboys Gwangi gets himself trapped in the fissure where he is knocked out by a rock fall. Returning to Zenith, the rodeo announces a new show, with a live dinosaur. The world's press arrives but Gwangi breaks free of his cage, killing some lions and devastating the town. Tuck manages to lead Gwangi to a rock ledge over a canyon, and T.J. drives a car into him, sending him over the cliff and into the abyss.

Returning to England with the script, I showed it to Charles, who also felt that the story had potential for an action adventure. Once we had obtained the rights, I began work on eight key sequence drawings whilst Charles commissioned screenwriter William Bast to develop the script. Additional material was written later by Julian More. Gradually we came up with a revised storyline based on the original screenplay, with Bast writing in my ideas for animation sequences. We gave the project the working title of *The Valley Where Time Stood Still*.

Although we had planned the project for Columbia Pictures, as the first script costing was higher than expected, they declined the offer, so we were forced to search for a new distributor. Fortunately, during *One Million Years BC* I had got to know co-producer Kenneth Hyman, whose father, agent Elliot Hyman, had just bought Warner Brothers. Following the success of the Hammer picture, Kenneth was well aware of the commercial potential of dinosaurs, and an agreement was signed between Morningside Productions and Warner Bros–Seven Arts.

Although the basic idea in the original *Gwangi* script was maintained, many new situations were added to enhance and update the storyline for modern audiences. The original screenplay had been set in the 1940s, contemporary with its writing, but we felt that it should take place at the turn of the century, eliminating the tired cliché of the army moving in with tanks and missiles, not to mention the atomic bomb. We took out certain characters and replaced them with more believable people. Professor Bromley was a good case in point. He added both a scientific aspect to the story and a much-needed touch of humour.

Somewhere south of the Rio Grande… At the turn of the century… a strange creature is brought back from the 'Forbibben Valley' and sold to a Wild West Show run by Champ Connors (Richard Carlson) and owned by T.J. Breckenridge (Gila Golan). Tuck Kirby (James Franciscus) arrives to buy T.J.'s high-diving show act for the Bill Cody Show, but when T.J. shows him the mysterious creature, he decides that it will make her show a world success. Identified by a British palaeontologist, Professor Bromley (Laurence Naismith), the mysterious creature turns out to be a tiny prehistoric horse called an eohippus. When the creature is stolen by gypsies, Tuck and the others decide to look for the 'Forbidden Valley'. Locating the hidden entrance they encounter a pterodactyl and later an ornithomimus that runs into the jaws of a 14-foot tyrannosaurus, which they call Gwangi. Whilst attempting to capture the creature by roping it, they are interrupted by a styracosaurus that fights Gwangi. During the battle the styracosaurus is killed and the cowboys flee the valley. Gwangi pursues but is stunned after a rock slide at the entrance. Transporting him back to the show they display him as 'Gwangi The Great' but during the first appearance, the tyrannosaurus escapes his cage and kills an elephant. Eventually Gwangi is trapped inside the town's cathedral, which is set on fire. Amid the flames of the crumbling cathedral, Gwangi dies in agony.

With the script now ready, Charles began to assemble a cast and crew. The much-respected James Franciscus was cast as the dashing hero Tuck. He was an acting rarity in as much as he accepted from the outset that this was an effects film. I always found him to be a pleasant man who gave much to his role as the cocky Tuck and who took an avid interest in the whole process of film-making. Gila Golan was cast as the heroine T.J., but as she originally hailed from Poland and was brought up in Israel, her accent forced us to completely redub her lines because it was felt that all the leads should be American. The veteran actor Richard Carlson was cast as Champ, a kind of father figure to T.J. Because from the early 1950s he had appeared in several cult science fiction films, including Ray Bradbury's *It Came From Outer Space* (1953), he never had any trouble with understanding what the special effects were to demand of him. As with most of our productions there was a strong British supporting cast. First and foremost was the always reliable Laurence Naismith playing the eccentric palaeontologist. Among the others in the supporting cast was the delightful Freda Jackson who played the gypsy Tia Zorina with a patch over one eye and a cataract in the other. Poor Freda was always handi-capped in our films; years later we cast her in *Clash of the Titans* as one of the three blind witches.

Spain was the obvious location for a story set in Mexico, so the production was mostly centred in and around Almeria and Cuenca, with the interiors photo-graphed in a television studio in Madrid. The unusual rock formations of Ciudad Encantada near Cuenca served as the 'Forbidden Valley'. Tabernas at the south-eastern tip of the Iberian peninsula was the plateau outside the valley, whilst Tabernas village would become the finale's Mexican town. For the two arenas seen in the film we used the bullring at Colminar for the first and another in Almeria for the second. Other locations were the sand dunes of Las Dunas de Cabo de Gata and the beautiful, centuries-old Cathedral of Cuencas, near Madrid, which served for the climax. As usual, we had a very tight location schedule strictly overseen by Charles, who had worked out every minor budgetary detail for the six-week location shoot. If anyone thinks we, or any other production, have ideal conditions when on location, think again. Even though everything is worked out in advance and you try to allow for snags, natural disasters and imperfections, there are always events that force us to simply make do. As a perfectionist I find this exasperating, but that's the way it is, and you have to do the best you can with the material that has been shot. On this production bad weather and lack of time produced some less than perfect background plates. Whenever I see the sequences for which I had to 'make do', I cringe, but few people in the audience seem to notice.

Apart from the arena diving ramp; Gwangi's cage, base and curtain; the entrance to the 'Forbidden Valley'; and the cave where the adventurers shelter, there was little set building on location. Most locations have to be 'slightly' modified to suit the action or to be more visually exciting. The valley's entrance only required partial construction, but the cave was almost entirely false, built to fit in with the surrounding rock formations.

After the live-action photography I returned to England to complete the models and miniatures, ready for animation and effects. Although Gwangi had been an allosaurus in Obie's version, I decided to make him more of a tyrannosaurus, and so I used elements from both species to make what I suppose could be called a 'tyrannosaurus al'. This combination allowed me a flexibility between aggressiveness and agility. If you like, he was glamorized. There was only one model, about 12 inches high, which required more detail and to be structurally more versatile because Gwangi had more to do in the film than any incidental animal. The eohippus was about 8 – 9 inches long by 7 inches high. There were two versions each of the pterodactyl and the ornithomimus, one for close shots (8 inches) and the other for distance (4 inches).

On 17 October 1967 I commenced animation. I was once again allocated my little studio, right at the other end of Shepperton Studios, in the parking lot, where I had previously shot *Mysterious Island* and *Jason and the Argonauts*. It had been altered for our films, and amongst other 'special' features had a projection tunnel that enabled me to obtain a longer throw from my projector.

Left hand page. Drawing for *Gwangi*. This was a drawing I made to sell the idea and it also appeared as the cover for Obie's drawings for his version of *Gwangi*. Notice that I emphasize how the name of Gwangi is pronounced.

Right. Gwangi attacks base camp. We constructed the top half of the cave, a ramp up which the cowboys could ride their horses and the ledge of wood and plaster to allow the men to fight Gwangi and the styracosaurus at their level. This shot was composed of the live action with a matte line drawn along the upper edge of the ledge into which I animated Gwangi to react to the cowboys' actions.

Above. The model of Gwangi. When the model had been completed, I photographed it from various angles for reference. This is the only one that survives and was shot on the floor in our house in London.

The first animation sequence I tackled was the complicated diving act performed by T.J. and her horse. The sequence was based on pictures in an old book about special equestrian acts. In it were photos of horses jumping from high platforms, including an act in 1902 of a horse jumping 40 feet into a 12-foot deep tank of water. This rather outrageous and eccentric idea appealed to me and seemed suitably spectacular and dangerous for an opening sequence. The ramp and platform were built full-size in the arena in Spain because it is seen in long shot during the Wild West show. A stunt girl substituted for Golan in the long shots of the horse and rider ascending the ramp, but the close shots of Golan on the horse were filmed on a separately built section. We then see Golan and the horse appear to jump in close-up (done from the mock-up platform) and then there is a cut to a wide shot of the jump, for which I substituted the real girl and horse with miniatures. Although I suspended the horse and rider on wires and animated them against the rear projection screen plate in the usual way, neither the model horse nor rider had any armatures. They were just a cheap plastic toy horse and rider (about three inches long) I had bought in a toyshop and painted to match the real horse and rider. The only thing I did was to cut the horses' back legs for the leap from the platform. When the miniature rider and horse hit the tank of water, they disappear behind a matte line, drawn on the rim of the tank. The splash was real. On location the effects man had rigged a smokeless charge inside the tank and in the animation studio I timed the shot to coincide with the explosion of water so the horse and rider hit the tank one frame before the splash.

The tiny and delightful eohippus is the first prehistoric creature we encounter in the picture. The name appropriately means 'dawn horse', and it was an ancestor to today's horse. In the original story there was a herd, but in our version we show only one, introducing the adventurers to the hidden valley. This also conveniently helped the budget, as the idea of animating a herd of eohippus would have been prohibitive, although with today's digital effects this wouldn't necessarily hold any problems. The eohippus is introduced, although not seen in the opening of the film, when we see a dying man struggling across treacherous terrain clutching a sack. Although we are aware there is something struggling in the sack (for which we used a dog), the first we see of the creature is at El Diablo on a table with T.J. and Tuck looking down at it.

It was another scene I dreaded animating, and I found myself postponing the task for as long as possible, worrying about animating a creature that could be compared with a living species. Animating a creature that cannot be compared with anything means that I can interpret what I think its movements would be. After all, who can really tell exactly how dinosaurs moved or how something totally fictitious like the hydra might have behaved. Because of this relationship to the modern horse, in the end I was able to incorporate some horse-like actions. For example, later in the film, during the chase, I had him stop and turn his head to look back at his pursuers and at the same time raise one of his front legs. I had witnessed this action during my study of horses, and it seemed to me that the movement gave the creature character. Another horse action is to look down, supposedly to see if anything is in its way, so I gave the eohippus a little glance downward and then up again before the animal moves forward. In the end the eohippus animation was executed in great haste, but it turned out to contain some of the smoothest and most natural animation I had ever done.

The key scene for the eohippus was the El Diablo tabletop sequence when we see the creature coming out of a tiny barn. The tabletop, including the barn and corral, were miniatures used for both the live-action shots with Gila, Jim and Naismith as well as for the animation. Using a cardboard cut-out of the eohippus, I would rehearse the actors, telling them that the creature would move from point A to point B, after which I would shoot the sequence without the cut-out. This footage was then used as the rear projection plate in front of which I animated the tiny eohippus on the table to match where they were looking.

After it is realized that the creature is a prehistoric creature, local gypsies steal it and release it from a sack near the Forbidden Valley. We shot a background plate of the actor kneeling down with the open sack and later, in the studio, I made a matte at the edge of the sack from which the animated model eohippus emerges. Pursuing the gypsies, Tuck and the other cowboys attempt to recapture the poor creature, and during the chase we used various cut-away shots containing many split screens with the eohippus model. However, in one very

Top. Pterodactyl flying away with boy. The boy seen in the clutches of the pterodactyl is a model. When the creature is forced to land, the boy escapes by crawling away, and shortly after he reverts once again to the real boy.

Left. Model of the ornithomimus. The poor little ornithomimus. He was not only described as looking like a 'plucked ostrich', but he also only appeared in the picture for a short spell, during which he is chased by cowboys and then eaten by Gwangi. He was thought a good introduction to Gwangi.

Above. The eohippus on the table. I have always thought this scene was charming. James Franciscus and Gila Golan were photographed in the studio in front of a miniature fence (seen behind the eohippus). The remainder – the model eohippus, the tiny stable on the right and the fence in the foreground – were all added later on the animation table in front of the rear projected image of Franciscus and Golan.

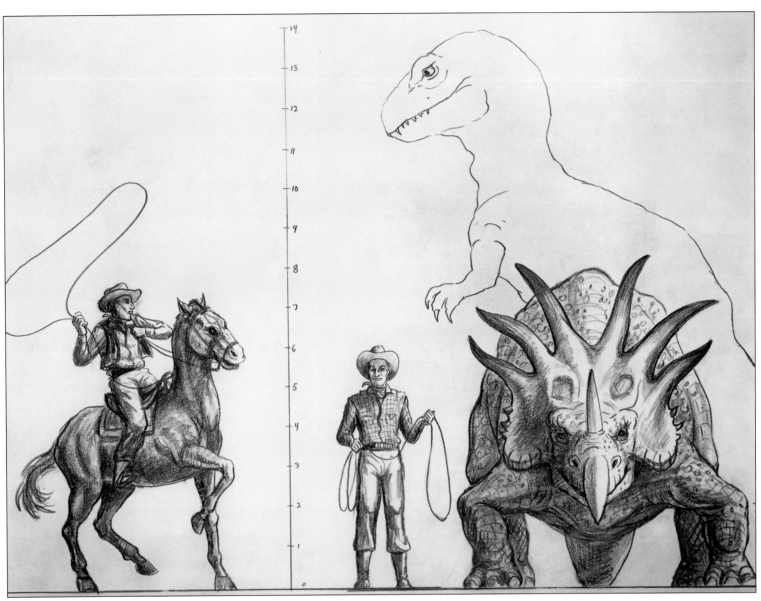

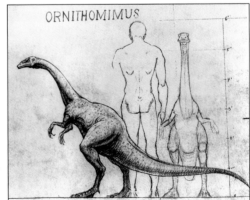

Above. Two drawings. These illustrate what would be the height of Gwangi, the styracosaurus and the ornithomimus compared with a human figure and a cowboy on horseback. These height comparison drawings were vital, not only for my reference, but also for the actors to visualize the creatures.

Left. Key drawing for the ornithomimus sequence. The ornithomimus was a prehistoric ostrich-like creature that grew to about 11 feet long and could move at up to 50 kph. It was the creature's ability to run fast, and its size, which encouraged me to use him, although sadly the story never gave him the chance to show what he could do.

quick long shot the creature is seen running from left to right. The distance made animating the model pointless, as it would have been far too small, so we obtained a baby goat with similar colourings to the eohippus and released it to run through the bushes. The size was exactly right and the bushes hid the differences.

Before the cowboys enter the valley, there is a night sequence in which a creature (a tiny model of a pterodactyl, seen only in long shot and masked by darkness) flies over the horses near the campfire. This was the first real hint the audience is given of prehistoric creatures lurking nearby, and in retrospect I wish we had expanded the sequence to allow the audience a stronger and more exciting anticipation of the extraordinary creatures they were going to see. However, once inside the valley the pterodactyl reappears when it swoops and plucks the boy from his galloping horse. During the live-action photography, the boy was hoisted into the air by means of a crane placed just outside the camera range. The cable on which he was suspended was painted out in the studio and I animated the model pterodactyl (which was 8 inches high and about 18 inches across) to correspond with the boy's struggling actions on the rear projection screen. Clutching the boy in its claws, the flying cycle of the reptile slows down as it struggles with the weight until finally it crashes to the ground where it flaps helplessly. As the boy crawls away, one of the cowboys proceeds to wring its neck. For the extreme close shots of its demise, we used a full-sized version of the pterodactyl built by the prop department in Spain. As with most such props, I was never happy with it, although it is difficult to get anything like that to look perfect. For example, when the cowboys leave the valley we used a

full-sized papier-mâché head of Gwangi when he is stunned by a rock fall. Even though its eyes moved and its body seemed to breathe, it still looked like it was made of papier-mâché.

For the long shots of the cowboy wrestling the pterodactyl, I used the animated model. I spent some time with the actor going through the motions of how it was going to look, and when we came to shoot, he acted out the movements without anything in his hands. Back in England, with the actor on the backplate, I carefully animated the model pterodactyl to correspond exactly with his movements.

The main adversary in the film was, of course, Gwangi, a huge carnivorous tyrannosaurus. As he was why the cowboys and audience were there, it was vital that the audience's introduction to him be special. My first idea was to have him jump out at the cowboys from behind rocks, a concept I had based on the original script. However, after sketching the scene, this seemed rather tame and mundane.

In *One Million Years BC* I had been unable to use the idea of a phororhacus being pounced on by the allosaurus, so after experimenting with various other concepts, I decided to use an ornithomimus, a creature never seen on the cinema screen before, as the means by which we introduced Gwangi. The cowboy explorers come across the ornithomimus grazing and they set about capturing it for T.J.'s Wild West Show. As the reptile runs up an incline between some rocks, Gwangi jumps out at it and grasps it in his mouth. The sight of this new terrifying creature stops the cowboys in their tracks, and in turn Gwangi reacts to their gunfire by chasing them so that the hunters become the hunted.

Following this introduction there was to have been a scene, modified from the original screenplay, that would have shown Gwangi falling into a pit. For some reason (probably the usual), I had been forced to drop it just before the commencement of location shooting. Like many things, I regret the loss of this sequence; as an exciting prelude to the roping, it would have presented an interesting fight between animal and man, as Gwangi's head would have been at ground level.

As I have mentioned, the roping sequence was the main reason I wanted to make the picture, and today it is still one of my favourite sequences in this or any other movie I have made. I am modestly proud of the look of it, although, as always, there are aspects I would undoubtedly change given the opportunity. Actors and horses had to be co-ordinated to be at a certain point at a precise time to ensure that I could animate the model of Gwangi to fit with their actions. The eye-line had to be spot on all the time they were riding, and to make it all work I had to use several old tricks and a few new ones.

The question of eyeline was, for the most part, easy. Throughout the film I used my old friend the monster stick. However, for the roping sequence I had to devise a 'moving' monster stick that would approximate the movements of the tyrannosaurus and at the same time give the impression that the ropes were straining as the characters lassoed the creature. I solved the problem by using an old jeep onto which we fixed a 15-foot upright pole. As the jeep had great manoeuvrability, it was able to get from one point to another with ease whilst the stuntmen lassoed the top of the pole, giving the impression of straining ropes. To prevent the ropes from slipping whilst the stuntmen were actually roping from their

Long Shot: (Dyn)The three men strain at their ropes as Gwangi moves from side to side. **402 C**

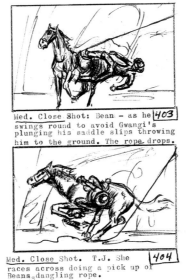

Med. Close Shot: Bean - as he swings round to avoid Gwangi's plunging his saddle slips throwing him to the ground. The rope drops. **403**

Long Shot: (Dyn) T.J. Pulls back. Gwangi strains against the three. Rowdy swinging rope throws it over Gwangi's head. **405 406**

Close Shot: (Dyn) GWANGI As he struggles against the ropes. **405A**

Close Shot: T.J. She sees Bean's accident and charges out of picture. **403A**

Med. Close Shot. T.J. She races across doing a pick up of Beans dangling rope. **404**

Med. Shot: TUCK AND T.J. As they pull at their ropes. **405B**

Med. Shot: Champ & Rowdy as they try to hold Gwangi still. **405 C**

horses, the pole had several horizontal spokes near the top and as an added precaution we occasionally had a man clinging to the pole to make sure the ropes attached themselves. In addition, I did my usual trick of acting out the actions off camera and shouting to the stuntmen and actors where the creature would be and where he was about to go.

You may say, where is the jeep on the rear projection plate? Surely it was too large to be hidden, even by such a creature as a tyrannosaurus? Of course, the jeep was too big to hide behind Gwangi, so to remove it along with the monster stick I shot the live action in two halves. First I photographed the right-hand side of the frame showing the cowboys lassoing and the ropes straining, whilst in the left-hand side of the frame was the jeep and the monster stick. Keeping the camera in exactly the same place, we then photographed on a separate reel of film the remainder of the cowboys roping and straining on the left with the jeep and pole on the right of the frame. Back in England the labs printed and combined the two

The total length of the roping sequence is nearly 4½ minutes but the animation took over five months to complete. Time and patience were expended on the intricate matching of the ropes and to effect the various 'contacts'. One of these 'contacts' shows Gwangi tugging a blanket held by one of the cowboys and pulling him to the ground. This was achieved by a wire attached to the edge of the blanket being pulled during the live action and matching it by animating Gwangi's actions so that it seemed the blanket was tugged by the creature.

pieces of film, and by means of a split-screen process, all that remained on the plate was the cowboys on either side with their respective ropes seemingly suspended in mid-air. This eliminated the jeep and the monster stick. The real ropes were now at the correct height on both sides, so that when I came to animate, I simply placed the model of Gwangi in front of the split screen join and matched the actual ropes on the rear projection with miniature copper wire ropes around his neck.

During the sequence I had Gwangi fall onto his side. If it had been a real animal or human, it would have been run-of-the-mill, but because it was a huge dinosaur, it caused me a few sleepless nights. Such an action, simple

though it sounds, has to be carefully planned, but even when I storyboarded the sequence, I had no idea how I was going to approach it. All I knew was that it would look good. The question I didn't consider was how do you trip a tyrannosaurus? I couldn't have him casually stumble over a rock or rope and fall flat on his face – it would have looked comical. After much thought I came up with the idea of a lasso somehow (either by intent or accident) landing on the ground, whereupon Gwangi 'happens' to step into it, after which it tightens around his foot, so pulling him over. I used twisted and painted copper wire for the lasso. The scene, although unlikely, does change the action, and is accepted within the pace of the

Left hand page. Key drawing of Gwangi leaping at a cowboy on horseback. This was my original concept for Gwangi's appearance, which I felt was not quite as spectacular as eating the unfortunate ornithomimus.

Above. Storyboard for the Gwangi roping sequence. It is perhaps the most exciting scene I have ever devised. This section of the storyboard shows how I intended the whole sequence to be edited together, a task that I usually did myself when all the filming was completed.

Far left. The famous monster stick. This is the monster stick for Gwangi, but it was one like this that I used on most of my films. On it you can see the feet marked, as well as an eye painted at the top to give the actors an eyeline reference for all the large creatures, including Gwangi. The set behind was the cleft in the rock, which turns out to be the lost valley. This was made of plaster and constructed in a ravine in Spain.

Left. The roping of Gwangi as it appears in the film. My one regret with this scene is that I didn't paint the real and miniature ropes white. The plain ones used made matching between the real and the miniatures difficult, and in the early stages of roping they could hardly be seen against the background. Perhaps it is a small thing to regret, but like all the 'mistakes', I find it very irritating when I see it today.

Below left. A set of extremely rare photographs of the cowboys roping the monster stick. This shows how the stuntmen playing the cowboys roped something that was not there. In three of the images you are able to see the monster stick mounted on the rear of the jeep and it is this that the horsemen are roping. In the final image a monster stick (probably the same one that appears in the still to the extreme left) is shown where the model of Gwangi will stand.

sequence. Incidentally, when we see Gwangi down, the ropes from each of the cowboys are being held in place by short poles in the ground. These were obscured by Gwangi during animation.

Where time allowed, I attempted to give Gwangi some elements of character, although it has to be said that to instil character traits into such a creature is difficult. Unlike the Ymir in *20 Million Miles to Earth*, or a Kong for that matter, tyrannosaurus belonged to the most violent species that ever lived. However, I felt sorry for him because all he wanted to do was to live his life and eat a few people along the way. The character I gave him was never to rest. His body is constantly on the go, searching for food or a way to escape.

Like the allosaurus in *One Million Years BC*, Gwangi possessed a powerful tail, and I used this to make him distinctive. The audience sees a huge lizard with a thrashing tail and is reminded of a vicious predator, a man-eater. The tail says everything, and if I had allowed him to just drag it along the ground or keep it fixed in the air, the result would have been dull. The constant movement helped to give his scenes pace and drama. Sound was another important element. Gwangi's roar was frighteningly primordial and the clashing of his teeth told us that he wouldn't hesitate to eat anything available to him. The roar was actually a camel slobbering, slowed and altered electronically. The sound of the jaws was created by the Shepperton sound effects department by constructing a set of metal teeth on two pieces of wood, clashed together like a clapperboard.

Next comes the fight with the stycosaurus. For the model of the styracosaurus, I recycled the armature of the triceratops from the previous film, keeping only the head of the original. I regretted not having time to design a better entrance for the beast. When we first see him, during the rush by the cowboys to escape Gwangi, he appears in the foreground with his back to the camera, followed a little later by a stand-off with Gwangi. However, following the attempt to rope Gwangi, there is a fight to the death between the two of them. For the fight I used a great deal of aerial brace to allow the Gwangi model to climb onto his victim's back and sink his teeth into the neck and back. 'Contact' was made between one of the humans and the styracosaurus by having one of the cowboys charge Don Quixote-like on his horse and spear the styracosaurus whilst Gwangi is on its back. The rider comes in from the left-hand side of the screen and embeds the spear into the unfortunate creature's side. I used the same trick of changing the real spear to a miniature at the point where the real one, in the rear projection, 'touches' the model. As with most 'tricks' of this type, the real spear has fallen behind the model on the rear projection plate.

it. If I had made the film on some of today's special effects budgets, I could have made a variety of models or puppets all able to do different actions, but in the late 1960s a typical effects budget for us would have barely been $35,000–$40,000.

Whilst stunned, Gwangi is tied up and by means of a hastily constructed wooden cart and taken to the town where he will be exhibited in T.J.'s Wild West Show. The sequence of Gwangi in the cart was constructed from a combination of shots. The long shots were of a full-size cart with a cut-out of Gwangi standing inside. The medium shots were of the model Gwangi in a miniature cart. For these I used a back projection plate shot on location that had the camera tracking alongside

> The cowboys' flight from the valley and the pursuit by Gwangi was originally planned to be a much more spectacular affair. As it is now, the only incident in the sequence is the death of one of the cowboys when he is snatched from his horse by Gwangi. It should have also included a scene where the cowboys encounter a long, deep ravine which they hope will slow Gwangi in his pursuit. Safely on the other side, the humans ride away, and although Gwangi momentarily hesitates, he does leap across. This scene would have bridged the flight from the valley and provided the chase with an extra edge of excitement.

We now arrive at the point in the film with which I have always been unhappy. It is the scene where Gwangi traps himself in the entrance to the valley and whilst trying to free himself starts a rock fall which knocks him out, so providing the adventurers with the opportunity to capture him. A very unconvincing model of Gwangi is seen sliding down an incline amongst the rubble. It looks awful. As the budget didn't allow us to build a bigger Gwangi model and photograph it at high speed (I would even have preferred a string or glove-like puppet), I had to settle on a compromise to get the film finished. I used a non-armatured, hard rubber model, and to disguise the fact that it was a lump of latex, I made sure we used a lot of dust, which went some way to obscuring the cheapness of it. When it comes to a standstill, lying on its side, we had to simulate a breathing movement. By attaching a wire underneath and pulling it gently, we managed to just get away with

the actors and horses. In the animation studio I placed the model Gwangi inside the cart and animated both the creature and the cart in front of it. However, it wasn't as easy as it sounds. I was faced with animating the cart wheels at the same speed that the men and horses were moving on the rear projection screen. To accomplish this I used a piece of camera tape (white fabric adhesive tape) on the rear projection screen to see how far, or at what rate, the objects (horses, shrubs, etc.) moved. Placing the tape at a certain point, perhaps a rock, gave me the rate by which everything moved. Once I had worked out the distance, perhaps a quarter of an inch, I would animate the wheels at the same measurement, achieving the same speed as the rear projection plate.

Once back in 'civilization', Gwangi is to be exhibited in the local bullring (Almeria's central bullring). The seats are packed with people waiting to see 'Gwangi', a title emblazoned on a huge balloon attached to an

Above left. Cowboy stabbing styracosaurus during fight with Gwangi.
During the fight between the styracosaurus and Gwangi, I had the latter climb onto the back of the poor styracosaurus to try and bite into its neck. The scene is full of movement, not just the bodies trying to gain the upper claw, but also in the tails of the creatures, especially Gwangi, as they whip the air. It resembles a wrestling match in which the action never fails to excite.

Above right. The cutout of Gwangi in cart on location. This was the full size mock-up of Gwangi in the cart that we used for some of the long shots.

Right. Gwangi in cart being led by cowboy. Here is the animated version that sees Gwangi trying to pull himself free of the ropes. The whole scene took some considerable planning, as I had to time each stop-frame movement to correspond with the movement of the real horsemen.

Left. The styracosaurus model. In the original 1942 script Gwangi fought with a triceratops, but as I had used that particular species in *One Million Years BC*, I opted for the more spectacular styracosaurus with its frill of horns like an oriental dancer's headdress.

equally huge curtain, which in turn covers the cage holding the creature. The idea was to have the balloon lift the canopy and spectacularly introduce the world's only living dinosaur. It was a variation of the scene in *King Kong* when he is first seen on stage. There are a number of shots of the balloon and canopy. The first was through a gateway for which I used a miniature of the balloon suspended on a wire 10–12 feet from the camera. Matching up the perspective in the camera, I carefully fitted it to look as though it was part of the full-sized curtain and base. For the low shots inside the arena I used a matte painting of the balloon and canopy, and for the high shots the balloon was a matte painting combined with the real curtain. The rising balloon and canopy were a miniature, which had to be animated along with Gwangi restlessly turning in his cage. Apart from one section of the cage that falls on Laurence Naismith, the whole thing was a miniature placed by means of a split screen onto the full-size base.

Animating the model inside the cage posed a few problems of its own. I built a false bottom in the animation table to precisely correspond with the edge of the model cage, and mounted the section on a camera dolly. The section had registration marks, which meant it would always be in the same place and allowed me to open and close the bottom without disturbing anything else, apart from Gwangi that is. Sitting on a cushion on the floor beneath the animation table, I lowered the false bottom to animate the model and raised it again to shoot the frame of film.

One minor 'touch' I gave to this sequence was in the fall of the section of cage, which, when it crashes to the ground, bounces and rocks backwards and forwards. This infinitesimal touch might seem insignificant, and most people would hardly register it, but it would happen in reality and it is worth spending those extra few hours producing the detail to bring the scene alive.

Before Gwangi escapes the arena, he is faced with fighting the performing elephant, which is also in the arena. I tried to give the action, during the whole arena sequence, some originality and perspective, so I carefully set up a variety of positions to give me the chance to animate at different heights and angles. For some low shots I made valuable use of circles painted on the arena ground, which supplied me with a natural matte line to insert the creatures. There were also some high camera angled plates looking down into the arena from the upper rows of seats. For these I constructed an animation table that corresponded with the natural curve of the arena in the rear projection plate. This gave the scene variety and depth.

The crowd scenes were a problem, as the budget didn't allow us unlimited extras. Even if it had, they would have been hard to come by. One day we would have 300, the next 100 and the day after 200. We never knew how many people we were going to have to play with. That's why some of the crowd shots of the panic outside the bullring are a little sparse. When the day came to film the presentation of Gwangi in the bullring (which had a capacity to hold thousands), we only had 300 extras, so we had to use them the only way we could: with the aid of special effects. Setting up the camera in one position we sat the extras closely together in one section of the arena and then photographed them acting out all the reactions the sequence would require (from calmly sitting to the panic and rush for the exits). When that was complete, we moved them over to the next section in the arena and filmed them again, and so on until we had covered all the necessary sections. We now had three separate pieces of film of the same extras sitting in different sections of the visible arena. Back in England the labs compiled these sections in the optical printer to make one shot of a full arena. Of course, the idea wasn't new; film-makers had been using this optical trick for years, although not always with visual success. In this case I think it worked rather well.

As the crowds leave the bullring, Gwangi pursues them into an exit tunnel. I placed him into this narrow space with his head touching the ceiling for a purpose. It makes the creature look twice as big as it towers over the people in the foreground (who were added by means of a travelling matte). Creating the illusion of mass is vital in these films, and by cropping the image within the confines of the walls, it reminds the audience of Gwangi's size. Angles are vital to encourage an illusion of size and they have to be selected very carefully. If I get too far back, the object can become ineffective, as the impression of size is reduced.

Once Gwangi escapes the confines of the bullring, he struts through the town creating understandable chaos. Surrounded by a human environment, his walk now becomes a feature and his other actions full of animal character. For example, as he stops, the weight of his body gently carries his upper torso slightly forward so that he appears to dip his head. I also had him constantly lifting his head to look at his surroundings, as though he was sniffing the air. These actions provided the audience, although hopefully subconsciously, with a feeling that they were looking at a real creature that was simply larger than anything they were used to. I had used similar actions for Gwangi when he was in 'his' valley, but here the movement seems accentuated because he is now in surroundings that are partially familiar to us as an audience.

As I have mentioned, I always try to find 'natural' lines and patterns in landscapes to create a matte line, which always saves time and money. One of these instances was in the square outside the church. Although the lines were not the reason why we chose the square (it was because of the church), the patterns in the stones did allow me to draw the matte lines for the split screen. Another good matte line that presented itself was as Gwangi enters the church. For that I created a matte line along the shadow being cast through the door. Of course, I carefully worked out where I wanted to place the lines in pre-production, but occasionally these changed, depending on the situation when we shot the live action.

Above. Three shots of how the matte for the balloon and curtained area was created. The first has only the base showing, along the top of which is the matte line, the second has the audience and Gwangi in cage, and the third is the combined scene.

Left. This still shows the miniature balloon being animated to rise in front of the rear projection of the arena. The balloon wasn't in the original screenplay but written in after I had come up with the idea because I wasn't keen on curtains simply being pulled back. I wanted something much more impressive.

Below. Animating the fight between Gwangi and the elephant in the arena. The seating area and overhang were photographed at the real arena and I used this plate for the rear projection. The arena floor, where all the action was to take place, was an animation table cut to the same curve as the arena in the rear projected image. On this I animated the fight between Gwangi and the doomed elephant. It is simple but very effective.

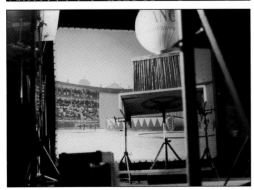

The performing elephant was originally to have been done by a real 15-foot pachyderm, but things didn't go according to plan. At the start of filming we had asked the production manager to obtain an elephant of that size. Weeks went by and no elephant appeared. 'It's coming,' he said. 'So is Christmas,' I said. However, because the Spanish circuses were working during the summer, they were not keen on letting out their prized elephants, so he told us he had to get one from England. Days went by and he assured me, 'It's coming, it is now in Bilboa.' More valuable time went by, and now it was two or three days before we were due to shoot the sequence. 'It's now around Seville and it's coming, it's on its way.' A day before the shoot I asked him again, this time trying not to show the desperation in my voice. The reply was, 'It's coming tonight, you'll see it tonight.' By this time both Charles and I were extremely nervous about this travelling elephant. It did arrive that night but was only 6 feet high, half the size we had asked for. You can't imagine the turmoil that went on in my digestive system! We debated the consequences for hours, trying to find an alternative, but in the end the only solution was to shoot the whole elephant sequence with a model, adding extra animation time to the schedule in England. Overnight I redesigned the sequence, hoping that inspiration for the beast would come when I began animation, and next day we shot a set of plates for the rear projection. In the end the result was a far better sequence than we could have achieved with a real animal. Fortunately, we did manage to use the real elephant in the parade at the beginning of the picture, which justified some of the cost of shipping the elephant to Almeria.

We wanted the demise of Gwangi to be a little more spectacular than that in the original 1941 storyline. However, try as we might, we couldn't seem to come up with a solution for an alternative ending. It was whilst I was on recce in Spain that I saw a church (in Cuenca) and suddenly realized that to end Gwangi's short career in such a building would suit the story far better than anything we had considered so far. As luck would have it, the church was being restored, and scaffolding was all over the front elevation, which for me gave the structure a primeval look – something we couldn't have anticipated. Arranging with the authorities to film in the town was never a problem. They were delighted that a Hollywood company was going to make them famous. However, gaining permission to photograph in a church was a different matter. Fortunately, because they were restoring the church, we offered a 'contribution', which broke down all barriers of objection.

As Gwangi would naturally force his way into the confines of the church, I designed the sequence so that we see him break in through the huge double doors. When I first saw these doors I knew this was another reason why the church was perfect. Gwangi pushes against the doors, which are being held closed by Tuck and others, with his huge tail. Eventually the beast wins over the humans and the doors are flung open. Gwangi turns, filling the height of the doorway with his lower torso and legs. Again, by using only the lower section of his body I was able to give the impression of size and the overwhelming odds of defeating such a creature. We didn't use the real doors but reproduced and set them up in front of a blue screen on the Spanish studio stage. As the doors are forced open, we can see Gwangi and the town beyond. These were added later, after I had animated Gwangi in front of a rear projection plate. I have always felt that the stalking of the humans in the cold, echoing church is very atmospheric, suggesting the sacred and profane.

The church will become the arena for Gwangi's death, but preceding that, Tuck has to ward off the tyrannosaurus from his interest in T.J. and the boy. We utilized the church's organ loft, enabling Jim Franciscus to be at the same height as Gwangi so that he could use a spear to distract the creature. Jim thrusts the spear at Gwangi's face, which he grabs in his teeth, tugs and then lets go of, making Jim fall back onto the organ's keyboard. The sound of the organ echoes through the building and distracts Gwangi long enough for Jim to throw the spear into the creature's neck and allow the humans to get away. As Tuck escapes the church with T.J. and the boy, he flings a brazier that bursts into flames in front of poor Gwangi. In his crazed confusion Gwangi knocks over a second brazier with his tail. The brazier was real, and I animated the tail to seem as if he was knocking it over. The images of Gwangi writhing in the flames were a composite of various shots. First of all we photographed the very back of the interior of the

Top. Model of elephant. The real elephant that we obtained was only half the height we originally requested, but because Gila Golan was sitting on its back at the beginning of the film, nobody notices that it is a different size to the model one that fights Gwangi. At least, I hope they don't.

Above left. Sketch of Gwangi chasing the hero up the cathedral steps. I was always intrigued by the idea that he stalks his prey within the confines of the arches of a church.

Above right. Stills of Gwangi climbing the steps to the cathedral from the final film. This again illustrates how closely my storyboards and concepts are to what appears in the final film.

Right hand page. The poster for *The Valley of Gwangi*. I have always considered this as a very good and exciting poster, but because Warner Bros threw the film away by putting it out on release as a second feature, the film didn't do as well as it should. Rather gratifyingly, the film today always plays to good audiences, whether on television or in cinemas.

COWBOYS BATTLE MONSTERS IN THE LOST WORLD OF FORBIDDEN VALLEY.

UNBELIEVABLE!
...creatures of a lost era challenge the best the West has to offer.

FANTASTIC!
...the Allosaurus, alive in the twentieth century.

AMAZING!
...a world that still exists as it did at the beginning of time.

TERRIFYING!
...enter Forbidden Valley at your own risk!

A CHARLES H. SCHNEER Production

THE VALLEY OF GWANGI

STARRING
JAMES FRANCISCUS · CO-STARRING GILA GOLAN · RICHARD CARLSON

ASSOCIATE PRODUCER AND CREATOR OF VISUAL EFFECTS RAY HARRYHAUSEN · MUSIC COMPOSED AND CONDUCTED BY Jerome Moross · SCREENPLAY BY WILLIAM E. BAST

PRODUCED BY CHARLES H. SCHNEER · DIRECTED BY JAMES O'CONNOLLY · Filmed in DYNAMATION® TECHNICOLOR®

A WARNER BROS.-SEVEN ARTS RELEASE through Warner-Pathe

church as a still. In the animation studio I constructed sections of the building in miniature, which I placed in front of the still. It was these miniatures that I set on fire and shot as a rear projection plate. The plate was then used on the rear projection screen, in front of which I animated Gwangi and then later printed in the foreground flames. The exterior of the burning church was part real, part miniature. The lower section, with the people watching, was real. The upper section and the flames were a miniature matched with the lower section.

I completed animation and effects on 7 October 1968 after shooting more than 400 stop-motion cuts for the film, more than any other film to that date. I had been animating for precisely ten days short of a year, an extremely long time to be cooped up with one subject. Apart from the regrets I have already mentioned, I am always upset with the perceptible colour changes of the models, especially Gwangi. Sometimes he goes through grey, green, brown and blue. The main reason was lighting. Colour needs considerable time and effort to match correctly, and there was just not enough time, with the volume of animation, for the opportunity to make as many tests as I would have liked. Because the various blue filters that we used to take the red out of the lamps were stronger than we would have preferred, the colour fluctuated. In my little studio I don't have the same facilities as a lab would have, so the test has to be sent out and you have to wait for it to be returned. This can take the best part of a day. If that test is not right, you have to carry out another one and go through the same process of waiting. There are so many scenes or cuts to film, that if I carried out this process on all the scenes, I wouldn't even shoot a frame a day, and would perhaps take two years to shoot them all. We didn't have that kind of budget, so I had to take the occasional chance, although I am loath to admit it. Working entirely on my own, the pressure was enormous, and I was often forced to take a gamble, so absolute perfection occasionally had to be sacrificed. However, I truly don't believe these colour changes deter from the excitement of the movie. Fortunately, with new electronic techniques Gwangi's colour can be easily corrected for home video and DVDs. I like to believe I was ahead of the palaeontologists who now believe that dinosaurs had vivid colours and that some could even change colours like a chameleon.

People ask me why Obie didn't receive a credit on the picture. Because there were various complex legal problems involved with the credits, we were prevented from crediting him as he should have been. In the end the film's credits only acknowledged writer William E. Bast, although there were two other writers working on it at various stages. I was never happy that Obie's name wasn't there somewhere, but something like this is a double-edged sword. Obie had died by that time, but if we had put his name on it without his widow's permission, Darlyne might have thought we were cashing in on his name. In any event, I had very little say in the matter, and the credits were worked out by Morningside.

Right up until January 1969 the film was to be called *The Valley Where Time Stood Still*, which was, we all felt, the perfect title. Unfortunately, the Warner publicity people thought it too long and complicated, and even after the strong objections from everyone involved, including James Franciscus, the title became *The Valley of Gwangi*. The problem with the title was that some people associated the word Gwangi with a Japanese man-in-a monster-suit picture, which is why we had avoided using the word in our title. In any event, the change of title didn't help it at the box office, but what really killed the picture was the change of management at Warner Bros. Just after we had completed the film, the Kinney Corporation bought out Elliot and Kenneth Hyman's Seven Arts at Warner Brothers and took charge in 1969. A new regime always wants to make a clean sweep, and as the film had been part of the previous executive's projects, it was decided that it didn't merit adequate publicity. The new management had apparently no interest in the picture and viewed it as a dinosaur picture and therefore 'old hat'. It was insanity, and angered both Charles and I, because whatever they felt, it didn't deserve its fate of being ignominiously released as the lower half of double bills with such forgettables as *Girl on a Motorcycle* or *The Good Guys & the Bad Guys* and *Seven Golden Men*. As the publicity people had opted to use the name *Gwangi*, the best way to have sold the film would have been to begin the exploitation with Gwangi's name on billboards. Later you add 'What is Gwangi?' to arouse curiosity, and so on.

Predictably, with such a tacky release the film received very mixed reviews on both sides of the Atlantic. However, a handful of reviews perceived it for the entertainment it was, amongst them one from *Film Bulletin*, which in April 1969 said, 'Marvellously entertaining for youngsters and young-at-heart elders.' The reviewer went on to say, 'a combination western-science fiction film that should enthral'.

I wish the film had been released five years earlier. If it had, I am convinced it would have been a success. The action kept the picture moving at a good pace, the photography was excellent and the cast delivered solid and believable characters. It is sound entertainment, and those people who see it today seem to enjoy it immensely, although I am always amazed how many people want to pick faults with the film.

The Valley of Gwangi was to be the last time that I would work with dinosaurs. Leaving aside my amateur efforts and *The Beast From 20,000 Fathoms*, where the Beast was not really a proper dinosaur, I have worked on only three dinosaur pictures. Today, however, some people remember my dinosaur pictures more than the others. I am also delighted to say that museums and even film-makers have used them to illustrate the prehistoric reptiles, and in 1995 I was invited to Canada to lecture to a group of palaeontologists about the films and taken on a dig – which was a great honour.

After the production my daughter Vanessa, who was about five years old at the time, coveted Gwangi (the one without the armature) as any other girl would cherish their Barbie doll. She took him to bed and had Gwangi on one side with a teddy bear on the other. He went everywhere with her. One day Diana went shopping at Harrods with Vanessa in her pushcart and Gwangi wrapped up against the cold with his head peeking out. All was well until an elderly lady discovered what Vanessa was hugging. She was shocked and admonished Diana for letting the child have such things. It's a good job she didn't know what other creatures lurked in the house.

There is an old Hollywood proverb, 'You're as good as your last picture', and with the box office disappointment of *The Valley of Gwangi*, Charles and I now decided it was time to return to the source of our greatest success: the stories of the Arabian Nights.

CHAPTER 9 RETURN TO LEGENDS

The Golden Voyage of Sinbad

One of the most frequently asked questions about my work is about how much I was involved in the directing of our films. Well, as I designed the effects sequences, it follows that I had to direct them because I was the only one who knew what they were about. As far as the remainder of the picture was concerned, the director was the director, although when he understood my role, I would work very closely with him. I must confess that occasionally I entertained thoughts of directing an entire feature, but in the end I knew it would have been far too strenuous to have coped with both the live action and effects. Besides, my 'performers' always do exactly as they are told with no backlash of temperament – which is more than can be said for some actors. However, there were times when I would look at the completed picture and say to myself, 'Damn it! If I couldn't direct better than that, I should quit the business.' Looking back, I chastize myself for not having been more demanding, but I hate confrontations and would always try to compromise. This was both a virtue and a drawback, especially if something needed to be done correctly.

What should be obvious by now is that our type of visual pictures were made on extremely restrictive budgets, so everything had to be pre-planned on paper before the first frame of film was photographed. Hence they were not what would be called a director's film. Because the director didn't fully realize my overall input or was used to 'effects' technicians only coming onto a picture towards the end of live-action photography, my involvement sometimes caused friction. The result was that one or two of them tried desperately to assert their authority, and at times it would seem as if we were shooting two different productions. Working with 'these' directors was extremely hard going, although I hasten to add that they were the exception rather than the rule. In fact, over the years I worked with some fine professional directors who realized instantly what my role was in the production, accepted it and got on with the task of directing the live action and obtaining the best performances possible from the actors. Often brought in after the pre-planning, some would even add fresh new ideas, approaching the project from a completely

new perspective. One such director would handle our next picture: Gordon Hessler. He possessed a constructive and positive feel for fantasy and his involvement was one of the key elements that helped shape the picture and make it the success it was.

The genesis of what would become *The Golden Voyage of Sinbad* had begun ten years before. The drawings I made included a giant guarding the entrance to the ancient city of Petra, an oracle, a centaur, a dancing Shiva and a magician creating a homunculus. Unfortunately, the key drawings didn't inspire a storyline, so I tucked them away until another opportunity arose. Fortunately, it wasn't long before it did.

In May 1965, just as I was beginning pre-production on *One Million Years BC*, a writer called A. Sandford Wolf contacted me. He had sent a script titled *Garden of Evil* to Morningside Productions, which Charles had rejected. We met and discussed my ideas, and he offered to develop an outline for a story progression based on my drawings.

Reading Wolf's outline today, I can see why it never progressed. It was far too complex, with too many levels of plotline all struggling to emerge, and in the end none really succeeded in bridging together my key drawings. The next time the project raised its head was in late 1965 when Jan Read (with whom I had stayed in touch) tried his hand at it. Although Jan's outline did contain the essence of the Arabian Nights stories, it was again far too complex, and because Charles was looking for something straightforward, he rejected it. Soon after that I began pre-production work on *The Valley of Gwangi*, so the project was returned to a drawer where it languished for a few more years.

Following completion of *Gwangi*, Charles and I found ourselves in the usual situation of looking for the next suitable project. By that time I had concluded that if there was ever to be another Arabian Nights story, it was going to be up to me to initiate a step outline. Although I had written the step outline for *The 7th Voyage of Sinbad*, I had never found it easy to come up with storylines, despite having several advantages on my side. The drawings were potentially sound as key sequences, I was probably more familiar

Left hand page top and bottom. Two key drawings for scenes in *The Golden Voyage of Sinbad*. The top is the step scene from the Kali fight and the lower drawing is the battle between the centaur and the gryphon. For some time I had wanted to resurrect Sinbad or find some other suitable Arabian Nights story, so in 1964 in an attempt to visualize some ideas I made a series of large drawings, of which these are two, in the hope that a story would materialize.

with the legends than anyone else and, most important of all, I knew how the story needed to develop in practical visual terms. My first task was to decide on a central character. After the previous attempts to find a new hero figure, I decided that Sinbad was the most suitable, as he really personified true adventure and was still the best known of the Arabian Nights characters. On 3 March 1971, after considerable agonizing, I submitted a rough step outline to Charles unimaginatively entitled *Sinbad's 8th Voyage*. The comments it contains occasionally seem apologetic, but my opening paragraph illustrates that I was not attempting to write a screenplay. 'The human element is left undeveloped as well as any possible love interest or humour. Apropos of the large black and white drawings, the main purpose is to establish the SPECTACLE and ADVENTURE side of the storyline.'

Arriving at a Middle East port, Sinbad's ship is boarded by the Sultan and his daughter Margiana. Watching in the shadows is a masked figure who releases a tiny creature which scrambles up the ship's tie rope. On board the Sultan is showing Sinbad a map, asking him to take him and his daughter to the island of Lemuria. He explains that when the Sultan was 5 years old, he and his half-brother Jaffa were taken there by their mother, where they drank the waters of The Fountain of Youth. Now the Sultan is 300 years old but he and Jaffa (who has turned to the black arts) need to replenish their supplies of the precious water and Jaffa wants
to marry Margiana and steal the throne. Suddenly the Sultan sees Jaffa's tiny creature, a homunculus. Sinbad manages to capture it in a glass jar and throw it into the sea but not before the eyes and ears of the homunculus have allowed Jaffa to learn of their plan. Following Sinbad's ship in his own, Jaffa creates a new winged homunculus which flies off to spy on Sinbad's ship. Arriving at Lemuria ('with its fallen temples, giant faces in the rock') they trek through the Valley of Vipers in search of the woman of knowledge who will tell them the location of the lost Fountain. Discovering a ruined temple hidden by the jungle [I have written 'similar to Angkor' in my notes] they encounter the oracle, a demonic face that appears above a well. He tells them that the tribe of the Blue People guard the temple of the Fountain. Once outside they encounter Jaffa with whom they reluctantly join forces. Travelling together they come to a great wall into which is built a massive face with stairs leading up to a huge open mouth, which in turn leads to the Blue People's domain. These strange people are led by a chief wearing a golden mask and their deity is the goddess Shiva [described as 'a large bronze statue with six arms']. Believing the intruders will defile the goddess, the chief makes the statue come to life. Sinbad and his men fight the six-armed statue, finally destroying it by smashing it into pieces. Meanwhile Margiana has been taken to be sacrificed to the God of the Underworld – Marisha. Lowering her into a pit she is taken deep into a cave system by Marisha, a one-eyed centaur. Sinbad and his men follow and arrive at the Fountain of Destiny.

My description of the Fountain of Destiny or Youth goes as follows: 'Jutting from the side of the wall of the cave are many carvings made by the ancient people. Water comes pouring out of an opening, cascading down into a large carved vessel spilling over the edge into the many cracks in the cave floor.' This description was inspired by a John Martin painting called *Sadak in Search of the Waters of Oblivion* (1812). Like all of Martin's work, it is striking and visual, illustrating his extraordinary pre-cinematic imagination.

The story continues:

By the Fountain awaits the centaur holding Margiana. Sinbad and his men fight the creature, saving Margiana and destroying the centaur by pushing him down a crevasse. Jaffa meanwhile has drunk from the Fountain's waters and becomes younger and younger, finally shrivelling to a mummy and dying.

The conclusion of the story remains unwritten. Apparently I had exhausted my imagination, and all I say is, 'The remainder of the story has yet to be worked out.' Although the outline is very basic (all step outlines are), on re-reading it I am surprised and gratified to discover that it contains many of the ideas used in the final film. It is no coincidence that my villain is named Jaffa. It was, of course, a tribute to Conrad Veidt's performance as the Vizier in Korda's *The Thief of Bagdad*, who I had always seen as the visual template for evil sorcerers. Even in some of the storyboards, when the sorcerer is named Koura and long before Tom Baker had been cast, the likeness to Veidt is unmistakable.

Sadly, one of the better ideas, the Valley of Snakes or Vipers, was never to see the light. I had planned to have a number of giant animated snakes in the foreground with real snakes slithering out of holes in the rock face in the background. I even went as far as making two drawings of the idea, but Charles has an aversion to snakes, and felt that it would upset pregnant women for some extraordinary reason, so the idea was dropped.

Charles was both excited with the outline's possibilities and confident that it would stand construction into a screenplay. So much so that several days later he commissioned Brian Clemens, a screenwriter with a reputation for fantasy (his credits included several Hammer Films and he was the creator of the hit television series *The Avengers*), to begin work on a treatment. The three of us began the inevitable sweatbox sessions, thrashing out how the project might evolve, adding new ideas and dropping bad ones. During these sessions we decided that the Vizier would be a victim, not an evil entity, and it would be for him that Sinbad would undertake the voyage.

One scene that did cause us problems was a pre-credit sequence. I sent a memo to Charles in which I suggested that almost the entire sequence be shot from a low subjective camera angle, implying something small and threatening moving through the palace:

In a palace corridor a cat hisses at something lurking in the shadows. From a very low point of view the camera moves forward until we see the legs of two guards towering above us. They guard a door, which is ajar. The camera enters and slowly glides over the floor towards a huge, richly covered bed. Moving

higher, we see a sleeping figure in the bed. On the wall behind is cast the shadow of a tiny humanoid figure that apparently begins to pour a liquid onto the face of the sleeping man. There is then a shock cut to the corridor as a shriek comes from the bedchamber. The door is flung open and a man runs down the corridor clutching his smoking face. The camera cuts to the shadows where we see the tiny humanoid with beady eyes, large ears and with a skin of scales.

This was to have been the dramatic introduction of the homunculus and the visual explanation of why the Vizier needed to find the Fountain of Destiny and restore his face. I make the point in the same memo that the Vizier is next seen wearing 'a golden stylized mask… giving him the appearance of something out of a robot world'. After much debate the sequence was dropped; it was felt that a faceless man would not be a good idea for a family film and might even gain the picture a more adult certificate. The faceless Vizier was reinstated at a later date, but the character only tells Sinbad how it happened. In my opinion the demise of the pre-credit sequence robbed the story of a shock opening, so presenting the audience with a mysterious other-worldly quality that perhaps the present opening doesn't completely possess.

On 14 May 1971 Brian produced a revised step outline entitled *Sinbad in India*:

In Marabia a legend foretells of a sailor wearing a golden amulet taking the Vizier and Margiana to the lost island of Cheduba to piece together six more tablets of gold to complete their destiny. Deep in a palace vault, Sinbad is told the legend and the Vizier reveals to him his face which is that of an ape.

The idea of a character being changed into an ape or baboon was a theme I had wanted to include in my original step outline. Although Brian used it here, it was later replaced with the faceless idea. The baboon, along with the carved stone face in the wall from my original outline, formed key sections of the plot for *Sinbad and the Eye of the Tiger*.

Sinbad, the Vizier and Margiana set sail but Jaffa sends an homunculus to sabotage Sinbad's navigation, enabling Jaffa to reach the island first and have an audience with a medium who provides him with directions to the Fountain of Destiny. When Sinbad arrives at the medium's temple, Jaffa brings a Shiva statue to life and whilst Sinbad overcomes the bronze giant, Jaffa manages to escape. Also during the fight Margiana is taken by a centaur and following the creature Sinbad arrives at the same time as Jaffa in the cave of the Fountain of Destiny.

In this early version the Fountain was a column of fire but subsequently became a fountain that changed from water to fire and back again, with a keeper of the Fountain rising on the water. This would have been spectacular but doubled the work required to insert the keeper. In the end the fire-fountain was dropped in favour of good old-fashioned water.

A griffin appears to fight the centaur and after a titanic battle the griffin wins and saves Margiana. Jaffa casts the golden tablets into the Fountain where they fuse into a huge key. Jaffa attempts to pick up the key but he turns into a toad. Sinbad reaches for the key and is not harmed and at that very moment the Vizier's face is restored.

Left hand page and left. Two key concept drawings for the unrealized sequence called the Valley of the Vipers. As a model animator one of my favourite creatures is the snake because the movements (especially in the tail) lend themselves to stop-motion animation.

Above. The griffin. A rough sketch for how I imagined the griffin (the word griffin would fluctuate between this spelling and gryphon, but in the end it was the latter that we used) would be introduced to the film as a stone statue, which was first suggested in May 1971.

Below. A section of the storyboard for the capture of the homunculus by Sinbad and the Vizier. In this section the homunculus is captured in a glass jar but this was changed in the final script. There were two armatured models: one 8 inches high which was used for the medium shots and the other a full 12-inch model that I used for most of the main animation sequences, including close-ups.

Sc. 81   CLOSE SHOT   SECTION OF CHEST (DYN) SINBAD shoves his sword under the chest in search of the HOMUNCULUS.

81 cont. The HOMUNCULUS quickly climbs the chest. as he disappears, SINBAD'S face can be seen looking under the chest in b.g.

Sc. 82   same as   CLOSE SHOT   SINBAD He sees it is useless and starts to get up off of the floor.

SC. 83   TOP OF CHEST   (DYN) The HOMUNCULUS climbs to the top and we pan with him as he runs along the top.   In b.g. is the VIZIER.

During subsequent sweatbox sessions we decided that the voyage to the island needed to be broken with an 'incident', and so in another memo to Charles dated 18 May 1971 I suggested that the figurehead on Sinbad's ship comes to life. 'The figure stirs from its position, climbing onto the deck of the ship. It smashes its way into the chart cabin, grabbing the ancient map which shows the island and its location.' I also place the creation of the homunculus by Jaffa onboard ship, after which he sets it free, 'releasing it to the wind'. My final suggestion in that memo was to have 'the griffin come from a stone statue'.

Everyone felt that the story now contained enough material to progress onto a screenplay, and between 16 and 22 August 1971 Brian wrote the first draft. The new innovations included Koura as the villain's name, a magic mirror, Lemuria as the island's name, and the multi-armed Goddess of the Blue Men named as Caro.

After spending some time dissecting this screenplay and discussing new ideas, Brian delivered a revised screenplay, dated 9–21 December 1971. In this version the story begins to smooth out, i.e. the plotline becomes more realistic in cinematic terms. The title had now become *Sinbad's Golden Voyage*, which would go on to be its shooting title.

The story had moved forward and the film we know today can be clearly identified. All the key Dynamation scenes are basically in place, as are the main characters. To round it off, the Blue Men have now become Green. Even though we had a relatively workable script, all of us continued with the process of smoothing situations and dialogue. Charles was almost as famous for his memos as David O. Selznick, but there is ample evidence that I also wrote many memos, suggesting improvements or additions, to both Charles and Brian. When I work on a project, I am continually thinking about the story and how to link the Dynamation as convincingly as possible. It is a never-ending process. In one memo I suggested that the Goddess should be changed to Kali because we had anticipated going to India for the principal photography. Dialogue was also uppermost in my mind. I wanted the main characters to have power and to seem more than ordinary. For example, I suggested that the Vizier say in the vault something like: 'Koura – his creation – his spy: an extension of his eyes and ears – a living homunculus!… Now he knows, Sinbad – as much as we…'. To explain how Koura creates his homunculus we are given a line on his ship, 'mandrake root and a few chemicals, Ahmed – is all that is needed'. Finally, as they see the temple in the jungle, the Vizier says, 'It is the temple of the Oracle… of All Knowledge… It is written – our path lies here…'. I felt that these few odd lines added reality to fantasy and conveniently explained as swiftly as possible how the creatures are created and how they come to be there. At one sweatbox session it was decided that the screenplay lacked Arabic references, so an expert in Arabic language was commissioned to write the special phrases that were used, mainly for comic relief. For example, 'I always trust in Allah, but always tie up my camel.'

Eventually, in June and July 1972 the final screenplay was completed by Brian:

Sinbad (John Philip Law) is returning from a voyage, when a strange flying creature is sighted circling the ship. An arrow is fired at it and the creature drops a golden amulet onto the deck. During a storm Sinbad experiences a strange dream. The ship reaches Marabia, where Sinbad meets the mysterious Vizier (Douglas Wilmer) who wears a golden mask to hide his burnt face and who also possesses an amulet. In a secret vault it is discovered that both amulets fit together forming a map to the lost island of Lemuria. Listening through his 'eyes and ears' – the homunculus – is the evil magician Prince Koura (Tom Baker). Sinbad, the Vizier and Margiana (Caroline Munro), a young girl who Sinbad has seen in his dream, set sail. During the voyage Koura steals Sinbad's map by bringing the ship's figurehead to life. However, reaching the island first, Sinbad and his crew discover the Temple of the Oracle of All Knowledge and consult the oracle (Robert Shaw) who tells that they must find the Fountain of Destiny where three (they must find the third) golden amulets will bring the bearer three gifts. Koura destroys the temple, sealing Sinbad and his companions inside. Escaping, they follow Koura to the Temple of the Green Men where the statue of the six-armed goddess Kali is brought to life by Koura. Sinbad and his men destroy her and amongst the smashed pieces is the remaining amulet. To avenge their deity, the Green Men offer Margiana as a sacrifice to the cyclopean centaur and Koura takes all the amulets. Finding Margiana in the Temple of the Fountain of Destiny they all look on as the centaur and a gryphon battle, with the latter losing because of Koura's interference. Sinbad kills the centaur but is too late to prevent Koura from placing the golden amulets in the fountain which restores his youth and gives him the cloak of darkness, rendering him invisible. Only able to see Koura's sword, Sinbad traps the magician in the fountain where the water makes him visible. Sinbad kills Koura. The waters give up a beautiful golden crown which Sinbad places on the Vizier's head, healing his face and restoring him to his rightful place on the throne of Marabia.

Conrad Veidt. Caroline Munro, an attractive and pleasant girl, was chosen to play Margiana. Being the early 1970s, her costume revealed a voluptuous display which up until that time was more than we were used to from our heroines. The part of the Vizier was played by Douglas Wilmer, a very accomplished British actor who had played Pelias in *Jason*. He possessed a majesty and dignity that is often difficult to find for such roles, and although the script demanded that he play almost the entire part behind a golden mask, he skilfully managed to give his character presence. Among the remaining members of the cast was a talented young actor called Martin Shaw, playing the role of Rachid, one of Sinbad's sailors.

Long before we had completed the screenplay, Gordon Hessler joined the team as director, bringing with him many original ideas. Gordon had worked with Alfred Hitchcock on the *Alfred Hitchcock Hour* as producer and director, and then gone on to direct a series of cult horror films. He was a perfect choice, mainly because he had the ability to extract the best from actors and guide them to believable performances.

Other production personnel were John Stoll, the production designer, and Fernando Gonzalez, art director and designer of the miniature sets. Designs for the more important props and sets are usually my domain, mainly because they have to fit the rest of the picture, especially on something like *Golden Voyage* where the overall concept is either Arabian/Moorish or Indian. One such vital prop was the Vizier's golden mask, based on a Persian warrior design. There were actually three masks made by Colin Arthur (the makeup artist) from my drawings and constructed from a cast of Douglas' face. All were made of fibreglass

Throughout pre-production we had intended to shoot almost the entire picture in India. The overall design, especially the Dynamation sequences, were conceived as being set in and around Indian locations carefully selected from history and travel books. As the lost continent of Lemuria is generally recognized as being located in the Indian Ocean, I conceived that the architecture on the island should resemble the Khymer in Western Indian. The 'lost city' of Angkor, in Cambodia, had captured my imagination many years before, and its obscure origins seemed to fit well with the parallel of Lemuria, therefore asserting a huge influence on the look of the picture. Aside from the design factor, there had been a more commercial reason for using Indian locations. Around that time many of the major Hollywood studios had invested large of sums money to photograph films in India, mainly because labour was inexpensive. However, once the money had been deposited, they found they couldn't withdraw it due to Indian laws, and were forced to search for possible productions to film there. Columbia Pictures had been no exception. They had a huge amount of frozen rupees that would have cut our production budget down considerably, so it seemed advantageous that we should use some, if not all, this money to enhance our meagre budget. However, as pre-production progressed, we began to hear frightening stories from producers who had filmed there, about the appalling red tape and bureaucracy they were forced to endure, and how extras accepted work on several pictures at the same time and then didn't show up when required. Without even going to India, and reluctantly forsaking the allure of those rupees, we decided the situation was not conducive to, shall we say, a realistic low budget picture such as ours. We therefore revised our plans and fell back on territory we knew: Spain. We chose Madrid and Majorca, and as it turned out, the scenic assets of Majorca were an excellent alternative, helping to convey a mood that perhaps may have been lost in India.

Now that we had a script, we began pre-production and casting. In the end the cast was one of the best we had ever managed to assemble, although finding Sinbad didn't prove easy. The last thing we wanted was someone with bulging muscles, but we did want an actor who possessed an athletic build and the rare ability to make such a fantasy character seem real. In the end we cast the very talented John Phillip Law. He made a convincing hero: tall and dashing in the swashbuckler tradition. His adversary, the evil magician Koura, was played by Tom Baker. Aside from his obvious presence on screen, it was his powerfully striking eyes that immediately caught our attention, reminding me of

for strength and lightness, with padding inside to prevent them from wobbling as Douglas moved. The masks had to be polished every morning to achieve a fresh, sparkling, burnished look, as the gold paint tended to tarnish almost overnight.

Ted Moore was director of cinematography, and his fine and professional expertise was yet another element that made the film special. Because we were dealing with mysticism rather than a magic lamp, we purposely avoided garish colours and a flamboyant storybook feel. We wanted a more realistic atmosphere than *7th Voyage*, so we asked Ted to mute the colours to give the picture a more subdued and natural atmosphere,

Sc. CLOSE SHOT MARGIANA She looks on.

Sc. 84 END OF CHEST (DYN) The HOMUNCULUS comes to the end of the chest, pausing Suddenly a large glass jar drops over him. VIZIER & MARGIANA move closer.

Sc. 85-88 FULL SHOT GROUP (DYN) We reveal that SINBAD has placed the glass jar over the HOMUNCULUS.

Sc. 86 CLOSER VIEW (DYN) VIZIER, SINBAD & MARGIANA see clearly the trapped little creature.

Sc. 85-88 FULL SHOT GROUP (DYN) We reveal that SINBAD has placed the glass jar over the HOMUNCULUS.

Sc. 86 CLOSER VIEW (DYN) VIZIER, SINBAD & MARGIANA see clearly the trapped little creature.

Sc. 87 CLOSE GROUP SHOT As they rise - they move slightly away from the table.

Sc. 88 FULL SHOT (DYN) The HOMUNCULUS overturns the glass jar and escapes. OUR VIEW moves with it. SINBAD & CO try to catch it.

Sc. 88 CONT. (continuation) As our view moves with the little creature.

Sc. 88 CONT. It finally lands on the floor. As it scampers out we see the large legs and feet of SINBAD & CO. In b.g.

Sc. 91-94 ANOTHER ANGLE (DYN) The HOMUNCULUS bounds into picture and quickly climbs up the drapery.

Sc. 92 CLOSE SHOT SINBAD He sees it getting away and throws an object at it, o.s.

Sc. 93 MEDIUM CLOSE SHOT (DYN) The object strikes the curtain causing H. to fall.

Sc. 94 ANOTHER ANGLE (DYN) As the body of the HOMUNCULUS falls into fire.

Sc. 95 CLOSE SHOT SINBAD, MARGIANA, VIZIER as they are blown by the wind.

Above. Further homunculus storyboard sketches.

Right. Koura bringing the homunculus to life. The origins and concept of the homunculus were established in ancient alchemy, being an artificially created miniature human form fashioned by use of chemical reaction and, of course, magic.

Left. Key drawing for the creation of the homunculus by a sorcerer. This drawing was rendered many years before when I was planning *The 3 Worlds of Gulliver* but the idea was never used. I resurrected the concept for *The Golden Voyage of Sinbad* and the scene in which Koura creates the tiny creature is very similar.

making everything look a little dusty and worn.

Accompanied by Diana, I flew to Madrid on 16 June 1972. Live-action shooting began on 19 June at Arta and moved to Palma on 27 June. From 3 July to 12 August we shot all the studio interiors and exteriors, including the travelling matte foregrounds, which were completed with the final shot on the deck of Sinbad's ship. We wanted to use the Alhambra Palace (as we had done for *7th Voyage*) for the live-action scenes inside the walls of Marabia, but the Granada authorities threatened to charge us so much for rental, we were forced to find an alternative. In the end we found the Palace Generalife Palma, Majorca, which

Majorca, which had been Sokurah's cave, was now used as the interior of the temple of the oracle. Torrente de Pareis in Majorca, with its striking cliffs and river mouth reached only through a solid rock tunnel, might be recognized as the scene where the dragon and Cyclops fight in *7th Voyage*. Good locations are always hard to find, and as these hadn't been used in nearly twenty years, we felt there was plenty of life left in them, especially if shot from different angles.

We used the facilities of the Verona Studios, up in the mountains near Madrid, to film the interior and exterior sets. Sinbad's ship, which had only two sides

the cave/Fountain of Destiny) were photographed on one of the stages at the Madrid studio. Yet for the miniature shots of Sinbad's and Koura's ships at sea, we travelled to the film complex at Rinella in Malta to use what was then the world's largest (400 feet by 300 feet) sea/marine tank. Constructed next to the sea, when filled with water the tank merges with the real sea behind, allowing a genuine horizon and natural skyline. An ordinary studio tank would have the sky painted down to the water line and makes the horizon always look too near.

After the live action was completed, I returned to England to begin effects and animation in the Goldhawk Studios in Shepherds Bush, West London. However, the small studio area was on the first floor, and to avoid vibration from the traffic outside (buses were the worst), we had a special concrete floor laid.

On 20 September 1972 I began animation. The first scene was of the tiny homunculus flying above Sinbad's ship. Some legends claim that the basis of its creation is the mandrake root, which has five appendages, resembling the human form, and that when pulled from the ground it was thought to scream. When the root is mixed with certain potions and the alchemist's blood, a homunculus is formed, ready to do the alchemist's bidding. After seeing the human homunculi in *The Bride of Frankenstein*, I had always wanted to use the idea of a homunculus in one of our films, although I realized it would have to be modified to meet the requirements of modern storytelling. They were created by Koura to act as an extension of his eyes and ears. Incidentally, the bat that appears in the dream montage during the storm was a similar model, which I constructed from one of the pterodactyls from *The Valley of Gwangi*.

The homunculus appears next in the vault sequence,

> The long shots of the city of Marabia were actually paintings by Emilio Ruiz del Rio, who specialized in painting effects for films. He was extremely talented and had provided painted cities and exotic location shots for many of the Italian 'sword and sandal' epics filmed in Spain. Usually these special shots were painted on glass or used a hanging miniature, but Emilio executed these paintings on a thin metal sheet (5–7 feet across), which had the advantage of allowing the camera to pan across it. He first of all noted what time of day we wanted to shoot the scene so that the shadows cast by the sun would match those in the painting. He then set up the metal sheet about 6 feet from the camera (the position marked on the ground), so that when we came back to shoot, perhaps two or three days later, the hanging painting would be in exactly the same position for the camera. Cutting the sheet to fit in with the contours of the landscape, including the trees, he then executed the details of the buildings to fit with the natural lie of the land. All extremely clever.
>
> For the shot of Sinbad's ship moored in the harbour in Marabia, Emilio painted the upper part of a scene, complimented by actors bustling around as though it was a busy harbour. It gives the illusion that the ship is in water and one of many vessels in the harbour by adding ships' masts. To set the whole thing off, he then painted the city in the background.

had been styled to resemble a Moorish village complete with an Alhambra-like palace. With a few cinematic modifications we managed to achieve a look that was in many ways superior to the Alhambra. While Manzanares, near Madrid, was used for the scenes of Koura's imposing castle, we also used two locations seen in *7th Voyage*. The Caves of Arta on

and was made mainly of plaster, was constructed on a hill with no sea anywhere near it. However, we built a section of the ship down by the sea for high shots in which water would be seen, and used other cinematic tricks to make it seem as if the ship was on the sea. All the miniature sets (exterior of the Temple of the Oracle, exterior of the Green Men temple, interior of

   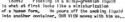   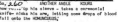 

Top left and right. A section of the storyboard for my original concept of how the homunculus comes to life.

Above. Matte painting. Spanish artist Emilio Ruiz del Rio standing in front of his wonderful painting for the city of Marabia. The detailed painting was executed on metal, mounted and cut out to fit into the contours of the background, so that when the camera was set up, the whole thing blended as one.

Above. Still of the ship. The full size set of Sinbad's ship built miles from the sea at the Verona Studios in Spain.

Right hand page, left and centre. Two of my key drawings for the figurehead. The image of Elsa Lancaster and her 'flared' hairstyle in *Bride of Frankenstein* provided some inspiration. Although a Moslem ship would have no figurehead (unless captured from the infidel), this theatrical idea stayed in the story simply because everyone seemed to like it.

Right hand page far right. Homunculus model.

Right hand page right centre. Homunculus sequence still. The birth of the homunculus parallels the birth of the Ymir in *20 Million Miles to Earth*, but this time I indulged myself by producing identifiable emotional characteristics.

Right hand page right bottom. The homunculus on the floor of the Vizier's vault. There were two armatured models of homunculi, one 8 inches high, used for the medium shots, and the other a full 12-inch model, used for most of the main animation sequences, including close-ups.

when Sinbad and the Vizier discover the secret of the amulets. The creature is knocked from its hiding place on a ledge and is chased around the floor. There were two reasons why the chase takes place on the ground. One was to give the audience a point of view of the room as seen by the creature. The effect of seeing everything as huge, especially the humans who tower over him, makes the whole sequence more powerful. The other reason is far more practical. If the camera is looking down, there is a potentially large area to match for the matte lines, so this problem was eliminated by having the creature break its wing and therefore confined to the floor. The less the floor is seen, the easier it is to create matte lines for the creature to run between.

Later in the film Koura creates another homunculus. This is one of my favourite sequences, and the emotions of the creature come through. For example, it looks around at its surroundings, paces up and down the table, reacts fearfully to Koura by making spitting noises, and finally it overcomes its fear and jumps onto Koura's sleeve. These reactions gave it charm and, to some degree, personality. The sequence slows the pace of the picture but this is sometimes important. In this case we witness the power of the sorcerer and the forces of magic, but it also illustrates how the homunculus is only a tool of Koura's evil. Most of the birth was executed on an animation table painted to resemble a small marble slab, but for the scene where the creature jumps onto Koura's sleeve, I drew a matte line along the top edge of Tom's sleeve onto which the homunculus appears to jump. For the shots of Koura and Achmed (Koura's assistant) looking down at the homunculus on the table in the foreground, we first of all rehearsed both actors with a stand-in model of the creature. This gave them the eye line and allowed me to illustrate

what I intended the creature to do. When they had mastered exactly where to look and how to react, we photographed the scene for real but minus the model. While Tom was convincing throughout the film, in this scene one really believes he is seeing and nurturing the creature. The scene is also enhanced by the music. As the creature began to flap its wings, composer Miklós Rózsa supplied a harp glissando, making the homunculus and the entire scene literally come alive.

The final appearance of the homunculus is in the cave of the Oracle. Just after Sinbad and his party descend into the cave, and as the last man leaves the frame, the creature appears at the top of the steps and looks down at them. I particularly like this appearance because the creature isn't expected to appear at that point. To keep the element of surprise, I wanted to allow the live action and the appearance of the homunculus to be continuous. To have used a cutaway would have disrupted the scene, so I drew a matte line along the top of the steps and allowed my homunculus to stroll into the picture. After Koura has sealed them all in, the homunculus makes his final appearance when he attacks Sinbad as he tries to escape by ascending a rope. This was done by photographing a rear projection plate of John climbing the rope, during which I would talk him through the actions of what the creature would be doing to make him lose his hold. When it came to the animation, I carefully timed John's movements as he tried to fend off the creature and then matched the model homunculus (on aerial wires) to the movements. At the end of the scene the homunculus is killed by an arrow. After a cutaway shot of the real actor releasing an arrow, we see the homunculus being speared with what was a miniature arrow. This arrow was constructed to allow a wire to pass through the length of its shaft,

on which it was mounted. The wire extended from off camera and into the model, and I animated its progression along the wire simultaneously with the movements of the model. Eventually I allowed it to pierce the homunculus' body.

From the animated to the inanimate, or should that be inanimate to the inanimate. It's all very confusing when everything I do is actually inanimate and only becomes animated when it is animated by me. Anyway, I am sure it is apparent by now that I have always had a fascination with bringing extraordinary creatures to life, but what fascinates me even more is bringing obviously inanimate objects to life. *In Golden Voyage* I was able to indulge myself with two examples. The first was the figurehead of Sinbad's ship, or as the publicity department inaccurately called it, the siren. The whole sequence came about as a device to enable Koura to steal the chart. In our case, it was not situated on the bow of the ship, but on the mast nearest the bow. This 'slight' alteration was necessary because I didn't want to animate the figure climbing onto the deck, which would have been cumbersome and not nearly as effective. Like everything, the design went through many changes.

The first indication we have that the figurehead is 'alive' occurs when a sailor is on watch at the prow of the ship. The figurehead (next to which he is standing) moves her outstretched arm down to her side. The sailor holds his drinking responsible for the illusion, but when the sculpture moves her head to look at him, he raises the alarm. The figurehead then proceeds to pull her entire body away from the wooden support. First of all we photographed the actor on the full set. This included the wooden section from which the sculpture tears herself away but with the full-size

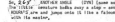

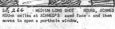

THE SIREN FIGUREHEAD

THE SIREN

figurehead removed. This was then used as a rear projection plate against which I aligned the model to appear as if it was in its correct position. Next I animated it so that it seems as if the figurehead was tearing herself away, jerking her body, specifically her shoulders, from side to side. The action and the noise of wood rending gave the whole pre-fight sequence a terrifying anticipation.

Having freed herself, the figurehead smashes her arm into the deck cabin to obtain the map. The destruction of the cabin was achieved on the full set. Wires were attached to sections designed to fall apart, and just after the sailor runs from the cabin, the wires were pulled and the cabin collapsed. Once again, I used this as the rear projection plate and matched the collapse of the cabin with the actions of the model. This gave the audience a subconscious feeling that what they knew to be real was linked to what seemed unreal. There are other examples of 'contact' in this sequence. In the ensuing fight an axe is thrown by one of the sailors and buries itself in the figurehead's side. The actor threw the real axe and as soon as the rear-projected image of the axe appears to touch the model, I substituted a miniature one. The real one continues its flight unseen on the plate, behind the model. Another example shows the figurehead being pushed back by a torch (fire was the only thing she would be afraid of) until she crashes through the ship's rail and plummets over the side. For the rear projection plate we photographed the actors shadow boxing in front of a

full-size rail with a section missing. In the studio I built a miniature of the missing section of rail and fixed it so that it appeared to fill the missing section on the rear-projected image. It was this that she crashes through. The final touch that enables her to disappear over the side was achieved by drawing a matte line behind the rail and it is behind this that she actually disappears.

The final scene in the figurehead sequence shows it plunging into the sea and sinking to the bottom. The plunge into the surface of the sea was shot in the sea tank on Malta but the underwater shots were photographed in a specially constructed five-foot by two-foot plate glass tank in the London studio. The water was clouded to make it seem as if it were the bottom of the sea, and to simulate bubbles we inserted an Alka Seltzer tablet into a hole in the back of the model.

The object of the story was to locate the other amulets, which in turn would allow the adventurers to achieve their destiny, but first they had to find the island of Lemuria. The ancient lost continent of Lemuria was purportedly pre-Atlantean, and like Atlantis, the science of geology refuses to acknowledge its existence.

Instead of constructing a model of Lemuria, as I had done for *7th Voyage*, we used real locations. For the first sight of the island I used a stock shot of an island near Tahiti. Originally it had been photographed with an anamorphic lens (widescreen or scope), and we decided to use the footage without un-squeezing it. This squeezed image provided us with exaggerated jagged peaks, giving the impression of a place never seen before.

Once on the island, the first stop is the Temple of the Oracle of All Knowledge, which Sinbad hopes will help them find the hiding place of the last amulet. The 39-inch miniature was beautifully constructed and mounted on a large table by Prosper (head of the Spanish set and miniature construction) and his crew. Because Koura demolishes the building, we constructed it in small, brick-like sections so that when shot at high speed it would seem to disintegrate outwards like large stone blocks. In the live action, explosives were used to destroy the doorway, but as we needed a safer method to collapse the miniature structure, Prosper had constructed the miniature with a hollow centre, accessible from beneath the table on which it was built. When we were ready to shoot, he pushed his hand up through the centre of the miniature, which in turn pushed the bricks outward. Because we wanted a selection of takes, the structure had to be rebuilt several times before we were happy with the result.

The action next moves to the Temple of the Green Men, or as it is better known, the Temple of Kali. I designed the temple so that its vast, shadowy Indian-like façade would fill the audience with awe and an anticipation of wondrous things to come. The imposing exterior was in fact a miniature that I would have preferred to have been much larger so as to compensate for the flames beneath the recessed statues, which looked far too big (even though they had been shot at high speed) in proportion to the building. Everything in the foreground, including the actors, steps and rock,

Above. Stills of figurehead as it appeared in the film. The first shows the figurehead as it would be seen on the prow of Sinbad's ship. The second is the figurehead on the animation table holding the boat hook, during the fight sequence.

Above right. A rough drawing on a location photograph to show where the faces and temples will appear as Sinbad and the others land on Lemuria. The landing on the beach was photographed at Torrentes de Paris, and I later added the gigantic stone faces in the cliffs and the ancient temples (which were 10-inch high plaster models)

by means of mattes. These images introduce the adventurers and the audience to the Indian-type culture of the island's ancient people.

Right hand page top. The faces and temples of Lemuria as they appear in the final film.

Right hand page bottom. Still of the exterior of the Temple of Green Men or The Temple of Kali. The imposing exterior of the Temple of Kali was in fact a 32-inch high miniature, into which the actors would be later added (sandwiched between the temple and the foreground miniature foliage) by means of a travelling matte.

was full-size and added in by travelling matte.

Once inside the temple, the focus is initially on the action between Koura, Sinbad and the Green Men, but in the background is the huge bronze figure of Kali, always dominating the set and commanding the attention of the audience, no matter what is being played out in the foreground. Kali is the Hindu goddess of destruction, also known as 'the dark mother', and was seen as the consort of Shiva. She possessed four arms and a belt of skulls or serpents symbolizing savagery and the cannibalism practised by her cult. For the purposes of our film I designed her with six arms, each wielding a sword, but otherwise I based it on traditional images, although we played down the cannibalism. There was only one model, of about 14 inches high, which is now in a very sorry state because the years have taken their toll on her latex body.

To demonstrate his powers to both the Green Men and Sinbad, Koura brings the bronze figure to life and commands her to dance for him. We were lucky to obtain the talents of the noted Indian dancer Surya Kumari, who interpreted what I wanted. Assisted by one of her students, whom we strapped to her back, we first shot the dance on black and white film stock to give me the reference for four of the six arms I would have to animate on the model. In addition, we also made a rear projection plate, the duration of which corresponded with Surya's dance, and consisted of Tom and others in exactly the same positions and nothing else (the full-size statue of Kali had been removed from the set). Miklós Rózsa did compose music for the dance sequence as part of his score, but by the end of production we felt that it required authentic Indian music. We therefore commissioned three Indian musicians to compose and play music to match the action, which they made an excellent job of. Rózsa did, however, write the score for the remainder of the film, including the fight sequence for which he

created a kind of musical Morse code. You can hear the staccato theme – dot, dot, dash – conjuring up the illusion that a telepathic message was being sent by Koura, who looks as though he is directing the whole fight.

The fight begins when Koura throws Kali his sword. As it flies through the air, I exchanged the real sword for a miniature. This 'sleight of hand' occurs as it passes behind the sword of Sinbad, who raises his weapon when Koura throws his sword to the statue. Of course, I couldn't just have the statue fight with one sword when she had six hands, so after Kali catches it in one hand, a separate weapon sprouts from each of the other hands. Straightforward enough, but how did the swords grow? The secret was cardboard. I made five separate cardboard swords painted to resemble the original and then photographed the whole thing in reverse. I counted the number of frames required for the sword to grow and then wound the film back and shot each frame in reverse. I would shoot a frame of the complete cardboard sword, carefully cut a section off the top and then shoot another frame of film. I continued with this until I was left with no sword, going through this process five times in all. When the film was printed in reverse and projected at the correct speed, it looked as if the swords were growing.

The staging of the sword fight was almost as complicated a process as the skeleton fight in *Jason*. When one describes the scene, it sounds fairly easy – a number of actors reacting to an imagined 8-foot high bronze statue with six lethal swords – but the reality was actually a nightmare. Every movement of the actors had to be carefully choreographed to ensure that each individual performed each movement with perfect timing so as to guarantee that they would be in a specific place at a specific time to enable me to animate the statue to their movements. When it came to the live action, our invaluable stuntman Fernando

Poggi carefully went through the moves to translate them into a viable professional sequence of fight actions. Poggi strapped three of his stuntmen together with a very large belt. This then simulated the six fighting arms of the statue. It was, of course, important that the men's arms were synchronized so that it wouldn't seem as though they were simply hacking away, and this is where the many long rehearsals proved their worth. As with other such sequences, the actors had to shadow box, but by now the routine was so ingrained in their minds, they could have done it with their eyes closed.

Left hand page top. Key drawing for the interior of the Temple of the Oracle of All Knowledge showing the oracle rising out of the well.

Left hand page bottom right. Key drawing for the Kali dance. The dance, which was basically Indian, needed some specialized choreography. I was specifically keen on the side-to-side head movements. As with all animation fights, and long before the live action, I had designed and sketched about 50 continuity drawings illustrating the overall pattern of the fight.

Left hand page, extreme bottom left and above. Kali thumbnail sketch and the model on the animation table during the photography of the fight sequence. Kali was the second of the three metal creations I animated during my career, and was by far and away the most active. Because of this, the animation took just over two months to complete.

Above. Stuntmen choreographing the Kali fight sequence. In this very rare still the stuntmen can be seen taking the place of what would be Kali during a run through of the fight action as choreographed by Poggi. When John Phillip Law and the other actors had picked up the movements, they were then required to go through the motions again, in other words shadow boxing.

Middle. Model of Kali.

Right. Still of Kali fighting Sinbad.

My one regret about the Kali sequence is that the full-size plaster statue that appears at the beginning and the end does not actually resemble my model. Long before we arrived in Spain to begin filming, I had sent a copy of the model, made from the original mould, to the Spanish construction department, on which they were to base a full-size prop. Unfortunately, something went terribly wrong, perhaps due to lack of communication. When Charles and I arrived on set the day we were due to begin shooting, I was horrified to see that the statue wasn't the same as my concept. Although the torso had its differences, it was the head that bore little resemblance to the one I had designed. The full-size version had a more masculine face. As filming was just about to begin, there was no time to change it, so we were forced to keep it, although it only appears out of shot, or at least in long shot. It was one of those events over which we had little control, and at the time reminded me of the elephant fiasco during the filming of *The Valley of Gwangi*.

During the fight there are one or two 'incidents' I designed to heighten the action and pace of the sequence. The first shows a sailor throwing a blazing brazier that hits the statue and falls to the ground. The brazier was real, mounted on a wire strung horizontally across the set. At a certain point the brazier was stopped in mid-air, after which it fell to the ground. In the studio I animated Kali to be in the exact spot where the brazier stops so that it seems as if the object bounces off the miniature. The only problem we had with the effect was that although the metal brazier stopped, the coals of the fire didn't. Fortunately, they seem to spray over the bronze statue in a way that looks as if they are hitting a solid object. Another enhancement occurs at the climax of the sequence. Kali is fighting Sinbad and his men on a short flight of steps leading to a stone platform. Some of the best fight sequences have taken place on stairs, and they always help the action.

I have to confess that when faced with the animation for such a complex sequence, I would wonder why I made life so difficult for myself. It was wonderful to dream and plan such effects, but how would I make them all work? Whatever doubts I had about this sequence, today I am extremely proud of it. Everything seemed to come together. The stunts were all first-rate and the action flows at a cracking pace.

Following the destruction of Kali, the Green Men, encouraged by Koura, capture Sinbad and prepare to sacrifice Margiana to their god by lowering her into a pit. From a cave emerges a huge one-eyed centaur. The idea of incorporating a centaur into a project had first raised its head during the preparations for *Jason and the Argonauts*. I decided to combine two legends and came up with a cyclopean centaur. Surprisingly, this worked perfectly, especially when it was decided to use the single eye design as a motif throughout the story. The eye, after all, is the window to the soul and therefore ideally suited to our tale of destiny. In the end I believe I achieved the correct balance, although some wag suggested at the time of the film's release that he looked a little like David Bowie because of the hairstyle.

At first, the audience doesn't see anything, we only hear hooves echoing on the rock floor. Eventually, in the depths of the tunnel a strange shadow is cast onto the wall, followed by the creature's appearance into light as he dips his head to avoid the top of the cave entrance. The interior of the tunnel was a miniature (about the height of the centaur) in which I animated the model to cast a shadow and then to appear. The whole thing was then matted into the main picture with Margiana, although when the centaur steps out of the tunnel into the main cave, it does so by means of a split screen.

All the opposing forces – Koura, the centaur with Margiana and Sinbad and his men – converge in the massive cavern of the Fountain of Destiny where the final battle between good and evil is to be fought. Because the Fountain of Destiny was just a fountain, albeit a very big one, I knew I would have to come up with a design that would kinetically enhance it. In the end I went for the protective shape of a circle of stone monoliths resembling Stonehenge, a monument that has always been seen as a mystical construction. Because stone circles also appear in various forms in other cultures throughout the world, their appearance in Lemuria seemed quite acceptable. The overall concept of the Fountain encased with its monoliths, inside a huge cavern lit by two shafts of light, gave the impression of a special place.

We had a tough time making the Fountain of Destiny look as if it was rising 50 feet. At first we tried a single jet of water, but it looked insipid, and after experimentation we settled for four separate jets of water clustered together, giving the necessary body the fountain required. To achieve the colour changes, coloured gels were used in the lights mounted behind the monoliths, but when Koura dies in the fountain, we also had to inject a red dye into the water to obtain a rich blood-like colour. Once again, we photographed the water at high speed to give the water 'weight'.

The scene is set for Koura to acquire, for his own evil ends, the secrets of the Fountain of Destiny, but there is still one more surprise: another mythological creature. Generally the gryphon was seen as the representation for the forces of good. This background made it a perfect adversary to the cyclopean centaur, and so in our story the gryphon is the guardian of the Fountain and represents good as opposed to the evil of the centaur, a conflict that parallels the one between Sinbad and Koura.

The battle between the gryphon and the centaur was another complicated sequence to animate. After all these years I was still incapable of designing a straightforward sequence. That would have been too easy. It wasn't just that I needed to astound an audience, it was that I was always trying to challenge myself by designing a sequence that was more spectacular than the last, and although the ideas always seemed good on paper, the reality of animation often seemed overwhelming. This time I was faced with co-ordinating eight legs, two arms, two heads, mouths, eyes, two tails and a pair of large and rather cumbersome wings, all of which had to be choreographed into a feasible fight. The wings presented the major problem because they had to be continually flapping

Above and right. Stills of centaur. Just thinking up the idea of a cyclopean centaur is a long way from reality, and I spent considerable time designing this creature, trying to achieve a believable half-man half-horse, but at the same time making him look aggressive. The model of the centaur is about 13 inches high, with ocelot fur for the horse section and a tiny doll's eye in his forehead.

Top and bottom right. Fight between the gryphon and centaur. The bottom image shows the models on the animation table and the top a scene of the fight from the completed film. I had originally conceived that during the fight the gryphon would fly up to the ceiling of the cavern, dive bombing the centaur, but when it came to shooting the sequence, I realized that the creature's design would make it far too heavy to fly, so I dropped it.

Left. The Fountain of Destiny (and how to get there). This was a map that I drew for reference to show where the miniature set of the Fountain of Destiny would appear in the cave. Notice that the stone gryphon is still a possibility, so it must have been drawn before the final screenplay was agreed.

Above. The miniature set of the Fountain of Destiny with a cutout of Sinbad for reference. The set was huge. The monoliths were 32 inches high and the fountain was constantly maintained at a height of 51 inches. The rock background was over 15 feet high and the whole thing was built on a wooden platform (32 inches off the ground), allowing access to the special pumps installed to supply the fountain.

Sc. 635-639 FULL SHOT (HS- MIN- DYN- TM)
As the CENTAUR backs away from SINBAD and his men.
The creature rears as the men stab him again and again.

Sc. 636 CLOSE UP SHOT (DYN2 TM4 MIN B.G.)
Again the men in f.g. swing their swords as
the CENTAUR in b.g. rears and bellows.

Sc. 640 CLOSE SHOT KOURA He sees
no chance of aiding the CENTAUR.

Sc. 641 SINBAD rams the sword into the
CENTAUR o.s.

Sc. 642 ANOTHER ANGLE DYN-TM-MIN B.G.)
The sword can be seen sticking from the creatures
chest as he rears and bellows in pain.

Top. Section of 'slaying of the centaur' storyboard. I have to confess that when I was animating the centaur, I had in mind an opera tenor in his final death throes. The idea was shamelessly over the top, but in this context it is hopefully accepted.

Below and opposite. A section of the storyboard for the appearance of the griffon.

Above and right. Sinbad slaying centaur. The two images above show John Phillip Law shadow boxing the centaur. The next image and the one on the right show the sequence with the centaur added as he is slain by Sinbad.

Right hand page bottom right. A close-up of the centaur.

Right hand page right. Various scenes from the film. These show the centaur attacking Sinbad with his giant club, lusting after Margiana and attacking Kurt Christian.

· THE FOUNTAIN OF DESTINY · 115 B

Sc. 626 (Dyn) MEDIUM SHOT CENTAUR IN F/G.
He hurls the rock at SINBAD. It shatters against
the monolith.- just missing SINBAD'S head.

Sc. 627. CLOSE SHOT MARGIANA (as she
turns to the fountain and says a simple
moving prayer. There is a sound......

Sc. 628 CLOSE SHOT CAVE on other side of large
cave. The Echo sounds of beating of wings and
a lion-eagle roar comes from the tunnel.

Sc. 631 CLOSE SHOT CAVE (same as 628)
As crashing out of the tunnel appears a live GRIFFIN
- half eagle-half lion - and awesome creature.
It roars.

Sc. 633 (Dyn) (Same as 626) SINBAD moves into
picture again watching the reactions
of the CENTAUR.

Sc. 633A CLOSE SHOT SINBAD as he watches
the irritated CENTAUR. He moves out of pic.

to achieve dramatic effect and to supposedly allow the creature to retain its balance.

The gryphon's death was due to Koura's intervention; he tips the scales in favour of the centaur when he slashes the creature's rear leg. This 'contact' between sword and model occurs between the rear projection plate and the model. The real sword is held by Tom on the rear projection plate, but at the point where it seems to touch the gryphon, I replaced the real sword with a miniature one suspended on wires. To add another touch to the incident, I slit the gryphon's leg, adding a mixture of Kensington Gore (artist blood) and glycerine (to thicken it), which I animated to produce flowing blood.

Once the gryphon is eliminated, it is the centaur's turn to be brought down, this time by Sinbad. The hero jumps onto the creature's back, which was achieved by a cut between the real Sinbad and a miniature Sinbad. From here he is able to plunge a knife into its neck. Dying, the centaur falls onto the body of the gryphon.

Whilst the fighting is in progress, and unseen by Sinbad, Koura drops two of the three amulets into the Fountain. The first grants him the gift of youth and the second a shield of darkness (invisibility). Believing himself totally invisible, he steps into the waters of the gushing Fountain where his outline can be seen by Sinbad. With one quick thrust Koura meets his demise and his blood turns the Fountain of Destiny red.

Now Sinbad has the last gift, he casts the remaining amulet into the waters. The surface becomes placid and in it we see reflected a Sinbad dressed in fine clothes and wearing 'the crown of untold riches', although his real image in the top half of the screen remains the same. The crown appears from the water,

but instead of taking it for himself, he places it on the Vizier's head. For the first time we are able to see Douglas Wilmer as his features are restored. Ray Bradbury always used to say to me, 'Why didn't we have him with a tear in his eye after he got his face back?' In retrospect Ray is quite right – it would have been a good touch to end on, but at the time no one thought of it.

During pre-production both Charles and I begin to anticipate who might write the music score for the picture. Since the exclusion of Bernie, it had become more and more difficult to find someone able to handle fantasy. This problem was still being mulled over when we completed the location shooting, and at the end of shoot party we were presented with a poem (I believe composed by someone in Charles' office) that alludes to the film's as yet unwritten score: 'Ray is good and what is more / vowed that he will write a score / Charles was speechless at the plan / said by golly if you can / Bernard Herrmann's lost the job / I'll even pay you thirty bob!!' I am glad to say that Charles never considered this option. Eventually he asked Miklós Rózsa. I had long admired his work, especially his beautiful score for *The Thief of Bagdad*, and knew that there could be no one better for our Arabian fantasy. Unfortunately, because of the budgetary restrictions, Miklós didn't get a full orchestra, and this was reflected in the magazine *Gramophone*. In their July 1974 review of Rozsa's record score accompanying the film's release, they said, 'A new score by Miklós Rózsa – and this is the first for several years – is always welcome, the more so in this case since the music was so poorly dubbed onto the actual film soundtrack: a strange fault in a film which depended so much on its

Sc. 629   CLOSE SHOT   KOURA as he looks towards the sound in the tunnel.

Sc. 630 (Dyn)   CLOSE SHOT CENTAUR as he glares in the direction of the o.s. sound.

Sc. 634   (Dyn)   In b.g. SINBAD runs for cover behind the CENTAUR and out of pic. CENTAUR rears.

music to bring Ray Harryhausen's special effects to life. Here the sound is clean and clear if not particularly bright and we can hear the music as it should have been heard on the film.' Rósza's music was a different style to that of Bernie: more romantic and traditional with rich, luxurious themes. His score for *The Golden Voyage of Sinbad* includes both vivid and memorable sections, with the magic working its spell, especially during the fight between the centaur and the gryphon (with its two bass tubas). Rózsa was a traditional writer, using strings and brass to achieve a depth of mystery and fantasy so vital in such a subject, whereas Bernie would use new techniques to achieve his sounds.

The film was completed for $982,351, a remarkably small sum, even for the early 1970s. Released in the summer of 1974, unlike the press reviews for *The Valley of Gwangi*, those for *Golden Voyage* were generally very good. It seems that we had hit the right time for such an adventure, with many of the reviewers making the point that this was a serious fantasy for both children and adults. The UK magazine *Films and Filming* was ecstatic: 'the film has most of what the Hollywood swashbucklers contained, and in some senses more'. Jay Cocks in *Time* magazine was also complimentary: 'These creatures have their origin in the imagination and the workshop of Ray Harryhausen… He brings

them all alive in a process called Dynarama, which would appear to combine equal portions of stop-action photography, elaborate multiple-exposures and a kind of gentle necromancy.' However, the review by Roger Ebert in the *Chicago Sun-Times* is the one I like best: 'I recalled a recent screening where a bunch of film buffs were waiting for an elevator and one said, "Seen any halfway decent movies yet this summer?" and the other said, "Only *Sinbad*". Halfway decent, because it did one of two things movies are supposed to do. It created and sustained a fantasy. It was exciting escapist adventure. It was fun.' No greater praise from a critic could anyone wish for their work.

The public also liked it. The film went on to become a runaway success all over the world, and as far as I am concerned, it is another personal favourite, one in which all the ingredients came together successfully. But just because the critics and the public like a film, it doesn't mean that the Academy of Motion Picture Arts and Sciences® does. Although many of our films were submitted to the Academy for a possible Special Effects award, none came even near to being nominated. In the case of *The Golden Voyage of Sinbad*, the Kali sequence was shown to the Academy judges, and I am told by a friend who was at the meeting that the committee members thought Kali was a full-sized

Below. A recording session. Miklós Rózsa, the film's music composer, with Charles and me at a recording in Rome. In the first image I seem to be looking up at Miklós in awe.

Right hand page. Poster. The poster for *The Golden Voyage of Sinbad*, which I think helped the film to be the huge success that it was.

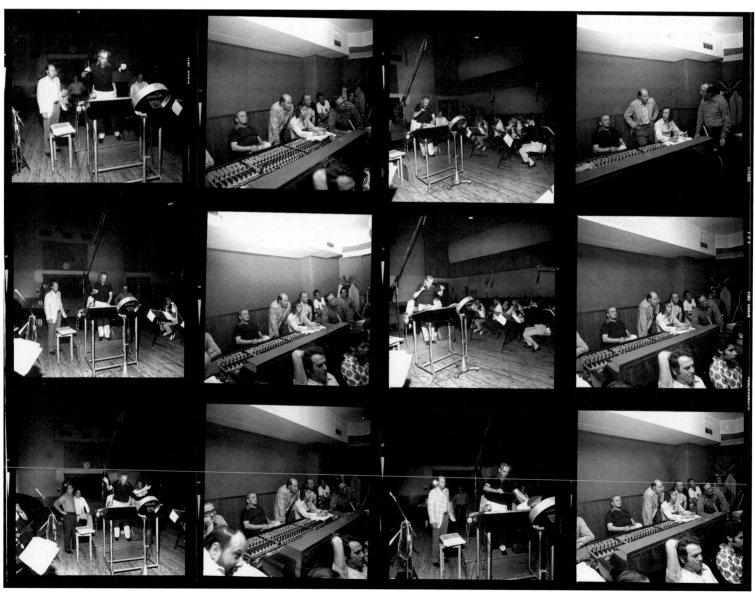

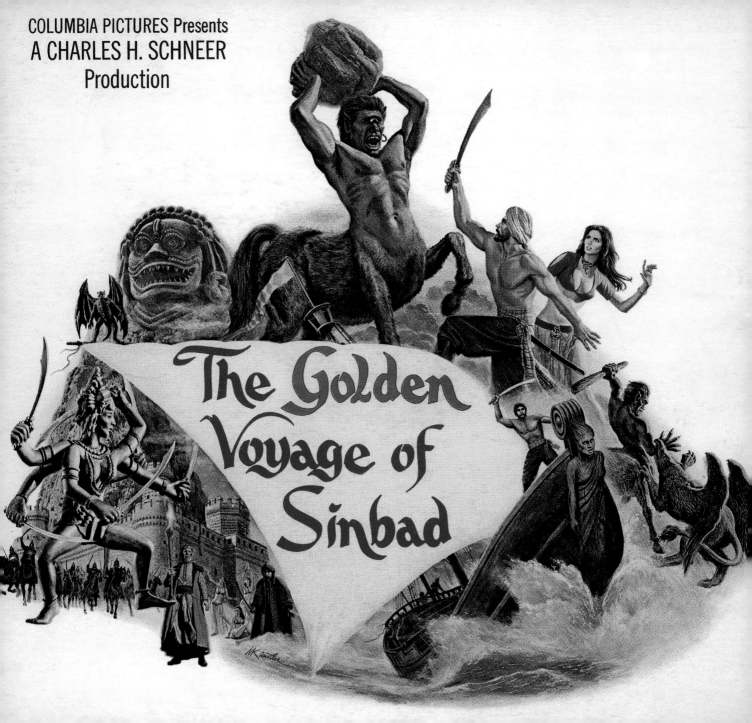

COLUMBIA PICTURES Presents
A CHARLES H. SCHNEER
Production

The Golden Voyage of Sinbad

mechanical statue! These judges were themselves effects people and must have been aware that it was stop-motion, so I don't know how they rationalized this assessment of my work. I have often wondered if our lack of acceptance by the Academy was because we were working in Europe rather than Hollywood. In any event, I don't believe the Academy ever really took our work seriously or judged stop-motion animation fairly. The only time that I am aware of stop-motion winning an award was in 1950 for Obie's *Mighty Joe Young*. in fairness to the Academy, I did receive a 'special' (*The Gordon E. Sawyer Award*) Oscar® for my work in 1992, which was presented by Tom Hanks and Ray Bradbury.

Following the completion of *Golden Voyage*, we looked at many possible stories. Among those considered were *Conan*, *The Hobbit*, *Skin and Bones* and *The Food of the Gods* (see Chapter 12, Lost Projects). However, when the popularity of *Golden Voyage* became apparent, both Charles and I realized that we were going to have to make another Sinbad adventure. As luck would have it, I had the perfect story.

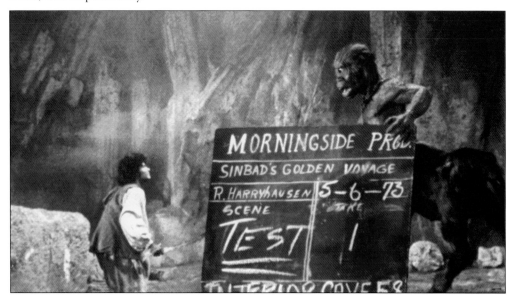

Above. The centaur waiting to 'perform' for the cameras.

CHAPTER 10 GOODBYE OLD FRIEND

Sinbad and the Eye of the Tiger

When you're on a roll, don't change course. Although an old Hollywood adage that seems to have become overused in recent years, since the beginning of pictures, film-makers have always made follow-ups or sequels. I suppose Charles and I were no exception. Having looked at the enormous success of *The Golden Voyage of Sinbad*, we realized we had to follow it up in some way, yet we were determined that it would not be a sequel. The decision was made even easier by already having the basis of a storyline that included key sequences intended for the previous film.

As mentioned in the previous chapter, the premise of a prince transformed into a monkey was originally conceived during the outline for *Golden Voyage*. The idea had been dropped because it made the story too cluttered, but when a further Sinbad adventure was discussed, I felt the idea might stand development into a separate story. So, based on that one premise I developed a fifteen-page step outline called *Sinbad In Hyperborea – An Adventure Fantasy*, and in May 1974 sent it to Charles, accompanied by some key drawings and a list detailing suggested animated figures, high speed miniatures and second unit location shots.

Included in that outline were many ideas that would find their way into the finished picture, for example the baboon prince, a colossal mechanical iron man and an iron boat, a miniature Zenobia who is carried to Sinbad's ship by a seagull, a giant walrus, a sabre-tooth tiger, Neanderthal man, the gate in the style of a huge face and the pyramid. However, some ideas never made it to the end, including a dwarf assistant for Zenobia, a mammoth elephant frozen in the ice, a fight between Neanderthal man and a huge viper and a final struggle between the iron man and Neanderthal man.

Like my outline for *Golden Voyage*, the premise for most of the final film was already in place, but as usual, I left the conclusion to others, believing this should be worked out during the inevitable 'sweatbox sessions', where, as the story strands develop, the ending usually finds its own conclusion. Inevitably, more of my ideas were dropped at this stage, for example the 'hot coals' powering the iron man, which incidentally was to have been uranium, not fossil fuel (later it would become a 'mechanical heart of bronze');

the serpent coiled around the tree, an idea I had for *The 7th Voyage of Sinbad*; the introduction of Neanderthal's family and companions; and finally the valley of the vipers, which had been optimistically included but was to fall by the wayside by the time of the second treatment.

I did not invent Hyperborea. It was said that the sun rose and set there but once a year, and perhaps because of this, it is placed by Virgil under the North Pole. The word itself signifies 'people who dwell beyond the wind Borea'. Some legends call the aurora borealis the light of Apollo, and so I conceived of a land at the centre of which would be a natural power force harnessed by the Arimaspi, the supposed inhabitants of that lost world.

Rather gratifyingly, Charles was pleased with the concept and immediately commissioned Beverley Cross to develop the outline and work with me to expand the principal effects sequences. Beverley came up with a treatment in June 1974 entitled *Sinbad Beyond the North Wind*, which now contained a feasible ending. It was a titanic battle of good against evil between one of the shrine's four 'guardians', a sabre-tooth tiger (brought to life by Zenobia), and Neanderthal man, who is killed and then avenged by Sinbad. Following many more 'sweatbox sessions', Beverley wrote one more treatment, *Sinbad at the World's End* (July 1974), which expanded the story in more visual terms and was accompanied by some of my key drawings. This package gained Columbia's approval to proceed with a screenplay.

The first screenplay was completed by 2 December 1974 and contained two new sequences. The first involved the zomboids, later known as the ghouls, which were conjured up by Zenobia casting 'a claw-like glass container' into the fire. The second sequence, conceived by me but eventually dropped, was the introduction of a worm-creature. This rather unattractive beast was unleashed onto Sinbad's boat by two zomboids (dispatched by Zenobia) from a giant clam-like shell. Once on board, the creature begins to consume the vessel's wood. Sinbad manages to cleave it in half but the sections form two separate creatures that are eventually roped by the sailors and pulled up on the rigging where they are shot full of arrows.

Left hand page. A key sketch for one of the snow scenes. Huge snow caves and ice bridges is how I envisaged the North Polar wastes that Sinbad must trek through.

On 6 March 1975 Beverley produced a revised screenplay bearing the rather uninspiring title *Sinbad III*. Three months later, on 9 June, he delivered the final shooting script called *Sinbad and the Eye of the Tiger*. Little had changed between these two versions other than dialogue:

Sinbad (Patrick Wayne) moors at Charak, intent on seeking permission from Prince Kassim (Damien Thomas) to wed his sister, the Princess Farah (Jane Seymour). He finds the city under curfew, and when he shelters in a nearby tent, he is attacked by three ghouls, appearing from a fire. Disposing of the ghouls, Sinbad learns from Farah that Kassim is still uncrowned because of a spell cast on him by their witch stepmother, Zenobia (Margaret Whiting), who wishes her son Rafi (Kurt Christian) to be Caliph. Knowing only that the prince is ill, he sails with Farah and a covered cage to find Melanthius, Hermit of Casgar, whom it is hoped can remove the spell. Zenobia and Rafi follow in a metal boat powered by the Minaton, a metal half man, half bull. During the voyage Sinbad discovers that the cage holds a baboon which Farah tells him is Kassim. Arriving at Casgar they find Melanthius (Patrick Troughton) and his daughter Dione (Taryn Power). The old man agrees to guide Sinbad to the frozen lands at the world's end and there they will find the ancient powers of Hyperborea which may restore the prince. Reducing herself to the height of a hand, Zenobia boards Sinbad's boat and learns of their destination. The baboon/prince sees her but she escapes when a wasp the size of a bird attacks Melanthius. Whilst Zenobia enters the land of Hyperborea through an ancient ice tunnel, Sinbad and his crew travel over the frozen wastelands where they encounter a giant walrus and later, in the tropical interior, a giant Neanderthal man. This primitive man, Trog, shows Sinbad the way to the centre of Hyperborea, through a great stone gate in the shape of a huge face. Once through they see a massive pyramid from which emanates a strange light. Zenobia has already arrived at the pyramid and by using the Minaton, forces her way inside, but in so doing the Minaton is destroyed and the temperature inside begins to change. When Sinbad and his party arrive Prince Rafi attacks the baboon and during their struggle, Rafi is killed. The baboon is hoisted into the light source and Prince Kassim is restored. Now the shrine's temperature is changing and a sabre-tooth tiger which had been frozen begins to stir and the creature's malevolent yellow eyes flicker open. Zenobia metamorphoses into the creature and attacks. During a terrible battle Trog dies but Sinbad manages to kill the tiger and along with it, the evil witch. Sinbad, Farah, Melanthius and Dione return to Charak to rejoice as Kassim is crowned Caliph.

Charles was eager to begin production as soon as possible, so during the later stages of scriptwriting I began looking for possible locations. Apart from Petra, which we had decided to use for Melanthius' home, we had no other definite locales aside from the fact that we were almost certainly going to shoot in Spain, even though the costs had increased considerably since our last film. The director and cast would come on board after we had completed the second unit photography. In retrospect it seems strange now that we didn't consider John Philip Law for Sinbad, although I recall that at the time Columbia wanted a different actor and that Charles and I were strenuously trying to avoid the label of sequel. After considering many American and British actors, for example Ben Murphy (from the TV series *Alias Smith and Jones*), Ron Ely (from the TV series of *Tarzan*) Michael York, Jan Michael Vincent, Timothy Dalton, Paul Jones, Robert Conrad, Terence Hill, Franco Nero, Joseph Bottoms and even Michael Douglas, we eventually decided on Patrick Wayne, son of actor John Wayne. He certainly looked the part, and his name offered a publicity opportunity. Another child of Hollywood was Taryn Power, daughter of Tyrone Power, who was cast as Dione. Meanwhile, Kurt Christian, who had appeared in *Golden Voyage* as one of Sinbad's sailors,

Above and left. Storyboard of creature climbing aboard. Looking at my sketches, I regret the demise of the worm-creature, which was due most probably to a similarity with the figurehead in the previous film.

changed sides for this one and played Zenobia's evil son Rafi. There was also, as usual, a strong British cast, this time led by Jane Seymour, giving a very credible performance as Princess Farah. Although we had originally considered Larry Naismith as Melanthius, he was busy on another production, so Patrick Troughton, who had played Phineas in *Jason*, was cast. While I had wanted the part to be something much more than how it turned out, Patrick's know-ledgeable but eccentric characterization of the alchemist was one of the best performances in the film. However, for me it was Margaret Whiting as Zenobia who held the picture. When I had produced the step outline I wrote: 'deliver us from the typical blonde floozy who is usually cast in such a role'. I had pictured her as a female Conrad Veidt, if there could be such a creation, and suggested that it needed someone of the calibre of Coral Browne or Viveca Lindfors to achieve the required degree of majestic evilness. I don't remember if either of these ladies was considered, but we did think

about Margaret Lockwood, Elisabeth Sellers, Dana Wynter, Anne Baxter, Patricia Neal, Mercedes McCambridge, Jean Seberg and Nanette Newman. In the end Bette Davis was offered the part, but unfortunately her fee was way out of our league. In the event we were fortunate to obtain Margaret, who delivered a dark performance of a woman obsessed with seeing her son ascend to the Caliph's throne and who would stop at nothing to achieve her ambition. Throughout the live-action photography Margaret played Zenobia without an accent, but Charles and I decided to get Margaret back to re record

her lines, this time with an accent, giving Zenobia that 'extra' dimension of character.

We looked around for some time for a director, considering Don Chaffey, Peter Hymes, Don Sharp, Mike Hodges, Ted Post, Monte Hellman, Jack Smight and even Gordon Hessler again, but for one reason or another they all dropped by the wayside. In the end Charles contracted Sam Wanamaker, a talented actor best known for directing for the stage but occasionally for film. Regretfully, he was probably not the ideal choice for a fantasy adventure, especially one in which he wouldn't have complete control.

To introduce Neanderthal man I suggested that he be seen trapped in a tar pit around which a sabre-tooth tiger prowled. This idea remained through many script developments but later suffered a metamorphosis when Neanderthal is surrounded by wolves. To visualize the scene I used a Spanish location photo on which I sketched both Neanderthal and the wolves. In an even later version, Trog (he was given this name when Neanderthal was dropped) fights an arsinoitherium, which he eventually pushes into the tar. Although Trog and the tar pit idea survived until almost the final script, it was eventually dropped in favour of Trog spying on the two naked girls, which was considerably easier to film and thought by some to be more exciting!

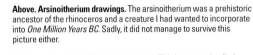

Above. Arsinoitherium drawings. The arsinoitherium was a prehistoric ancestor of the rhinoceros and a creature I had wanted to incorporate into *One Million Years BC*. Sadly, it did not manage to survive this picture either.

Left. Rough drawing of the worm creature. This is a more detailed interpretation of how I saw the worm creatures. A cross between the moon calf and one of my early alien designs.

Above. Drawing of gateway. The immense gates were inspired by *King Kong*, although the idea for the face with the door as its mouth was inspired by an article in a magazine about a park in Italy where there was a carved face in the rock that had water coming from its mouth. I simply put the two ideas together and produced a fantastic gateway looking as if it was the entrance to an unearthly kingdom.

Left. The gateway miniature. The miniature gateway with the pyramid in the background. In the foreground are cut outs of the characters who will appear in the final scene. These are placed as reference for the animation and travelling mattes.

Right hand page top. Drawing for Zenobia's palace. This is my original key drawing for how the palace might finally look.

Right hand page centre. Almeira coastline. This was the location for Zenobia's palace, which I had photographed whilst on a recce.

Right hand page bottom. How Zenobia's palace looked in the final film. The exterior of Zenobia's palace was a 16-inch model matted into the Almeria coastline, with the actors standing on rocks. The moon (which was unused footage from *Golden Voyage*) and the mist were both double printed over it.

Right hand page far right. Still of Jane Seymour in a bikini. During the filming of the North Polar wastes in Malta, Jane Seymour found the right solution to the heat by wearing a bikini under her fur coat.

Second unit photography began in winter 1974 at Picos de Europa in the Pyrenees, where I directed Sinbad's trek through the North Polar wastes. As none of the actors had been cast at that stage, we used doubles for the long shots and in addition photographed plates, allowing us to later add the real actors into the shots by means of travelling mattes. This method is never ideal, but when working with such budget restrictions, travel costs have to be saved. Later I also double printed in arches and bridges of snow, giving the long shots a more exotic look.

The next second unit location was Petra in Jordan, the home of Melanthius. Its location is deep in the Jordanian desert and dates from the 11th century BC. Like something out of a fantastic legend, it is surrounded by mountains and contains stunning, elaborate temple façades and tombs carved from the rose-red rock.

Whilst planning *Golden Voyage* I made a drawing that showed a version of a troglodyte guarding the entrance to Petra. Because the narrative of that story changed, the idea and therefore the location were dropped. Now I had a second opportunity to realize its inclusion and couldn't wait to see it again.

During the recce, Nadim Sawalha, who was to play Hassan, acted as a go-between with the Jordanian authorities and King Hussein. We flew to Amman where we packed everything – lights, cameras, costumes – into trucks to transport to the village of Eliji, near the entrance of Petra. Once there, we were then faced with taking all the equipment down through a narrow gorge that in places was only 3–5 feet wide and towered 200–300 feet on either side. The only way it could be done was to pack most things onto mules and donkeys, but for the heavier equipment we were able to use an army jeep, which could just about drive through the gorge's confines. Once in the valley, we stored the equipment in a tomb, guarded overnight by Jordanian soldiers. As most of the scenes were long shots, we again saved on travelling expenses by using stand-ins dressed to resemble the real actors.

Principal photography, with Sam as director and a full crew and cast, began in Spain on 16 June 1975. The locations included a return to some familiar spots. The city of Avila was used as the basis for the city of Charak. Manzanares, with its weird rock formations, waterfalls and pools, became the sheltered valley of Hyperborea, and in Toledo we found a beautiful 12th-century Jewish synagogue for the dramatic backdrop for the Caliph's aborted coronation at the beginning of the film. The coast near Almeria became the location for Zenobia's palace and was also where we photographed Zenobia's metal boat. Unlike the vessels in *Golden Voyage*, we had to build Zenobia's boat so that it could actually go to sea. As the budget wouldn't stretch to building a proper vessel, we built a shell over oil drums, allowing some room in the stifling interior for rowers to work the oars. Although

Although the studio facilities on Malta were excellent, we didn't use them for the live-action interiors, exteriors and blue-screen shots. For a fraction of the studio cost we hired a disused RAF airfield on the island, called Halfar, where we used a huge hangar as our sound stage and Quonset huts for the blue screen photography of Zenobia in the bottle. The hangar was rigged to accommodate several small interiors plus the enormous section of the shrine's interior, which would have been difficult to construct on the usual sound stage. A few sets, including Sinbad's cabin, were constructed inside a very large tent on the runway. Even some exterior sets were shot on the runway. For example, the live action snow scenes, which would be cut in with the second unit footage shot in the Pyrenees, were filmed on a set constructed of polystyrene snow and painted backdrop. Shooting snow scenes in the middle of summer on an open runway was hard on the crew but even harder on the actors, who had to wear thick fur coats. With the glare of the sun reflecting off the white of the set and no shade, the temperature exceeded 110 degrees! No wonder one of the actors fainted.

it was constructed at Carboneras with cost in mind and equipped with two motors, because of regulations we were forced by the Spanish Marine Authorities to use tow tugs. These unexpected items cost an extra $10,000, and with other construction problems the final bill was an amazing $64,000. To add insult to injury, at the end of five days' filming it fell apart.

We had originally intended to film the entire picture in Spain. However, long before the boat fiasco it became apparent that costs had risen too much, so we decided to look for another base. During the filming of *Golden Voyage* we had 'discovered' Malta, an island possessing excellent studio facilities and a wide and varied landscape that included towns and cities in many styles and periods. So in September 1975 the production moved to Malta to complete the remainder of the location and interior set photography.

To enable us to comfortably photograph the live action that takes place on Sinbad's ship, the deck and one side was built alongside the quay in the studio complex at Rinella. The studio tank was again used to photograph the miniature versions of Sinbad's and Zenobia's ships (each 5-foot long scale models, operated with wires and remote control motors), as well as the iceberg sequences. The Rinella studio facilities were also used to build and photograph the miniature sets, including the 6-foot high ice cave, the exterior of the pyramid and the great gateway (which was 4–5 feet high and some 20 feet deep).

For some weeks Ted Moore and I photographed the miniatures from different angles. To anticipate the positions of the characters and creatures I would eventually place into the miniatures by means of travelling mattes and rear projection plates, I used cut-outs to act as a guide for how they would appear within the shot. Shooting still photographs or footage, I used these as references to line up the travelling mattes so that I obtained the correct proportion between the actors, animated models and miniature sets. If I didn't do this, the camera might be too far back and produce smaller characters than required. These reference transparencies of frames of the film were stuck in the camera when we were producing the travelling mattes. They would supply me with the knowledge of where everything was supposed to be and make sure I got the perspective correct.

The shots of the city of Charak were not, as some people believe, paintings. For some reason I produced all these shots myself using real locations and making composites that included models. In long shot the real buildings of Medina on Malta were matted in above the walls of Avila and combined with 8-inch high miniatures of minarets and domes to give it an Arabian architecture.

Once principal photography was complete, I returned to England to begin what would be thirteen months of animation and effects. This time we hired a small studio area at Lee International Studios in Ladbroke Grove, West London. The first animation to be filmed was the ghouls conjured up by Zenobia from the flames of a fire. I had originally planned for four, but costs had to be cut, so four became three. The inspiration came from an anatomy book where there was a rather gruesome picture of a body with no skin, just the muscles. To this basis for the creatures, I added the distinctive 'bug' eyes. I had to consider many things when designing the ghouls, primarily whether they looked believable, and secondly making sure they didn't look like men in suits. In fantasy films there is a very thin line between realism and comedy, and in the end it comes down to what people will accept. If it is too extreme, the audience will laugh. To imbue the sequence with a more menacing atmosphere, I designed it to take place at night. Even the action

inside the tent is lit only by the fire, and once the fight progresses outside, the moonlight provides only a basic light that creates pockets of inky blackness, so providing a necessary link between these 'children of the night' and the forces of darkness.

The fight with the ghouls includes several 'contacts'. One of these has a ghoul using a flaming torch as a weapon. To achieve this effect, the rear projection plate for the animation was exposed twice. With the invaluable assistance of Poggi, we carefully choreographed the live action, with Pat Wayne fighting thin air. Then using the same set, but this time draped in black, one of Poggi's stuntmen, also draped in black, held the lit torch and went through the necessary movements to match Pat's movements. The camera would only pick up the flame of the torch, seemingly floating in mid-air. Both these sequences were photographed several times to enable us to select the best shots. Later in London I would time the various takes, selecting the best to superimpose over the first image of Pat. This combined print of Pat fighting a moving flame gave me a rear projection plate against which I animated the model of the ghoul holding a miniature torch handles. I matched all the actions of the flame with the model and torch handle so that it

seemed as if he was holding a lit torch. In other words, the movement of the flame dictated how I was able to move the ghoul.

Early on in the fight, one of the creatures hurtles flaming embers at Sinbad. It was filmed much like the torch sequence. We first filmed the live action and then, without moving the camera, the lights of the set were turned off, whereupon a stuntman dressed entirely in black threw the flaming embers towards the spot where Sinbad had been. This plate was later double printed into the live action scene, and I timed and animated the ghouls to fit into the action contained in the combined plate. In another 'contact' scene near the beginning of the fight, one of Sinbad's men rams a sword through a ghoul's chest and, as its back is towards us, we see the point of the blade emerge from its torso. For this I substituted a miniature sword at the point where the real sword would enter on the rear projection plate. This is immediately followed by a shot, in medium close-up, of the unimpaired ghoul gazing down at the wound in its chest. The attempts at trying to wound the ghouls confirmed that they were immortal and that Sinbad was going to have to find an ingenious method of disposing of them, but like the skeletons in *Jason*, how do you kill something

that is already dead? This time we opted for the dramatic death by logs. As the fight nears its climax, the action makes its way towards a huge stack of logs. The logs are held in place by a rope, which Sinbad cuts, so allowing them to squash the ghouls. For this we first of all photographed the miniature 12-inch logs at high speed for the background plate, then filmed an actor (it was a double) against a blue screen striking at the spot where the rope would be. Following this, these two images were combined as a travelling matte. The next shot sees the ghouls enter from the left and get crushed by several miniature logs, animated on wires from above. These logs corresponded with the high-speed logs on the plate.

Although the ghouls sequence flows relatively well, I have never been truly happy with it. As the opening Dynamation sequence it should have set the pace, and it simply doesn't, because it lacks both excitement and drama. However, there is another character with which I am very happy: the baboon. From what I have read, a real baboon is almost impossible to train, let alone teach to play chess. At one point the creature was to have been a mandrill, but I realized that its physiognomy was much too extreme. In the end I settled for a regular African baboon. Someone once

Left hand page. The three ghouls emerge from the fire. The ghouls were fleshier versions of the skeletons, just muscle and bone, and were meant to look as if they lived in torment amid the fires of Hell. This was a simple split screen with the background and the foreground fire as the split areas. The three ghouls were then animated to rise from what would have been the fire in the foreground.

Left. Model of ghoul. In early sketches I portrayed the ghouls with tiny antenna on their heads, but dropped the idea, as it gave them a comical aspect.

Above. Still of ghoul 'holding' torch. An example of 'contact' in the fight with the ghouls involved one of them using a flaming torch as a weapon.

SC. 36 CLOSE SHOT ZENOBIA & RAFI
ZENOBIA looks on with excited interest – her eyes
are wide with tension.

SC. 37 FULL SHOT (DYN) SINBAD
and his men retreat as the ZOMBOIDS run after them.

SC. 39 FULL SHOT QUAYSIDE (TM-MIN-DYN
SINBAD covers the retreat of HASSAN and the MATE.
Behind him is a high pyramid of sawn, timber logs.

SC. 41 CLOSE SHOT SINBAD He looks
around for an escape route then turn toward the
pyramid of timber logs.

SC. 43 MED. SHOT SINBAD & LOG PYRAMID (Tm
He moves toward base of logs and slashes with his
sword at the ropes lashing the logs to their base

SC. 44 FULL SHOT (TM-MIN-DYN) (SAME
SINBAD clears the rolling logs as they thunder
down over the ZOMBOIDS.

SC. 46 ANOTHER ANGLE QUAYSIDE (TM-MIN
As the pyramid collapses, the logs knock the
ZOMBOIDS over like ninepins, burying them.

Top. Section of the storyboard for the log sequence. I not only drew the images but also typed out all the descriptions to tie in with the scenes. Also you will note that I labelled each shot with abbreviated references to show how the shots would be achieved by, for example, travelling matte (TM), Dynamation (DYN) and miniature (MIN).

Above left. Drawing for the baboon chess sequence. I had originally had the idea of a man playing chess with the creature. The chess scene became the inspiration for the entire story; it was also the first clue to the tragedy that had befallen the prince and the key to what would become the characterization of the baboon/prince.

Above right. The chess sequence as it appears in the film. Jane, the chess table and half the chessboard are in the rear projection image. The model baboon and the stool were set up in front of the rear projection screen to match the same perspective. To play chess, the baboon had to pick up at least one piece from the board. By making a matte line that crossed the board, I created a split screen. Behind the bottom of the split I placed the chesspiece on a tiny platform, level with the matte line, and it is this which the baboon picks up.

Right. Metal armature for baboon.

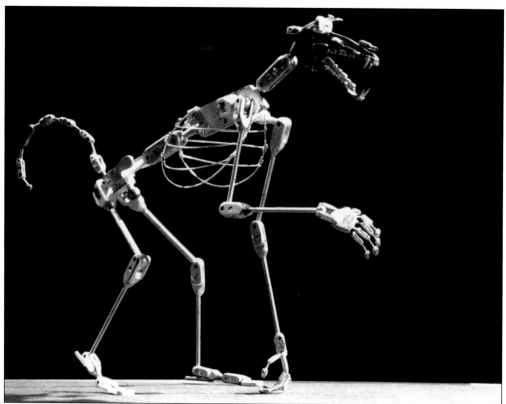

asked me why I didn't base him on a charming monkey, giving me the opportunity to make him comic, but I felt the choice of a rather ugly ape would bring a touch of pathos to the character. It was important to the story to have a creature that would produce sympathy, a kind of animal Quasimodo, conveying a feeling that it had once been handsome and intelligent but was now reduced to something ugly and stupid.

In all my animation, especially where real animals are involved, it is extremely important that the model projects inspiration and stimulates the action. In the case of the baboon, it went through many changes before I was happy with it. The sculpting was begun by Tony McVey, who produced an excellent rendition of the furless animal. However, I was aware that for animation its hands were too big and that the shape of its face was not quite right. I therefore began to re-sculpt it into something that would still resemble a real baboon, but at the same time possess qualities that would give me that extra something so vital when animating. There were two baboon models, one of just 5 inches, but the 24-inch one was constructed with tiny levers so that the lips, eyebrows, eyes, etc. could be animated to achieve facial expressions.

Although I have touched on the problem before, one of the most difficult elements of moving such a model during animation is the fur. A number of methods can be used to prevent this happening. First and foremost, I always try to handle the model on a side away from the camera where it will not show. Also, when the animator is in very close proximity to the model, the fur is sometimes disturbed by the animator's breath. To prevent this happening, I use hair spray to stiffen the fur.

The inspiration for the chess scene came from a picture in a volume of *The Arabian Nights*, which shows a monkey playing chess with a sultan. We replaced the sultan with Jane Seymour who was much more visually exciting. The sequence was achieved, as always, in stages. Jane and the chess table appear on the rear projection plate, which was photographed at a slightly higher angle to allow for the top of the table and its chess pieces to be seen. The baboon was mounted in front of the projection screen on a fixed miniature stool, and animated to correspond with Jane Seymour's actions. Of course, I couldn't simply have him sit there waiting to move the next piece, so I gave him a combination of animal and human actions, including scratching and putting his hand on his chin. Although most movements have to be pre-planned, sometimes an action materializes quite naturally when I am standing in front of the model. In the case of the baboon, I knew I was going to have him look into the mirror, but when I planned the scene, I didn't know he would shed a tear. This human trait occurred when one movement led to another, until it seemed like the most natural thing for him to do. Likewise, when I was shooting the chess scene I knew only that he would play chess; all the other intricate, almost unnoticeable actions, like scratching himself and raising his eyebrows, were thought of on the spot. If animation movements are pre-planned too rigidly, there is a risk of shutting the door on creativity. I never question if the ideas will come, as I know they will when I am faced with them. It is one of the fascinating elements of model animation. If you get the poses and gestures in your mind correctly, when you reach the end of the pose, that pose will suggest another, one that you may not have conceived originally. It is an instant creation of movement.

Later in the film I did the same thing as I had done with the chess game, with a piece of meat picked from a rock. I made a matte line along the top of the rock, placed the meat (a piece of liver) on a stick, and it is this that the model picks up.

As the baboon was supposed to be a human in an ape body, human contact with him, either directly or indirectly, was doubly important. Licking Dione's hand and the chess scene are such examples, but there were others. The examination of the baboon by Patrick Troughton shows the creature lying on a table in the foreground and then being pushed up from behind by Troughton. Following on from that, the baboon proceeds to shake hands with Troughton. During live-action photography, Troughton mimed the lifting and shaking hands and later, with the model lying on the animation table, I moved the model to correspond with Troughton's movements. Later in the picture, whilst the baboon/prince is playing chess on the open deck of Sinbad's ship, he becomes so frustrated that he sweeps the pieces off the board with his hand. To place him into the frame I animated him on a miniature hatch cover that hides the real one on the rear projection screen. During the live-action photography, the chess pieces were knocked over by means of a wire operated off-screen. Later in the studio I counted

The baboon's actions, along with all creatures based on living animals that appear in our films, are the result of a great deal of study. For this film I visited London Zoo, and spent hours observing the baboons and tigers, making sketches and filming them on 8mm. I was able to discern certain movements that offered clues to the species, for example how they hold their tails and turn their heads, movements I humanized for the baboon prince. The tigers were a different story. They have a slow feline prowl and are always stalking with their muscles poised to pounce. For animation, such slow movements have to be condensed, with gestures kept to a minimum so that the essence of what you want to say is in the movement.

Below. Large and small baboon models. The effect of the fur moving during animation (by the animator's fingers) became a characteristic of *King Kong*, but whereas that was acceptable, I didn't want to make the same mistake, so I always tried to move them from behind, although there is always some unavoidable movement.

Right. Animating the baboon. This clearly shows the animation process for the baboon playing chess, with me moving his arm and the chess piece. Compare it to the image from the final scene on the previous page.

the number of frames required for the baboon's hand to correspond with the movement of the chess pieces, and then animated it so that it also covered the wire on the rear projection plate. I again used a wire in another scene when he is seen to knock a book from Dione's hand. One of the things that monkeys do best is peel bananas! In the hands of the baboon the action becomes delightful and poignant. The miniature fruit (about 1½ inches long) was made of rubber sections internally strengthened by wire. The model's hand supported the tiny object and I animated the banana at the same time as I animated the baboon's hands.

While the baboon required character, Zenobia's

agent of strength required only the impression of power. The Minaton was based on the Minotaur, half-man, half-bull, from the Greek legend of Theseus, although here he is a mechanized bronze giant. Whilst the Minaton is seen mostly as an animated model, there are some scenes where the character only required minimal movement. To avoid unnecessary and time-consuming animation, we had Peter Mayhew (who had played Chewbacca in *Star Wars*) don a cumbersome fibreglass suit based on the model, and play him in mostly background scenes.

The demise of the Minaton occurs too soon and his potential was a wasted opportunity. Arriving at the

pyramid, Zenobia commands him to remove a huge block from the structure, but in the process of pulling it out, he is crushed beneath it. Minaton should have been a far more important character and woven more intricately into the story as a terrifying tool of evil. As it is, he is often seen just standing somewhere in the background and only occasionally 'coming to life'. The saddest thing of all is that I now realize all this would have been acceptable if only we had gone for a climax that saw Minaton and Trog fighting to the death. I can only blame myself for this, as I was the one who decided that the tiger and Trog were the best opponents for the fight.

To spy on Sinbad, Zenobia changes herself into a seagull (originally I had in mind an albatross) to enable her to get to Sinbad's ship. Once she is safely onboard she changes back but shrinks herself to remain hidden. Some full-size props were used, but the majority of scenes showing the miniature Margaret Whiting are travelling mattes photographed in Malta with a wide angled lens. The capture of Zenobia in a glass container was a very complex shot. First of all we photographed a real jar on the table of the full set with the actors talking and reacting to it. Later the glass was matted out to enable the image of Margaret (who had been photographed at the correct perspective against a blue screen) to fit

---

I had originally conceived an elaborate introduction for the Minaton by designing a sequence resembling something from Dr Frankenstein's laboratory. The Minaton's construction would have shown Zenobia's Shadowmen (zombie-like creatures) assembling the bronze giant in a hellish-like underground vault. In Beverley's first draft screenplay he describes the laboratory and the Shadowmen:

… there are furnaces, steam and the steady pounding of hammers… forges, cooling-vats and huge, primitive presses – and, working silently, a dozen anonymous figures. They are frightening, faceless slaves, Shadowmen… obscene parodies of humans – stunted men without will or soul. They are grey, hairless, and their eyes have the substance of phlegm.

This scene could have been very atmospheric, a kind of cross between *Frankenstein* and Dante's *Inferno*, but unfortunately neither time nor budget would allow for such a sequence. All we see in the final film is the completed Minaton ready for his mechanical heart.

inside. We then shot a special glass bottle against black and double printed this over Margaret to make her look as if she was inside the real glass jar on the table.

While she does escape, Beverley wrote in a moral point so the audience knows evil doesn't pay. On return to her own boat, most of Zenobia's body resumes its original size, but because there was not enough potion, one foot retains the shape of a gull's webbed foot. The

first 'foot' made for Margaret looked too much like a Donald Duck appendage, so this was rejected and another, hopefully more frightening one was made. When we went to dinner with Margaret after she shot that scene, she would take great pleasure in saying out loud, 'Not enough, not enough', the lines uttered when she sees her misshapen foot and realizes that there is not sufficient potion.

To enable Zenobia's escape we came up with the idea of a wasp that causes chaos when it grows to the size of a bird. So many sharp-eyed fans have pointed out that Melanthius first shows us a bee, which when it grows becomes a wasp. The only excuse I have is that a wasp wasn't available, so we were forced to use a bee, but I always like to think that the bee perhaps metamorphosed during its growth. Its growth was

Sc. 85   EXT. ZENOBIAS CASTLE   DAY
(Miniature Inlay)   It is a sinister fortress built on black rock near the sea.

Left hand page top. Minaton on the metal boat. In all these images the Minaton is the animated model added in by means of a matte or split screen. In some close shots, where there was only a minimum of movement, we used the actor Peter Mayhew, who was extremely tall, inside a fibreglass suit.

Left hand page bottom. Drawing of Zenobia's metal boat. The idea was that the Minaton would 'power' the oars of the vessel from the deck.

Top. Wasp sequence. During its growth on the table, achieved with a zoom lens, I kept the creature moving in tight circles as a real wasp might move.

Middle right. Wasp model. The model was 8–9 inches long with a 10-inch wing span and covered in a light fur.

Left. A section of the Minaton assembly storyboard. This shows the shadow men working in a hell-like laboratory to build the Minaton. I wanted to look like a scene from a James Whale Frankenstein movie. Sadly, my vision of the Minaton's construction was deemed too time-consuming and expensive.

Below and left. Minaton model. The model of Minaton is just over 16 inches high, about the same size as Talos, and required stiff but at the same time fluid movements.

Sc. 89   MED. TWO SHOT   ZENOBIA AND RAFI
With the bench and the sheeted figure in the foreground.   (Dialogue)

Sc. 90   SHOCK CLOSE SHOT   MINATON'S HEAD
The creature of bronze has a head fashioned in the likeness of a monstrous bull.

Sc. 92   INT. LABORATORY OF ZENOBIA   DAY
As the whistle SOUNDS the SHADOWMEN leave their forges and bellows and shuffle sluggishly to

Sc. 92   CLOSE SHOT   SHADOW MEN AS
they turn into OUR VIEW, walking sluggishly past the camera.

Sc. 94   FULL SHOT   TREADMILL   Watched by ZENOBIA AND RAFI, TWO SHADOWMS begin to work a huge treadmill...........

Sc. 99   ANOTHER ANGLE   RAFI   as he places the mechanical heart in the Minaton's chest. He bolts down the oven breast-plate

Sc. 95   M.S. TREADMILL   As it begins to revolve...............

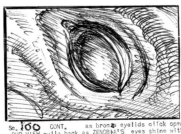

Sc. 100   CONT.   as bronze eyelids click open OUR VIEW pulls back as ZENOBIA'S eyes shine with triumph.

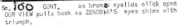

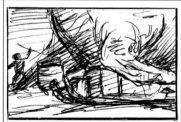

Sc.412.It continues to advance, smashing the precious stores and equipment.

Sc.413.MED.SHOT(DYN)
One SAILOR is killed,a second is thrown high in the air.

Sc.414.ANOTHER ANGLE
He breaks his back as he falls and disappears through a hole in the lake.

Sc.416.ANOTHER ANGLE.
SINBAD snatches up a line of rope and an axe.

Sc.417.419.421.427.ANOTHER ANGLE(DYN)
SINBAD,coiling the line of rope as he goes,advances on the giant Walrus.

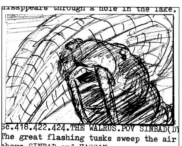

Sc.418.422.424.THE WALRUS.POV SINBAD(D)
The great flashing tusks sweep the air above SINBAD and HASSAN.

Sc.420.423.426.FULL SHOT(DYN)
in the extraordinary combat.

Sc.429.ANOTHER ANGLE(DYN)
The wounded walrus begins to slither back towards the hole in the ice.

Top. The model walrus. The model walrus is about 20 inches long, with bristles for whiskers and tusks made of resin. Because of the layers of latex that covered the armature, achieving realistic movements was extremely difficult.

Above. A section of the storyboard for the walrus scene. Some critics found the walrus rather unexciting, but what might seem a straightforward sequence in the film is in effect quite a complex set of animation techniques, which took a great deal of time to produce.

Right hand page. Original key drawings for the walrus scene. Although I considered several fictional and non-fictional creatures to break up the trek, among them a Yeti (which would have been fun) and a mammoth, I eventually decided on the reputedly aggressive walrus.

achieved by placing the model against a blue background and photographing it with a zoom lens. The lens was calibrated for stop-motion and moved fractionally as the wasp was animated for each frame of film. The one drawback with the zoom lens is that throughout the growth sequence the correct horizon has to be constantly checked, otherwise it can move out of place. By means of a travelling matte the footage was combined in the optical printer with the background that included Patrick Troughton.

During the trek across the frozen wastelands, Sinbad's party encounters an immense walrus that emerges from beneath the ice. When writing my outline I knew that we would need some kind of Arctic creature to break the trek. He is, of course, huge, so to justify him being a giant walrus we had Melanthius (incorrectly) call him 'Walrus Gigantica', suggesting

that it was a hangover of a prehistoric age. Because there was so much latex rubber surrounding its armature, it could only make very limited movements, but I managed to solve the problem to some extent by cutting away some of the unseen latex to relieve the stress on the armature.

The travelling matte shot of the creature rising up through the ice behind the actors included a massive splash of water, supposedly pushed up by the beast, and great slabs of ice that slide away. We filmed the splash using high-speed photography, by dropping a stone into a four-foot barrel of water against black and then double printing it over the model. The slabs of ice were made from Styrofoam mounted on wires, and at the same time the model was rising, these sections were animated separately to fall away. During the fight with the walrus the humans throw spears and

snowballs in an attempt to repel it. The snowballs, which were on the projection screen, were replaced by wads of cotton animated along wires to impact with the beast. The net Sinbad's men throw over the creature was a fine mesh fish net strengthened by wires, which allowed for animation – very similar to the ones I had used in *20 Million Miles to Earth* and *Jason and the Argonauts*. Some critics found the walrus rather unexciting, but what might seem a straightforward sequence in the film is in effect quite a complex set of animation techniques, taking a great deal of time to produce.

Troglodyte, or Trog as he became known, is a character I am very pleased with. Although conceived as the guardian of Petra in my early drawing, he turned out to be the perfect character for this story. As everything in Hyperborea was supposedly ancient,

I therefore conceived that a character based on a real cave dweller would be ideal. However, to enable him to be kinetically suitable for a fantasy adventure, I designed him to be much bigger than a real troglodyte would have been, and as an additional touch gave him a horn in his forehead, making him look aggressive, even though he was a bit of a softy. When the film was first released, some people actually thought he was a man in a suit. While I suppose I should consider this flattering, in retrospect I should have designed him with something similar to the cloven hoof I had given the Cyclops, which would have been almost impossible for any real man to walk on. Having said that, early on in pre-production we did consider using a man, but by the time you composite everything, it would present more problems. Like the baboon, the Trog model was unusually detailed, with tiny levers built into his face, especially around the mouth and eyebrows, allowing him complex facial expressions and therefore a greater variety of emotions. I also took the time and effort to instil extra personality into his character. Even when he is just standing, listening and looking

on, he is always moving with subtle actions and reactions that are on the edge of being human. Whereas in a fight scene one action usually leads naturally to another, Trog's delicate movements were often far more difficult to produce because they needed much more thought and concentration. This 'animated passivity' is extremely time-consuming, but the end result, especially in the case of Trog, was well worth the effort. I have always been dismayed that few critics, or indeed fans, ever mention the animation of Trog. To me he represented some of the most detailed character movements I have ever achieved.

As the travellers approach Hyperborea, they witness the manifestation of Arimaspi power, the aurora borealis, emanating from the shrine of the four elements. We first see the structure at a distance, and it seems to be smooth sided, like the pyramids at Giza in Egypt. However, when we get closer it becomes apparent that its overall structure is stepped like that of the oldest pyramid in Egypt, Pharaoh Djoser's at Saqqara. As far as I am aware, there are no 'hollow pyramids' in Egypt, which would in reality be

impossible to build. The overall effect of the internal towering walls together with the shaft of light shining down from the apex and ending in swirling liquid was hopefully impressive and suggested that the adventurers were in the presence of knowledge beyond mere mortal men.

The shots of the full interior with the actors in the foreground were achieved through travelling mattes against a miniature of the shrine's interior, but we also constructed a section of the shrine that looked more spectacular than any Cecil B. DeMille production, in the Malta aircraft hangar. It included the massive sculptured Styrofoam statues carved by the very talented Janet Stevens, as well as a section of the steep circular steps which led up to the light. The power beam of the Arimaspi was actually made of dental floss! We mounted dozens of floss fibre strands around a cylinder-like construction made of a 3–4 foot piece of gauze. The whole thing was then suspended on a revolving mechanism and mounted in front of black velvet. Then we pulled it out of focus, giving us a round shimmering shape like a shaft of

Left. Model of Trog. The model on the far left is a hard rubber stand-in that possesses only a wire armature. This saved undue wear and tear on the metal armatured Trog. Trog was about 16 inches high, dressed rather modestly in an animal hide with a miniature club to complete his caveman regalia. Sadly, Trog is one of my creatures that no longer exists, at least not in his original form, because all I have of him is a non-armatured copy that I cast from the same mould. During the making of *Clash of the Titans*, we were pressured for time and what was Trog is now Calibos. It always breaks my heart to have to cannibalize my models. It's like losing a close friend.

Below. The demise of the Minaton. This is an excellent photograph to demonstrate how Dynamation was achieved, as if you didn't already know. The rear projection screen shows Margaret Whiting making her way along the edge of the pyramid (note the top doesn't exist) and I am animating the model Minaton on his animation table. The table is aligned just below a proposed blacked out matte line on the same level as the one Zenobia is standing on.

Right hand page. A set of key drawings that illustrated the exterior of the pyramid, the destruction of the Minaton and the pyramid's interior.

light, and I ran an inky dinky light up and down the revolving gauze and floss, creating reflections on the strands. This was our magical power source! The swirling water in the raised well of the shrine was produced by simply swirling the water in a tank, photographing it at high speed and then double printing into the set.

When it came to the tiger, I found that animating the movements of a large feline animal posed some difficulties, as it required precise and minuscule advancements in movement throughout its body. As well as tigers, I also studied domestic cats, and by so doing managed to achieve a combination of mannerisms represented by both. The overall impression is of latent ferocity and a lust for blood, but at the same time there are also slow, graceful movements that pmask the creature's power. When we first see the interior of the shrine, the audience only sees what looks like a large lump of ice on a plinth and is not aware that the tiger is underneath. Only when Zenobia transfers her being into the creature does it become apparent. To encase the tiger in what looks like ice, I covered it with cellophane, then sprayed it. As the tiger struggles to free itself of its ice cocoon, I used sections of clear acrylic resin that had to be individually animated on wires to seem as if they were falling away. The plinth the tiger stands on was part of the full-size set, and to place the creature on it, I drew a matte line along the top edge of the plinth, giving me a split screen between which I animated the model. When he leaps to the ground in front of the steps, he lands in a shadowed area. This shadow provided a natural line with which to create a split screen – another example of how important it is to shoot the live footage around a natural line, but that if a line doesn't occur, create one. Hence the shadow.

The following fight scene between Trog and the tiger was the final animation sequence to be photographed, and I was forced to rush it in order to get it in the can

Steps have always been, for me, a dramatic means to portray power: the more steps, the more power. Witness the hundreds of steps in *First Men in the Moon*. Here, within this shrine of immense power for good and evil, it was only natural I should design it to convey the path to ultimate power. Rafi meets his death on these steps following a fight with the baboon, and they were so steep that poor Kurt was forced to wear heavy padding when he tumbled down them whilst clutching a dummy baboon. Fortunately, it was done in one take and he wasn't hurt, but the incline would have put me off attempting such a stunt. In my original concept for the steps I had included four different creatures at the four corners representing the four mystic elements – earth, fire, air and water. Somehow this ideal was lost during script developments and we ended up with only one guardian: the tiger. It's a pity they were lost, as the guardians were to have been other prehistoric and legendary beasts.

Top. A section of the original storyboard for the fight between Trog and the tiger. It was always important to plan the sequences carefully and in great detail, so everything was worked out before any photography began.

Right. A sketch for the emergence of the tiger from the ice.

Right hand page top. Model tiger. The model tiger was designed to reveal its savage musculature power, and was a combination of a living tiger and the sabre-tooth tiger as painted by Charles Knight.

Right hand page bottom. Trog and the tiger face off. In a battle between good and evil Trog and the tiger face each other in a fight to the death. The model tiger (here suspended on aerial wires) and Trog are placed in front of the rear screen projection of the live action.

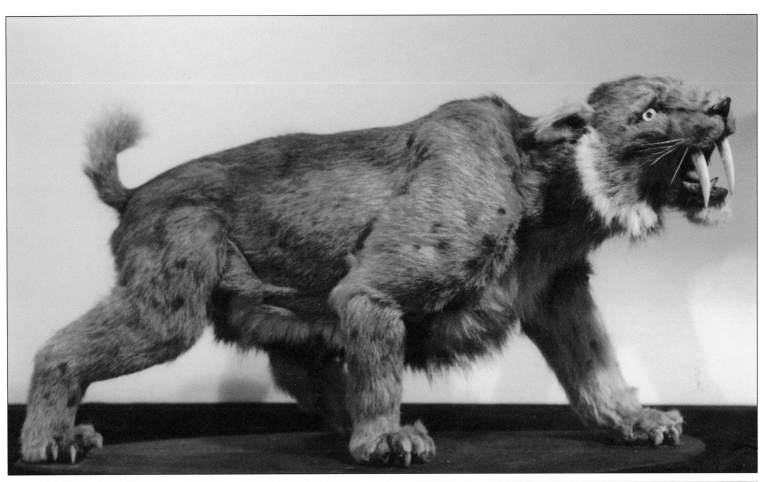

on time. The sequence has always worried me because it ends badly. Trog had been such a central character that I would have preferred him to have met his death differently, but as it is, he departs the picture far too quickly, without any kind of grand gesture. Having said that, I have to admit that I did enjoy animating the fight because it allowed me the opportunity to provide Trog with some final human-like actions in the form of sparring, wrestling clinches, roll-overs and head-butting. Such actions were lifted from fights I had seen but other stances were derived from sculpture. Sculpture can be an inspiration for the animator, especially where exaggerated actions might be required. When I see a particular piece that is full of energy, it leads me to wonder what actions might have been

required to arrive at that one stance and to leave it. In my library I have a statue that depicts a gladiator with his knee in the back of a lion's neck. It is full of action, and for some time I had wanted to put a sequence of movements into a film that would reflect the pose. The Trog/tiger fight gave me that opportunity, and I was able to recreate it to some extent where Trog holds the tiger around the neck and pulls him from behind.

Following Trog's death, the ensuing struggle sees Sinbad forced back up the steps in an attempt to gain the advantage over the tiger. Although Sinbad was photographed on the rear projection plate, I had to show the creature advancing up the steps towards him, so I built a miniature flight of steps situated just outside the frame, on which I animated the model.

Perspective was an important ingredient in the scene, indeed, one of the secrets of Dynamation, and it has to be carefully worked out so that the humans do not look too large or small against the models. The demise of the tiger takes place on the steps when it leaps at Sinbad and he impales it on a spear. As the fight progresses, the tiger is now on the steps above Sinbad, looking down at him. Once again, I placed the model on a miniature section of the steps painted the same colour as the rear projected steps, and supported it from the side of the animation table. Although the tiger's death required a dramatic placement, such a set up is not ideal because the colour matching between the model and real steps can be a problem. This was no exception. Each test had to be

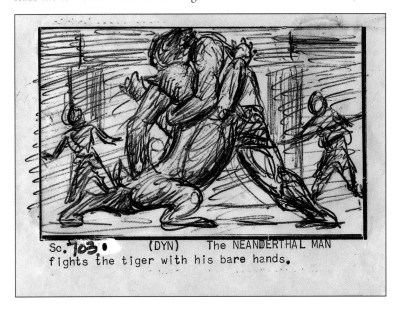

Sc. 703. (DYN) The NEANDERTHAL MAN fights the tiger with his bare hands.

Sc. 704. 706 ANOTHER ANGLE (DYN). A final slash of the TIGER and TROG is dead. SINBAD moves in with the large HARPOON.

Sc. 705. 707. CLOSE SHOT SINBAD He struggles to his feet gripping the abandoned harpoon.

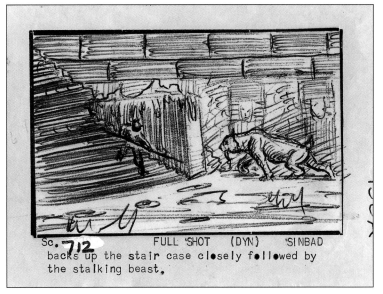

Sc. 712 FULL SHOT (DYN) SINBAD backs up the stair case closely followed by the stalking beast.

Left hand page top. A sketch for the Trog/tiger fight.

Left hand page bottom. The tiger and Trog during animation. In this still the model of Trog is about to attack the tiger.

Above. Storyboard for the fight between Sinbad and the tiger.

Right. The baboon ascending the staircase. This is another good example of Dynamation. I am moving the baboon on the animation table seemingly going up the stairs, whilst the real stairs are on the rear projection screen.

Above. Drawings of tiger scene death. The tiger's death was, I suppose, a more dramatic version of that of the young allosaurus in *One Million Years BC*.

Right hand page. Poster for the movie.

Below. I get a helping hand from a key member of staff.

sent to the labs, and if the colour didn't match, I would have to do it over again, losing a whole day. Colour matching is done with the eye, but often what the eye sees is not a match on celluloid.

Sinbad and the Eye of the Tiger took three years to complete and cost $3.5 million, almost three times as much as *The Golden Voyage of Sinbad*. Released in the US in May 1977, it was a worldwide success with audiences, although not quite so popular as the previous film. Reviews for our films in general were never heart warming, but those for *Sinbad and the Eye*

of the Tiger were certainly not good and in some cases grossly insulting. The most acidic comments focused on the acting and the direction, and only occasionally remarked on the technical effects. *Variety*, which was unrelenting about the film, said: '*Sinbad and the Eye of the Tiger* is a technically adroit but childishly plotted hokum adventure fantasy…', although the review goes on to say, 'When the fantasy creatures have center stage, the film is enjoyable to watch. Such beasties as skeletons, a giant bee, an outsized walrus, a mechanized golden behemoth, and a primitive man are marvellously

SINBAD AND THE
EYE OF THE TIGER

vivified by Harryhausen… the care taken with the effects shows despite the overall corniness of the film.' The critics had missed the point that this was fantasy and that for such a picture reality has to be suspended, but I have to admit that this film did have many faults and is one of my least favourite. The basis for the story is fine – it had all the hallmarks of an exciting adventure and could have surpassed *Golden Voyage* – but it demanded more time and effort spent on it to make it something worthwhile. I blame no individual for this. If anything, I blame myself for agreeing to certain alterations and not ensuring that enough work was done. I will just say that it was a concoction of missed opportunities.

Even though *Sinbad and the Eye of the Tiger* made its money back quite quickly, it came to the market during cinema's fashionable turn to science fiction. Expensive, well-made films such as *Star Wars* (1977), with their explosive excitement every five minutes, were all the rage with both adult and younger audiences. It wasn't that the era of heroes had totally vanished (although that would also disappear), it was that the style of the movies was beginning to change. Regrettably, *Sinbad and the Eye of the Tiger* was to be my final association with Sinbad, a point in my life that is perhaps reflected by the final words uttered by Melanthius in an earlier version of the script. 'Do you think anyone will believe us? No, only a legend now, as, in time, we will be… "Sinbad the Sailor" they'll say, "He was never real, only an improbable hero from an incredible Arabian Night's tale." That's how the world goes, my friend, men don't really care for the truth…'.

Once Charles and I had completed the film and made the usual round of publicity appearances in the US and Europe to promote the picture, we sat back and looked at the response to the film and realized we would again need to change subjects. Science fiction was the current box office craze but we had no desire to go down that path again. As mentioned many times, Dynamation is suitable only for a narrow band of subjects, so what could we now turn to that would be suitable and acceptable for audiences in the late 1970s? The answer was in a film we had made nearly thirty years before: ancient mythology. *Jason and the Argonauts* had not been a great success at the time of its release, but by the late 1970s it had achieved commercial, critical and cult status. We therefore decided to research the possibility of shooting another Greek legend, and it was Beverley Cross, who had worked all those years before on *Jason,* who came up with a story he had been working on for some years.

Clash of the Titans

I suppose the two subjects I am best known for, in cinematic terms, are dinosaurs and mythology. Greek and Roman myths contained characters and fantastic creatures that were ideal for cinematic adventures, which few, if any, film-makers had considered. Gradually I began to explore the possibility of adapting some of them for the screen and realized that if some of the adventures were combined with 20th-century storytelling, a timeless narrative could be constructed that would appeal to both young and old. One such story, that of Perseus and his quest to kill the Gorgon Medusa and save Andromeda from a sea monster, was perfect for such a project. I first considered adapting the story in the late 1950s and then again after *Jason*. Aside from being a wonderful tale, the main attraction was the creatures, especially Medusa the Gorgon, a unique character who lent herself perfectly to Dynamation. However, what held me back from developing it into a workable outline was the tricky question of rationalizing the complex quest and the hero's name. I'm sure I could have eventually overcome the first problem, but the name Perseus was too close to Percy, which at that time was associated in America with a sissy. To avoid ridicule, therefore, I felt I either had to change the hero's name or drop it completely. Both would irrevocably alter the legend, so I let it slip into the back of my mind, as other, more concrete projects materialized.

The story reared its head again in 1969. Whilst living on Skiathos (a Greek island near an area of the Aegean that had been associated with Perseus), Beverley Cross wrote an outline called *Perseus and the Gorgon's Head*. Unfortunately, we were already planning *Golden Voyage of Sinbad*, so unable to develop it, but during the making of *Sinbad and the Eye of the Tiger*, Beverley again suggested the idea. Needless to say, I was very keen, and we all felt the time was right for another Greek legend and that the name problem wasn't the hurdle it might have been decades before. Charles obtained National Film Development Fund finance to develop the story further, and all three of us began to enhance the outline by working out a compromise between Beverley's story and my key visual concepts. I made a

number of drawings: the Stygian Witches' lair, Medusa and Perseus, and various concepts of the Kraken, Pegasus and the witches. I also sculpted a bronze of Perseus slaying the Gorgon, which was not only essential in working out an entirely new concept of Medusa's appearance, but allowed Beverley to visualize the sequence and assisted in selling the whole idea during the budget presentation to potential backers.

Like the story of Jason, the original legend of Perseus is complex and convoluted, so we had to manipulate events, stealing from one legend and putting it in another. This modification is essential to take advantage of what the film medium has to offer. It's not that we feel we are better than Plato, it is just a question of making a suitable film that will hold an audience's attention. For example, in the original legend the winged horse Pegasus springs from the blood of Medusa's head, an event that occurs towards the end of the saga. Beverley wanted the winged horse as one of Perseus' tools in his quest to save Andromeda, so he constructed a sequence that sees Perseus capturing and taming the creature. This introduced the horse and made for a spectacular early sequence that establishes a bond between Perseus, who we see as a strong idealistic hero, and the beast. However, the idea of a creature, or for that matter creatures, springing from the blood of Medusa was far too good an idea to discard, so Beverley decided to include a sequence in which giant scorpions spring from her blood.

As it was my task to visualize the story's events, I was conscious that we had to avoid the same situations seen in *Jason*, especially in the sequence featuring the gods of Olympus. After reading an early treatment by Beverley, I felt it required a transition between the gods and the mortals, similar to the chessboard used in *Jason*, which communicated to the audience that a deadly game was being played by the gods for the hearts and lives of the Greeks. I came up with the idea of using a miniature arena. Behind this 'arena of life' were niches containing hundreds of other characters reflecting all the Greek legends. Zeus would put the figures in the arena, where the gods would control their destinies. It was a vital tool in introducing the characters of our story, which is evident when Zeus takes the figure of Calibos and commands that 'He shall become abhorrent to human sight', whereupon the shadow of the tiny statue transforms into a monstrous creature. This tells you much about Zeus, and everything about Calibos, before the audience even sees him.

When we felt we had a workable screenplay and enough key scene illustrations, Charles approached Columbia Pictures. At first they were very excited and in principle approved the idea. However, as the picture progressed, it became evident that it would have to be an expensive production if we hoped to complete the picture in the way we wished, and as costs rose, Columbia decided to pull out. To say that their decision was a huge setback would be an understatement, but we firmly believed the project was commercial. Charles approached other major companies but one by one they declined, because, I think, they were unable to visualize the film's full potential. Fortunately, after years of inactivity MGM were setting up as a production company again, and after reading the script and seeing the drawings, the head office rang Charles and said that our project was exactly the kind of picture they were looking to produce – namely good, exciting family entertainment. In fact, they wanted to make it on a much larger scale than even we had envisioned, and put up extra money for star names. After all those years working with tiny budgets, Charles and I faced the prospect of working amongst premiere film stars, although I hasten to add that this didn't mean the effects budget would be in proportion to the stars' salaries.

After months of pre-production, working on designs, models, storyboards, overcoming the problems of effects and with Beverley fine-tuning the script to incorporate the stars, everything was now ready to begin shooting. *Clash of the Titans* (the name had changed when we went to MGM) was set to be my sixteenth feature and the twelfth in association with Charles. Rather interestingly, its $16 million budget exceeded the sum total of all the Schneer/Harryhausen collaborations up to that point.

Whilst we usually had a wish list of actors for the prospective parts, casting them, however, was never straightforward. Although some people think you just go out and merrily get everyone you think you should have, on our pictures that was never true. Because of budget, or more often the type of picture we were making, star names were usually reluctant to participate, so the task of casting was frequently a compromise. Nevertheless, the actors on our pictures were always professional, it is just that we never seemed to secure the actor we originally envisaged in the role. *Clash of the Titans* was the exception to the rule. Harry Hamlin was chosen by Charles and director Desmond Davis for the part of Perseus from over 300 candidates, including Malcolm McDowell, Michael York, Leigh Lawson and Richard Chamberlain. Harry had made only one picture but had considerable stage experience. Not only was it felt that he would be able to handle the role and the effects, but he also looked the part. Before MGM took the project on, several distributors suggested that we cast Arnold Schwarzenegger (long before he became a star) as the central character. However, his muscled physique would have reflected the 1950s and 60s Italian epics, which was an image we desperately tried to avoid. Although the ancient Greeks depicted their heros as athletic, they were certainly not musclemen (with the exception of Hercules). Perseus had to look the part of a hero, not because of muscles, but because of his ability to fight and defeat his adversaries, whether through strength or cunning.

Apart from Hamlin, there was only one other key American actor in the film, the delightful Burgess Meredith, who played Ammon. We originally wanted Michael Hordern or Peter Ustinov, but MGM felt there were too many British actors and that American audiences would think it was a foreign film. We therefore agreed to Burgess being cast as the frustrated poet, and on reflection he was a perfect choice, giving the part a unique, eccentric 'pixie' quality. Leslie-Anne Down had first been considered for the part of Andromeda, but we decided that Judi Bowker, a relative newcomer, should be our heroine. Her beauty and vulnerability convinced us that she was perfect as the innocent pawn of almost everyone in the story.

As casting progressed, we had to ask ourselves, who do you secure to play the part of the father of the gods? We had considered John Gielgud, Orson Welles and Sir Ralph Richardson, but in the end Zeus had to be played by Laurence Olivier, who delivered much dignity and authority to the part. However, it was Maggie Smith as Thetis who had some of the best

---

After his daughter Danae (Vida Taylor) gives birth to a son which she calls Perseus, by the god Zeus (Laurence Olivier), King Acrisius (Donald Houston) of Argos has both cast into the sea in a casket. Zeus saves them and commands Poseidon (Jack Gwillim) to unleash the Kraken and destroy Acrisius and Argos. Years pass and Perseus (Harry Hamlin) grows to manhood. Thetis (Maggie Smith), angered when Zeus turns her son Calibos (Neil McCarthy) into a misshapen beast, transports Perseus to the city of Joppa where he meets Ammon (Burgess Meredith). After receiving three gifts (a helmet, sword and shield) from the gods, he travels to Joppa where he falls in love with Andromeda (Judi Bowker), daughter of Queen Cassiopeia (Siân Phillips), whose suitors are required to answer impossible riddles or be burned at the stake. Using his helmet, which makes him invisible, Perseus sets out to solve the latest riddle and sees Andromeda carried off during the night by a giant vulture. With Ammon's help, Perseus captures and tames Pegasus, last of the winged horses, and flies after Andromeda to the lair of Calibos. Perseus learns the answer to the riddle, but as he leaves, Calibos sees footprints in the dust and during a fight with Perseus, Calibos' hand is cut off. At the betrothal of Perseus and Andromeda, Cassiopeia foolishly declares her daughter more beautiful than Thetis herself, and the vengeful goddess orders Andromeda to be sacrificed to the Kraken. Having only a few days to seek a means of defeating the Kraken, Perseus seeks out the Stygian witches with the aid of Bubo, a mechanical owl sent by Athena (Susan Fleetwood). The three witches (Flora Robson, Freda Jackson and Anna Manahan) advise Perseus to kill Medusa, the last of the Gorgons who lives on the Isle of the Dead. Paying Charon to row him there Perseus defeats the two headed dog Dioskilos and then cuts off the head of Medusa, whose look can turn living things to stone. On the return journey Calibos releases the blood of the Medusa's head which mutates into three giant scorpions that Perseus and his men slay along with Calibos. As the Kraken rises from the sea, Perseus uses Medusa's head to turn the creature to stone. Perseus and Andromeda are reunited and are immortalized in the stars by Zeus.

Above. The cast of *Clash of The Titans* on the set of Mount Olympus.
Front (left to right): Susan Fleetwood (Athena), Ursula Andress (Aphrodite), Laurence Olivier (Zeus), Claire Bloom (Hera), Maggie Smith (Thetis). Back (left to right): Burgess Meredith (Ammon), Pat Roach (Hephaestus), Jack Gwillim (Poseidon), Harry Hamlin (Perseus), Judi Bowker (Andromeda).

Right hand page. Medusa's eyes. I used what I call 'Joan Crawford lighting', which was especially effective in the 1945 film *Mildred Pierce*. The lighting simply highlighted her eyes to show her emotions, but with Medusa it emphasized the power to turn men to stone.

lines in the picture. For example, she says of Zeus, 'so many women… And all these transformations and disguises he invents in order to seduce them! A shower of gold, sometimes a bull or a swan… Why, once long ago, he even tried to ravish *me* – disguised as a cuttle-fish!' When Hera asks if he succeeded, Thetis bitchily replies, 'Certainly not!… I beat him at his own game – I simply turned myself into a shark.' Only Maggie Smith could deliver lines like that and get away with it. Also in the cast was an old friend and a fine actor, Jack Gwillim, previously King Aeetes in *Jason and the Argonauts*, who this time played Poseidon.

Director Desmond Davis was chosen by Charles for his impressive handling of *Girl With Green Eyes* (1964). We did not want a modern approach to the story, but it had to be converted to the screen with just the right balance of reality and fantasy. It was felt that Desmond would be able to achieve this, and as it turned out, he handled the subject especially well. I found him easy to work with, and although it took a while, he accepted the importance of the effects.

In April 1978 Charles and I began the all-important location recce, taking us to Sicily, Greece, Italy and Turkey. The journey was not as fruitful as we had hoped. The only location we decided upon was the amphitheatre in Ostia Antica, which was eventually used for the theatre in which Perseus encounters Ammon. In trying to find the perfect location for Medusa's temple, we looked at many exotic and fascinating ancient sites, but none seemed suitable. They were either too ruined or too commercial or both. In the end we decided to return to the tried and tested Spanish and Maltese locations where we knew we could guarantee good dramatic backgrounds, plus a few Southern Italian locations used so successfully in *Jason and the Argonauts*.

Principal photography began on 14 May 1979 at Pinewood Studios on Stages D and M, shooting the Olympus sequences, the Queen's apartments and Hephaestus' foundry. A week later we began the location photography in Spain, starting at a remote area called Guadix that was to be the 'Wells of the Moon'. We then went on to Mesa Loc for the desert scenes and finally to the mountains of Antequerra to shoot the journey to the witches' lair. On 14 June the production moved to Italy. Travelling there proved to be more of a problem than anticipated. To carry the

cast and crew, Charles had chartered a plane but about 1½ hours into the flight it developed engine trouble and the pilot had to 'feather' one engine, leaving us with only three. Eventually we landed safely at Perpignan, where we had to await repairs before flying on to Rome. Burgess Meredith and Terry Sharratt (the boom operator) refused to continue the flight on the same plane, and instead flew to Paris, then Rome.

Following completion of those scenes set at Ostia Antica in Italy, we moved south to what was left of the once uncrowded beaches at Palinuro (used in *Jason*) to film the River Styx and the Isle of the Dead. In a dried-up riverbed near Palinuro we filmed the scorpion sequence, then the temples at Paestum for the Dioskilos and Medusa sequences. Finally we flew to Malta on 6 July for a three-week schedule photographing the remainder of the locations and the interior sequences (Medusa's lair), which were shot in the aircraft hangar at Hal Far Airfield. The long shots of the city of Joppa were actually Cospicua harbour enhanced with miniature temples, a palace and a large statue in the foreground. The market place was shot in Fort St Elmo, and other scenes in Fort Rocco. The procession and the Kraken/sacrificial sequence was filmed mainly in the Malta tank, with additional rock scenes shot on Gozo island. On 31 July 1980 the main unit moved back to Pinewood Studios in England to film the remaining interior work, including the palace of Argos, the swamp and lair of Calibos, and the temple of Thetis. These were completed on Stage D, whilst Andromeda's bedroom was shot on Stage M, and the lair of the Stygian witches and the travelling mattes on the old *007* stage. We also had a second unit at Kinance Cove in Cornwall waiting for rough seas for the opening scenes. Live-action filming eventually wrapped on 1 September 1979 and by that time my workshop was ready.

For nearly eighteen months my working home would be the old effects sound stage at Pinewood, converted to accommodate the set-ups for animation. Occasionally I would work around the clock, sleeping on a cot in the studio office. In case you haven't guessed it by now, animation can be exhausting. Apart from the fact that the animator walks miles in a day, back and forth between camera and the model for each single frame exposure, there is the mental

strain of moving the models to ensure a 'flow' in the animation, and on top of that there are hundreds of other equations to consider. So the process becomes physically gruelling, although when there is a high and the scene is going well and one action naturally follows another, there is a 'rush' of adrenaline and you only become aware of the tiredness when the scene is complete.

Because of the extra pressures on the production, I brought in Janet Stevens, who had worked on sculptures for *Sinbad and the Eye of the Tiger*, to assist me with most of the models, particularly Medusa and the Kraken. Janet was extremely skilful in transforming my sketches into three-dimensional clay entities. Part of her talent was a genius for detail, which is crucial in the creation of stop-motion models. Without detail, models can lack conviction and look plastic. Witness the ones made by Warner Bros for *The Animal World*. Janet was a pleasure to work with and her unique contribution on those last two films was invaluable, adding a style that made them something special.

As always, the actual animation models I completed myself, assembling the armatures after dressing down, filing and soldering all the units together. When completed, I cast the foam latex by 'cooking' them, much as I had done since the days of *7th Voyage of Sinbad*. I then finished off the skin or covered them in a fur, inserted the eyes and made the teeth, tongue and ears. Sometimes models would require repair, so I would restore them overnight in my workshop at home, ready for the animation table next morning. I had to, so as to avoid delays in animation, and after all, they were the stars of the picture. Since I knew the models better than anyone, it made sense that I should assemble and look after them in times of need. This applied especially on *Clash*, when for the first time I had two animation assistants. As with the sculpting, it soon became apparent that the animation work would be too much for just one pair of hands. Charles was concerned that the animation would overrun its budget if I spent the extra time doing it all myself, so I reluctantly agreed to make enquiries about an assistant animator. Only one person could fit the bill as far as I was concerned, Jim Danforth, who Charles approached in 1978 to see if he would be interested. Jim is a meticulous

Above left. Me discussing what I wanted for Medusa with Janet Stevens. Janet had also worked on the sculptures for *Sinbad and the Eye of the Tiger*.

Above middle. With Steve Archer and the armatured model of Bubo.

Above right. Jim Danforth and myself getting to grips with making Pegasus fly. The tiny model of Harry can be seen on the model's back.

craftsman whose stop-motion animation work includes *The Wonderful World of the Brothers Grimm* (1962), *The Seven Faces of Dr. Lao* (1964) and *When Dinosaurs Ruled the Earth* (1971). Unfortunately, he was preparing *Conan* and unavailable, so for a while, whilst other tasks were completed, we ignored the potential problem. Following the completion of the live-action photography the issue raised its head again, and so we decided to talk to three UK animators. One of these was Steve Archer, who I had met some time before as a young fan when he had shown me an 8mm film of clay and wire animation. Steve's humorous, Puckish style stuck in my mind and I asked him to come to the studio in late 1979 to shoot a test with some of the models from *Eye of the Tiger*. Although his style was different from mine, he possessed a great talent. However, I was still very reluctant to lose complete control of the 'hands on' animation. I remembered how Obie had ended up by overseeing and doing little, if any. I didn't want that. It was not how I worked. The art of actually creating an artificial life-force in the characters themselves was always my first love and the organization just a means to an end. After much deliberation I decided to try and continue to do all the work myself. Barring accidents and misadventures, I believed it was still possible.

By late February 1980 I had finished most of the Pegasus roping sequence, a good deal of the Calibos footage and nearly all of the scorpion and vulture shots. However, due to technical problems with the film stock sprocket holes (the punch kept wearing and caused inaccuracy in second and third exposures), the work fell a month behind schedule. It eventually dawned on me that I would not make up the lost time and so, after discussions with Charles, decided to hire Steve, who started on 4 March 1980 animating several vulture flying sequences shot against blue-backing. Even with Steve now on board and both of us flat out on the animation, by the middle of summer we were still running behind schedule and Charles was becoming more and more anxious. In August 1980, as luck would have it, Charles received a call from Jim, who was apparently at a loose end after a project had fallen through. He arrived in the UK in September 1980 to begin animation on the Pegasus flying scenes and Dioskilos sequence. Although I couldn't have completed the film on time without both Jim's and Steve's invaluable assistance, I still managed to complete the majority of the hands-on animation myself. It wasn't that I wanted to say that this was my picture – not one film I have worked on can I truly say is 'mine', as all pictures are team efforts. The real reason was that I preferred to work alone. In my mind I had the sequences laid out in rough, and I suppose I didn't want to impose what I envisaged on another animator. I had never wanted to animate with someone looking over my shoulder, so to do that to another was suppressing their talent.

The opening scenes of the film take the audience to Olympus, the citadel of the Greek gods. Working with Frank White, the production designer, we created an Olympus that combined the look of paradise and a realistic dwelling for supreme beings, a reflection of the ancient Greek image of the home of the gods. We went for outsized columns (of which we could only see the bases), suggesting massive structures that could only be guessed at. To add scope and grandeur,

I also suggested a backdrop showing a city (influenced by John Martin's imaginative picture *Joshua Commanding the Sun to Stand Still*) extending over the peaks of Mount Olympus. Unfortunately, the beautifully painted backdrop is never clearly seen because there was too much stage smoke obscuring it. The long shot of Olympus was a model, constructed at Pinewood, measuring about 20 feet across.

The first Dynamation creature to appear in the film was the gigantic Kraken, a sea monster, the mutant offspring of a prehistoric reptile that had mated with one of the mighty Titans. There are many interpretations of what it looked like, but I wanted it to be at least part humanoid, making Andromeda's sacrifice to it more acceptable, much like Fay Wray was to King Kong. If all it had wanted was lunch, the creature would simply devour Andromeda and then return to the sea. His design was a combination of

mythical merman, with his fish tail, and four arms resembling the tentacles of an octopus and various prehistoric creatures, which I hoped would make him appear more grotesque.

There were two armatured Kraken models. The first, about 18 inches high and almost 4 feet long from head to tail, was used for 95 per cent of the animation. The second was only the upper torso of the creature, and at 4 feet from the navel up was the largest armatured model I had ever constructed. Because of its size, the amount of latex over the armature made it extremely difficult to move. It required the muscles of a Greek wrestler to animate it. Fortunately, it was used only for detailed close-ups, namely in the final sequence when it fills the entire frame behind Pegasus and Bubo. Another armatured model of the creature's lower arm and hand was used for detailed close-ups. There were also two 4-foot non-armatured Krakens,

Top. Painting the backdrop. The backdrop to Olympus showed a city influenced by John Martin's imaginative picture *Joshua Commanding the Sun to Stand Still*. It was painted by the wonderful technicians at Pinewood Studios.

Bottom. The Olympus model. The long shot of Olympus was a model, constructed at Pinewood, measuring about 20 feet across. This is a publicity photograph in which I seem to be standing over the home of the gods like Zeus himself.

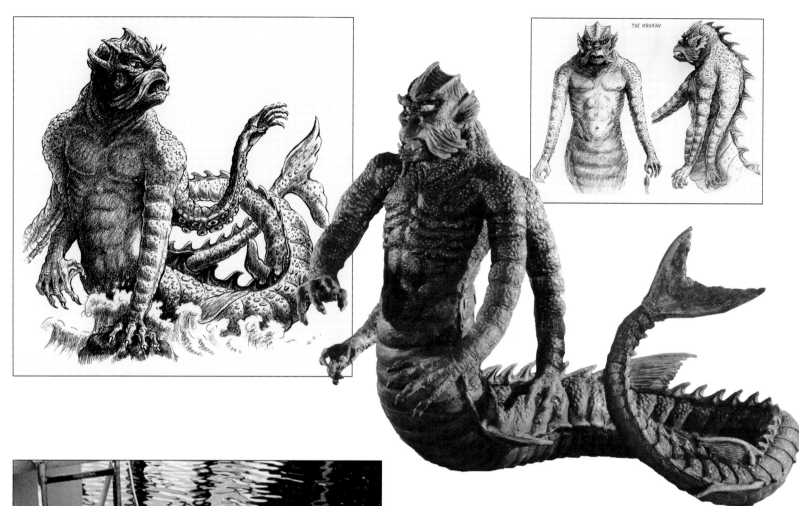

Top left and top. Drawings of the Kraken. The Kraken was a sea monster, the mutant offspring of a prehistoric reptile that had mated with one of the mighty Titans.

Above. A model of the armatured Kraken. There was another armatured model, which was just of the torso and head with his four arms. This was used for extreme close-ups, such as when Pegasus flies in front of him.

Left. Still of Kraken rising out of the sea. Any scenes that necessitate animation and a backdrop of water create huge problems, and this one of the Kraken rising out of the sea was no exception. In this shot I overcame some of the water problem is by having him appear from behind a promontory, and the water splashes were added later.

Far left and below. Stills of this Kraken in water tank. Colin Arthur's 15-foot Kraken, which he constructed specifically for the underwater scenes. Colin also did all the makeup for the picture.

one of solid latex used as a stand-in, whilst the other was made of sponge rubber, inside which was a rough support frame that rested on a teeter totter so the whole thing could be kept upright during the high speed photography of the creature rising from the sea.

The Kraken's release so that it can destroy Argos is performed by Poseidon. As we didn't want to ask Jack Gwillim to perform his scenes underwater with his mouth open, we photographed him at high speed on a stage in front of a blue screen at Pinewood. To make it appear as if his hair and clothes were being moved by the water, we used a wind machine and overprinted footage photographed through a glass tank filled with water and other elements to seem as though he was deep underwater.

Any scenes that necessitate animation and a backdrop of water create huge problems. In the climax of the picture the Kraken is seen pulling himself up, by his four arms, over rocks. Once emerged, I inserted the sea background plates with split-screen rear projection and completed it with churning water matted into the scene. The churning water was actually multiple exposures of controlled underwater explosions set up by Brian Smithies. They were photographed in the Malta tank at high speed (between 48 and 72 frames per second) against a blue sky from which, with some touching up, I made a matte. The explosions were then double printed three or four times so they looked bigger. These same

splashes were also used in the first Kraken scene as he rises from the sea off Argos. Of course, if you have water, the creature in it must look wet. For this I covered the entire model with glycerine, but because it dries out rapidly under studio lights, I had to reapply it every two or three frames, slowing everything down. Glycerine also has the side-effect of reacting with the rubber of the models, and this, combined with the intense heat of the lighting, has made them liable to disintegration over the subsequent years.

Producer Sam Goldwyn is credited to have uttered to one of his screenwriters the immortal lines, 'What we want is a story that starts with an earthquake and works its way up to a climax…'. In *Clash of the Titans* we endeavoured to follow his advice, beginning the story with the total destruction of a city by a wall of water created by the Kraken. Argos is not mentioned in the original Perseus legend, but in our version Zeus avenges the treatment of Perseus' mother by ordering the destruction of Argos, home of King Acrisius, Perseus' grandfather. Beverley chose Argos because it was one of the oldest Greek cities. We naturally visited the actual city when we were looking for locations, but it turned out to be very disappointing. Today it is nowhere near the sea, although it may have been once, and the surviving ruins are partially buried under what looks like a modern rubbish dump. In the process of trying to find 'our Argos', we visited a

number of walled cities in Greece and Turkey, even considering Palmyra in Syria and Leptis Magnus in North Africa, but none suited. In the end we used the Malta studio walled fort for live sequences, and a Maltese town enhanced with miniature Greek temples for the long shots.

When the cataclysmic wave hits the city, buildings, statues and people are swept away. Some scenes were achieved with real water and those on a larger scale with mattes. The former were all photographed within the fort's walls by using dump tanks. Where dump tanks and real people are used together, great caution is needed and everything checked and double-checked to make sure nothing can go wrong. On consulting the stuntmen, they were happy with the arrangements, but during the shooting one of them fell under the weight of the water and fractured some ribs.

Although I had overseen the destruction of sections of cities in my earlier career, the entire destruction of a city, albeit ancient, was a new challenge. On *Clash*, for the first time I had a budget that would allow me to film the entire sequence at high speed. No more animated crumbling buildings, this was the big league. The wave that rushes towards the unfortunate city begins with a series of stock shots (some of which were unused from *Jason and the Argonauts*) and completed by an artificial wave created in a special floor tank on one of the stages at Pinewood. To enable us to matte the wave(s) into whatever we liked, the entire tank was painted black with black velvet mounted behind. Into this we released water from dump tanks (also painted black), which we hoped would give us the required wave. Unfortunately, it didn't. The water just rushed flat along the bottom of the tank. I solved the problem by having a two-foot baton (again painted black) nailed at the base of the dump tank chute, so that when the water hit it, it would start to roll into a two-foot wave. It worked perfectly, and with the camera mounted low on the ground, giving it yet more height, the wave seemed 100 feet high.

For the long shots of the city's destruction by the wave, we constructed a more or less complete miniature of Argos in front of a painted backdrop and then matted the tank shots of the wave in front. For the closer shots Cliff Culley and his crew built sections of the city on the backlot at Pinewood. The 5-foot miniatures, which included temples and a large statue, were all constructed in block sections, allowing them to crumble realistically when several tons of water hit them. Between 23 and 28 April 1979, using two cameras, the destruction of the miniatures was shot at high speed. With miniature sets you are always at the whim of the dump tanks. Everything is over in a second, and water once released can do the unexpected. Because things didn't always collapse as planned or perhaps part of the set moved as one, we had to rebuild the miniature several times whilst the tanks were refilled and the ground dried out.

The human figures seen fleeing before the wave and falling beneath collapsing buildings were shot in the studio against blue-backing and then optically composited into the miniature. There was a lot of blue screen work on this picture, and ironically we had to send almost all of it to the States to be put together. One of the reasons we originally came to England was to use Rank Laboratories' travelling matte system, but by the time of *Clash* they had closed

---

For the opening underwater scenes we build a 15-foot Kraken. Colin Arthur, who had worked for us on the last Sinbad movie, began its construction in his living room, but it grew so enormous that it went right on through into his dining room and in the end had to be shipped by truck. Under the supervision of underwater cameraman Egil Woxholt (who had worked on *Mysterious Island* and also shot the aerial footage for *Clash of the Titans*), the model was towed in and out of a submerged cage set built in Camino Bay, on Malta. I watched the proceedings from the surface through a mask and snorkel. Unfortunately, there were unforeseen problems working with such a model underwater. Because it was made of sponge rubber, the wretched thing always wanted to float. To cure this problem it was weighed down with hundreds of pounds of lead, but this in turn led to another unexpected problem. After the first day's shoot we left the model on the beach, but by the next morning the lead had been pilfered, so we had to buy more to ballast it again. Everything went from bad to worse, and try as we might, the model just didn't look right. In an attempt to get movement into the creature, we tried to use a diver in a Kraken suit, but this too proved disastrous. While the idea sounds good, in reality the diver's movements were restricted by the cumbersome rubber suit, and he couldn't control his actions. Because MGM wanted footage for a preview trailer, some shots were used, but few remained in the final film.

Above. Still of the miniature square of Argos. This still shows the miniature square being filmed before its destruction by the tidal wave.

the operation. Frank Van der Veer in Hollywood completed some composites and Technicolor did others, although towards the end of production Roy Field joined us at Pinewood to complete the rest of the mattes.

The first Dynamation creature seen in detail is the giant vulture: the servant or agent of Calibos that carries Andromeda's astral image in a golden cage. In Beverley's original script it was to have been a huge bat or marsh hawk, but I felt that was a little too mundane. I suggested that it should be something ugly (I don't consider a bat ugly – perhaps that says something about me), something totally opposite to the beauty of Pegasus. After many discussions I came up with the vulture, a repellent image to most people and one which paralleled the concept of darkness and decay that Calibos represented. There were two models of the vulture, one some 10 inches high, with a wingspan of just over 20 inches and covered with crow feathers, used for close-ups and detail shots like the balcony scenes. The second was about 5 inches high with a 10-inch wingspan, and because it was

used for long shots, it was moulded entirely in latex, including the feathers. I obtained the crow feathers, along with all other natural furs, from various taxidermists, mainly the Hudson Bay Company near the London Embankment. I didn't go out and procure them by direct means. I always dreaded going into their emporium because it had the double effect of amazing and frightening me. There were so many furs hanging up I always wondered how there could possibly be any animals left alive in the world.

The vulture is first seen from inside Andromeda's bedroom where it places a cage on the balcony and then perches on the balustrade. This entire sequence was matted into the background area of the full set. Following the arrival of the creature, the astral image of the princess moves onto the balcony. The camera angle is now reversed and we see the vulture, this time in the foreground with its back to us, still perching on the balustrade. The live action was photographed on the real set, which I then used as a background plate. Next I constructed a miniature balustrade, placed it in

the foreground and animated the vulture with its back to the camera.

If Medusa was the main reason I wanted to film the story of Perseus, the flying horse Pegasus came a very close second. Since seeing the wingless flying horse in Korda's *The Thief of Bagdad*, I had been fascinated with the concept.

In total there were three Pegasus models. Two, approximately 12 inches high with 18-inch wingspans, were used for long shots. I did begin to build a third as a standby, but this only got to the armature stage before I realized it wasn't necessary. Then there was a larger model of about 18 inches high with a wingspan of $2^1/2$ feet, which was constructed when we realized that a more detailed model for close-ups would be required. In addition, I constructed a fully armatured 7-inch high model of Harry for the aerial shots of Perseus on the back of Pegasus. I chose the skin of unborn goats to cover all the models because the pelts had small pure white hairs in proportion to the size of the model. The carefully armatured wings were from a white dove.

I was intrigued to find out if an animated model of Pegasus could achieve even better results than that of the flying horse in Korda's film. I knew how I didn't want it to look. Some years before, I had seen an Italian epic that had used a real horse with very small wings. It seemed totally impractical, especially with a large, muscular man sitting on its back. A horse can weigh up to half a ton, therefore I had to find a logical balance between the proportions of the creature and its wings, even if everyone knows a horse can't really fly. Having studied a variety of references for the horse movements, including motion studies and photographs, I realized the best way was to simply watch them. However, I couldn't just copy their movements. To make Pegasus fly would need a motion that was part real and part pure imagination. If I didn't eliminate certain movements, the action would have looked mechanical. In essence, I had to compromise and take certain liberties. The main problem was what to do with the legs whilst the horse was flying. After several tests, which included posing the legs gracefully, tucking them under its belly and just letting them dangle, nothing seemed quite right. Eventually we hit on the straightforward gallop, allowing Pegasus to tread the air like a racehorse.

So. 30 EXT. PART OF THE CITY OF ARGOS. DAY (H.S. MIN - TM - MALTA TANK) As great waves of water thunder over the walls and into the city. People on the parapet and on the beach flee for their lives.

So. 30 Cont. The waves dash against and break into the city walls. (Note: People on parapet and beach to be added by TM.)

Top. Storyboard pictures of destruction of Argos. A section of the storyboard showing how I originally conceived of its destruction. Beverley Cross chose Argos to be destroyed because it was one of the oldest Greek cities.

Above. Two scenes from the final film showing buildings collapsing and people being swept away. The one on the left is the model being destroyed by the water and the one on the right shows people (who were inserted by travelling matte) perishing under the wall of water and buildings.

Right and above right. Two stills showing the Argos miniature buildings on the backlot at Pinewood Studio. The top shows the technicians working on assembling the sections of buildings that would fall apart when the water hit them. In the top right of the still can be seen the dump tanks full of water. In the lower still the water has been released and the sections have been swept away.

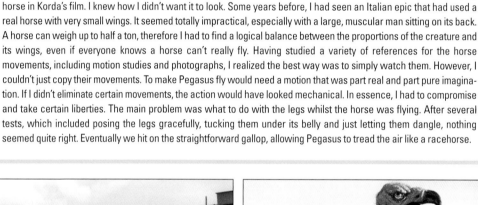

Above. Still of the model vulture. This is the more detailed of the two models with its wing span of over 20 inches and crow feathers. The giant vulture was the servant or agent of Calibos, which carries Andromeda's astral image in a golden cage.

Right. Drawing of how I had originally envisioned the vulture. In Beverley's original script the vulture was to have been a huge bat or marsh hawk, but I felt it was a little too mundane so I came up with the repellent vulture who seemed to embody decay.

The most visually exciting and challenging Pegasus sequence was the capture and taming of the flying horse by Perseus. The live-action plates for the sequence were shot day-for-night at the Guadix location chosen for the mountains in the background. The two trees and the pool in the foreground were added to lend a certain mystery to 'The Wells of the Moon' where the winged horses lived. The sequence shows Perseus roping the horse whilst wearing the helmet of invisibility, given to him by Athena. Thus all we see is a rope apparently moving on its own. To achieve this the rope was painted white and attached to thin wires at either end, which in turn were fixed off screen at the end where the horse was and kept taut by one of the crew at the other end. When photographed against the sky, the wire disappeared, leaving the rope seemingly suspended in mid-air. During the fight, Perseus' helmet of invisibility is knocked off and he appears, pulling on the rope. Perseus' sudden appearance was a dissolve, and at the point where he begins to become visible, I changed the real rope to a miniature one. During the live-action photography I had shown Harry how to mime the actions of pulling on a rope without holding anything, and back in my studio I animated the model of Pegasus with a section of wire painted white (to resemble the rope around its neck) and aligned the rest of it to match Harry's hands on the background plate.

The close shots of Perseus on the horse in the air were a combination of mattes. First we photographed Harry against a blue screen astride a beer barrel, where the camera was dollied past to simulate flying past the camera. Later the sky and Pegasus' wings were added, making a double travelling matte. The wings seen in these shots were real duck wings (each

wing about three feet across), which had been treated by a taxidermist and fitted with armatures. For animation purposes they were attached to a board. After timing the Harry Hamlin live action, we animated the wings from different angles and at varying tempos so that they would always be moving up and down at the same speed as Harry on the blue backing.

Unlike most of my flying sequences, we opted for a rigid rod mount rather than the usual aerial wires because the model was far too heavy and wouldn't have given us a firm registration for a more realistic effect, particularly for the gallop. The mounting shaft or rod came up from below and was attached to the left-hand side of the model, which is why we mostly see him flying left to right. The scenes in which he is flying right to left were reversed optically. The up and down motion of the shaft was done manually, securing it each time with a locking device. In addition to that, there were three swivels in different planes, situated where the shaft connected to the model. This gave us up and down, left to right, and rotation. The linear movement was achieved by mounting the shaft rig on a borrowed 5-foot screwed lathe track that allowed the model to move along. The rod mount was optically lost with a variation on the method used to lose the wires in the *Superman* films. Mounted on the shaft was a V-shaped mirror that reflected the blue screen behind. The point of the V was towards the camera so that it couldn't be seen. This then reproduced the blue screen and later, when the sky and clouds were added, obscured the metal shaft. Jim Danforth was assigned to carry out most of the Pegasus aerial scenes, and his professionalism certainly showed through in enhancing the rather difficult sequences.

Calibos, Lord of the Marsh, was another creature not found in Greek mythology. The character's name was lifted by Beverley from Shakespeare's *The Tempest*, fashioning him after Caliban, the savage and deformed slave. A perfect Dynamation character, half man, half beast, like all the creatures, he went through many changes in both the script and on my drawing board. As always with a humanoid figure, one of the most important elements of the design was to make him *not* look as if he was a man in a rubber suit. Therefore I gave him a demonic look accentuated by a cloven hoof and a reptilian tail.

Throughout pre-production the character of Calibos was to have been dumb. This was to avoid spending vast amounts of time attempting to animate the model to dialogue. However, just before the final shooting script was written, it was decided that he had to communicate, and after much deliberation the problem was solved by using an actor in Calibos makeup for close-ups when dialogue was required. Based on the model and my drawings, Colin Arthur created the wonderful makeup for British actor Neil McCarthy, who possessed a good basic facial structure for the character. The model therefore only appears in medium and long shots where the legs and tail are seen. As it was the first time a Dynamation character had lines, I was a little apprehensive about whether or not the two extremes of model and actor would work. I needn't have worried. Neil played the part beyond all expectations, and when seen edited together, Neil and the model blend perfectly. Perhaps one of the best examples of the intercuts between animation and live footage is during the swamp sequence where Calibos wrestles with Perseus. I employed a number of medium shots of the model in close 'contact' with Harry Hamlin, an effect that necessitated accurate

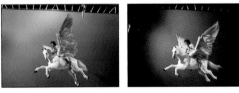

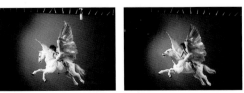

Above left. Harry Hamlin roping Pegasus. During the live-action photography I had shown Harry how to mime the actions of pulling on a rope without holding anything. Later back in my studio I animated the model of Pegasus with a section of wire painted white (to resemble the rope around its neck) and aligned the rest of it to match Harry's hands on the background plate.

Left. Stills of Pegasus model on rod and track. We used a rigid rod mount and track to make Pegasus 'fly'.

Above. Drawing of Calibos. Calibos's name was lifted by Beverley from Shakespeare's The Tempest, fashioning him after Caliban, the savage and deformed slave.

Right. Still of Neil McCarthy in makeup. Based on my model and drawings, Colin Arthur created the wonderful makeup for British actor Neil McCarthy, who possessed a good basic facial structure for Calibos.

choreography in the plate photography and precise alignment of the model during animation. This was all made much easier by Poggi, who was again in charge of stunts and swordplay on the picture. Working together we choreographed the sequence with a stuntman who had to always keep himself in front or to the side of Harry (it was here that I would insert the model). We rehearsed the action three or four times and then, when everyone was happy and Harry knew how to hold his arm, we shot the scenes with Harry shadow boxing. In the animation studio I then matched the movements of the Calibos model to the struggling actions of Harry Hamlin. To add an extra realistic element to the fight, I planned to have splashes made in the water during the live-action photography. These would have then been matched to where the model's legs and tail would have made contact with the water. Sadly, time didn't allow me that little luxury, but on reflection I don't believe the exciting atmosphere of the sequence suffers from the loss.

There are two Calibos models. The largest, about 18 inches high, was constructed from Trog. I reluctantly stripped him down to the armature, altered one of the foot armatures and added the tail armature. There was also a smaller model used for the long shots in which he appears with Pegasus and for the poignant scene in the temple where we see him pleading with his mother Thetis for revenge against Perseus. This was a favourite scene of mine because we see Calibos display both vulnerability and extreme hatred, telling us much about the character.

There was some concern that audiences might miss Calibos' cloven hoof, so to emphasize this I dramatically introduced the deformity when he first appears to Andromeda by having him step into frame. From that point the audience know they are going to see something abhorrent, but then the camera pans upwards, showing the back of Calibos, whereupon they realize the full extent of the deformity and how vindictive Zeus had been.

Although it looks simple, shots such as the pan up can involve much planning, time and patience. It would have begun during the live-action plate photography where Judi is in the background and the camera panned upwards. In the animation studio I would match the pan upwards by panning up the model, which was on a miniature foreground set in front of the rear projection screen, at the exact same rate. Of course, I couldn't move the camera, so I mounted the model and the miniature set on a table, which was in turn mounted on a crane device. As the rear projection pan progressed, I would mark a point, perhaps a rock, on the rear projection screen with tape, giving me the correct measurement to lower the table on the crane. I would lower the table a fraction of an inch to match the rate of pan up on the rear projection plate, at the same time as animating the model's movements.

If Calibos was the villain, the owl sent by Athena to help Perseus was the comic relief. Bubo gave us a rare opportunity to instil some gentle humour into the story, although I was a little concerned, remembering the mistakes made in *Mighty Joe Young*. However, I was persuaded and reassured by Beverley that the balance between the heroics and the comedy would be necessary and appropriate. In the event Bubo was perfect for the story, and I must confess that the gentle humour it allowed was crucial. Contrary to what some critics said at the time, Bubo was invented before R2D2 from *Star Wars*. This inference irritated all of us involved in the story development.

There were three different armatured models of Bubo: a detailed 18-inch high model for close-ups, a medium 4-inch high model for the flying sequences, and a tiny 1½-inch model for long shots. The first was constructed mainly of fibreglass covered with brass 'feathers', but the wings were armatured, covered in latex and painted to resemble the larger model. The medium model was made entirely of latex over an armature and again painted to look like brass. Only when we had shot a lot of the flying footage did I

construct the tiny model, made entirely of metal and with simple copper wings without an armature. For the aerial photography we constructed a mechanism precisely machined to run along an overhead wood track. Three aerial brace wires ran from this, holding the model from above, but for extra stability during the animation, we ran a fourth wire from the bottom of the model to a paper cup filled with sand. To save time we also used a radio-controlled mechanized model constructed by Colin Chivers and David Knowles. Like the main armatured one, it was about 18 inches high, and used mainly in scenes where the actors were seen handling him. Although limited, its movements included flapping its wings, revolving its head, spinning its eyes and opening and closing its beak, accomplished with tiny motors inside the body.

Steve worked on much of Bubo's animation and gave the character the impish personality that made him one of the special features of the film. From Bubo's first appearance, it is established that although he has been sent from the gods, he is a funny little character. Perseus and his men are in a desolate landscape, relieved only by a gnarled tree. Slowly, from the distance Bubo flies towards them and lands on a tree branch that snaps, sending him toppling to the ground. For the long shots we used the smallest model, then the medium model for the next shots of him hovering and descending to the branch, and finally the full model for the landing and fall. Apart from the model of Bubo and the branch on which he lands, everything else was back projection. The tree itself was matted out to enable us to fix the branch by means of a rod hidden behind the matte of the tree. After the animation, the tree was replaced by a second pass through the camera and background plate.

With the help of Bubo, Perseus finds his way to the lair of the Stygian Witches. These ladies were an amalgamation of the Stygian Nymphs from whom Perseus had to obtain the means of defeating Medusa, and the Gorgon's three sisters who share a single eye.

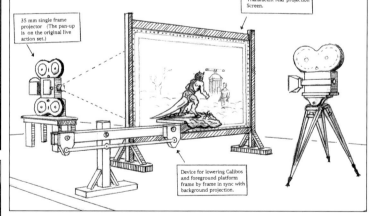

Top left and left. Stills of Calibos. The large 18-inch model of Calibos was constructed from Trog. I reluctantly stripped him down to the armature, altered one of the foot armatures and added the tail armature.

Above. A drawing showing how the first appearance of Calibos was achieved. The first time we see Calibos is when Andromeda arrives in the swamp and a cloven hoof steps into the picture. This may look simple on the screen but was in fact quite complex. For it I constructed a crane-like device that lowered the model frame by frame to match the rear projection plate of Andromeda.

Right. Calibos' cloven hoof steps into the picture. A still of how the effect looked in the final film.

Top right. Sketch of Bubo with wings open. One of my earliest sketches for Bubo.

Far right. Still of model Bubo. This was one of three armatured models of Bubo and in addition to that there was also the radio-controlled model.

These marvellous characters were played with great gusto by Flora Robson, Freda Jackson and Anna Manahan. Despite the live rats running about the set and problems with their cumbersome makeup, which made it very difficult to see properly, so causing Freda to fall over and Anna to set fire to her costume, they hugely enjoyed playing the three old crones squabbling over the eye. To help keep the sequence as light as possible, we inserted some amusing visuals, including a hand coming out of the cauldron, which is pushed back in by one of the witches. Originally this was to have been a skeleton hand, but we thought the real one worked much better.

The witches tell Perseus that to find Medusa he must cross the Styx to the Isle of the Dead. Normally one would have to be dead to cross the Styx, but in our story Perseus pays Charon, a miser who ferries the dead, to take him and his men to the other side. This was shot on the beach at Palinuro, near the rock arch used for the Talos sequence in *Jason and the Argonauts*. The Isle of the Dead itself was a natural island off the coast called Scoglio del Coniglio, on which I matted a temple and an extension to make it seem larger. The swirling mist was added later. Once on the Isle, the men climb up through a passage that leads them to a temple (one of the three at Paestum in southern Italy used in *Jason* for the Phineas/Harpy sequence). Here they would encounter the first of the two creatures living in that place of the damned.

The first of the creatures is the guardian of Medusa's shrine, Dioskilos, a two-headed dog. He was actually based on Cerberus, a three-headed dog (sometimes described as possessing fifty heads) who guarded the entrance to Hades, or the shores of the Styx, to prevent the living from entering and the dead from leaving. Originally we wanted to keep the three heads, but although I struggled to sculpt a realistic model, it looked far too grotesque and top heavy and was therefore totally unbelievable. Even with two heads we had to manipulate the design quite extensively to arrive at a beast that retained a feel for mythology but also kept a sense of proportion. The Dioskilos model was about 7 inches high, 11 inches long and covered in very exotic Siberian rabbit fur that was prone to movement during animation.

When originally conceived, the Dioskilos sequence was intended to be longer and more violent. It was cut down when we realized we had two key sequences back-to-back, and the violence was scaled down so that it wouldn't alienate a younger audience. Some examples of what we removed from the sequence included a scene in which the creature was to have bitten into a man's arm and Perseus cutting off one of the creature's heads even though it doesn't stop it. This last scene was dispensed with because of the violence and its similarity to the Medusa sequence immediately following it. In the final film one of the heads is 'killed' but not actually cut off. This was

achieved by animating the model in front of the rear projection screen and letting Harry's sword appear to go into the creature from the side. As the action continues, blood oozed from the wound. The second thrust by Harry is delivered to the creature's chest by substituting a miniature sword at the point of entry. Another dropped feature was the conclusion of the fight on a stone spiral staircase in the temple, showing Dioskilos and Perseus plunging from its summit to the temple floor. I suspect everyone thought it too similar to the skeleton fight in *The 7th Voyage of Sinbad*. It's a pity, because in the final analysis the sequence required a more spectacular climax. Although I had designed the sequence, a lot of the animation was completed by Jim assisted by Steve. Considering how it was altered and cut down in favour of the next sequence, Dioskilos had much originality and excitement.

Dioskilos was always meant to lead us into, what was for me, the most exciting sequence in the film: the conflict with the Gorgon Medusa. The Medusa sequence is perhaps the second most famous sequence from all our films and one of my most satisfying – as near perfect as I was ever able to achieve. One of three Gorgon sisters, Medusa had once been beautiful, but after a violation in the temple of Athena (in our story it was Aphrodite), the goddess turned her hair into serpents and gave her the curse of turning all living things that looked at her into stone.

DIOSKILOS

Above. Still of Bubo landing on branch. From Bubo's first appearance, it is established that although he has been sent from the gods, he is a funny little character.

Above right. Drawing of Dioskilos. Dioskilos was actually based on Cerberus, a three-headed dog (sometimes described as having fifty heads, which would have been an impossible animation task to set myself) who guarded the entrance to Hades, or the shores of the Styx, to prevent the living from entering and the dead from leaving. In our film he guards the temple of Medusa.

Right. Model of Dioskilos. The Dioskilos model was about 7 inches high, 11 inches long and covered in exotic Siberian rabbit fur that was very prone to movement during animation.

Far right. Armature of Dioskilos. This armature is a good example of exactly how complex they were. Since my father's death in the early 1960s I had ordered the ball and socket joints and struts from a manufacturing company and then assembled them myself for whatever creation I had in mind.

Bottom right. Dioskilos on the animation table.

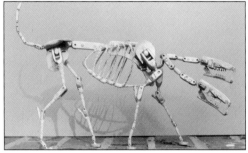

To develop Medusa into a workable Dynamation character, I began by researching how art, literature and films had portrayed her, and I was often surprised to discover that most representations of her had been as a beautiful woman with serpents in her hair. The two paintings that best represented her were Caravaggio's *Medusa* and Leonardo da Vinci's *Testa di Medusa*, but even in these gruesome portrayals she is seen as attractive, making it extremely difficult for me to believe that she could turn anyone to stone. I felt we needed a striking and yet unconventionally hideously ugly demon. In Florence there is a stunning statue by Cellini of Perseus holding the severed head of Medusa at arm's length. It is a frightening yet beautiful rendition of the legend, and the one on which I based the face of my Medusa. Taking the effect Cellini had produced, I designed her to possess a mesmerizing ugliness built on a beautiful bone structure.

The torso would have to complement her facial ugliness. In most renditions of Medusa it is unseen, but when shown (as in the Hammer film *The Gorgon*, 1964), she is usually wearing a diaphanous gown,

which would have been impossible to animate. I decided to give her a non-human body and expose as much of it as dignity would allow. In fact the drawing of Medusa was the earliest I completed for *Clash* (dating back to 1977), and it shows her wearing a discreet boob tube. However, when it came to designing the model, I experimented with her wearing a bra-like garment, but it looked vulgar, so in the end everyone agreed that the offending garment should be removed (I suppose one could say she was the first lady to burn her bra) and Medusa's potentially offending nipples were painted to blend in with the rest of her torso. The bow and arrows were not only an aid by which to kill, but by firing the arrows she was able to attract the full attention of her victims to look directly into her deadly eyes.

The number of snakes on her hair was a matter of some debate before a compromise was reached between aesthetics and practicality. The fewer we had, the less complicated animation would be, but I didn't want to destroy the appearance by having too few. After all, who wants a Gorgon that's skimpy on snakes? I eventually opted for twelve. Instead of

making them emerge from the skull, I 'laid' them on her head to take up more space. Because she possessed snakes for hair, it seemed an obvious progression to complement these by designing her lower torso as that of a huge snake, to which I added a rattlesnake tail, giving the opening scenes a sense of foreboding.

My early drawing of Medusa also portrayed her within the columns of the temple where Dioskilos is encountered, but as the development of the story progressed, we decided that Perseus and his men should descend into a vaulted chamber, a kind of ante-chamber to the underworld. The design of the chamber reflected this idea. It is a dark, mysterious place, with squat columns, ancient symbols and deep strong colours; a nebulous affair based mainly on the Palace of Knossos in Crete, but enhanced with flickering fires, shadows and a selection of Medusa's motionless victims. Lighting, as in all such sequences, played a huge role in achieving the right atmosphere. The full set (constructed and photographed in the hangar on Malta) was lit with flickering flames, casting ominous moving shadows in every corner and a mood of subtle menace. Grotesque shadows on

Above far left, top and above. Stills of model Medusa's face. Taking the effect Cellini had produced in his statue of Medusa, I designed her to possess a mesmerizing ugliness built on a beautiful bone structure. The model was so detailed that she still looked good in extreme close-up.

Left. Drawing of Medusa with her bow and arrow. This drawing of Medusa was the earliest I completed for Clash (dating back to 1977), showing her wearing a discreet boob tube.

Right, right hand page near right and far right. Three pages of the storyboard for the appearance of Medusa. I had always intended the appearance of Medusa to be slow and terrifying, as her shadow is cast by the flickering light onto a wall and then she emerges from the darkness into the light.

So. 474. INT. THE SANCTUARY NIGHT
PERSEUS and his TWO COMPANIONS circling the ritual pool.

So. 475. THE PLATFORM ANOTHER ANGLE (DYN)
OUR VIEW is moving through a forest of columns. A shadow appears across the surface of one column – it quickly disappears but we see it is the hideous silhouette of a woman.

So. 475 Cont. OUR VIEW moves on until the shadow again appears across a smooth wall. We now see it is the shadow of a woman with writhing hair.

So. 476 THREE SHOT PERSEUS AND COMPANIONS
PERSEUS signals to the TWO OFFICERS to raise their shields to cover their eyes.

So. 477. THE PLATFORM (DYN) On the platform the silhouette glides to a halt. We see the figure has the lower limbs of a monstrous snake... The head turns – looking, searching.

SC. 478 SHOCK CUT TO C.S. MEDUSA (DYN)
A sudden terrifying vision – the face of MEDUSA with writhing snake – hair, suddenly comes forward

So. 478 Cont. (dyn)
into the light. The mad staring eyes, the fanged teeth and reptilian green skin. Her eyes eminate power.

So. 479 FULL SHOT PERSEUS AND COMPANIONS
At the front of the staircase backing away with their shields held high covering their faces.

the chamber's walls and columns herald the arrival of Medusa, and when she finally appears in full frame, her face is lit with what I call Joan Crawford lighting. If you look at many of her films, for example *Mildred Pierce*, you will notice that Crawford moves in and out of shadows, or when stationary has a light across only her eyes. The technique has the effect of dramatizing a point ideally suited to highlighting Medusa's eyes. Lighting also has to be matched between the background plate and the miniature foreground, whether it is a continuation of a full-size set, the reflection of sunlight or shadows. With Medusa's lair the flickering light cast by the real brazier fires had to be reproduced onto her torso. To achieve this I used a technique that I had developed for *Hansel and Gretel* where we see Gretel looking into the witch's oven. I constructed an 18-inch round Plexiglas plate into which I cut various sizes of hole, and over these were taped various red and orange cells that would produce different densities of light on the figure. I mounted the whole thing on a 5–6 foot stand and placed it in front of a light with the lens taken out. When the wheel was

moved, it would cast a varying light on Medusa, making it appear as if she were lit by open fires. To animate the whole thing, I fixed a special screw to the centre of the wheel, allowing me to move it a fraction of an inch at a time to co-ordinate it with the animation of Medusa. When projected, the model of Medusa is seen bathed in the same flickering light as the background.

Like all my creations, Medusa needed to move in a special way. Her snake-like lower torso would dictate certain movements, but she had a human upper torso that would in effect make her top-heavy. Even when I was setting up for the animation, I had no idea how she was going to move, but then a long forgotten image from the 1932 Tod Browning film *Freaks* surfaced, and I knew how to approach it. In this film a legless man is seen pulling himself around by his hands, an action I found rather disturbing at the time, but I could see that Medusa (a freak created by the gods) would also possess such a grotesque action as she struggled to pull the unnatural weight of her half-human, half-snake body around. It would exaggerate her deformities.

The full appearance of Medusa is anticipated by silhouette shots of her tail rattling in anticipation of her prey and the outline on a column of her upper torso with her hair writhing. The tension increases when we see the whole chamber from Medusa's point of view as she searches for the intruders. The first 'action' has Medusa firing an arrow at the shield of one of Perseus' companions. Therefore I had to 'connect' the model in the foreground with the man who appeared in the rear projection. This began on the live set in Malta, where Brian Smithies rigged a real arrow on a wire, shot by him off camera so that it hit the shield. The smoke trail effect that came from the arrow was also created at this time. Later I animated the Medusa model in front of the rear projection of the real arrow. The model was placed very precisely so that I could animate her letting off a miniature arrow, which after leaving the miniature bow was taken away when the real arrow on the rear plate appears. Originally it had been intended to have Medusa dip the arrow heads into an open wound, as her blood was deadly poison, but we decided that dipping the arrows each time was a little

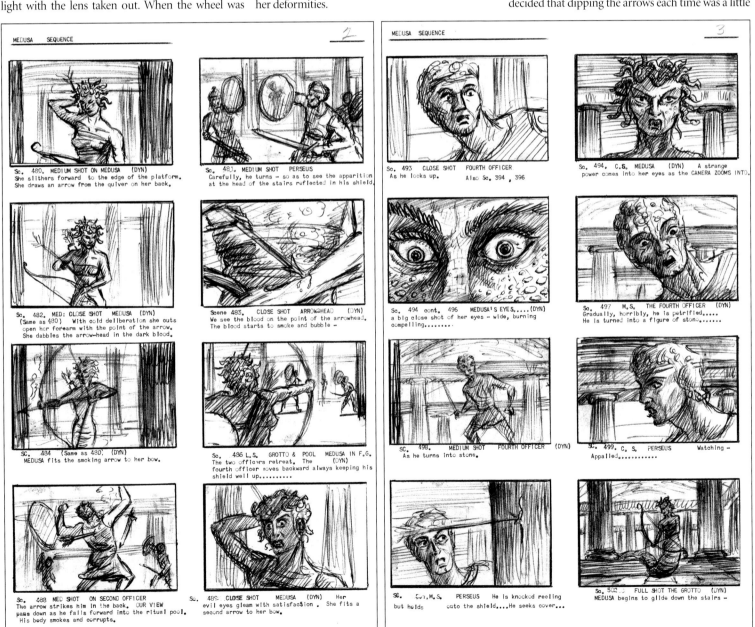

too grim. After the arrow hits his shield, the man makes the fatal mistake of looking at Medusa, whereupon her eyes turn him to stone. This effect was achieved by double exposure. When the man falls down and looks back, I matted out the area of the real actor except his cloak. I then made a small miniature model of the actor's pose, which I then dissolved into the matte. The clothing did not change, only the figure.

In an early screenplay Medusa was to have been slain by Perseus' shield. The shield, with a serrated edge, was to have been thrown like a Frisbee across the chamber to slice off the Gorgon's head. Today I can't believe we even considered this over the sword, but at the time we were concerned that the film wouldn't get an appropriate certificate because it might be considered too violent to simply chop off her head with a sword. We figured that somehow the shield would divorce Perseus from the act of decapitation. It was Harry who pointed out that the sword would work much better than an overlarge Frisbee. The scene now shows Harry swinging the sword, which slices through the neck, and the head lifts into the air

and tumbles out of shot. Using the same Medusa model as I had for the rest of the sequence, I detached the head at its neck armature joint and suspended it on wires. Thus I could animate it simultaneously with the torso. Once the sword has done its work, a reddish goo, her blood, pours from her neck. The goo was actually shot separately. We constructed a tube that would match the neck of the model and mounted it in front of black velvet. After mixing a red-tinted wallpaper paste, my assistant poured it down the tube so that it oozed out, and then matted it into the scene.

In her death throes Medusa manages to make a parting statement by scratching her nails down a nearby column. Suggested by Steve, it was an action and sound designed to send shivers down the audience's spine. We built a special miniature column out of cardboard, and as I animated the model's hand, I scratched the marks of her nails into the soft cardboard. It was the sound, of course, that made it seem like stone, added later by the sound department. At first they didn't quite get the proper effect. I kept telling them 'nails scratching on a blackboard' but the sounds they came up with were nothing like it. In the

end they got exactly the right resonance by scratching something on a blackboard. Strange how the obvious is sometimes the best way to achieve what you want.

There was just the one model of Medusa, 14 inches high and 24 inches long to the tip of the tail. She possessed 150 armatured joints and was large enough to allow us to shoot close-ups of her face, tail and lower body. Originally we had planned to build a large head for close-ups, but even though I hate to get too close to a model because it usually means we have to use bag filters, I decided that if we built one full model big enough, we should be able to get away with it. In the end my hunch was right and she looked good in close-up.

The Medusa sequence required enormous patience. It took days of animation to achieve apparently simple feats such as raising her arm to reach the bowstring and yet more days for the arrow to leave it. Then there were the natural actions of her arms, mouth, eyes and fingers, and the not so natural rattling of her tail. In addition, I had to continuously and convincingly animate the twelve tiny snakes on her head (twenty-four movements

So. 520   MED. FULL SHOT MEDUSA (DYN)
She quickly turns around just in time to receive ....

So. 520   cont.   the sharp spinning shield through
her neck. With a 'cut-off' brief scream, her
head severs from her body.

So. 521   CLOSE SHOT PERSEUS
Even he is shocked by the sight O.S.

Above. A section of the storyboard of the shield cutting off Medusa's head. Originally when I had executed these storyboards, the shield, with a serrated edge, was to have been thrown like a Frisbee across the chamber to slice off the Gorgon's head, but later this concept was changed to Perseus cutting off her head with his sword.

Top and above. Animating Medusa's decapitation. In the bottom still I am working on the model, which stands on the animation table. Behind is the rear projection screen (with no background image) and just out of the picture, behind the camera, is the disc that produced the flame flicker onto the model.

because the heads and tails were separate) and one on her arm. Like the skeletons and the Hydra, when there were so many movements required for each frame, it all got quite complicated to remember everything, particularly if I had drunk too much coffee and nature called.

The Medusa sequence is perhaps the one I am most proud of. Everything in it – the model, the actions, the pace, the lighting – works so perfectly. As with most Dynamation sequences, I edited it myself, with perhaps a modification or two by the editor and Charles. The editing process would begin with the editor, who would rough cut the live action according to the script and continuity. During animation I would keep referring to this cut, and as I completed the Dynamation scenes, I added them into the rough cut. Once everything was finished, I would then go through a process of refinement. When director Desmond Davis saw the completed sequence, he kindly called to congratulate me.

The film now moves to the return journey and Andromeda's rescue. Calibos, knowing the power of the Gorgon's blood, attempts to seek final revenge on Perseus, and whilst the exhausted men sleep, he punctures the bag containing the Medusa's head. Blood oozes onto the ground and from it appear a repellent combination of maggots and a trio of scorpions, the latter growing into huge, deadly creatures.

I had always wanted to design a sequence with scorpions but had never found a suitable opportunity, even though they are wonderful antagonists and their crab-like legs and pincers are well suited to Dynamation. When we discussed possible sequences to fit into the Perseus legend, I suggested scorpions, an idea that fitted perfectly with what would become the final battle between our hero and Calibos. We built three 18-inch models embellished only very slightly with larger and therefore more menacing pincers. We studied and photographed the movement of several live ones, but either the lights made them languid or they would do the opposite of what we wanted. In the end I simply used my imagination, basing most of the movements on those of the crab. I completed the majority of the sequence early on in the animation

Top left. Still of just the armature on the wall in my garden. The Medusa armature possessed 150 armatured joints.

Above. Medusa's eyes. Some more shots of the lighting used for the head of Medusa.

Top right. Still of model of Medusa. There was just the one model of Medusa, 14 inches high and 24 inches long to the tip of the tail, and it was large enough to allow us to shoot close-ups of her face, tail and lower body.

Right. Me with the prop Medusa Head. The Medusa sequence is perhaps the one I am most proud of but the full size head was always a disappointment to me, as it didn't resemble the model's face. In any case, it did show what might happen to my actors and actresses if things didn't go according to plan.

Sc. 554A 558 ANOTHER ANGLE
(dyn) PERSEUS & men are faced
with the monster SCORPIONS.

Sc. 555 M.S. SCORPIONS (DYN)
The huge creatures advance,
their stinging tails clicking.

Sc. 555A. C.S. PERSEUS & GROUP
They slash at the O.S. monsters.

Sc. 555B. C.S. SCORPIONS (DYN
They snap at the o.s. men.

Sc. 556. CALIBOS (DYN)
He limps through the trees to
scatter the horses with his whip.

Sc. 557. ANOTHER ANGLE (DYN)
The first officer is stung to
death.

Sc. 559. C.S. Men As they
slash at the o.s. monsters.

Sc. 560. ANOTHER ANGLE (DYN)
PERSEUS kills one SCORPION..
turns in pursuit of CALIBOS.

schedule, whilst I was still working alone. Generally, I like to get into a particular sequence and stick with it until it's finished, but because of the number of animated creations, I jumped around a bit at the beginning and filmed a little of each character, just to get a visual résumé of the picture as we were cutting it. Afterwards I would go back and complete the sequences.

I used the same zoom trick to produce the scorpions' rapid growth as I had for the wasp in *Sinbad and the Eye of the Tiger*, animating the model as I zoomed in with the lens. Only one model was used for the growth, shot at different angles with the zoom to make it seem as though there were three. To allow the men 'contact' with the scorpions I employed a few old tricks. The first has Tim Pigott-Smith cutting off a pincer. I choreographed Tim so that at a certain point he slashes down with his sword. With

the model scorpion on the animation table and Tim projected on the rear plate, I timed the sequence by counting the frames, so that when Tim's sword came down, the scorpion's pincer was seemingly cut off. I detached the limb by cutting the latex and pulling apart the armature joint below the pincer, which I then suspended on wires so that it fell to the ground at the same speed as the action of the model. To give it a little extra realism at the moment of severance, I added a mixture of makeup blood and glycerine. I went through the same procedure when Perseus slices the sting from the tail of another creature. Later I reassembled the armatures and glued the latex, as I had done with Medusa's head.

The demise of the last scorpion is brought about by Perseus when he plunges his sword into the top of the creature's body. On the live-action plate Harry is plunging into nothing, but I had calculated

approximately where his hands should stop as if they had reached the skin of the creature. I stood the model in front of the rear projection screen, and as the real sword appears to enter the body, I replaced it with a miniature. I also animated a downward motion with the model to make it seem as if the sword was actually entering its body and pushing into it. During the scorpion fight, Calibos kills Tim Pigott-Smith's character by stabbing him in the back. This was done in basically the same way as I had filmed the fight in the swamp. On location we photographed Tim pretending to be held around the neck and then sinking to the ground as if he had been stabbed. Back in the studio I animated the model of Calibos in front of this location plate so that it seems as if he is holding Tim and stabbing him.

Finally Calibos and Perseus stand alone to fight one last battle. Using his whip, Calibos attacks Perseus. We see Calibos in the foreground with his back to the camera, and the whip lashing out at Perseus who appears on the background plate. It seems that the whip connects with the hand of Perseus, but of course it doesn't. Actually Harry held nothing, he simply positioned his hand as though he was pulling on a whip. I then animated the miniature whip (which had a wire inside and an aerial wire to support the tip) to match with Harry's hand. If his hand moved, I would match it with a corresponding movement in the whip. Perspective was vital, so I designed the whip with a taper, giving the illusion of

Although the live-action plates for the scorpion sequence were shot day for night, we were cursed with extremely bad weather, suffering long downpours that made everything look gloomy and overcast. The sequence was scheduled for the last day of the Italian shoot and the production was due to catch a specially chartered plane to Malta the next day, so I was faced with little or no room to manoeuvre. The sequence had to be photographed then or be dropped from the film, whether it was raining or not. Once back at the studio in England, I tried rebalancing the colour of the plates with an orange filter in the projector, and although it worked to some extent, the sequence looks murky and grainy. If I had been more temperamental, thrown my hat on the ground and jumped on it, I might have got another day's shoot. But it would have cost the company a lot of money to delay the cast and crew and I didn't want a confrontation. Some people might call that artistic crucifixion!

Left hand page. The scorpion storyboard. A section of the storyboard for the scorpion sequence showing their appearance from the blood of Medusa and how the early scenes were to be cut together.

Above and above right sequence. Stills from the scorpion fight. When we discussed possible sequences to fit into the Perseus legend, I suggested scorpions, an idea that fitted perfectly with what would become the final battle between our hero and Calibos.

Right. Still of a scorpion model. There were three models but I only used one for the growth of the scorpions, shot at different angles to make it seem as though there were three. They were combined into the one shot by means of a travelling matte.

Sc. 624 (Same as 604 FULL SHOT SACRIFICIAL ROCK
The great KRAKEN appears between the (Dyn)
rocks of the cove — face to face with ANDROMEDA.
He glares down at her as she twists and turns
in torment.

Sc. 625 Med CLOSE SHOT Men on rocks reacting.

Sc. 627 CLOSER SHOT KRAKEN & ANDROMEDA (DYN)
As his huge head moves down into ....

Sc. 629 Cont. our view as camera pauses
on ANDROMEDA.

Sc. 627 Cont. As the huge head moves down
into our view — ANDROMEDA struggles with her
chains. She turns away from him in terror.

Sc. 629½ EXT. ROCK AND CLIFFS As PEGASUS (Dyn-Tm)
appears with PERSEUS. He is still clutching the
head of MEDUSA in the scarlet cloak.

Sc. 630 CLOSER MOVING SHOT PERSEUS &
PEGASUS (DYN- TM)

Sc. 631 MD. SHOT THE KRAKEN - Watching -
Suspicious. Ready.......

distance between model and man. Calibos is finally killed when Perseus manages to grab his sword and throw it into his opponent's stomach. Originally, I animated a shot of Calibos writhing in agony, but Desmond considered it a little too melodramatic.

The finale sees Perseus rescuing Andromeda by holding up Medusa's head and turning the Kraken to stone. Harry's hand is actually holding nothing, while the head was in fact a detached miniature, which I suspended in front of the rear projection plate of Harry by six wires, three at the top and three at the bottom, achieving absolute stability. As soon as the Kraken looks into Medusa's eyes, he turns to stone and crumbles back into the sea. To do this I made a special plaster replica of the model, constructed in sections, so that when it was shot at high speed, we could collapse it. We then inserted it into the scene with a travelling matte.

The sacrifice sequence has always seemed visually wrong. After all the other spectacular encounters, it seems to lack, amongst other things, a visual sense that we are witnessing the wrath of the gods. I did plan to add threatening clouds, giving the sequence a dark and brooding effect, but it would have taken more time than the schedule would allow. Another element that always looked far too mundane was the full set, built on the edge of the sea tank in Malta. My first design for the sequence included people on the shore looking at the spectacle behind barriers, or half cages, to protect them from the beast. The idea was discarded in favour of people just standing there. It wasn't right. Perhaps another reason for my lack of enthusiasm for the sequence is that whilst I was shooting the animation, my hand slipped and hit a metal drill press, injuring my finger. It didn't even break the skin, but the next day, I couldn't bend the digit. As my fingers are the tools of my trade, I rushed off to the doctor who said it was only bruised. Even so, it was impossible for me to animate, so Steve took over the completion of the sequence. I must say he made an excellent job of it. For the next two or three weeks I attempted to busy myself with other tasks. As it got better, I did attempt some animation, but found it difficult without the full mobility of all my fingers. To this day I believe the doctor was wrong and that I had cracked a bone. I had never injured myself before during production, so it is strange and fortunate that the one time I did, there were other animators to hand. Curiously, just before my accident Steve also injured his hand in a tripod and had to go to hospital.

After sixteen months of work (preceded by eighteen months of preparation) the animation was completed in mid-January 1981. Even then I didn't have time to rest. The next few months were spent in the editing room and then working in the capacity of associate producer alongside Charles to oversee the recording of the sound effects and score. Laurence Rosenthal's thrilling and soaring symphonic music adds so much to the picture, enhancing the action rather than dominating it. He seemed totally at home with fantasy. A perfect example of this is in his music for the capture of Pegasus. It is magnificent, highlighting exactly what I had in mind when animating and reflecting the essence of the struggle and ultimate conquest of the beast. His composition for the Medusa sequence was even better. The sound effects department had wanted to drop the music because they thought the sound effects of the rattle and the slithering on their own would be more

Left hand page. A section of the storyboard for the Andromeda sacrifice sequence. Once again it can been seen how closely the storyboard resembles the scene in the film.

Above. A still of sacrifice sequence. After all the other spectacular encounters, the sacrifice sequence seems to lack, amongst other things, a visual sense that we are witnessing the wrath of the gods. What I had intended was to shoot a special dark, threatening sky with lightning that would have been matted in behind the Kraken, but

time and money didn't allow for it. However, the end sequence would have been far less impressive without Laurence Rosenthal's music, which helped to bridge some of the sequence's inadequacies and lent it a spectacular feel.

effective. Good though the sound effects were, it needed Laurence's wonderful music. The end Kraken sequence would have been far less impressive without his music, which helped to bridge some of the sequence's inadequacies and lent it a spectacular feel. Laurence used to come down during the animation to get a feel for the creatures, whereupon I would impart the ideas running through my head. He knew exactly what we wanted and composed a score that was a perfect meld of fantasy, spectacle and romanticism. Between 28 November 1980 and 30 January 1981 the score was recorded with the London Symphony Orchestra, following which both Charles and I went straight into a long promotional campaign. This took us on a month's tour of America, to Europe and even Japan. The film finally opened in the US in June 1981 and in Europe the next month.

Most critics were kind to the film, with the best reviews coming from America. The *Pennsylvania Times* said, 'Those who love movie magic will thank heaven for *Clash of the Titans*! It's a magical experience!' The *Washington Star* commented, '*Clash of the Titans* is a welcome old-fashioned trek through an ancient world of Gods and Heros. That old master of fantasy, Ray Harryhausen, has finally been given full rein to display his teeming imagination on the screen. It works!' and finally '*Clash of the Titans* is Ray Harryhausen's *Gone With the Wind*', wrote the *Bergen Record*, New Jersey. My favourite was the *Chicago Sun-Times*, where Roger Ebert wrote, '*Clash of the Titans* is the kind of movie they aren't supposed to be making anymore: a grand and glorious romantic adventure, filled with brave heroes, beautiful heroines, fearsome monsters and awe-inspiring duels to the death.' He went on to say the kindest comment about the effects: 'The real star of the movie, however, is Ray Harryhausen… when Perseus tames Pegasus, it sure looks like he's dealing with a real horse.' He concludes by saying, 'it is perfect as summer entertainment. It's a family film and yet it's not by any means innocuous: It's got blood and thunder and lots of gory details, all presented with enormous gusto and style. It has faith in a story-telling tradition that sometimes seems almost forgotten, a tradition depending upon legends and myths, magical swords, enchanted shields, invisibility helmets, and the overwhelming power of the kiss. I had a great time'. He knew what the film was all about, and most audiences seemed to agree with him, thank God. This approval was not shared by other reviewers, who could not see the adventure, fantasy and imagination. Perhaps they didn't have an imagination, as some seemed to revel in tearing it apart, writing not only aggressive, but down right vicious and opinionated reports. When I came to read the *Variety* review where they called it 'an unbearable bore' with 'flat, outdated special effects', I became very disillusioned. I gave the film so much of myself that when it was vindictively and unconstructively torn apart, the passion of film-making seemed to die.

Following *Clash of the Titans*, Charles and I started to search for the next Dynamation subject. Several were considered, including two that would have returned to the Sinbad legend and a project called *Force of the Trojans*. Both were heavily researched and scripts written (see chapter 12), but there were no buyers. Even though *Clash* had proved itself at the box-office, the trend for fantasy had now shifted to the anti-hero with his passion for violence and mayhem, and our subjects where no longer considered commercially viable. The age of the hero was dead. *Clash* was destined to be my last picture, and looking back, the decision to end my career at that point was absolutely right. With all the problems involved in production, and the knowledge that I was losing precious control of solo animation, I was forced to concede that it was time to stand aside for others and their new

This page. Two examples of the artwork for the film poster.

Right hand page. My favourite artwork. This poster not only contains action and excitement, but also shows how good the cast was.

An Epic Entertainment Spectacular!

CLASH OF THE TITANS

Metro-Goldwyn-Mayer presents A CHARLES H. SCHNEER Production CLASH OF THE TITANS

starring HARRY HAMLIN as Perseus JUDI BOWKER as Andromeda

BURGESS MEREDITH · MAGGIE SMITH · URSULA ANDRESS · CLAIRE BLOOM

SIAN PHILLIPS · FLORA ROBSON and LAURENCE OLIVIER as Zeus Produced by CHARLES H. SCHNEER and RAY HARRYHAUSEN

Creator of Special Visual Effects RAY HARRYHAUSEN Written by BEVERLEY CROSS Music by JOHN BARRY Directed by DESMOND DAVIS

DOLBY STEREO   MGM   United Artists

COMING FOR THE SUMMER OF 1981

technology to take over. The industry was on the threshold of revolutionary changes, all of which I would have been unhappy with. CGI is a wonderful tool that continues to fascinate me, but I know, deep down, it would never have suited me. Perhaps my fate would have been significantly different if it had been CGI that had brought Kong to life. I might not have been so inspired and could have ended up as a plumber! The use of CGI is now so commonplace that almost all major (and some not so major) movies have embraced the technology and now it is overused. Three-dimensional stop-motion model animation created a fantasy world that was so rare.

The way the creatures moved encouraged a sense that one was watching a miracle, but when the miraculous becomes commonplace, the concept of the miracles cease to be miraculous. In any event, my time had passed: there would be no room for a maverick who worked on his own in a small back room making it up as he went along.

But the technology wasn't the only problem. It had become harder and harder for me during those last few pictures to sustain my enthusiasm. A despondency had crept in when it was time to begin working alone in my small animation studio. What had once sustained me during the tedium of animation, namely viewing the rushes to see if I had achieved what I wanted, ceased to be intriguing. I felt that it was time to call it a day. By the end of *Clash of the Titans* I had reached the grand old age of sixty-one, and had been working since I was a teenager. Moviemaking takes so much out of one's life. You have to live, eat and breathe pictures, not just during production, but before and after. I hardly saw my family during the endless months of production, and there eventually comes a point when you say, 'Is this worth it?'

Having said all that, I regret none of it. I love the films I was fortunate enough to have been involved with, and although the years spent on them were sometimes tiring, they were also fun. They were certainly not wasted years. How could they be? It is gratifying to know that my work bridged the years between Obie's pioneering work and the new science of computer special effects and that the films have given so many people so much enjoyment and inspiration. While I don't miss the stress and strain of moviemaking, I regret that I shall not now be able to put on celluloid some of the other creatures, lost lands and adventures still lurking in my imagination. It won't be me, but maybe one day someone will again have the courage to make a picture that is pure imagination and adventure with real heroes and villains, two of the greatest assets in the history of moving pictures, or for that matter, any visual storytelling. Once again, I should allow the gods the final word. In *Clash of the Titans* Hera asks of Zeus, her husband, 'What if one day there were other heroes like him? What if courage and imagination were to become everyday mortal qualities?' Zeus replies, 'We would no longer be needed. But, for the moment, there is sufficient cowardice, sloth, and mendacity down there on Earth to last forever.' Perhaps this might suggest that I really do have a Zeus complex!

Above. Perseus and his shield. Harry Hamlin made a good Perseus. He was not only a good actor, but also looked the part and was certainly better than Arnold Schwarzenegger, who had been suggested for the role during the early days of the project.

CHAPTER 12 LOST PROJECTS, LOST WORLDS

The A–Z of Unrealized Ideas

Left hand page. **An oil painting I executed for my project** *Adventures of Baron Munchausen*. In it he has just arrived on the moon.

Below. **An early plaster model of the Baron.** This was based on a Doré concept for the character.

Below right. **The Baron's meeting with the Moon Giant for** *Adventures of Baron Munchausen*. This rare still is from my 16mm colour test for the meeting between the Baron and the Moon Giant. It was the only time that I was to experiment with having the animated models talk.

Inevitably, over the years there are many ideas, concepts, stories and projects that never see the light of day. Some were not very good, which would explain their inability to mature into a moving picture, while others became strands in realized projects. There are, however, some that I believe could have made exciting, innovative and commercial pictures, and it is these 'lost worlds' that I have set down in this chapter. Reading them now after perhaps half a century has elapsed, I find some of them dreadful, but on the whole most of the concepts have some spark in them that might have gone on to greater heights. For every great idea in a screenplay, a dozen are rejected. Our films are not unique in this destructive ratio: undoubtedly there are far more unmade scripts lying about in Hollywood than were ever actually turned into viable productions.

The working titles are listed in alphabetical, not chronological, order. Dates are difficult to pin down, as most of the ideas, in one form or another, grew over a number of years. Wherever I can, I have supplied dates, although I would ask the reader's indulgence, as I have had to recall nearly sixty years in the business.

THE ABOMINABLE SNOWMAN

I had considered this idea very early in my career, possibly post war and again in the mid-'50s, but I was unable to sell it to Charles or anyone else. He almost saw the light of day when I was planning *Sinbad and the Eye of the Tiger*. Instead of Sinbad fighting the giant walrus, I had considered a Yeti as the antagonist, but the idea was squashed during a sweatbox session.

ADVENTURES OF BARON MUNCHAUSEN

I first considered this way back in my amateur days when I originally discovered Gustave Doré's wonderful illustrations for the adventures of the outrageous Baron. The idea (which I considered at various points between 1938 and 1950) had seemed ideal for a fantasy film and a natural for stop-motion animation.

Although I had played around with the idea of making a film and had produced various notes on how to go about it, it wasn't until about 1949–50 that I produced several short step outlines of a few of the Baron's adventures. I always intended to produce a series of short films based on the stories. I chose as the first film the Baron's adventures on the moon, in which he discovers a three-headed eagle, the 'Moon Cheese Factory' run by a giant, and returns to Earth on a large slab of cheese. Even with only one story to tackle, I realized the project would be a major undertaking, so I asked Charlotte Knight to develop the screen story. Whilst she was doing that, I settled down to sculpt a figure of the mendacious Baron (for sketching purposes) and draw a series of continuity sketches for a test scene showing the Baron accidentally falling into a vat of cheese, following which the giant cuts it open and discovers him curled up like an embryo in one of the holes. He gets out of the cheese and begins to talk with the giant.

The conversation between the giant and the Baron was to have been synchronized, an ambitious departure from my usual Fairy Tales without lip-synch, only narration and extreme expressions on the models. After considering the *Puppetoons* system of separate heads to produce separate words, I rejected it, as it had always seemed a little awkward. I then developed my own solution, building a 7–8-inch diameter rubber face for the giant, which I padded out with sponge to give it substance and coated in a layer of latex. This 'special' face possessed little levers with which I was able to manipulate and obtain a smile or lip movements that made up lines of dialogue. It also had eyelids I could animate and so obtain the vital element of realism for the close-up face. I then photographed it in stop-motion to match the dialogue and rear-projected it behind the small animated model of the

Baron. This enabled them to converse directly. It was the first time that I experimented with animation and dialogue, and because of the time and effort, it was the last.

The subject raised its head again soon after *Jason and the Argonauts*. I was talking with Don Chaffey about ideas and mentioned Baron Munchausen, so he looked at the German film version *Baron Prasil* (1940) and was so impressed that he suggested we work on it together to try and develop it for Dynamation. Sadly, the project evaporated after we both went our separate ways on other projects.

AESOP'S FABLES
I had intended some of these wonderful imaginative fables as part of the Fairy Tale series. However, the only one I tackled was *The Tortoise and the Hare*, which I shot some tests for in 1952. After a gap of fifty years, the film has now been completed.

ATLANTIS
The legend of the fabled lost continent of Atlantis has always inspired my imagination. I began designs and a storyline way back in the late 1930s, although it never matured beyond two drawings and a step outline that is now lost. From memory, the premise was the destruction of the island of Atlantis (or Lemuria), and the two drawings (one of which is based on a John Martin painting I completed in the 1940s) show dinosaurs attacking classical buildings whilst volcanoes erupt in the background.

Above. Drawing for the project *Atlantis*. I completed this in the 1940s and it is based upon a John Martin painting showing a dinosaur attacking classical buildings whilst volcanoes erupt in the background.

BEOWULF
The idea to film this mythical adventure was first muted in about 1960, when Charles and I were searching for a new idea. It was seen as uncommercial and abandoned almost before it had begun. I again raised the concept with Michael Winner in 1971, but our discussions petered out, presumably for the same reasons. I never seemed to have made any drawings or sketches, so the images in my mind at the time are now lost.

CONAN
Soon after completing *Valley of Gwangi*, Charles and I looked at the Conan stories, a potentially different type of mythology in the form of sword and sorcery, which seemed to hold possible avenues for Dynamation. Perhaps because of the rights situation, or maybe because we decided it was not right for us, we dropped the idea, although something constructive did come out of it. Because no fresh ideas presented themselves, I sat down and wrote the basics for *Golden Voyage of Sinbad*.

DANIEL IN THE LION'S DEN
This was to have been another possible story for the Fairy Tale series. Despite being a story from the Old Testament, I thought it might fit nicely into the series. There was no storyline as far as I remember, but I did complete a rough set of storyboards.

DANTE'S INFERNO
The influence of Gustav Doré, who had vividly illustrated the story, led me naturally to this subject from a very early age. I have always considered it perfect for stop-motion animation, although it would have been completely different from my other features. There would be people turned into trees, harpies flying through the woods of the underworld, bat people, a minotaur, tormented souls pushing bags of gold up a hill and others being attacked by serpents. It would have been a real Harryhausen spectacular. I would have based my designs on an image from Doré's Bible called 'The Lustful' that show thousands of tormented souls whirling up through a crevasse, with Virgil and Dante watching them. It would be an interesting sequence but a huge special effects problem with so many elements to tackle. Each tormented soul would have to be individually animated for each frame of film as they drift up through the void. At the *Jason* pace, that would amount to about a tenth of a frame a day, a frame every two weeks for that one sequence. The cost would have been astronomical even by today's standards.

When I thought about it seriously, I felt that maybe the audiences wouldn't sit through $1^1/_2$ hours of tormented souls. I was obviously wrong. Today, people seem to be able to sit through two or three hours of it!

Above. Still of Satyr from *Daphnis and Chloe*. The Satyr which I sculpted for *Daphnis and Chloe*, I suppose it is a prototype for the Cyclops in *The 7th Voyage of Sinbad*. He had goat's legs, pointed ears and prominent cheekbones (his face was based on Conrad Veidt and his character in *The Thief of Bagdad*). The pose is very dramatic and was based on pictures of Nijinsky performing 'L'Après-midi d'un faune'.

DAPHNIS AND CHLOE
This very early project was conceived as a short at about the time as *Evolution*. I sculptured a Satyr for it, a prototype of the Cyclops with goat's legs, pointed ears and prominent cheekbones (his face was based on Conrad Veidt in *The Thief of Bagdad*). I had planned to set the story to the music of Ravel, and made a few notes, but only these and the model survive from the project.

DAVID AND GOLIATH
The idea for animating the Old Testament story of David and Goliath occurred to me about the time I was doing my early Fairy Tales in the late 1940s. Inevitably, it was Goliath, the giant, that appealed to me, although I had planned to animate all the characters. With the assistance of Cecil Maiden I completed a four-page outline consisting of five key sequences, the fourth of which was the titanic but one-sided battle between the boy David and the Philistine warrior Goliath. To accompany this outline I also produced several large key drawings that reflect Doré's influence.

Above. Two drawings from *David and Goliath*. I produced several key drawings for *David and Goliath* that reflect the influence of Doré on my work. That influence was never very far away when I was executing drawings and even storyboards.

DELUGE
I suggested this intriguing idea to Michael Carreras at Hammer Films soon after the completion of *One Million Years BC*. When I was very young I had seen the 1933 film, based on a novel. Both had set the main body of the adventure after a worldwide deluge, concentrating on the post-civilization world breaking down into lawlessness. I suggested to Michael, that we rethink the idea and develop a new storyline, setting the action in London instead of New York and with

the catastrophe as the centrepiece of the film. In a letter to Michael I wrote, 'The title and it's suggested general world destruction by another great flood and earthquake is about all that could be retained of the novel… A much more important new story line would have to be developed, placing the visual destruction of the world cities in the middle or near the climax of a new concept.' I went on to say, 'A film of this nature has not been on the screen for a long time', meaning that a revival of the 'disaster' genre was long overdue. This prediction anticipated *The Poseidon Adventure*, a film that began a cycle of 'disaster' movies that has yet to end. Michael wrote to me in April 1971 saying, 'I honestly can't get excited about it.' Today all that remains is a title drawing of the destruction of London by a huge tidal wave and a few notes.

DICKORY DICKORY DOCK

This was another idea for the Fairy Tale series and one which was to have been a segment of a further set of 'Mother Goose' stories I was trying to develop during the summer and autumn of 1946.

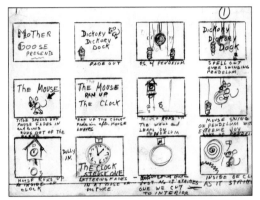

Above. A (very) rough storyboard for *Dickory Dickory Dock*.

DINOSAUR GRAVEYARD

This only exists as a one-page outline of lost dinosaurs, fabulous treasure and weird cavemen. The action takes place in South America and the Pacific islands. A young archaeologist finds an old manuscript telling of a tunnel built in ancient times between Easter Island and Peru to link two civilizations. In the centre of the tunnel is a huge cave where the dinosaurs, and by some means whales, come to die (much like the elephants' graveyard), and living in the caves are a race of blind men that guard a fabulous treasure. That's as far as it goes and sadly there are no drawings to remind me of what exactly I had in mind.

THE FALL OF THE HOUSE OF USHER

This was a project I had tried to develop at about the same time as shooting the test for *Baron Munchausen*, in the late 1940s, early 50s. Originally I had intended to make three Edgar Allen Poe stories. The above, *The Premature Burial* and *The Pit and the Pendulum*. As a boy, Poe had been another of my favourite authors because of his vivid and frightening imagination, and some of the tales were, I felt, more than suitable for model animation. The idea was to produce an eerie feeling with the tales, and I vaguely remember that I was going to create the characters as elongated images, rather like El Greco figures. The project only got as far as making one rough sketch.

Above. Drawing for *The Fall of the House of Usher*. Although I had always wanted to make a film of Edgar Allen Poe's classic story, sadly, *The Fall of the House of Usher* only got as far as making this one drawing.

FOOD OF THE GODS

Following the completion of *Mighty Joe Young*, Obie had kept up his association with Merian Cooper, and one day in 1950 he rang me to say that Cooper was interested in filming the H.G. Wells' story *Food of the Gods*, with Obie supervising the effects. This strange story concerns a substance that once eaten makes everything grow to a tremendous size – chickens, wasps, rats and even humans. Obie kindly asked if I would be interested, which of course I was, and for a time I became involved as his assistant. He produced some designs, as did I, but in the end the project was dropped.

Over the years I tried to resurrect the idea many times, mentioning it to Charles when we were short of an idea. In about 1961 I completed a drawing of giant chickens towering over a house, but Charles discovered that the story had already been sold to a pop star who was trying to find finance. In 1965 a film called *Village of the Giants,* apparently based on Wells' book, was produced by Bert I. Gordon, who made it again in 1976 under its original title *The Food Of The Gods*. I have to say that the story deserved much better.

Below. Drawing of giant chickens from *Food of the Gods*. In about 1961 I completed this drawing of giant chickens towering over a village for H.G.Wells' *Food of the Gods*.

FORCE OF THE TROJANS

This was planned as the next project I would do with Charles, following *Clash*. It was the story of the quest (populated along the way with various mythological creatures) that led to the founding of Rome. Beverley had developed the idea in 1980 and submitted an outline in January 1981, which at that time had the working title of *Aeneas*. Based loosely on Virgil's *Aeneid*, it told the story of Aeneas, warrior and Prince of Troy. In November 1983 Beverley completed a screenplay for Morningside Productions entitled *Force of the Trojans*. The story had been expanded, and while most of the salient points of the outline were kept, much had changed, including the creatures that would inhabit the quest. Among the key sequences were the fatal flight of Daedalus and Icarus, a colony of cyclops, Furies, jackal men, the Sphinx of Phrygia, the evil goddess Hecate (possessing three hideous faces and six hands, each holding a different weapon) and Scylla and Charybdis ('a monstrous mutation of octopus, triton and sea serpent').

I completed a number of illustrations of Scylla and Charybdis and a rough storyboard of the sequence. In addition I fashioned a clay model of the Sphinx with her bat-like wings and hanging breasts, dragon's tail and hideous deformed body.

It was suggested that to take some of the burden off my shoulders, we should use the facilities at Industrial Light & Magic. Sections of the Sphinx and Pandora's Box were to be done by them, as were nearly all the opticals. With Steve Archer as my proposed assistant, I was to have completed the remainder in England, including the wooden horse of Troy, the Icarus and Daedalus flight, the Furies, the Sphinx, Scylla and Charybdis and of course the Four Horsemen.

The project received some keen interest from MGM, and although we hired directors and recced locations, as with so many projects before it, the enthusiasm waned. At the time we were looking for production backing, audience tests revealed that the public had turned to more violent subjects loaded with sex and muscles. Mythology simply could not be converted into this type of 'entertainment' and MGM lost interested. As the money was not forthcoming and as we couldn't find new backers, the project slowly faded away.

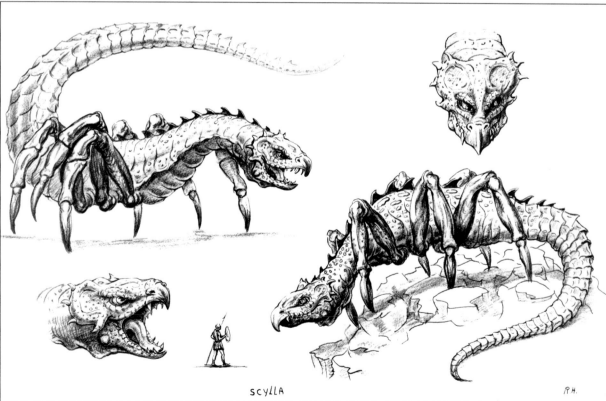

Above and left. Drawing of Scylla and a key drawing for Charybdis. Scylla and Charybdis (a monstrous mutation of octopus, triton and sea serpent) were intended for the proposed project *Force of the Trojans* I was to have made with Charles and Beverley.

Below. The clay sphinx. The sphinx was one of the antagonists in *Force of the Trojans*. She was basically Egyptian in look but also possessed bat-like wings and a hideously deformed body.

SCYLLA

FOUNTAIN OF YOUTH

I wrote this curiosity sometime in the early 1950s. There are no drawings or sketches, but I do have a very brief outline of the story:

A millionaire who is terrified of death seeks immortality by abducting an archaeologist to help him locate the Fountain of Youth. Amongst his collection of ancient artefacts is an old parchment which supplies clues to the whereabouts of the fountain. Travelling to the four corners of the Earth, including India [even then I had designs to travel to exotic locations], they eventually arrive in Egypt and discover the fountain in the centre of a lost pyramid. The waters are enhanced by cosmic rays to produce immortality in anyone who bathes in it.

How the story ends I don't know. As with most of my early ideas, I felt it was wise to leave that to someone else. However, I do make a note that immortality can only be found within one's self – a deep statement from my misspent youth! The idea of the fountain or force being discovered in a pyramid was an idea I resurrected for *Sinbad and the Eye of the Tiger*.

FRANKENSTEIN

Sometime soon after the 1925 *The Lost World* and at various other times over the subsequent years, Willis O'Brien developed a concept of having the monster perform in the stop-motion process, but it was made with the very capable Boris Karloff, so Obie was forced to drop the idea. I also played around with the idea of reviving it, although the *Frankenstein* story had been made and remade so many times that it would be difficult to instil any enthusiasm into a producer for the subject. After Abbott and Costello met the titled character, I felt it could never be taken very seriously again.

THE FROG PRINCE

Supposedly another in the Fairy Tales series, it was ideally suited to stop-motion animation. I completed a two-page outline in June 1947, which related the story of a princess who promises a frog anything he desires if he retrieves her ball from the pond. She reneges on the promise but the creature follows her to the palace, and when the princess throws the frog against a wall, it turns into a handsome prince. I altered the original tale by disposing of the kiss, but in the end everything turns out happily ever after and the two are married. Apart from this outline, the only evidence that remains of the idea are two drawings.

Above. One of the two drawings I did for *The Frog Prince*. All that remains of the project are the two drawings and a short outline.

GULLIVER

Not an idea of mine, nevertheless it is a curiosity. In the late 1950s there was a proposal for a television series based on the character as seen in *The 3 Worlds of Gulliver*, using optical effects to create a world of large and small people. In 1963 a pilot, which I wasn't involved in, was produced by Charles for Columbia Screen Gems, with John Cairny stepping in for Kerwin Mathews and Christina Gregg playing his girlfriend. Although NBC was reportedly interested, the series was eventually dropped.

THE HOBBIT

The idea of filming *The Hobbit* and *Lord of the Rings* came up separately and as a combined project several times over the years. I have to confess that I struggled with the narrative of *The Hobbit* and eventually gave up, deciding that it was not suitable for Dynamation and lent itself more to the cartoon medium. How wrong I was!

ILYA MUROMETZ

I had always wanted to make a film about the great Russian folk hero using Reinhold Glière's wonderful symphonic tone poem. The piece has remained one of my favourites. The scale of the story would have necessitated a huge production and been prohibitively expensive, but its originality and depth would have made a unique and wonderful feature.

Bernie Herrmann and I often talked about making a film where he would have written a score and then I would have designed animation sequences around it – the exact opposite of the usual process. I suppose it would have been Dynamation's *Fantasia*.

THE ISLAND OF DR MOREAU

Yet another H.G. Wells story I fell in love with when I was very young, and was another project considered many times over the years. My first encounter with the story was the 1932 film *Island of Lost Souls*, which was based on the book and starred Charles Laughton and Bela Lugosi. Since then it has been made many times, but never as successfully as that first version. The creations of Moreau would have given Dynamation wonderful opportunities to produce mutated creatures that couldn't possibly be men in costumes and makeup.

JACK AND JILL

Again, this was to have been a segment of another 'Mother Goose' set of stories, and from my storyboards looks as though it would have been fun to make.

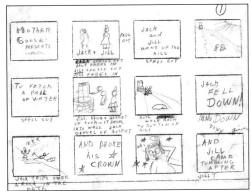

Above. A section of my storyboard for *Jack and Jill*. It was to have been part of the Mother Goose Stories and it is obviously my first thought on what I wanted for the film.

JACK SPRAT

Another possible segment for the 'Mother Goose' stories, today it seems a curious subject to choose, although looking at the surviving storyboards, apparently I intended to overcome the downside of the story by developing the comic side.

JOHN CARTER OF MARS

The stories of John Carter had been kicking around Hollywood for years, and Charles and I received an outline of the above soon after we had made *The 7th Voyage of Sinbad*. It was an Edgar Rice Burroughs story, and while we had long wanted to make a film of one of his books, we felt that the story simply wasn't strong enough, a feeling confirmed by the fact that nobody made it.

KING KONG

In 1970/71 Michael Carreras at Hammer Films was considering re-making *King Kong*. He wrote a letter to me whilst I was in the States asking me to 'drop in and have a drink' to discuss it. Although my answer to him said, '…if your intentions are to produce the film in the near future I would be most pleased to talk to you about it…', I remember hesitating at the thought of re-making such a classic, which up until then had definitely been a no-go area as far as I was concerned. I didn't see how one could improve on the original except by making it in colour and smoothing the animation, but in the end it still wouldn't be the same picture. However, if anyone was to be involved in a re-make, I was determined it was going to be me. I felt that at least I would respect Obie's original work and attempt to transfer some of its values. Nevertheless, I suspect that to this day I would have been trying to live down the fact that I had remade a timeless classic. Perhaps fortunately, Michael found the rights impossible to secure from RKO, who were reluctant to relinquish them, and the project faded away until 1976 when Dino De Laurentiis remade it in colour but without the advantages of stop-motion animation.

THE LABRINTHODON

This was a wonderful idea by Obie, although I don't know exactly when he conceived it. During the production of *Mighty Joe Young* he showed me several drawings of the concept, which basically told the story of a group of explorers who discover the lost graveyard of the whales in an undersea land (Obie and I seem to have been obsessed with finding this graveyard). His sketches for the whales and the submarine were magical, and the images have remained with me all these years. In late 1968 and early 1969 I suggested the idea to Charles, and whilst in Los Angeles during the promotion for *The Valley of Gwangi*, I approached the Nasseur brothers, who had bought the rights for the story and drawings from Obie. Sadly, it didn't progress beyond that, as the purchase price was far too high.

LITTLE GOOGIE

This little clown idea came about in 1949/50 when I played around with the idea of animating a series of shorts based on his adventures in Vaudeville. I built a model with a set of expression heads, for which my mother made the costume.

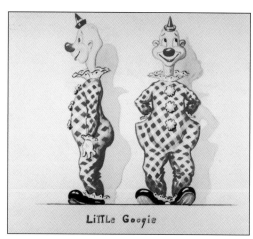

Above. Watercolour designs for *Little Googie*. I always regret that I never shot any footage of this character because I must confess he is one of my favourites.

THE LOST CITY

I had this idea about the time as *The Beast from 20,000 Fathoms*. All that remains of the idea are scribbles on a scrap of paper:

An archaeologist and his sister discover a statue of a centaur on which are inscriptions to an underground city where the centaurs lived. Along with their guide they search for the buried city in a remote area of Italy. Eventually they find the city which is hidden under another city (like the excavations of Ur) and discover a huge, seemingly bottomless dark pit. Somehow they find a way down (either by rope or a pathway) and find themselves in a lost world populated by living centaurs.

This is as much of the story as I detailed in my notes. The rest, including the ending, remains lost to time.

MARY HAD A LITTLE LAMB

This idea again was to have been one of the Fairy Tale films, but I didn't develop it beyond a few very rough storyboard sketches.

THE MONSTER STORY

In the never-ending quest to find a story that would allow me to animate dinosaurs and fantastic creatures, I came up with this little story. Although it had possibilities, I have to say it was not terribly original in its concept. The action takes place high in the Rockies. Two brothers, David and Al Winder, welcome David's publisher Eleanor Landing to their log cabin for a short stay. Overnight David's dog disappears and a trail of blood leads them to a hidden valley where they discover Professor Paul Hendrix. Hendrix has been experimenting with a new weapon called A-2 that alters the molecular structure of animals. Many years before he released his weapon on the valley and has discovered a cave that apparently didn't exist during the experiment. The four enter the cave and discover a giant ant and spider, which David kills. Later they witness a fight between a brontosaurus and pterodactyl, and finally a Neanderthal man who has mutated from another scientist trapped in the valley during the experiment. In the conclusion Al is killed by the Neanderthal man and David and Eleanor just manage to escape the valley before another A-2 weapon explodes, destroying the valley. David writes the story, but

as Eleanor points out, everyone will consider it science fiction. As I said, not the greatest storyline in the world.

THE NIGHT BEFORE CHRISTMAS

Originally I had thought of this delightful tale as a separate story and film. I developed a first draft script on 12 August 1946, but looking back on it, the story would have worked better within the framework of the Fairy Tales.

PEOPLE OF THE MIST

This project (not be confused with *Valley of the Mist*) came about in 1982 when Michael Winner, the British director, rang me and asked if I would be interested in discussing a project he had purchased for filming. I flew to Spain to meet with him and we went through the already written script but it was clearly not suitable as a basis on which to shoot a film. Armed with a few of my ideas, Michael set about restructuring the storyline and rewriting the dialogue whilst I produced a set of drawings and sketches.

The original story was a rather obscure tale written by Sir H. Rider Haggard. Although I have never been able to find a copy of the book, I am aware that the screenplay (which is actually rather similar to *She*) was a loose adaptation of the book:

Two brothers lose their heritage in England and travel to Africa to seek a new fortune. One is killed saving a woman from a lion and in return she leads the other brother on a quest to find the Land of the Mist, situated on a huge undiscovered plateau, where the largest rubies in the world are to be found. Arriving on the plateau they see a holy mountain shrouded in mist and encounter a race of soldiers and priests dressed in ancient costume. In the City of the Mist they are given food and, left to their own devices, find their way to the strange mountain where they find the rubies and a mural that tells of the slaying of the gods. A mist descends and before the brother becomes unconscious he sees weird forms in the swirling clouds. On waking the priests accuse the brother of desecration and sacrifice him to their god Jal, a massive statue whose mouth forms the platform from which he is pushed into a sacred pool. He survives the fall and below the statue he discovers a chamber containing flickering screens, switches and blinking lights and it is here that we learn the secret of the mist. Alien beings are controlling the people and mankind began its evolution in the valley. Unfortunately these beings are now corrupt and somehow the brother escapes to tell the people what he has seen. He tells them that he can destroy these man-eating creatures by diverting the pool's water into their chamber. The people dam the river and as the water rises other creatures appear and begin killing the people. The waters reach the mountain's dormant volcano which begins to erupt, and although the brother escapes to return to England, the City and Valley of the Mist are destroyed along with the alien creatures.

My role, apart from designing the key sequences, was to enhance the fantasy element, a task I naturally achieved by suggesting various scenes, some of which would incorporate prehistoric creatures I hadn't used before. The use of dinosaurs would imply that they had been brought to earth by aliens and now, after millennia, only this valley retained the species. I suggested that when the adventurers reach the plateau, they see a small dinosaur pursuing a tribe of pygmies, whom they save by shooting the beast. Another idea, although not new to my repertoire, was a pterodactyl flying away with a native in its claws.

Later, near the sacred mountain, there is a fight between a stegosaurus and two vicious dryptosaurus, which when animated would have made a wonderful sequence in the story as an introduction to the uniqueness of the plateau. Looking at the drawing now, the concept reminds me of the final action sequence in *Jurassic Park* (1993) where the velociraptors fight with the tyrannosaurus inside the building.

To add spice to the sacred pool scenes, I suggested that carnivorous prehistoric animals, perhaps plesiosaurs, who devour the victims, occupy it. I built a small clay model of the proposed huge, grotesque sacrificial statue, which had a gong fixture on its flat head that would presumably summon the beasts below. This, of course, is another 'tribute' to the huge gong in *King Kong* that when struck summoned the ape.

In addition to the dinosaurs I incorporated many other ideas into the story. Some old, like the man-eating plant with tentacles. I also injected the idea of the people of the plateau capturing the adventurers by using flying creatures (at one time pterodactyls were suggested, but I designed a mutation that resembled something between a prehistoric beast and a huge eagle), an idea not too far removed from *War Eagles*.

Although I had originally suggested that the aliens be unseen, this was changed in a script written by Michael, so I had to come up with an alien concept.

Because the dinosaurs were to be a prominent part of life on the plateau, I designed the alien to partially resemble a lizard-like creature that possessed elements of dinosaurs within its makeup. Finally, I felt there needed to be a liaison between the UFO people and the humanoid tribe, so I suggested we use an alchemist/mystic as the link.

Even with a few of the above ideas being incorporated into the screenplay, I was never happy with some of the characters and dialogue, and on several occasions voiced my reservations to Michael. Reading

my notes today, I find that I was becoming increasingly sceptical as to the project's viability, and in a letter to Michael dated April 1983 I boldly state that, 'This script seems to fall somewhere between a Bob Hope type send up and a Maria Montez *Queen of Atlantis*. Some of the monsters still appear to be injected into the story just for the sake of having more and more monsters.'

In any event, after audience tests were carried out on the concept, it was discovered that this kind of picture was no longer popular.

Left hand page bottom. A key drawing for a scene in *People of the Mist*. It shows a scene in the story that has humans travelling on the back of flying creatures (a cross between a prehistoric creature and an eagle) in an Aztec-like city.

Left. Another key drawing. This shows a stegosaurus being attacked by two vicious dryptosaurus for *People of the Mist*. It would have made a great sequence.

Below. Two clay models of a creature and statue for *People of the Mist*. The statue was to have been a huge sacrificial monolith on the edge of a lake, which had a gong fixed on the head that was to have summoned the creatures living in the waters. The gong was, of course, another small tribute to *King Kong*.

Below far left. A key drawing of a man-eating plant. I resurrected my old idea of a man-eating plant for possible use in *People of the Mist*. If at first you don't succeed...

Bottom. Key drawing of a pterodactyl with a native in its claws. Yet again, this was intended for *People of the Mist*.

THE PRINCESS BRIDE

In early 1982 I had some communications with British producer Milton Subotsky who had run the highly successful UK-based Amicus Productions but who was at that time heading Sword and Sorcery Productions. Amongst other subjects, he was keen on the book *The Princess Bride*, which he strongly believed could be made into a successful film. While the brief synopsis of the book had possibilities, on reading Milton's screenplay I was not impressed with the way it had been handled and felt that my involvement could only be minimal. Milton understood my reservations and attempted to correct the screenplay, but it never became a reality, although it was eventually made into a good film in 1987 by Rob Reiner. Other projects that Milton suggested were *Slan*, to be based on the 1953 novel by A.E. Van Vogt, and *Another Fine Myth*, another sword and sorcery idea. I got on well with him but we never did get together on a project, the main reason being the lack of a suitable subject and a realistic budget.

R.U.R.

Whilst waiting to be mustered out of the army in New York in 1945, I had time to do some research at the New York Public Library concerning a Czech play by Karel Capek that interested me. It was called *R.U.R.* (Russom's Universal Robots). The idea of robots had sparked my interest, even though I had never seen a production of the play.

Set some time in the near future, R.U.R. is a factory that produces robots 'for tasks mankind has found dull and boring'. The latest model proves to be cleverer than its makers. These superior robots unite and like Frankenstein's monster seek to kill their creators and all of mankind. In the epilogue, Alquist, the one-time head architect at the factory and the only survivor, sends a couple of robots that have fallen in love out into the world, telling to them 'Go Adam, go Eve. The world is yours.'

The more I read the play, the more I realized that this was an ideal subject for a motion picture, especially one using stop-motion techniques. To visualize my enthusiasm I executed several rough pre-production drawings and a storyboard for a possible presentation, but I abandoned the project in favour of the Fairy Tales, which were more affordable and commercial.

In the 1940s it would have been a fresh subject, but since then a number of films have been made on the subject of androids, making the original seem clichéd. Nevertheless, the basic concept of robots taking over the world is still a good one.

THE SATYR

This very early project was written after my return from the Yucatan, Mexico. I was so impressed with the ruins and the similarities between Egyptian and Mayan pyramids, I wrote a brief outline linking them to a mythological 'underworld', a subject that was to haunt me over the years.

The story was a cross between *The Lost World*, *Gwangi* and ancient mythology, and I suppose was the basis of some ideas that would eventually realize themselves in *The 7th Voyage of Sinbad*. I nearly resurrected the idea in the early 1950s with another story which I titled *The Lost City* (see above):

A circus owner who is travelling through Mexico hears a legend of great caverns, known in mythology as 'the underworld', in which still live creatures that have a direct connection with the pyramids of Mexico and Egypt. Financed by a millionaire and accompanied by two adventurers who are looking for deposits of oil, they discover a ruined pyramid in the deepest part of the jungle under which is a shaft – the entrance to the underworld. Lowering themselves into the abyss they discover a nightmare world of caverns in which live creatures of legend who have been waiting to escape into the upper world. A sphinx, a cyclops, a mermaid, a griffin [I made a note in the margin to include a snake-headed Medusa] and finally a satyr of enormous size. It is this last creature that is the personification of evil and is feared by all other creatures and gods in the underworld.

Dynamiting his way through the caverns, the circus owner releases the creatures and they fight each other and some of the explorers are killed. Those that are left flee, closely pursued by the satyr, but although the adventurers seal the entrance with dynamite, the creature breaks through 'like a giant genii'. Somehow the circus owner and his colleagues capture the creature and display him in the circus, but during a performance he breaks loose, fighting and killing an elephant. After destroying the town, he makes his way back to the caverns of the underworld, where he seals himself inside, away from the eyes of mankind.

SIMPLE SIMON

Part of the proposed Fairy Tale series, this was to have again been part of a new set of 'Mother Goose' stories. One of the two rough storyboards is dated 1946 and shows an amusing little interpretation on the story.

Left. A rough sketch for *The Satyr*. Here a group of adventurers have discovered the entrance to the mythological underworld and released a giant satyr.

SINBAD AND THE SEVEN WONDERS OF THE WORLD

This was another subject considered in 1981, immediately after *Clash of the Titans*, and had the potential to be a fascinating project. Several outlines and treatments were developed (although I did no illustrations) by Beverley Cross. In May 1982 I wrote to Charles with a list of Dynamation sequences. The tone of my letter reflects scepticism about the way Beverley had written it, and I offered my own suggestions and thoughts:

Sinbad attends the coronation of the Caliph of Egypt who sends him on a quest to assemble a small gold pyramid, the sections of which are hidden within the seven wonders located in the four corners of the ancient world.

1. *The Pharos in Alexandria where he meets Ali Baba.*
2. *The pyramids in Giza where Ali Baba discovers the entrance by using the word 'sesame'.*
3. *Olympia and the Games. Within the temple of Zeus the giant statue of the god created by Phidias comes to life after Sinbad takes the pyramid section from its hiding place beneath the throne.*
4. *To Rhodes and the submerged head of the Colossus within which hides the dragon of Rhodes, a huge deadly eel.*

I didn't like the idea of an eel but to offset that I suggested in my letter to Charles, 'Perhaps on the surface we could still see the remains of the legs and some other broken parts [of the Colossus].'

5. *To Halicarnassus and the Mausoleum and the Warrior of Ashes – frightening skeletal horses.*
6. *Ephesus where he does battle with the Amazons and their goddess Hecate.*

In my letter I say, 'I cannot visualize a very effective and different sequence. We might explore the possibility of going to hell itself. At the time of *Jason* we had Medea take Jason to hell to bathe in the elixir of protection against the might of the Hydra. In this instance he may need some protection from the formidable Sphinx.' Of the sphinx I observe, 'I know you dislike riddles, but the Sphinx has always been associated with them.'

7. *Finally a journey to Babylon and the hanging gardens with Ganesa and Garuda. In all the locations he finds a section of the golden pyramid which, with the last, assembles into the book of the dead.*

Like so many of our ideas and projects, it gradually faded away as other, seemingly more commercial ideas came up. Perhaps the cost of good original locations such as Egypt, Greece, Turkey, South America (the Hanging Gardens), Mexico and Jordan were prohibitive and led to the idea's downfall. As I have said, it is a pity, because the premise of using the seven ancient wonders is an excellent idea, one I am sure someone will successfully translate into a film one day.

SINBAD GOES TO MARS

aka **Sinbad on Mars**, aka **Sinbad's Voyage to Mars**

The very mention of this project almost never fails to bring a polite smile to the face of anyone I mention it to. I really can't imagine why! The idea, a kind of space opera/swashbuckling pulp story, was a result of the science fiction boom of the late 1970s and was considered a viable project to follow the success of *Sinbad and the Eye of the Tiger.*

The concept of marrying Sinbad with space had originated some years before, but I never got around to producing a believable outline, as the very idea of an ancient sailor (no matter how brave he was) meeting an advanced civilization was extremely difficult to resolve. This problem would dog all attempts to bring it to the screen. However, at the time the idea seemed viable enough. In early 1977 Charles commissioned Kenneth Kolb (the writer of *The 7th Voyage of Sinbad* screenplay) to produce a treatment, which he did in January 1978, followed by a revised treatment in May of the same year. Unfortunately the treatment read like a Flash Gordon serial and did nothing to make Sinbad leaving earth in any way credible. Basically the plot began with Scheherezade relating the 1002nd tale, which begins with a light emanating from the great pyramid in Egypt.

Other than a three-armed genie and a tentacled plant, there was very little in the way of Dynamation in the storyline, and most of my work would have been in creating spaceships and destroying Mars in a cataclysm of fire. Interestingly, the man-eating plant was another attempt by me to use my design for *Mysterious Island* and was yet again to emerge in suggestions for *People of the Mist.* The storyline didn't inspire us, even with Ken's revisions, and so Charles asked Beverley Cross to see if he could build on Ken's premise and solve the problems. Beverley produced a treatment in April 1979 with subsequent revisions, and although this treatment came up with the idea of the civilization on Mars being the basis of the ancient Egyptian religion and myths, an idea that was similar to the successful 1994 film *Stargate*, it still fell short of overcoming the earlier problems:

The Caliph of Alexandria camps near the great pyramid and during the night the structure glows and weird figures with animal heads appear and kidnap the Caliph's daughter – Princess Tanila. Returning to his palace he summons Sinbad to find his daughter. Along with his companion, Ali Baba, Sinbad enters the pyramid where the genie Sesame appears. The genie tells Sinbad that the Princess has been taken to the planet Mars. Sinbad commands the genie to take them there and by means of a shimmering mirror they are transported to a similar pyramid near a ruined city. Mars is ruled by an evil Queen who seeks immortality, and the planet, once verdant, is now ravished by hordes of monstrous moths. Making their way to the Queen's underground palace, Sinbad, Ali and Sesame encounter and kill some of the terrifying moths.

Once at the palace they are greeted by the Queen who explains that the Princess has been taken in order to succeed to the Martian throne, as she is a descendent of the last Egyptian Queen – Cleopatra. In reality the evil Queen wants the girl's blood which will guarantee her immortality. Sinbad soon realizes this and they try to escape but are challenged by a half mummy, half Frankenstein monster and then are captured by the Queen's surgeon-priests. Sinbad is accused of desecration and sentenced to be sacrificed to the Martian sphinx. Sinbad destroys the creature with fire and returns through a labyrinth as a volcano erupts and begins to consume the palace. The

Queen is killed in the eruption but the Princess is saved. All three are taken to the pyramid by Sesame, who has transformed himself into a giant Roc bird, and once there are transported off the dying planet and returned to the great pyramid on Earth.

In subsequent revisions Beverley very cleverly enhanced the idea that the Egyptian civilization began as a parallel Martian civilization by changing the Queen to a Martian Pharaoh and his surgeon-priests into Anubis, Horus and Sebek, ancient Egyptian deities. He also named the Pharaoh's city/palace Sebeth which is Thebes (an ancient Egyptian city) spelt backwards and further suggested it should be filmed in the Yucatan or an Inca location. He also describes the Martian spaceships as obelisks. In the story there are creatures that would benefit from Dynamation: the Martian Sphinx, the Roc and after some discussion with me, a Canal creature (which would look like a giant moray eel) and a monster jellyfish that Sinbad encounters whilst sailing along the canals of Mars.

Although I was heavily involved in the development, I made no drawings or sketches for the project, mainly because I was involved with *Clash of the Titans.* That task was given to the very able space illustrator Chris Foss, who designed several spacecraft, monsters and sets, and to Seamus Flannery, the production designer, who delivered some very original designs, visualizing Ken's, and later Beverley's, fantastic ideas to help sell the project.

Even Beverley's attempts at solving the problem of an ancient mariner fighting aliens didn't seem to work. While there were further efforts to translate the idea into a working screenplay, the overall result was a slightly comical premise, which was what we had begun with. If I were to be truthful, I would say that it would have been better to have dropped Sinbad altogether. After more than two years' work, the subject was eventually shelved because by then the fantasy/science fiction genre had become more brutal than any of us would have imagined.

SINBAD PROJECT (Untitled)

An idea for a Sinbad project, I considered this somewhere between making *One Million Years BC* and *The Valley of Gwangi.* Theoretically it would have given us a wonderful commercial combination of Sinbad journeying through a forgotten land populated with dinosaurs. I don't remember the details of the plot (I am not even sure there was one), but I do remember that originally it was to have been set in Mexico, although looking at the three drawings completed, India or the Far East seemed to be more in favour.

Above. Drawing for an untitled Sinbad project. This key drawing was intended to promote an untitled Sinbad project in which the legendary adventurer travels through a land populated with dinosaurs. Again, it would have made a great film, but there were no takers.

SKIN AND BONE

This was a project that had it been filmed would have been a complete oddity, although at the time I was extremely keen on its possibilities. In late 1962 Diana read the 1936 novel by Thorne Smith, the author of the Topper stories, and mentioned that it might make a great film. I read the book and thought it would make a very unusual, if eccentric, comedy, which would have required careful handling by the proper writer and director:

A photographer, Quintus Bland, experiments with developing chemicals. One day he accidentally inhales a compound, and although it doesn't kill him, it affects his body in a very peculiar way. Every time he takes a drink of alcohol, his body becomes invisible except for his skeleton. His adventures, complicated with the fact that he occasionally resumes his flesh at unexpected moments and finds himself naked in public places, end with the compound wearing off, and he and his wife living happily ever after.

The end is rather nebulous and would have been required to be a bit more coherent. Although the adventures he gets into are somewhat repetitious, the whole piece is generally very entertaining.

I made only one key drawing, of the skeleton getting out of bed with the photographer's wife screaming. I showed it to Charles, along with a few notes of an outline. He liked the idea and made contact with Methuen, the publishers, and after receiving their approval, approached Columbia, who at first were excited with it but ultimately decided to drop it as uncommercial. To my knowledge the story has never been made into a film, which seems a pity. The idea did raise its head again after *Sinbad on Mars* fell through, but by the mid-1980s the project seemed unsuitable for more discerning audiences.

Left. Drawing for *Skin and Bone.*
The only key drawing I made for a proposed project based on a novel by Thorne Smith.

SLEEPING BEAUTY

This again was to have been a complete story as part of the Fairy Tale series, but my work in features in the early 1950s took over and it was never made. I have no storyboards, but there are several rough drawings I made of the exterior and interior of the castle.

Above. Drawing for *Sleeping Beauty*. This is how I envisaged the castle for *Sleeping Beauty*.

SOUTH AMERICAN ADVENTURE

This project never received a title. Written at about the same time as *The Elementals*, in the early 1950s, it was another attempt at a 'lost valley' theme. A young couple, Joe and Toni, are sent to explore for oil in the Guatemalan jungle. Deep in the jungle they discover a tribe who worship a stone idol that bears a striking resemblance to a carnivorous dinosaur. Learning of a valley some miles away that is forbidden to the natives, the explorers set off. There they discover a rich fertile valley with more idols. Next day they begin their survey and discover a huge cave, near which they set off explosives to test for oil. When the sound of the blast dies down, they think they hear sounds from the cave, which they intend to explore the next day. That night a huge beast destroys their camp and the next day they enter the cave and discover a lake of oil. From its blackness rises a huge allosaurus, and running for their lives they drop the torches which set fire to the oil. The creature writhes in agony and slowly sinks back into the blackness.

It doesn't really have any huge exploitation ideas and it certainly would have required much more development. I suppose the real reason for writing it was to travel to South America. As far as I can remember, I never developed the idea and never offered it to anyone.

TARZAN AND THE ANT MEN

The 1923 *Tarzan and the Ant Men* by Edgar Rice Burroughs came to my attention in about 1960 when I spotted an illustration in the book when browsing through some old titles in a bookshop. The illustration, along with the idea of Tarzan being shrunk to a tiny Lilliputian size by a sorcerer to help battle an army of marauding ants, seemed full of Dynamation possibilities. With the resurgence of popularity in Tarzan at that time, it had all the hallmarks of a successful, exciting film. I began to pursue the idea of shooting it and talked with Charles about the story and the animation possibilities. However, after some enquiries we discovered that there were problems, mainly with obtaining the rights from the Burroughs estate. With that the project faded.

THE THREE BEARS

Another proposed individual Fairy Tale short that might well have been one of the best. I did a lot of work on the project, but due to feature commitments it was filed away in a drawer until I rediscovered it nearly fifty years later.

Left. Drawings for *The Three Bears*. The idea of *The Three Bears* was to have been another in the Mother Goose series.

THE TIME MACHINE

After my *War of The Worlds* project disintegrated, I was searching for another story subject other than dinosaurs and monsters on the loose, which I knew could not go on repeating themselves indefinitely. *The Time Machine* seemed to have possibilities, although the story was not the ideal medium for Dynamation. However, I would have animated the Morlocks and the crab-like monsters that appear when the traveller goes forward millions of years.

TO LIVE FOREVER

aka **You Can't Live Forever/Never Live Forever/ The Sun Chariot/Quest For the Sun Chariot**.

This was only ever a rough step outline originally written by Tudor Gates. Tudor initially offered it to Charles, who in turn asked me to read it. I don't recall when it was proposed but I think it might have been in the late 1960s.

It was a science fiction fantasy set sometime in the near future that told of a group of international scientists who discover a huge cavern (that sounds familiar) beneath the pyramids of Giza. Travelling the tunnels, then a subterranean river takes them to 'The Land of the Dead' where they discover the bones of human giants and evidence of the lost civilization of Atlantis. Here the world is hollow, with all life existing on a concave surface. Having found a walled city they are welcomed by a race of people who are the descendants of the Atlanteans. They show them a spaceship and it takes off, revealing to them the history of the human race. Spacemen came from Tau Ceti and made the Egyptians their slaves. Atlantis invaded Egypt to purge Earth of the invaders but their efforts resulted in a nuclear war which in turn created a great flood. Finally Atlantis is submerged in the deluge and the inhabitants go to live beneath the crust of the Earth. Having all this revealed to them, the spacecraft goes out of control and crashes into the ocean and all the members of the expedition are saved but each has forgotten the secrets revealed to them.

Today the whole idea seems too complex and heavy-going for either Charles or I, and presented little in the way of Dynamation techniques. We rejected it, and what became of the project I don't recall, although some of the ideas, like spacemen in Egypt, seem very familiar.

THE TORTOISE AND THE HARE

Perhaps *The Tortoise and the Hare* (2002) should be in the record books as the film that took fifty years to make. It was begun in 1952 as a solo effort as the sixth film in my *Fairy Tales* series. However, because of feature commitments, I sadly only shot about three minutes of footage and then I just didn't get time to complete it. For nearly fifty years those three minutes of colour footage languished in my cellar in London, although it was never forgotten. Over the intervening years the project seemed to play on my mind as something that I never completed, and I always like to finish anything I begin. Several times I considered getting the camera out to photograph the remaining seven or so minutes, but I never did. Since my retirement I have found it difficult to work up enthusiasm for animation again. The times have changed and my art has to some extent been superseded by CGI.

On several occasions, though, I did talk with various film-makers and producers about completing it and getting someone else to film the animation, but like so many projects before, the discussions came to nothing. Fortunately, most fans knew of this unfinished film, and one day I received an offer from two young animators, Mark Caballero and Seamus Walsh, who are based in Burbank, California. They offered to finish the film as far as the building of the sets and animation were concerned. Seeing some of their work, I decided that their style would suit mine and that they would be the perfect choice to complete the project. I settled down to write a script, design storyboards and key drawings, as I had done in most of my other projects. Like the other *Fairy Tales*, I wanted to make this Aesop fable a simple moral tale with touches of humour. It tells of an arrogant hare that challenges a tortoise to a race, but in the end, despite obstacles put in his way, the tortoise wins because the hare is too confident.

I organized and kept control of the production via phone, fax and letters, and on three or four occasions I travelled to Burbank to keep an eye on developments. Slowly the film came together and I even animated several scenes myself – my first real hands-on animation for over twenty years. Mark and Seamus are great animators and technicians. They built the sets and the model of the tortoise, which had gone missing many years before. The other characters, the hare and the fox, were my originals, and surprisingly stood the rigours of animation very well. Mark and Seamus also managed to integrate my original footage, which mostly covered the beginning of the race, with their newly shot footage. The balance of colour and style was miraculous. They even managed to keep my early trademark of a bird or two flying across the scene.

The 11-minute film was completed in early 2003 and I must confess that it has been a great joy to round off something that began so long ago.

Right hand page above. A key drawing for *The Tortoise and the Hare*. The only one of my lost projects not lost anymore. Begun fifty years ago when I only completed 3 minutes of animation footage, *The Tortoise and the Hare* was finally finished in 2002 and incorporated those original 3 minutes of footage.

Right hand page below. *The Tortoise and the Hare* completed. The same scene as shown in my key drawing is brought to life, or at least three-dimensional form.

UGALA

This was a little idea I came up with in that period in the early 1950s just after *The Beast* and just before I met Charles. It is a lost world scenario, very like *Gwangi* in many ways. All I have of my step outline is one page which tells of a scientist who organizes an expedition by means of a helicopter to the lost canyon of Boranca de Cobra in Mexico where he finds 13-foot men (the missing link), dinosaurs and fights a giant spider. Whether I offered the idea, or even mentioned it to anyone else, I can't remember. In any event, I don't think it proceeded beyond a few pages and there are certainly no drawings to visualize it.

THE VISITATION

Dating from about December 1950, I wrote a treatment entitled *The Thing From Beyond*. It tells of a ship whose passengers witness the crash of a flying saucer into the sea. There is a sequence in which a hatch in the craft slowly unscrews and from this darkness emerges tentacles and then an evil-looking alien (which reflects that I still had Wells' Martian invasion in my head). The being misinterprets the humans' intentions and begins to destroy them until finally only the engineer and a girl survive and watch from a lifeboat as the ship blows up and sinks.

Either in 1951 or 1952 I then co-wrote a treatment based on my original idea with a friend, Cecil Maiden, who went on to write screenplays for several films. In this the story shifted to a more esoteric level, separating the alien creature into two living entities, one good, the other evil, but both with the same mind.

A ship is found drifting in the Pacific ocean with no one on board. The story flashes back to the people on the ship witnessing the crashing into the sea of a flying saucer. They manage to haul the craft on board and during the cover of night an evil presence emerges from the interior. This entity breeds evil and slowly the crew and passengers discover their dark side emerging and taking over the good side. In the end amid much killing and chaos another entity is discovered onboard the saucer and this turns out to be all that is good. The good being restrains the evil one and tells the three people left onboard that he is an alien and they have been observing Earth. On his planet their good and evil have separated to become two beings with the good dominating evil. The alien returns to the skies with the three earthlings to teach them to return to Earth and educate mankind to do good.

Although my original treatment would have allowed for animation, the second treatment hardly has anything in it. The only item would have been the spaceship. However, the idea of a being that has a separate good and evil perhaps would have appealed to me at that tender age. Nobody seemed interested in such a complex project, even with the interest in science fiction in the 1950s. I did try to resurrect the idea in the early 1970s when I offered the project to Michael Carreras at Hammer. In a letter dated 2 April 1971 he commented, 'I must admit that I find it intriguing, but at the present time nobody is having any success with this type of science fiction subject, so I know there is no point in me delving into it any further.' The word 'intriguing' was probably a euphemism for 'terrible'.

WAR EAGLES

My first meeting with Obie was whilst he was working on the *War Eagles* project at MGM. In 1938 the project began its short life when Merian C. Cooper began preparations for another fantasy to rival *King Kong*. Obie was brought on board to design and create the effects, and Ernest Schoedsack would direct from a script by Cyril Hume. The project fell into trouble early on when Hume had to rewrite large sections of the story three times, altering the hero from a professor to a young pilot. Eventually the production was shelved in March 1940, two months after Hume's final revised screenplay:

Slim is a young pilot who, while flying over Antarctica, encounters a bank of fog and crashes into a valley protected by mountains warmed by volcanic activity. He is found by a native girl, Naru, and becomes a member of a tribe of warriors who fly on giant eagles, which they call Erns. The tribe are descendants of a Viking called Einar who came to the valley many thousands of years before. Capturing his own eagle, a huge white bird, Slim becomes a member of the tribe and helps them to destroy a herd of allosaurus that have terrorized the tribe for centuries. After many months of trying to repair his radio, which is the one thing that survives his crash, he hears that New York is being attacked by an evil nation intent on taking over the world. It is using a ray that debilitates all engines by cutting off the electricity, so that the American military cannot retaliate.

Slim, along with the other war bird warriors, flies to New York where they are just in time to see a massive dirigible containing the ray fly over the Manhattan. A dog fight ensues with the war birds winning and with the dirigible destroyed with one of its own bombs. The last shot sees the military might of America chasing the other bombers over the Atlantic watched by Slim, Naru and the white eagle from the Statue of Liberty.

Having been impressed with the original artwork and the exciting and intelligent screenplay, I always thought the basic story, with some alterations and updating, would make an excellent fantasy/adventure picture. Several times during my career, whenever a meeting came up to discuss possible projects, I would suggest the old O'Brien project, and on two occasions it progressed to a point beyond just talk. The first was about the time we began to consider *Gwangi*, and the second, and by far the most serious, was after *Clash of the Titans*, when we were riding high with MGM. Charles, who was very interested in it, managed to get the three different original scripts from the old MGM library. After reading them, MGM told us that they thought the idea old-fashioned and so the project was dropped.

Unfortunately, I never produced any artwork for the subject (aside from my flying creatures in *People of the Mist*, an interpretation of the eagles), but I do have some copies of wonderful artwork by two artists, Leland Curtis and Duncan Gleason, which visualize in Doré fashion the imaginative screenplay and make one long to have seen a completed picture.

Obie did make several colour tests for the project from which, to my knowledge, only stills survive. They show not only landscapes of pure Doré, but dinosaurs and one very good close-up of an eagle.

Above. An original drawing for *War Eagles*. This was one of the pre-production drawings by Duncan Gleason of an attack by an allosaurus for Obie's unrealized 1938/40 version of *War Eagles*.

WEE WILLY WINKIE

Again, all I have is a few storyboard sketches that are embarrassingly rough. The story would have been perfect for part of the 'Mother Goose' stories.

Above. Poster artwork designed by Hammer for *When the Earth Cracked Open*. Although most of my designs and sketches set the story in prehistory, or at least contemporary times, Hammer's poster suggests that it might be set in the future. However, I understand that this is not unusual, as a Hammer poster is only designed to sell an idea, or in this case a girl in a space helmet.

WHEN THE EARTH CRACKED OPEN
aka **The Day the Earth Cracked Open**

After my involvement with Hammer on *One Million Years BC*, there were several suggestions from Michael Carreras for projects that would utilize stop-motion animation. *When the Earth Cracked Open* was one of the more concrete proposals. It began life as *The Day the Earth Cracked Open*, and the pre-production poster artwork suggested that it might be set in the future. It reminds me of my suggestion to remake *Deluge* (Hammer were rather prone to throwing everything into the artwork to raise the finance, even though what appeared might not be in the completed film).

My involvement with the project began in late 1970, and working with Don Houghton, who was writing an outline, we spent some considerable time,

Top. Selected sketches from the rough storyboard for *When the Earth Cracked Open*. In these a girl is attacked by a swamp creature, the only part of which we can see is a tentacle.

Above and left. Sketches for *When the Earth Cracked Open*. These sketches show a dinoasaur-like creature chasing a group of people who appear to be dressed in modern clothes.

March–April 1971, developing various ideas. At that early point I produced six drawings of a creature (dinosaur-like in appearance) emerging from the ground and chasing what look to be sailors, and all my other sketches, storyboards and outline indicate that the story was to have taken place in a prehistoric setting and relates nothing of a tidal wave.

I even budgeted for shooting and animating a trailer or promotional piece, quoting two to three weeks to animate a giant tentacle sequence. The story was fairly basic and followed more or less the same themes as the previous Hammer prehistoric adventures. It was to have opened with a montage showing Earth's pre-history from the Ice Age to the first Neanderthal man, which takes us to the River people whose leader is Rabbala. One day, whilst the men are fishing, the Fire Warriors, led by Za'Ama, attack the camp, killing the old men and children, and take the women. Rabbala and his men follow through the Poison Swamp where they encounter strange creatures (for this sequence I was to have animated a swamp creature with tentacles and a giant toad). Meanwhile the Fire Warriors make their way across a desert, and when the River People follow, they are faced with a giant 'Sand Crab' (or a Triceratops, Anklosaurus, Giant Sloth or a giant Beetle), which leads them to a chasmic gorge. Once on the other side they find themselves in a dense jungle where they are attacked by giant soldier ants and are saved only by a rainstorm that sweeps the creatures away. As though that wasn't enough, they encounter a lake of salt and sulphur in which lurks a serpent and a Primord-Reptile that Don describes as 'a cross between a gorilla and a lizard' (which would have been comical). Finally the River People catch up with the Fire Warriors in their home – an active volcano – and by pushing huge rocks into the volcano they create an eruption. During the confusion Raballa and his men are reunited with their women and escape across an ever-widening chasm (thus the title), into which crumbles the volcano and the Fire Warriors.

In a memo from Don dated 12 May 1971, following a meeting with myself and Josephine Douglas at Hammer, it was resolved that there would be only four specific 'monster effects': the swamp creature, a giant stag beetle, a giant armadillo and the giant soldier ants, although I was to create the climax of walls of lava and volcanoes. It was at this point that I roughed out some storyboards.

The demise of the project came about on 19 July 1971 when Michael Carreras wrote to me announcing, 'the production of this subject has, for various reasons, had to be postponed until Spring of next year'. This was the last I heard of it, so presumably Michael was unable to obtain the necessary backing or some other project took its place. Reading it today, the whole thing looks like *One Million Years BC – Part II*, and perhaps it is best that it was never realized.

Looking back over the years I have been lucky to have been involved is so many exciting projects, the best of which I suppose did mature and grow into full-length feature films. Of those above and elsewhere in this book, there are not many I really regret not making, although if pressed, I think I would have liked to have realized H.G. Wells' *War of the Worlds*, if only because I had worked so hard at producing a storyboard and key drawings. Even now, in the beginning of the 21st century, I believe the story still has great power and so much to offer a modern audience. George Pal made an excellent adaptation of the story in 1953, but it surprises me that no enterprising producer has taken the original story, in its original Victorian setting, and made a modern interpretation of the conflict between two worlds.

All of the above original stories, characters and plot situations, unless otherwise stated to be owned by production companies or individuals, are © Ray Harryhausen, 2003.

Filmography

All features are listed under the release dates.
Tests and other experimental films are not generally
mentioned, but appear in the main text.

Ray Harryhausen
Born 29 June 1920 in Los Angeles, California, USA.
Married to Diana Bruce in 1963.
Daughter Vanessa Harryhausen, born
Westminster, London in 1964.

1935–36 Cavebear
16mm, b/w.

Experimental Dinosaur Films

1937 **The Jupiter Project** (Unrealized)
16mm, colour, 1 minute of test footage shot.

1938–40 **Evolution of the World** (Unrealized)
16mm, colour, some footage shot.

1940–42 **The Puppetoons** (Madcap Models)
35mm, colour.
Series of shorts (of which RH only worked
on thirteen) produced by George Pal for
Paramount Pictures.

Western Daze (1941)
Dipsy Gypsy (1941)
Hoola Boola (1941)
Gaye Knighties (1941)
Rhythm in the Ranks (1941)
Sleeping Beauty (1941)
Jasper and the Watermelons (1942)
The Sky Princess (1942)
Mr Strauss Takes a Walk (1942)
Tulips Shall Grow (1942)
The Little Broadcast (1942)
Jasper and the Haunted House (1942)
Jasper and the Choo-Choo (1942)
(with Willis O'Brien)

1941 **How to Build a Bridge**
(aka **How to Bridge A Gorge**)
16mm, colour, 5 minutes.
A demonstration film illustrating the possible
use of stop-motion animation for training films.

1942–45 Various work for the Army Signal Corp
under Frank Capra, notably:
Why We Fight series (US War Office)
Prelude to War
Nazi's Strike
Divide and Conquer
Battle of Britain
Battle of Russia
Battle of China
War Comes to America
Negro Soldier

Snafu
Modelled statue for cartoon series.

Guadalcanal
16mm, colour, 10 minutes.
Made to illustrate the use of stop-motion.

1945 **Lucky Strike Cigarette Commercial**
16mm, colour, 2 minutes.
Made to sell the idea of using stop-motion
as an advertising medium.

1946 **Mother Goose Stories**
16mm, colour Fairy Tales (for the sake of
continuity we have called the film a Fairy Tale,
but actually the four separate stories were
Nursery Rhymes: 'Little Miss Muffet',
'Old Mother Hubbard', 'The Queen of Hearts'
and 'Humpty Dumpty'), 9 minutes 57 seconds.
Associate: Fred Blasauf.
Costumes: Martha Reske
Produced by Ray Harryhausen

Silver Dollar Commercial
16mm, colour.
Made for an investment company.

Religious Film (working title The Three Crosses)
16mm, colour.
Made for an unknown religious organization.

Kenny Key
16mm, colour.
Television commercials for real estate company.

1949 **Mighty Joe Young**
RKO, b/w, 94 minutes.
Producer: Merican C. Cooper and John Ford
Director: Ernest B. Schoedsack
Screenplay: Ruth Rose (from an original story
by Merian C. Cooper)
Technical Creator: Willis H. O'Brien
Second Technician: Peter Peterson
Technical Staff: George Lofgren,
Marcel Delgado, Fitch Fulton
Cinematographer: J. Roy Hunt
Art Director: James Basevi
Editor: Ted Cheesman
Photographic Effects: Harold Stine, Bert Willis
Optical Effects: Linwood Dunn
Music: Roy Webb
Cast: Terry Moore, Robert Armstrong,
Ben Johnson, Frank McHugh, Douglas Fowley,
Regis Toomey and Mr Joseph Young as himself
Main on-screen credit: First Technician

War of the Worlds (Unrealized)
16mm, colour, test.
Shot approximately 4 minutes of test footage.

Food of the Gods (Unrealized)
Only one drawing made of giant bee/wasp.

1950 **The Valley of the Mist** (Unrealized
Willis O'Brien project)
RH completed 3 key drawings for the project.

The Story of Little Red Riding Hood
16mm, colour Fairy Tale, 8 minutes 22 seconds.
Associate: Fred Blasauf
Costumes: Martha Reske
Narrative: Charlotte Knight
Narrator: James Matthews
Animation: Ray Harryhausen
Producer: Ray Harryhausen

Adventures of Baron Munchausen (Unrealized)
16mm, colour test.
Approximately 50 seconds of test footage shot
of Baron meeting and talking with the Giant
in the Moon.

1951 **The Story of Hansel and Gretel**
16mm, colour Fairy Tale, 9 minutes 47 seconds.
Associate: Fred Blasauf
Costumes: Martha Reske
Adaptation: Charlotte Knight
Narrator: Hugh Douglas
Producer and Director: Ray Harryhausen

1952 **The Story of Rapunzel**
16mm, colour Fairy Tale, 10 minutes 25 seconds.
Associate: Fred Blasauf
Costumes: Martha Reske
Narrative: Charlotte Knight
Narrator: Del Moore
Producer and Director: Ray Harryhausen

The Beast From 20,000 Fathoms
Warner Bros, b/w, 80 minutes.
Producers: Hal Chester and Jack Deitz
Associate Producer and Editor: Bernard W. Burton
Director/Art Director: Eugene Lourie
Screenplay: Lou Morheim, Fred Frieburger
Suggested by the *Saturday Evening Post* story
by Ray Bradbury
Cinematographer: Jack Russell
Music: David Buttolph
Cast: Paul Christian, Paula Raymond,
Cecil Kellaway, Kenneth Tobey, Donald Woods,
Jack Pennick, Lee Van Cleef, King Donovan
Main on-screen credit: Technical Effects

1952 **The Elementals** (Unrealized)
RH wrote the outline story and shot 2 minutes of 35mm tests on colour stock. He sold the idea for development to Jack Deitz in 1953. The rights for the story have now reverted back to RH.

The Tortoise and the Hare (Unrealized)
16mm, colour Fairy Tale. Only 3 minutes were shot of the tortoise preparing to race the arrogant hare, while the fox as the starting master looks on (see also 2000–02).

1953 **The Story of King Midas**
16mm, colour Fairy Tale, 9 minutes 45 seconds.
Associate: Fred Blasauf
Costumes: Martha Reske
Narrative: Charlotte Knight
Narrator: Del Moore
Producer and director: Ray Harryhausen

1955 **It Came From Beneath the Sea**
Columbia Pictures, b/w, 80 minutes.
Executive Producer: Sam Katzman
Producer: Charles H. Schneer
Director: Robert Gordon
Screenplay: George Worthington Yates, Hal Smith
Story: George Worthington Yates
Cinematographer: Henry Freulich
Art Director: Paul Palmentola
Editor: Jerome Thomas
Music: Mischa Bakaleinikoff
Cast: Kenneth Tobey, Faith Domergue, Donald Curtis, Harry Lauter, Ian Keith
Main on-screen credit: Technical Effects

1956 **The Animal World**
Warner Brothers, colour, 82 minutes.
Writer, Producer and Director: Irwin Allen
Cinematographer: Harold Wellman ASC
Art Director: Bert Tuttle
Music: Paul Sawtell
Supervising Animator: Willis O'Brien
Main on-screen credit: Animation

Earth Vs the Flying Saucers
Columbia Pictures, b/w, 83 minutes.
Executive Producer: Sam Katzman
Producer: Charles H. Schneer
Director: Fred F. Sears
Screenplay: George Worthington Yates, Raymond T. Marcus (Bernard Gordon)
Screen story by Curt Siodmak, suggested by *Flying Saucers From Outer Space* by Major Donald E. Keyhoe
Cinematographer: Fred Jackman, Jr
Art Director: Paul Palmentola
Editor: Danny D. Landres
Music: Mischa Bakaleinikoff
Cast: Hugh Marlow, Joan Taylor, Donald Curtis, Morris Ankrum, with the voice of Paul Frees.
Main on-screen credit: Technical Effects

1957 **20 Million Miles to Earth**
Columbia Pictures, A Morningside Production, b/w, 82 minutes.
Producer: Charles H. Schneer
Director: Nathan Juran
Screenplay: Bob Williams, Christopher Knopf
Story: Charlotte Knight
Cinematographer: Irving Lippmann, Carlos Ventigmilia
Art Director: Cary Odell
Editor: Edwin Bryant
Music: Mischa Bakaleinikoff
Cast: William Hopper, Joan Taylor, Frank Puglia, Thomas Browne Henry
Main on-screen credit: Technical Effects

1958 **The 7th Voyage of Sinbad**
Colubia Pictures, A Morningside Production, colour, 89 minutes.
Producer: Charles H. Schneer
Director: Nathan Juran
Screenplay: Kenneth Kolb (based on an original story by Ray Harryhausen)
Cinematographer: Wilkie Cooper
Art Director: Gil Parrendo
Editors: Edwin Bryant, Jerome Thomas
Technical Assistant: George Lofgren
Music: Bernard Herrmann
Cast: Kerwin Mathews, Kathryn Grant, Torin Thatcher, Richard Eyer, Alec Mango, Dany Green
In DYNAMATION The New Miracle of the Screen
Main on-screen credit: Special Visual Effects

1959 **The 3 Worlds of Gulliver**
Columbia Pictures, A Morningside Production, colour, 100 minutes.
Producer: Charles H. Schneer
Director: Jack Sher
Screenplay: Arthur Ross, Jack Sher
Based on *Gulliver's Travels* by Jonathan Swift
Cinematographer: Wilkie Cooper
Art Directors: Gil Parrendo/Derek Barrington
Editor: Raymond Poulton
Music: Bernard Herrmann
Cast: Kerwin Mathews, Jo Morrow, June Thorburn, Lee Patterson, Basil Sydney, Mary Ellis, Gregoire Aslan, Charles Lloyd Pack, Martin Benson, Peter Bull
Filmed in SUPER DYNAMATION
Main on-screen credit: Special Visual Effects

1960 **Tarzan and the Antmen** (Unrealized)

1961 **Food of the Gods** (Unrealized)
Only one drawing made of a giant chicken towering over a house.

Mysterious Island
Columbia Pictures, colour, 101 minutes.
Producer: Charles H. Schneer
Director: Cy Endfield
Screenplay: John Prebble, Daniel Ullman, Crane Wilbur
Based on the novel *L'Ile Mysterieuse* by Jules Verne
Cinematographer: Wilkie Cooper
Underwater Photography: Egil Woxholt
Art Director: Bill Andrews
Editor: Frederick Wilson
Music: Bernard Herrmann
Cast: Michael Craig, Joan Greenwood, Michael Callan, Gary Merrill, Herbert Lom, Beth Rogan, Percy Herbert, Dan Jackson
Filmed in DYNARAMA
Main on-screen credit: Special Visual Effects

1963 **Jason and the Argonauts**
Columbia Pictures, A Morningside Production, colour, 104 minutes.
Producer: Charles H. Schneer
Director: Don Chaffey
Screenplay: Jan Read, Beverley Cross
Cinematography: Wilkie Cooper
Art Directors: Herbert Smith, Jack Maxsted, Tony Sarzi Braga
Editor: Maurice Rootes
Music: Bernard Herrmann
Cast: Todd Armstrong, Gary Raymond, Nancy Kovack, Honor Blackman, Nigel Green, Michael Gwynn, Douglas Wilmer, Niall MacGinnis, Laurence Naismith, Jack Gwillim, Patrick Troughton, Andrew Faulds, Fernando Poggi
Main on Screen Credits: Associate Producer; Creator of Special Visual Effects

1963 **Skin and Bone** (Unrealized)
Only one drawing made.

1964 **First Men in the Moon**
Columbia Pictures, colour, 103 minutes.
Producer: Charles H. Schneer
Director: Nathan Juran
Screenplay: Nigel Kneale, Jan Read
From the story by H.G. Wells
Cinematographer: Wilkie Cooper
Photographed in LunaColor and Panavision
Art Director: John Blezard
Editor: Maurice Rootes
Music: Laurie Johnson
Cast: Edward Judd, Lionel Jeffries, Martha Hyer, Miles Malleson, Peter Finch (uncredited as the Baliff's Man)
Filmed in DYNAMATION the miracle of the screen
Main on-screen credit: Associate Producer; Creator of Special Visual Effects

1966 **One Million Years B.C.**
A Hammer Film Production, colour, 100 minutes.
Producer: Michael Carreras
Associate Producer: Aida Young
Director: Don Chaffey
Screenplay: Michael Carreras
Adapted from an original screenplay by Mickell Novak, George Baker, Joseph Frickert
Cinematographer: Wilkie Cooper
Art Director: Robert Jones
Editor: James Needs, Tom Simpson
Prologue Designed by Les Bowie
Music and Special Musical Effects: Mario Nascimbene
Cast: Raquel Welch, John Richardson, Percy Herbert, Robert Brown, Martine Beswick
Main on-screen credit: Special Visual Effects

1969 **The Valley of Gwangi**
Warner Bros-Seven Arts, colour, 95 minutes.
Producer: Charles H. Schneer
Director: James O'Connolly
Screenplay: William E. Bast, additional material by Julian More
Inspired by the 1941 unrealized project 'Gwangi'; co-produced by Willis O'Brien and John Speaks, script by Harold Lamb and Emily Barrye
Cinematographer: Erwin Hillier
Art Director: Gil Parrondo
Editor: Henry Richardson
Music: Jerome Moross
Cast: James Franciscus, Gila Golan, Richard Carlson, Laurence Naismith, Freda Jackson, Curtis Arden
Filmed in DYNAMATION
Main on-screen credit: Associate Producer and Creator of Visual Effects

1973 **The Golden Voyage of Sinbad**
Columbia Pictures, colour, 105 minutes.
Producer: Charles H. Schneer and Ray Harryhausen
Director: Gordon Hessler
Screenplay: Brian Clemens
From a story by Brian Clemens and Ray Harryhausen
Cinematographer: Ted Moore
Art Director: Fernando Gonzalez
Special Masks: Colin Arthur
Editor: Roy Watts
Music: Miklós Rósza
Cast: John Phillip Law, Tom Baker, Caroline Munro, Douglas Wilmer, Martin Shaw, Gregoire Aslan, Kurt Christian
Filmed in DYNARAMA
Main on-screen technical credit: Creator of Special Visual Effects

1977　**Sinbad and the Eye of the Tiger**
Columbia Pictures, colour, 113 minutes.
Producer: Charles H. Schneer and
Ray Harryhausen
Director: Sam Wanamaker
Screenplay: Beverly Cross
Story by Beverly Cross and Ray Harryhausen
Based on an original story by Ray Harryhausen
Cinematographer: Ted Moore
Art Directors: Fernando Gonzalez/Fred Carter
Editor: Roy Watts
Music: Roy Budd
Cast: Patrick Wayne, Taryn Power, Margaret
Whiting, Jane Seymour, Patrick Troughton,
Kurt Christian, Nadim Sawalha
Filmed in DYNARAMA
*Main on-screen technical credit: Creator of
Special Visual Effects*

1981　**Clash of the Titans**
MGM, colour, 118 minutes.
Producer: Charles H. Schneer and
Ray Harryhausen
Director: Desmond Davis
Screenplay: Beverley Cross
Cinematographer: Ted Moore
Assistants to Ray Harryhausen: Jim Danforth,
Steven Archer
Special Miniatures: Cliff Culley
Model Maker: Janet Stevens, Colin Chivers
Special Opticals: Frank Van Der Veer, Roy Field
Masks: Colin Arthur
Art Directors: Giorgio Desideri, Peter Howitt,
Don Picton, Fernando Gonzalez
Editor: Timothy Gee
Music: Laurence Rosenthal
Cast: Harry Hamlin, Judi Bowker,
Burgess Meredith, Laurence Olivier,
Maggie Smith, Claire Bloom, Jack Gwillim,
Ursula Andress, Siân Phillips, Flora Robson,
Freda Jackson, Anna Manahan,
Donald Huston, Tim Pigott-Smith,
Neil McCarthy, Susan Fleetwood, Pat Roach
*Main on-screen credit: Creator of Special
Visual Effects*

Sinbad and the 7 Wonders of the World
(Unrealized)

Sinbad on Mars (aka **Sinbad Goes to Mars**)
(Unrealized)

1983　**People of the Mist** (Unrealized)

1984　**Force of the Trojans** (Unrealized)

1996–98　**The Story of Odysseus** (Unrealized)
For Carrington & Cosgrove Hall Productions.
Consultant on story development and
character design.

1998　**Dairylea Dip Commercial**
Advisor and Consultant on animation.

1999　**Working with Dinosaurs**
(UK television documentary for Channel 4)
Photographed 28 seconds of animation in
which one of the skeletons from *Jason and the
Argonauts* stands from a crouching position to
face me, shot against a blue screen.

2000–02　**The Tortoise and the Hare**
16mm, colour, A Ray Harryhausen Production.
This is the completion of a short subject begun
in 1953. Conceived and written by RH, and
based on his story and designs, the film was
animated and photographed in the US by Mark
Caballero and Seamus Walsh using all the
original models except the tortoise, which had
to be rebuilt, as the original had been lost.

Additional
Spies Like Us (1985)
Directed by John Landis.
Guest appearance with others, including special
effects technician Derek Meddings. Seen as a
surgeon in tent sequence.

Beverley Hills Cop III (1994)
Directed by John Landis.
Guest appearance in bar sequence.

Mighty Joe Young (1998)
RKO/Walt Disney Productions.
Guest appearance with Terry Moore
(leading lady in the original version) in
reception sequence.

Glossary

Aerial Brace: See *Wire Brace*.

Anamorphic Process or Widescreen: A lens that in a camera squeezes a wide picture onto a standard film (usually 35mm); used on a projector it unsqueezes the image to fill a cinema widescreen (usually a 2.45:1 aspect ratio). Examples of this process are Cinemascope (the first commercial title), Panavision, Warnerscope and Dyaliscope.

Armatures: A metal skeletal framework on which a latex body or similar outer appearance is built up. The armature is constructed of ball-and-socket joints (see below) to allow for articulation or manual movement.

Aspect Ratio: The ratio of width to height of the image both on film and screen.

Backcloth: Usually a black velvet-like material in front of which effects can be photographed. This allows the effect to be optically composited into the action. For example, the fireworks used for the ray in *Earth Vs the Flying Saucers*.

Bag Filter: A slang expression for the defusing filter, which is sometimes used in the camera to soften lines around the actor's eyes.

Ball-and-Socket Joints: Sections of the metal skeleton armature that relate to human joints and which allow movement. Such joints occur when the metal armature corresponds with the hip, wrist, ankle or knee, so enabling the model character to attain natural movements. It consists of a ball over which is held tightly (allowing just enough movement to hold a pose) a separate clamp section. The principle is that the friction on the ball permits the model character to hold its position while one frame of film is photographed.

Blue Backing: This primarily uses a huge blue screen against which the actors stand, being careful not to use the same colour blue in their clothing. A standard camera then films the action. A system of mattes and counter-mattes is developed, eliminating the blue in favour of black, which is then used to print the actor onto the second element (i.e. a background scene). The process is accomplished in the optical printer. Because of the number of steps necessary to produce the mattes and counter-mattes, plus the variable quality of film stock, the precise positions of the filmed objects sometimes changed microscopically. If not precisely aligned when composited, the elements can 'fringe' with a leftover blue halo.

Camera Registration Pins: A mechanical means of registering one frame of film in a motion picture camera for exposure during filming. A very important necessity for the multiple exposures of motion picture film stock.

Camera Tape: Special white (usually) fabric-backed tape. Commonly used for sealing exposed film cans, it is adaptable for many other tasks. For example, I often used it for marking a spot on the rear projection screen to estimate the number of frames for foreground movement.

Colour Cells: See *Gels*.

Cut-out (Full): A full-size cut-out of a creature used in rehearsals. When we weren't using a monster stick, we would use a cut-out to enable the actors to keep their eyeline and to understand what they were meant to be seeing. For *The Valley of Gwangi* I sometimes used a cut-out, especially for the sequence where Gwangi gets stuck in the entrance to the valley. I also used one for the two-headed dog in *Clash of the Titans*.

Cut-outs (Miniature): Miniature cut-outs as stand-ins for lighting a miniature set, obtaining the correct perspective in respect to the size of the character in relation to the miniature.

Day For Night: A technique of photographing in daylight but using techniques such as underexposing the film stock, using dark filters or during printing, with the result that the final print looks as if it was shot at night.

Dioramas: Miniature three-dimensional sets in which models and figures are placed, usually for displaying prehistoric landscapes.

Dissolves or Mix: A change of scene accomplished by a gradual exposure of a second image (or the next scene) over the first. The second image will then dominate the first and the first will fade completely.

Dolly: A trolley in which a camera can be moved smoothly. Can be mounted on rails or thick plywood.

Dolly Shots: A shot that is accomplished by using the dolly, giving movement to an otherwise static picture.

Double Printing or Double Exposure: When two or more images are recorded on the same section of film in an optical printer or in the camera.

Flashing: This involves exposing the stock (film) to a low-level light before it is exposed. This lowers the contrast, which results in a slight fogging of the negative so that the deep blacks and other dark colours will photograph less as a mass of darkness and more as a pattern of light and shadow.

Foam Injection Method: A method of injecting a latex rubber foam solution into a mould. This can either be done by mechanical pressure or by simply pouring the liquid into a hole in the mould. To create the hardened sponge effect the mould is placed into an oven, where it swells to a foam.

Fog Filter: A camera diffusion filter (similar to a translucent screen) that creates an appearance of fog or a mist effect on the image.

Gamete Test: Running a test at many different stops on the lens to arrive at the correct exposure. In the case of stop-motion, in order to achieve a good depth of focus on a miniature it is necessary to use a one-second exposure with the lens stopped down to, say, F16 or F22. Stopping the iris down always gives the depth of focus, so that the models may move closer or further from the lens and still stay relatively sharp.

Gel: Coloured sheet (usually gelatine) that is placed in front of a light source as a filter to colour illuminations.

Glass Painting: This dates back to the early days of cinema. It enables the film-maker to add to the existing location or set by creating tops to buildings or the upper section of an interior. A large sheet of plate glass is placed before the camera, on which is painted the added section of the set or location. The process was replaced by matte painting, which can be executed in the studio.

Guide Tracks: This usually applies to sound tracks made during the live photography and later used as a guide for dubbing, but I used the term to describe a filmed sequence, usually shot in black and white, which included the actors, stand-ins or stuntmen acting out their scenes. This guide track has no models but is used by the animator to help him with actions and positions to which he can animate the models.

Hanging Miniature: A three-dimensional miniature that is suspended in front of the camera to complete a set or image. By using this method a full set can be built of the lower half of a building (for example, the floor and bases of columns in a temple) and a hanging miniature can be constructed of the upper half to complete the image.

High Speed Photography: By speeding up the rate at which the film stock is passed through the camera (usually 96 frames per second) to achieve, as far as miniature work is concerned, a natural appearance of water, smoke or an explosion, in relation to the size of the model.

Latex: A substance made from the rubber tree, which is mixed with certain chemicals to enable it to retain flexibility. In model making there are three forms: plain, foam and hard rubber latex. The foam is created by beating the liquid with an egg beater; the hard rubber is created by the addition of chalk or various chemicals.

Light Gels: See *Gel*.

Matte or Matt: A technique of combining two separately photographed scenes into one picture, which enables actors in a studio setting to be combined with locations or effects. It is achieved by a partial masking that prevents light from reaching a certain area of the film, and is used to block part of the lens of the camera during shooting, or part of the aperture in the printer. Part of another image will later go into the unexposed area for the creation of a composite image. See also *Travelling Matte*.

Matte Painting: A detailed painting that is combined in the optical printer to represent a complete image of a desired landscape or architectural structure.

Monster Stick: A term describing a pole that usually represents a large creature (such as a dinosaur), to enable the actors and extras to understand how tall the creature is and where its head and torso will be. This simple device enables them to react to it. The size of stick or pole is determined by the size of the creature. For *The 7th Voyage of Sinbad* I built a 20-foot monster stick with the top painted red for the head, the middle blue for the torso, and so on. Sometimes we would have the prop man carry the stick out of camera range to simulate movement so that the actors could keep the eyeline. See also *Cut-outs*.

Negative: Basic film stock that when exposed in the camera and then developed is the reverse of positive stock, making it possible to produce multiple positive images for use in the projector. The dark and light areas of the recorded image are reversed, and in colour photography the images are recorded in complementary colours. Through a dye process in the laboratory a complementary negative is produced, from which multiple positive colour prints are made.

Optical Printer: A film printing system in which the images from a negative or a positive are projected onto new film stock. In effect it is the same principle as that recorded in a camera or produced by a projected image.

Pan or Camera Pan: A shot in which the camera rotates horizontally or vertically by following the action.

Pins: See *Stability Pins*.

Plate: See *Rear Projection Plate*.

Pointers: See *Surface Gauges*.

Positive: A film stock that has been developed from the negative, thus producing a normal photographic reproduction of the images. The light areas on the negative produce dark areas on the positive, and the dark areas produce light areas in black and white photography.

Rear Projection: The projection of either a moving or still image onto the rear of a translucent screen in front of which models can be animated to perform actions that correspond with the action on the screen.

Rear Projection Plate: A moving image shot during live action photography for animation or a live-action rear projection screen. New methods have been devised to make these plates with much less contrast than normal, making the rephotographed image on the screen a much less realistic image when combined with a model.

Rear Projection Still: High-grade still photographs used for a rear projection screen. Usually backgrounds of buildings, clear skies, etc. See *The Beast From 20,000 Fathoms* (Chapter 2).

Recce: A reconnaissance to find locations for filming sequences.

Rotoscope or Rotoscoping: Rotoscope actually means to copy. It is the tracing on paper of a pre-shot projected image of a live-action figure. It acts as a guide to realistic cartoon images. The Disney cartoon animators used the technique to produce natural movements in their animation drawings, particularly where humanoid characters were involved.

Second Camera Pass: A process in miniature rear projection where a section of the picture is matted out with black paint on a foreground glass. An animation model or miniature building is added to the scene, and after recording the combination, the film and projected image are rewound in the camera. The previously blacked out portion is then exposed using an opposite matte and the final image gives the impression that the model or miniature is part of the original scene. See also *Split-Screen Technique*.

Sodium Backing or Yellow Backing Travelling Matte Process: Developed by Rank Film Laboratories in 1956, it reduced the number of steps required to obtain a proper travelling matte. The actors, lit by standard lighting, perform before a white screen illuminated by sodium-vapour lights, making the background yellow. A special beam-splitting prismatic camera produces two images in two separate apertures on two different reels of film. The standard colour negative records the detail of the live action and the second high contrast image is sensitive to sodium light, this turning the background area black with a transparent light area where the action is. This produces a moving matte, which can produce a counter-matte. The foreground action is then combined with a proper background in the optical printer. See also *Travelling Matte*.

Split-Screen Technique: A technique used in a photographed composition in which part of the image is masked off, leaving that part of the frame unexposed. The film is rewound and exposed a second or third time, but now masking out the already exposed area and only exposing the previously unexposed area of the composition. This can be done in the camera or on an optical printer.

Sprocket Holes: The perforations along the edge or edges of film stock, which are engaged by the teeth of sprocket wheels to move the film through the camera, printer and projector.

Stability Pins: In the process of substitution puppet animation, a series of perhaps twenty-five figures are necessary for two steps. A small pin is placed on each of the twenty-five figures in exactly the same place beneath the foot. When the second foot touches the ground, this process is repeated on the new foot. A small hole is drilled on the set, which gives the foot that is on the ground perfect registration for each puppet. George Pal's *Puppetoons* are a good example of this technique.

Stand-In Model: A solid (non-armatured) model that allows the animator to light and prepare a miniature set.

Step Outline: The earliest development of the script or screenplay. The story is written in progressive steps to allow the writer to determine if the overall plot will work.

Stock: The raw film stock. Usually 35mm, 16mm or 70mm.
35mm: the standard stock for professionals. It is 35 millimetres in width, with four perforations (or sprocket holes) along both sides of the frame. It is projected at 24 frames per second.
16mm: generally used by the amateur cinematographer. It is 16 millimetres in width, with usually one row of perforations (or sprocket holes), whilst the other side carries the sound track.
70mm: the widest commercial gauge of film stock, generally used for release prints of large-scale productions because it possesses excellent definition.

Stock Footage: Footage photographed for a previous production and brought in (usually from archive libraries) to incorporate into another. Most of our early films used stock footage to save on costs.

Subjective Camera: The photographing of a scene where the camera assumes the point of view of a character in the story. In other words, the camera is the character. The best example of subjective camera is from the 1946 film *The Lady in the Lake*, in which the entire film is seen through the eyes of a private eye. Another good example is the 1935 Frederick March version of *Dr Jekyll and Mr Hyde*, in which the opening scenes never show the actor, only his point of view, until he looks into a mirror. We used the technique several times, namely in *The Golden Voyage of Sinbad* in which we see the Vizier's secret chamber through the eyes of the tiny homunculus at ground level.

Surface Gauge: This consists of a heavy metal base on which a pointed, moveable metal arm is mounted. When the camera shutter is closed, the point is placed somewhere on the animation figure to allow the animator to judge how broad a move he should make. If the animation character is complicated, it is sometimes necessary to use several 'pointers' or gauges. They are naturally removed before the exposure of the next frame of film.

Sweatbox Session: A name we used for pre-production meetings (and believe me, we did often sweat) to discuss story development, key sequences and characters. Usually involved were Charles, myself and the scriptwriter, although sometimes the director (if he had begun on the production) would also participate.

Teeter-Totter: This is my name for a miniature arm or crane-like device that raises or lowers a model or animation camera vertically whilst keeping the platform on which the model or camera is mounted always perfectly horizontal. An example of its use was in *Clash of the Titans* when the Kraken rises from the sea.

Travelling Matte: Elements from different images are matted together to form a composite picture. In simple matting procedures stationary or static mattes are employed to block out part of the image during printing and then to fit a new picture element into the unexposed area of the negative. In more advanced systems the mattes change shape from one frame to the next (hence the term travelling), thus allowing the moving action to be combined with other picture elements. The process allows the combination of live action with models.

Treatment: A stage between a step outline and the development of the final screenplay. This precedes the writing of the draft scripts so that story faults can be discarded and the necessary alterations made.

V-shaped Mirror: A reflective material used on a rod or pole holding an animated model that is photographed against a blue background. The support of this material is a vertical V-shaped cardboard covering the rod or pole, which when combined with the reflective material reflects the blue from the blue backing, thus eliminating the support rod or pole from the camera. For example, Pegasus, the flying horse in *Clash of the Titans*, was supported in such a manner: the rod that supported the model was erased from the film by the reflection of the blue backing on the V-shaped reflective material attached to the rod.

Wide-Angled Lens: This lens creates an increased depth of field, thus keeping both foreground and background in focus. It is effective in showing simultaneous planes of action or playing an action or playing a character in the foreground against the immediate environment or against other defined characters in other sections of the image.

Wire Brace (Aerial Brace): Wires held by a specially constructed rig fixed above the animation table, which in turn support the model creature(s), for example the harpies in *Jason and the Argonauts* or the pterodactyls in *One Million Years BC*. In some of my early films wire braces would be used to suspend bricks, as in the case of *Earth Vs the Flying Saucers*. To make the wires 'invisible', they are hand-painted out on every frame of film to match the background.